Bilingual VISUAL dictionary

TOP-FLITE XL
Titleist

Bilingual VISUAL dictionary

A DORLING KINDERSLEY BOOK

LONDON, NEW YORK, MELBOURNE, MUNICH, DELHI

Senior Editor Angela Wilkes
Managing Art Editor Christine Keilty
Production Editor Lucy Baker
Production Controller Rita Sinha

Designed for Dorling Kindersley by WaltonCreative.com

Hindi Edition
Senior Editor Rohan Sinha
Editor Saloni Talwar
Design Manager Arunesh Talapatra
Senior DTP Designer Harish Aggarwal
DTP Designers Dheeraj Arora, Jagtar Singh
Production Manager Pankaj Sharma
Art Director Shefali Upadhyay
Head of Publishing Aparna Sharma

Hindi Translation by Yatra Books

First published in Great Britain in 2008 by
Dorling Kindersley Limited, 80 Strand, London WC2R 0RL

A Penguin Company

10 9 8 7 6 5 4 3
005-HD160-Jun/08

CIP catalog records for this book are available from the British Library and the Library of Congress

UK ISBN: 978-1-4053-3163-0

Printed by L Rex Printing Co. Ltd, China

Discover more at
www.dk.com

contents
viṣaya sūchī
विषय सूची

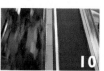

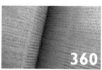

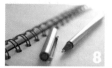

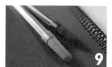

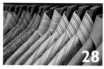

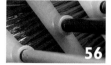

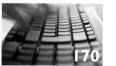

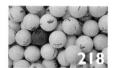

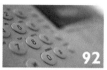

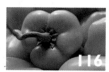

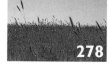

about the dictionary

The use of pictures is proven to aid understanding and the retention of information. Working on this principle, this highly-illustrated English-Hindi bilingual dictionary presents a large range of useful current vocabulary in the two languages.

The dictionary is divided thematically and covers most aspects of the everyday world in detail, from the restaurant to the gym, the home to the workplace, outer space to the animal kingdom. You will also find additional words and phrases for conversational use and for extending your vocabulary.

This is an essential reference tool for anyone interested in languages – practical, stimulating, and easy-to-use.

A few things to note

The Hindi in the dictionary is in the Devnagari script and this is accompanied by a romanization, showing you how to pronounce each word. The entries in the dictionary are always presented in the same order – English, the romanization, then Hindi. Where no suitable Hindi words exist, or are not commonly used, we have retained the English words, but the romanization has been adapted to show how native Hindi speakers pronounce them. You can find out more about this in the Hindi pronunciation guide on page 324-327.

Verbs are indicated by a (v) after the English, for example: **attend (v)**

There is an English index at the back of the book where you can look up a word and find out on which page it appears.

शब्दकोश के बारे में

तस्वीरों के ज़रिए किसी जानकारी को समझना और उसे ग्रहण करना हमेशा सहायक सिद्ध होता है। इसी सिद्धांत के आधार पर तैयार किया गया यह चित्रात्मक द्विभाषी शब्दकोश अंग्रेज़ी और हिन्दी भाषा में बड़ी संख्या में लाभकारी शब्दों को प्रस्तुत करता है।

यह शब्दकोश विषयों के आधार पर विभाजित है और इसमें रोज़मर्रा के जीवन से जुड़े अनेक पक्ष समेटे गए हैं, जिनमें रेस्तरां से जिम, घर से दफ़्तर और अंतरिक्ष से लेकर प्राणी जगत तक के क्षेत्र शामिल हैं। शाब्दिक क्षमता और बातचीत के कौशल को निखारने के लिए इसमें अतिरिक्त शब्द और वाक्यांश भी दिए गए हैं।

भाषाओं में दिलचस्पी रखने वाले व्यक्तियों के लिए व्यावहारिक, उत्साहवर्धक और प्रयोग में आसान यह संदर्भ पुस्तक एक अत्यावश्यक उपकरण सिद्ध होगी।

ध्यान देने योग्य बातें

इस शब्दकोश में हिन्दी मूल देवनागरी लिपि में लिखी गई है। शब्दों के उच्चारण को स्पष्ट करने के लिए उनका रोमन लिप्यंतरण दिया गया है। इस शब्दकोश में शब्दों को इस क्रम में प्रस्तुत किया गया है– अंग्रेज़ी, फिर हिन्दी रूप का रोमन में लिप्यंतरण और फिर देवनागरी में हिन्दी रूप। ऐसी स्थितियों में जहां अंग्रेज़ी शब्दों के समुचित हिन्दी पर्याय नहीं हैं या उनका आम चलन में प्रयोग नहीं होता, वहां हमने मूल अंग्रेज़ी के शब्दों को ही रखा है। हां, उनके रोमन लिप्यंतरण को उनके हिन्दी उच्चारण के अनुसार लिखा गया है। हिन्दी शब्दों के उच्चारण संबंधी विस्तृत जानकारी के लिए पुस्तक के अंत में (पृष्ठ संख्या 324–327) दी गई लिप्यंतरण गाइड देखें।

क्रियाओं को अंग्रेज़ी शब्द के बाद (v) के द्वारा बताया गया है, जैसे: **attend (v)**

इस शब्दकोश के अंत में अंग्रेज़ी तालिका दी गई है जिसमें किसी भी शब्द को देखकर आप उसकी पृष्ठ संख्या जान सकते हैं।

how to use this book

Whether you are learning a new language for business, pleasure, or in preparation for a holiday abroad, or are hoping to extend your vocabulary in an already familiar language, this dictionary is a valuable learning tool which you can use in a number of different ways.

When learning a new language, look out for cognates (words that are alike in different languages) and false friends (words that look alike but carry significantly different meanings). You can also see where the languages have influenced each other. For example, English has imported many terms for food from other languages but, in turn, exported terms used in technology and popular culture.

Practical learning activities

• As you move about your home, workplace, or college, try looking at the pages which cover that setting. You could then close the book, look around you and see how many of the objects and features you can name.

• Challenge yourself to write a story, letter, or dialogue using as many of the terms on a particular page as possible. This will help you retain the vocabulary and remember the spelling. If you want to build up to writing a longer text, start with sentences incorporating 2–3 words.

• If you have a very visual memory, try drawing or tracing items from the book onto a piece of paper, then close the book and fill in the words below the picture.

कोश का प्रयोग कैसे करें

आप भले ही व्यापार के लिए, शौक़ के लिए या विदेश में छुट्टी मनाने जाने के लिए कोई नई भाषा सीख रहे हों या पहले से सीखी हुई किसी भाषा का अपना शब्द ज्ञान बढ़ाना चाहते हों, आपके लिए यह शब्दकोश काफ़ी सहायक होगा और आप कई तरह से इसका प्रयोग कर सकते हैं।

कोई नई भाषा सीखते समय इस भाषा में प्रयोग होने वाले समानार्थी शब्दों (वे शब्द जो दूसरी भाषाओं में भी एक जैसे हों) और भिन्नार्थी शब्दों (वे शब्द जो एक जैसे दिखते हैं, परंतु उनके अर्थ अलग होते हैं) पर ध्यान ज़रूर दें। आप यह भी देख सकते हैं कि भाषाएं किस तरह एक–दूसरे को प्रभावित करती हैं। उदाहरण के लिए अंग्रेज़ी भाषा में खाने संबंधी अनेक शब्द यूरोपीय भाषाओं से लिए गए हैं जबकि इसने संस्कृति व तकनीक के क्षेत्र में बहुत से शब्द उन्हें प्रदान किए हैं।

सीखने के लिए व्यावहारिक अभ्यास

• आप अपने घर, दफ़्तर या कॉलेज में घूमते हुए, उन पन्नों को देखने का प्रयास करें, जो इन क्षेत्रों से संबंधित हैं। फिर इस पुस्तक को बंद करके अपने आसपास नज़र दौड़ाएं और यह देखें कि आपको कितनी चीजों के नाम याद हैं।

• किसी एक विशेष पन्ने पर दिए गए शब्दों का प्रयोग करके छोटी कहानी, पत्र या संवाद लिखने का प्रयास करें। इससे आपको शब्द और वर्तनी याद रखने में मदद मिलेगी। अगर आप कोई बड़ा आलेख लिखना चाहते हैं, तो दो–तीन शब्दों को मिलाकर छोटे–छोटे वाक्य बनाकर शुरुआत करें।

• यदि चित्रों की सहायता से आपको अधिक याद रहता है तो इस कोश में दिए गए चित्रों को अलग काग़ज़ पर बनाएं और बिना देखे उनसे संबंधित शब्दों को लिखें।

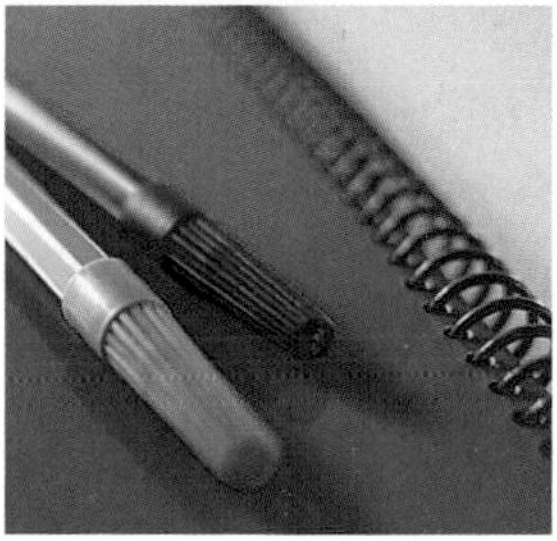

people

log

लोग

body • śarīr • शरीर

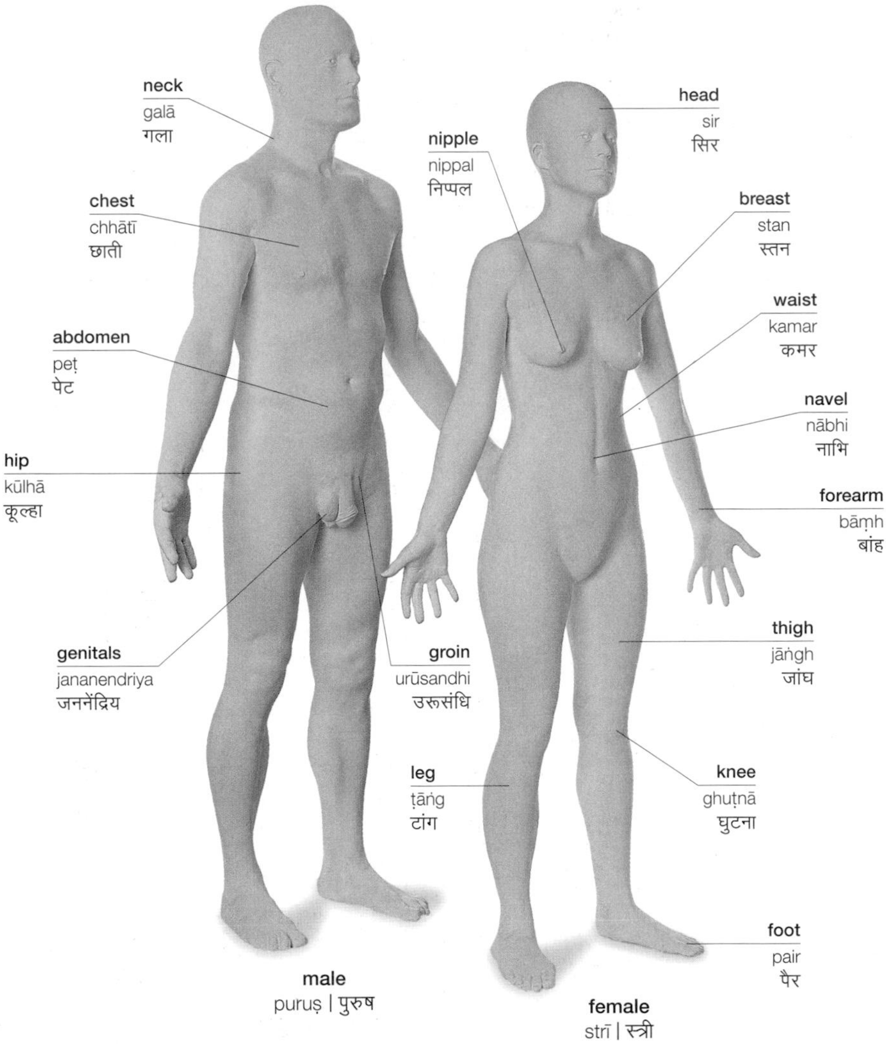
neck
galā
गला
head
sir
सिर
nipple
nippal
निप्पल
chest
chhātī
छाती
breast
stan
स्तन
waist
kamar
कमर
abdomen
peṭ
पेट
navel
nābhi
नाभि
hip
kūlhā
कूल्हा
forearm
bāṃh
बांह
thigh
jāṅgh
जांघ
genitals
jananendriya
जननेंद्रिय
groin
urūsandhi
उरूसंधि
leg
ṭāṅg
टांग
knee
ghuṭnā
घुटना
foot
pair
पैर
male
puruṣ | पुरुष
female
strī | स्त्री

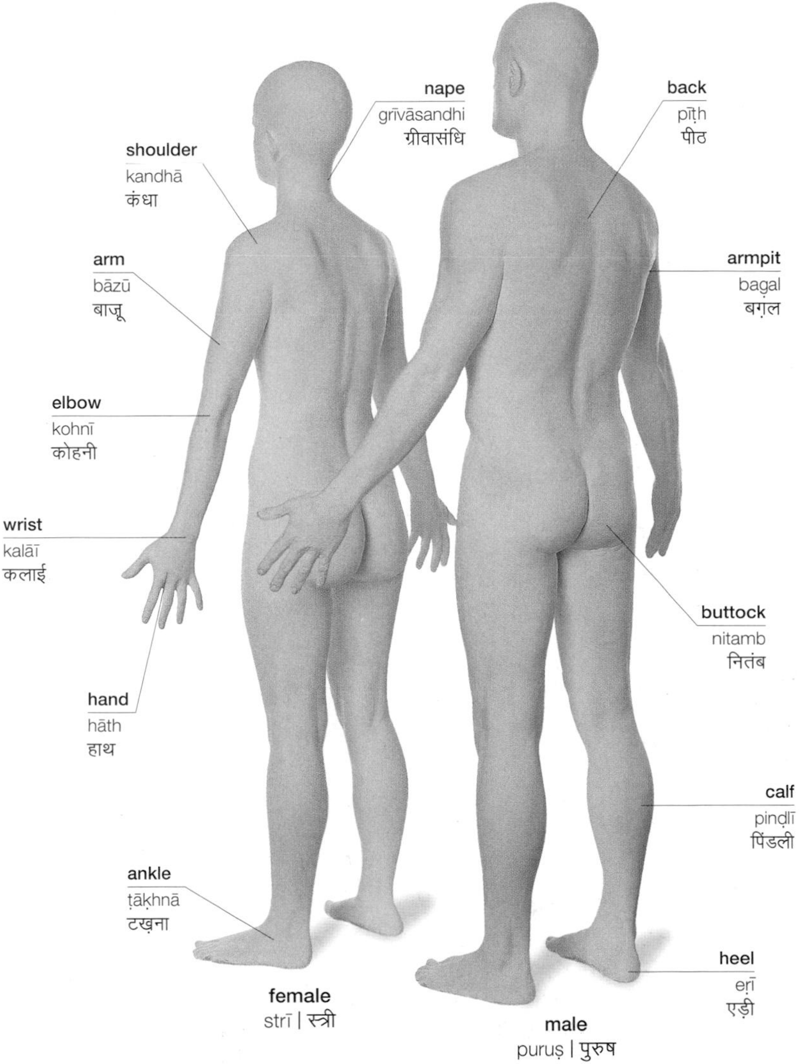
nape
grīvāsandhi
ग्रीवासंधि
back
pīṭh
पीठ
shoulder
kandhā
कंधा
arm
bāzū
बाज़ू
armpit
bagal
बग़ल
elbow
kohnī
कोहनी
wrist
kalāī
कलाई
buttock
nitamb
नितंब
hand
hāth
हाथ
calf
pinḍlī
पिंडली
ankle
ṭākhnā
टख़ना
heel
eṛī
एड़ी
female
strī | स्त्री
male
puruṣ | पुरुष

face • chehrā • चेहरा

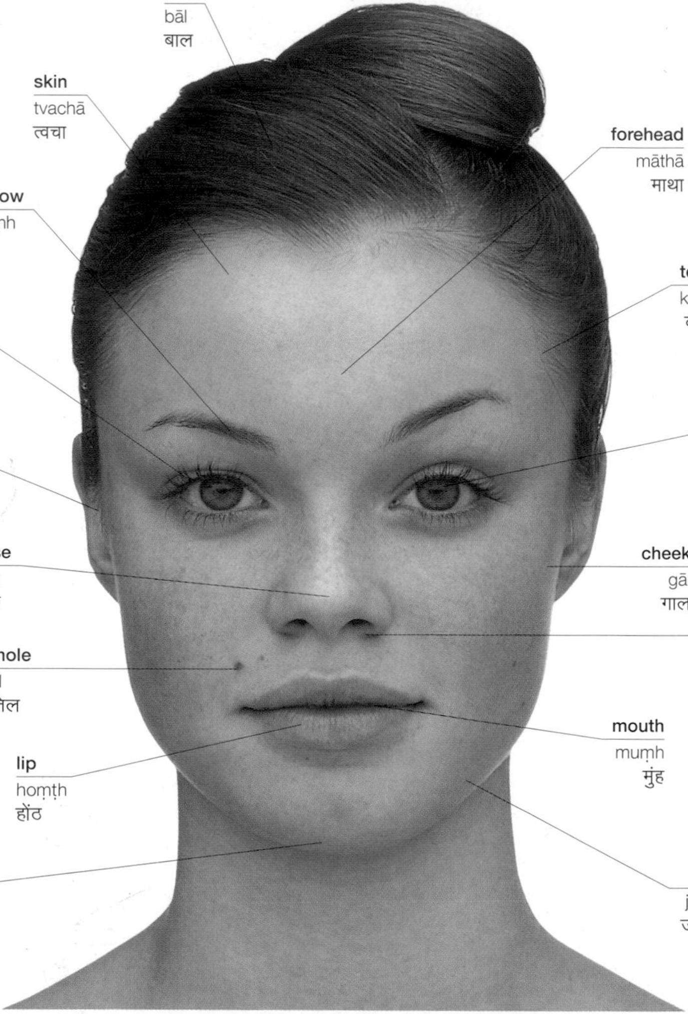
hair
bāl
बाल
skin
tvachā
त्वचा
forehead
māthā
माथा
eyebrow
bhauṃh
भौंह
temple
kanpaṭī
कनपटी
eyelash
palak
पलक
eye
āṃkh
आंख
ear
kān
कान
nose
nāk
नाक
cheek
gāl
गाल
nostril
nathunā
नथुना
mole
til
तिल
mouth
muṃh
मुंह
lip
hoṃṭh
होंठ
chin
ṭhoṛī
ठोड़ी
jaw
jabṛā
जबड़ा

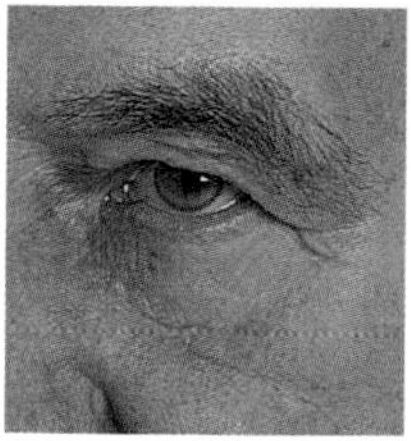

wrinkle
jhurriyāṃ | झुर्रियां

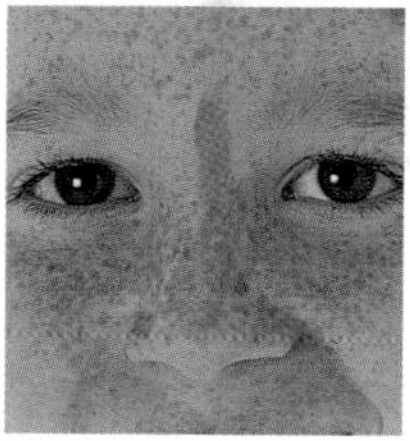

freckle
jhāīṃ | झाईं

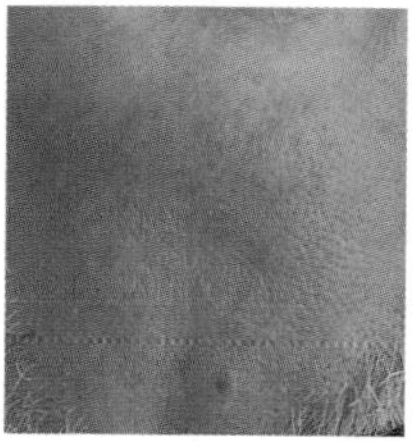

pore
rom chhidr | रोमछिद्र

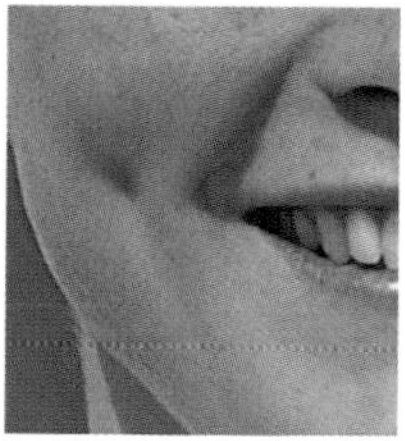

dimple | gāl kā gaḍḍhā | गाल का गड्ढा

hand • hāth • हाथ

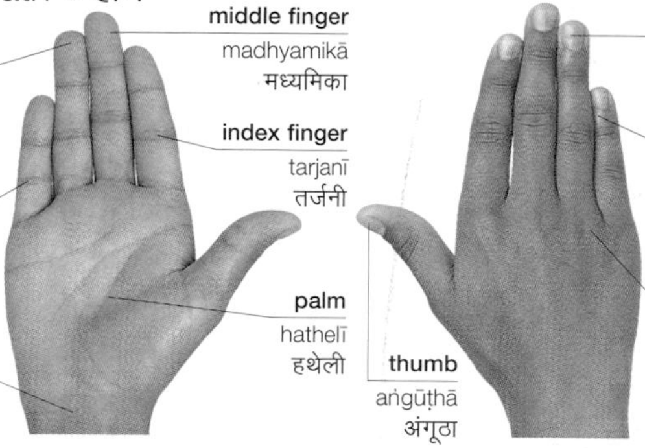
ring finger
anāmikā
अनामिका
middle finger
madhyamikā
मध्यमिका
index finger
tarjanī
तर्जनी
little finger
kaniṣṭhikā
कनिष्ठिका
palm
hathelī
हथेली
wrist
kalāī
कलाई
thumb
aṅgūṭhā
अंगूठा
nail
nāḳhūn
नाख़ून
cuticle
jhillī
झिल्ली
knuckle
uṅglī sandhi
उंगली संधि

fist
muṭṭhī | मुट्ठी

foot • pair • पैर

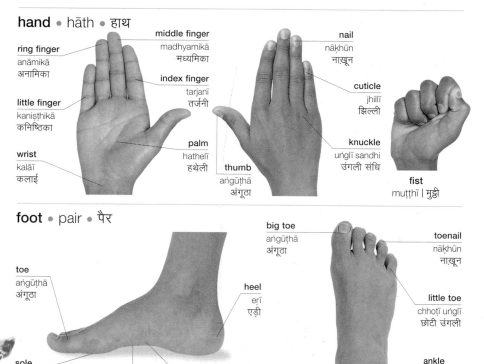

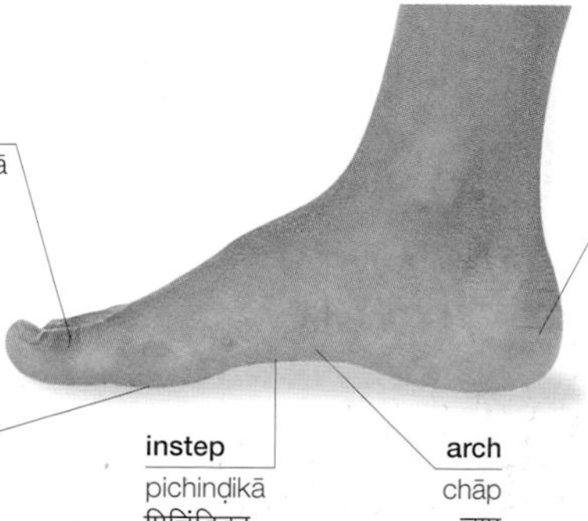
toe
aṅgūṭhā
अंगूठा
heel
eṛī
एड़ी
sole
talvā
तलवा
instep
pichinḍikā
पिचिंडिका
arch
chāp
चाप

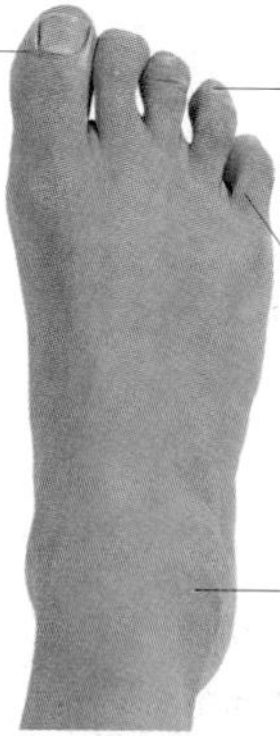
big toe
aṅgūṭhā
अंगूठा
toenail
nāḳhūn
नाख़ून
little toe
chhoṭī uṅglī
छोटी उंगली
ankle
ṭaḳhnā
टख़ना

muscles • māṃspeśiyāṃ • मांसपेशियां

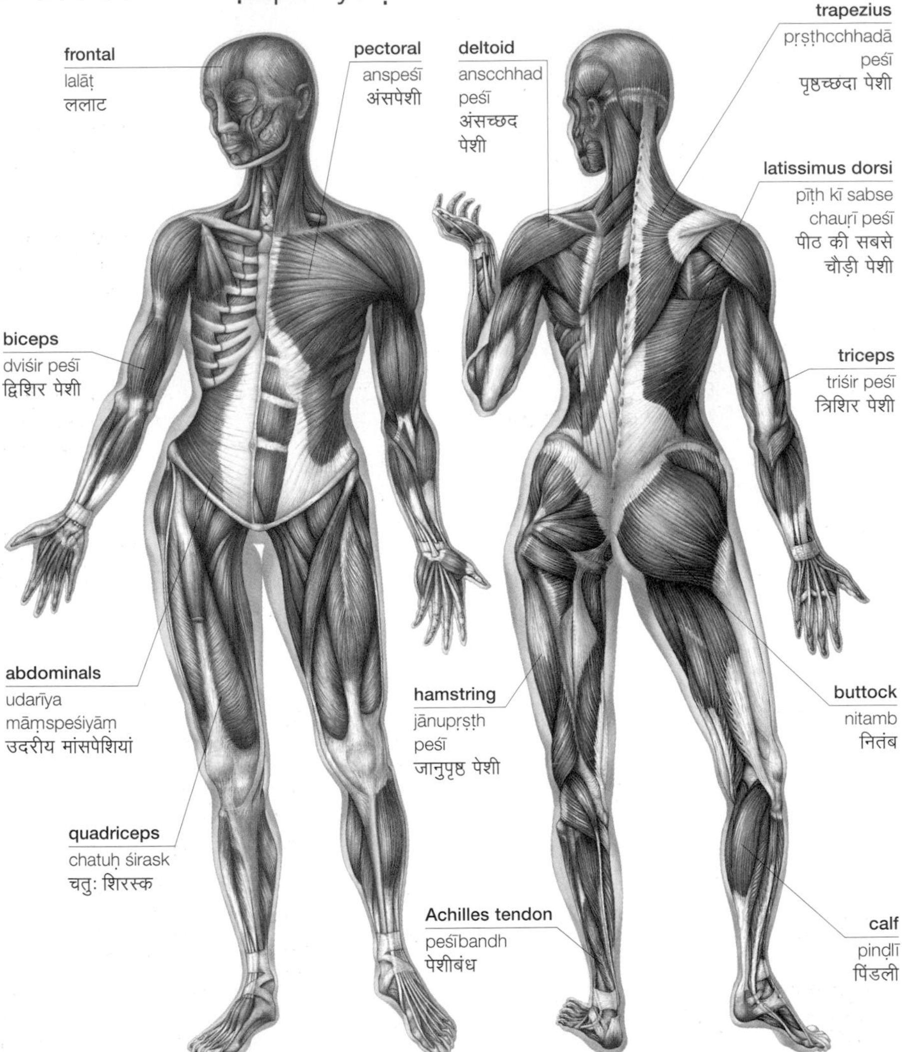
frontal
lalāṭ
ललाट
pectoral
anspeśī
अंसपेशी
deltoid
anscchhad peśī
अंसच्छद पेशी
trapezius
prṣṭhcchhadā peśī
पृष्ठच्छदा पेशी
latissimus dorsi
pīṭh kī sabse chauṛī peśī
पीठ की सबसे चौड़ी पेशी
biceps
dviśir peśī
द्विशिर पेशी
triceps
triśir peśī
त्रिशिर पेशी
abdominals
udarīya māṃspeśiyāṃ
उदरीय मांसपेशियां
hamstring
jānuprṣṭh peśī
जानुपृष्ठ पेशी
buttock
nitamb
नितंब
quadriceps
chatuḥ śirask
चतु: शिरस्क
Achilles tendon
peśībandh
पेशीबंध
calf
piṇḍlī
पिंडली

skeleton • asthipanjar • अस्थिपंजर

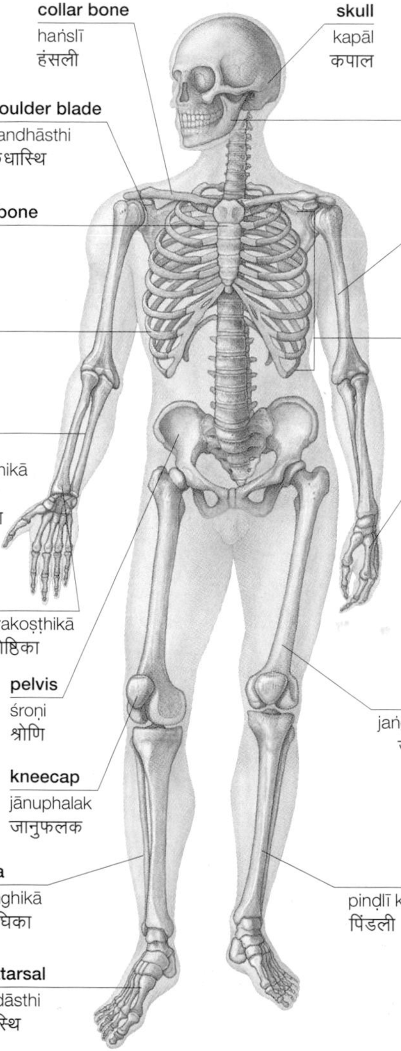
collar bone
haṅslī
हंसली
skull
kapāl
कपाल
shoulder blade
skandhāsthi
स्कंधास्थि
jaw
jabṛā
जबड़ा
breast bone
urosthi
उरोस्थि
humerus
pagaṇḍikā
पगंडिका
rib
paslī
पसली
rib cage
paslī panjar
पसली पंजर
ulna
antaḥ
prakoṣṭhikā
अंत:
प्रकोष्ठिका
metacarpal
panje kī asthi
पंजे की अस्थि
radius
bahiḥ prakoṣṭhikā
बहि: प्रकोष्ठिका
pelvis
śroṇi
श्रोणि
femur
jaṅghāsthi
जंघास्थि
kneecap
jānuphalak
जानुफलक
fibula
upjaṅghikā
उपजंघिका
tibia
piṇḍlī kī haḍḍī
पिंडली की हड्डी
metatarsal
prapdāsthi
प्रपदास्थि

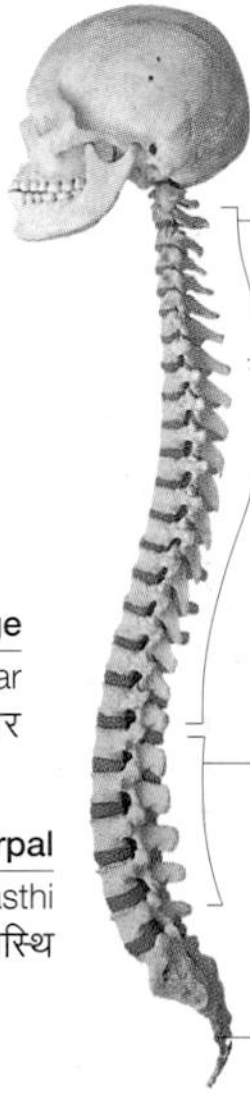
cervical vertebrae
grīvā kaśerukāeṃ
ग्रीवा कशेरुकाएं
thoracic vertebrae
vakṣīya kaśerukāeṃ
वक्षीय कशेरुकाएं
lumbar vertebrae
kaṭiparak kaśerukāeṃ
कटिपरक कशेरुकाएं
tailbone
puchhāsthi
पुच्छास्थि
spine
merudaṇḍ | मेरुदंड

joint • joṛ • जोड़

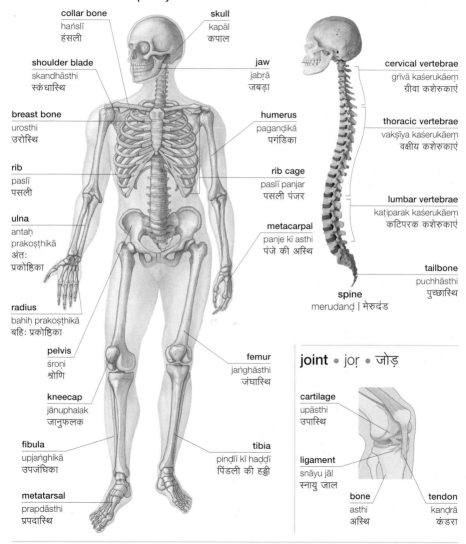

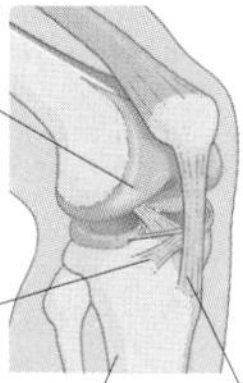
cartilage
upāsthi
उपास्थि
ligament
snāyu jāl
स्नायु जाल
bone
asthi
अस्थि
tendon
kaṇḍrā
कंडरा

internal organs • āntarik aṅg • आंतरिक अंग

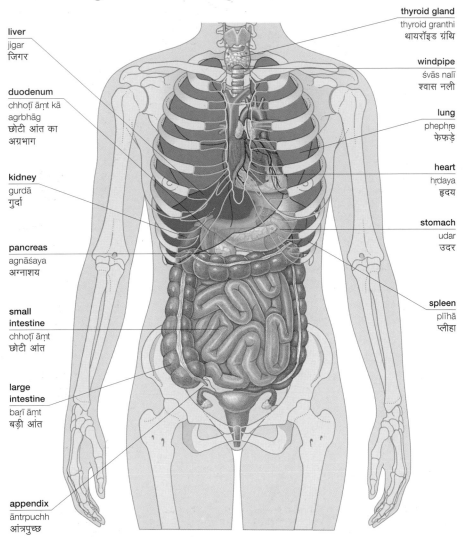

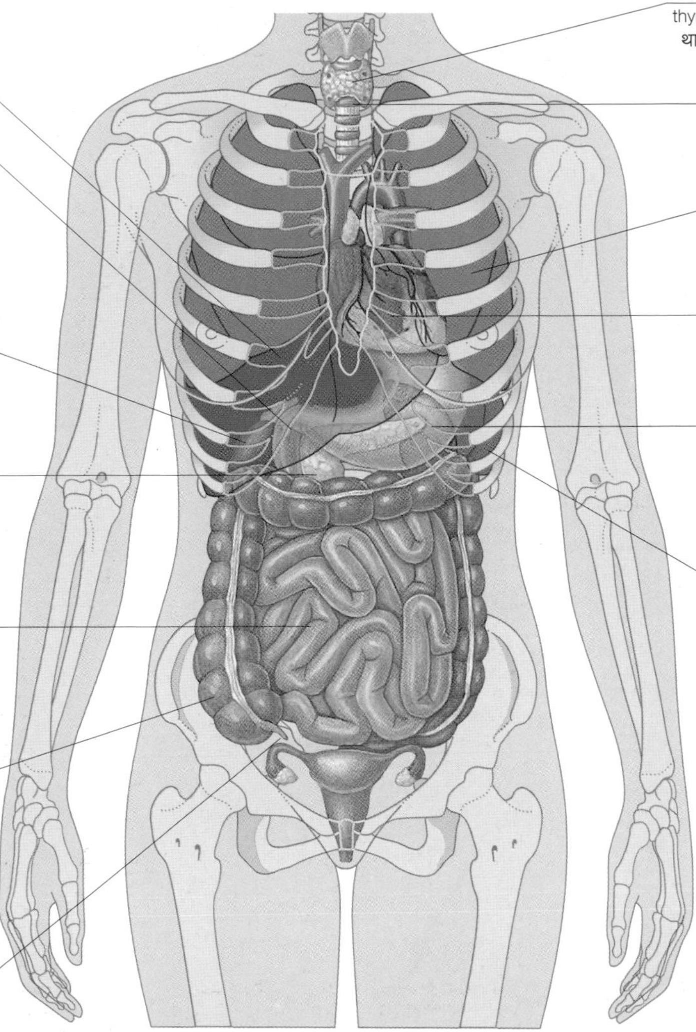
liver
jigar
जिगर
duodenum
chhoṭī āṃt kā agrbhāg
छोटी आंत का अग्रभाग
kidney
gurdā
गुर्दा
pancreas
agnāśaya
अग्नाशय
small intestine
chhoṭī āṃt
छोटी आंत
large intestine
baṛī āṃt
बड़ी आंत
appendix
āntrpuchh
आंत्रपुच्छ
thyroid gland
thyroid granthi
थायरॉइड ग्रंथि
windpipe
śvās nalī
श्वास नली
lung
phephṛe
फेफड़े
heart
hṛdaya
हृदय
stomach
udar
उदर
spleen
plīhā
प्लीहा

head • sir • सिर

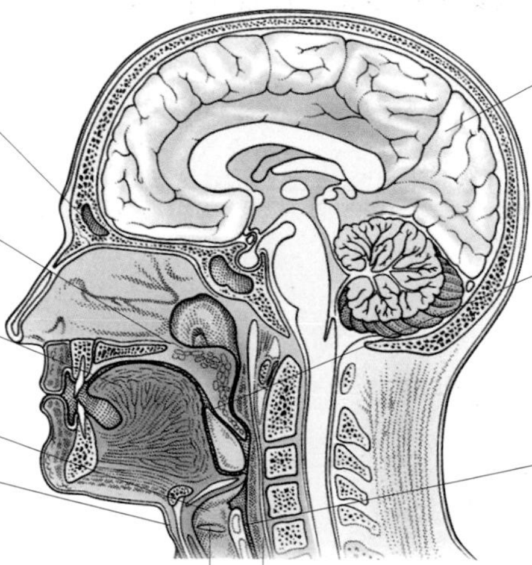
sinus
nālīvraṇ
नालीव्रण
palate
tālū
तालू
tongue
jībh
जीभ
larynx
kaṇṭh
कंठ
Adam's apple
kaṇṭhmaṇi
कंठमणि
vocal cords
svar tantr | स्वर तंत्र
brain
mastiṣk
मस्तिष्क
pharynx
śvās nalī
श्वास नली
oesophagus
āhār nalī
आहार नली
throat
galā | गला

body systems • śarīr tantr • शरीर तंत्र

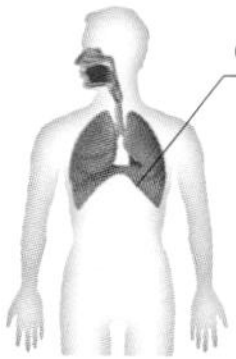
diaphragm
madhyapaṭ
मध्यपट

respiratory
śvasan | श्वसन

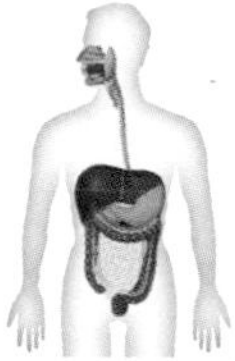

digestive
pāchak | पाचक

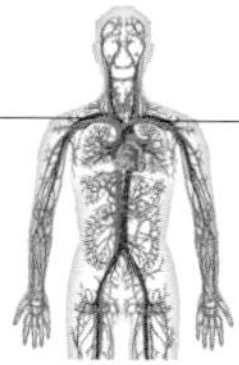
vein
nas
नस
artery
dhamnī
धमनी

cardiovascular
hṛdaya evam raktvāhinī
हृदय एवं रक्तवाहिनी

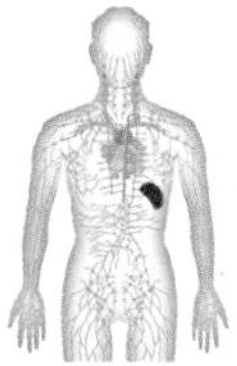

lymphatic
lasikā
लसिका

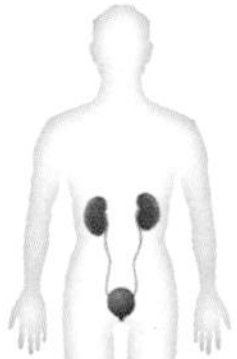

urinary
mūtr | मूत्र

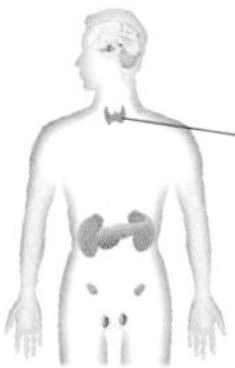
gland
granthi
ग्रंथि

endocrine
antaḥ srāvī | अंतः स्रावी

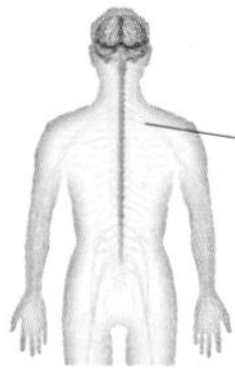
nerve
tantrikā
तंत्रिका

nervous
snāyu | स्नायु

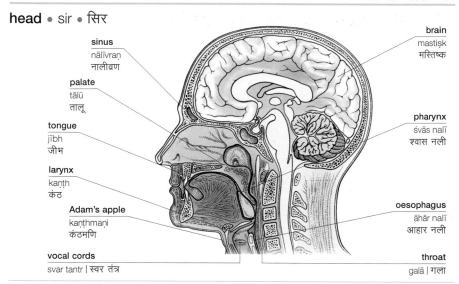

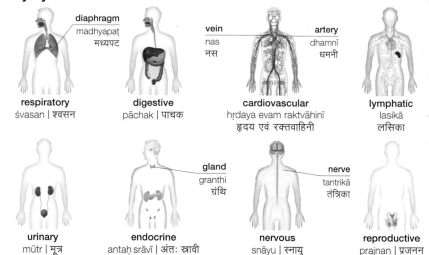

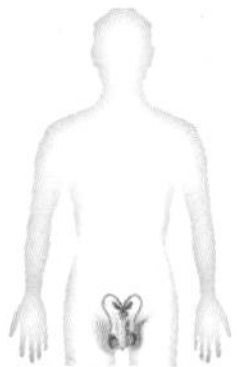

reproductive
prajnan | प्रजनन

reproductive organs • prajnanīya aṅg • प्रजननीय अंग

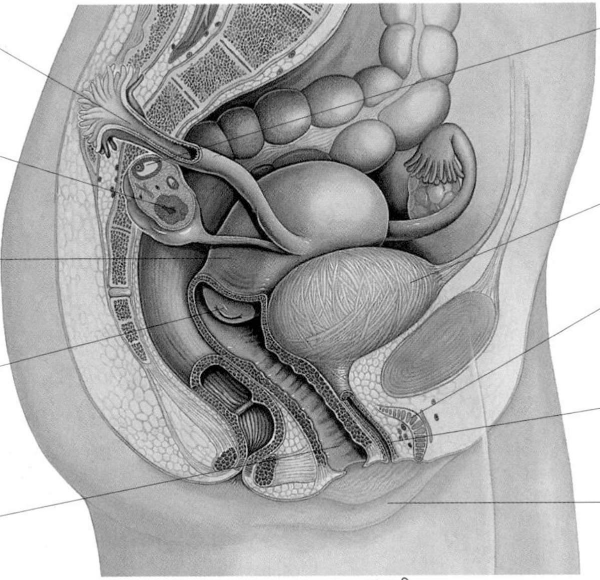

fallopian tube
ḍimb vāhinī
डिंब वाहिनी
ovary
aṇḍāśaya
अंडाशय
uterus
garbhāśaya
गर्भाशय
cervix
garbhdvār
गर्भद्वार
vagina
yoni
योनि
follicle
puṭak (jhillīdār chhoṭī thailī)
पुटक (झिल्लीदार छोटी थैली)
bladder
mutrāśaya
मूत्राशय
clitoris
bagśiśinikā
भगशिश्निका
urethra
mūtrnalī
मूत्रनली
labia
bhagoṣṭh
भगोष्ठ

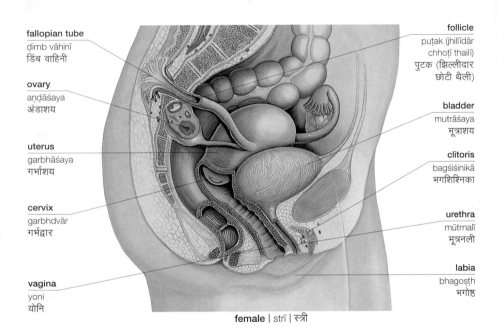

female | strī | स्त्री

reproduction • prajnan • प्रजनन

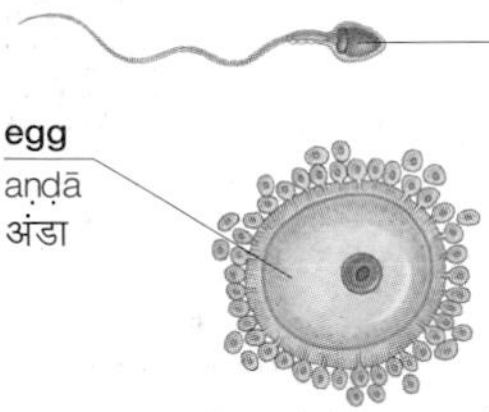

sperm
śukrāṇu
शुक्राणु
egg
aṇḍā
अंडा

fertilization | niṣechan | निषेचन

vocabulary • śabdāvalī • शब्दावली

hormone
hārmon
हारमोन

impotent
napunsak
नपुंसक

intercourse
sambhog
संभोग

ovulation
bīj janan
बीज जनन

menstruation
māhvārī
माहवारी

sexually transmitted disease
yaun rog
यौन रोग

conceive
garbhdhāraṇ karnā
गर्भधारण करना

fertile
urvar
उर्वर

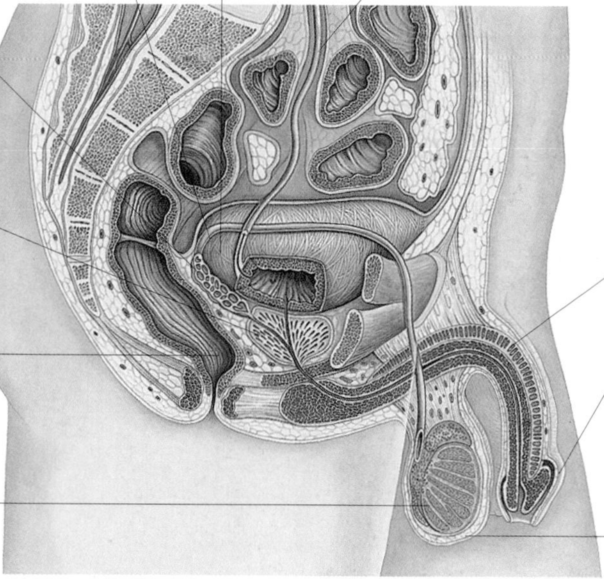
ejaculatory duct
skhalnīya nalī
स्खलनीय नली
vas deferens
śukravāhinī
शुक्रवाहिनी
ureter
mūtrnalī
मूत्रनली
seminal vesicle
śukrāśaya
शुक्राशय
prostate
puraḥsth granthi
पुर:स्थ ग्रंथि
penis
śiśn
शिश्न
rectum
gudā
गुदा
foreskin
śiśncchhad
शिश्नच्छद
testicle
aṇḍgranthi
अंडग्रंथि
scrotum
aṇḍkoś
अंडकोश

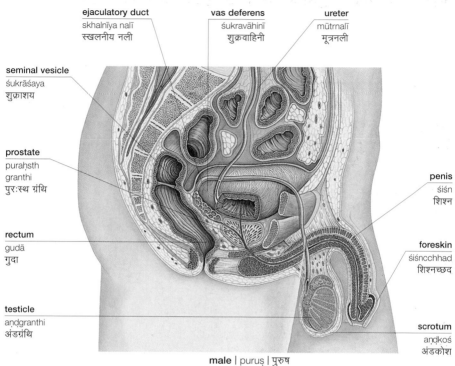

male | puruṣ | पुरुष

contraception • garbhnirodh • गर्भनिरोध

cap
kaip
कैप

diaphragm
ḍāyafrām
डायफ़्राम

condom
kanḍom
कंडोम

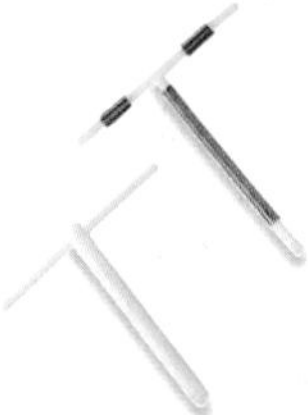

IUD
copper-ṭī
कॉपर–टी

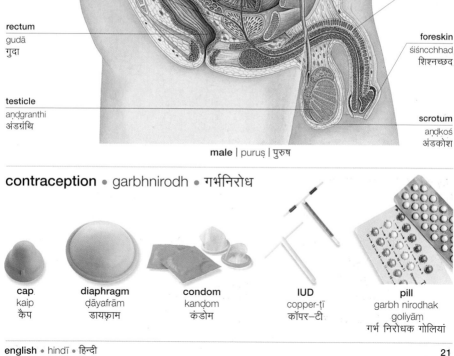

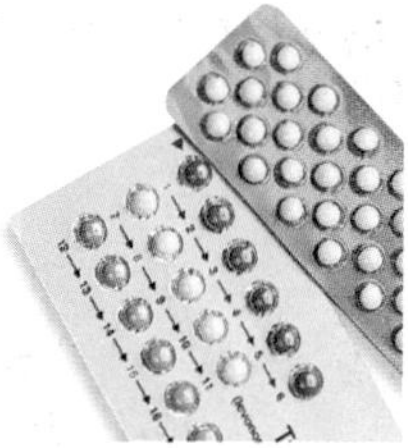

pill
garbh nirodhak goliyāṃ
गर्भ निरोधक गोलियां

family • parivār • परिवार

grandmother
dādī | दादी
grandfather
dādā | दादा
uncle
phūphā | फूफा
aunt
buā | बुआ
father
pitā | पिता
mother
mātā | माता
cousin
phūpherā bhāī | फूफेरा भाई
brother
bhāī | भाई
sister
bahan | बहन
wife
patnī | पत्नी
daughter-in-law
bahū | बहू
son
beṭā | बेटा
daughter
beṭī | बेटी
son-in-law
dāmād | दामाद
grandson
potā | पोता
granddaughter
potī | पोती
husband
pati | पति

vocabulary • śabdāvalī • शब्दावली

relatives riśtedār रिश्तेदार	**parents** mātā-pitā माता–पिता	**grandparents** dādā-dādī/nānā-nānī दादा–दादी/नाना–नानी	**stepfather** sautele pitā सौतेले पिता	**stepson** sautelā beṭā सौतेला बेटा	**generation** pīṛhī पीढ़ी
partner sāthī साथी	**children** bacche बच्चे	**grandchildren** nātī-nātin/potā-potī नाती–नातिन/पोता–पोती	**stepmother** sautelī mātā सौतेली माता	**stepdaughter** sautelī beṭī सौतेली बेटी	**twins** juṛvāṃ जुड़वां

mother-in-law
sās | सास

father-in-law
sasur | ससुर

brother-in-law
sāṛhū | साढ़ू

sister-in-law
sālī | साली

niece
bhānjī | भानजी

nephew
bhānjā | भानजा

titles • sambodhan • संबोधन

Mrs
śrīmatī
श्रीमती

Mr
śrīmān
श्रीमान

Miss
kumārī
कुमारी

stages • avasthāeṃ • अवस्थाएं

baby
śiśu | शिशु

child
bacchā | बच्चा

boy
laṛkā | लड़का

girl
laṛkī | लड़की

teenager
kiśorī | किशोरी

adult
vayask | व्यस्क

man
ādmī | आदमी

woman
aurat | औरत

relationships • sambandh • संबंध

manager
prabandhak
प्रबंधक

assistant
sahāyak
सहायक

business partner
sājhedār
साझेदार

employer
mālik
मालिक

employee
karmchārī
कर्मचारी

colleague
sahyogī
सहयोगी

office
karyālaya | कार्यालय

neighbour
paṛosī | पड़ोसी

friend
dost | दोस्त

acquaintance
parichit | परिचित

penfriend
ḳalam mitr | क़लम मित्र

boyfriend
puruṣ mitr
पुरुष मित्र

girlfriend
mahilā mitr
महिला मित्र

couple | yugal | युगल

fiancé
maṅgetar
मंगेतर

fiancée
maṅgetar
मंगेतर

engaged couple | bhāvī var-vadhū | भावी वर–वधू

emotions • bhāvnāeṃ • भावनाएं

smile
muskān
मुस्कान

happy
ḳhuśī | ख़ुशी

sad
dukh | दुख

excited
uttejnā | उत्तेजना

bored
ūb | ऊब

surprised
āścharya
आश्चर्य

scared
bhaya | भय

frown
tyoriyāṃ
chaṛhnā
त्योरियां
चढ़ना

angry
ġussā | ग़ुस्सा

confused
asmanjas | असमंजस

worried
chintā | चिंता

nervous
ghabrāhaṭ | घबराहट

proud
garv | गर्व

confident
ātmaviśvās | आत्मविश्वास

embarrassed
lajjā | लज्जा

shy
śarmīlā | शर्मीला

vocabulary • śabdāvalī • शब्दावली

sigh (v)
āh bharnā
आह भरना

shout (v)
chillānā
चिल्लाना

laugh (v)
haṃsnā
हंसना

cry (v)
ronā
रोना

shocked
sadmā lagnā
सदमा लगना

yawn (v)
ubāsī lenā
उबासी लेना

upset
pareśān
परेशान

life events • jīvan kī k̤hās ghaṭnāeṃ • जीवन की ख़ास घटनाएं

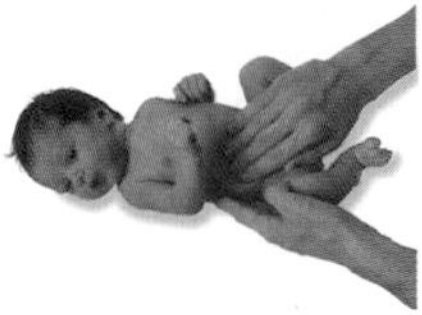

be born (v)
paidā honā | पैदा होना

start school (v)
skūl jānā | स्कूल जाना

make friends (v) | dost banānā | दोस्त बनाना

graduate (v) | snātak honā | स्नातक होना

get a job (v)
naukrī pānā | नौकरी पाना

fall in love (v)
prem honā | प्रेम होना

get married (v)
śādī karnā | शादी करना

have a baby (v)
santān honā | संतान होना

wedding | vivāh | विवाह

divorce
talāḳ | तलाक़

funeral
antyeṣṭi | अंत्येष्टि

vocabulary • śabdāvalī • शब्दावली

christening
īsaī nāmkaraṇ
ईसाई नामकरण

bar mitzvah
yahūdī upnayan
यहूदी उपनयन

anniversary
sālgirah
सालगिरह

emigrate (v)
utpravās karnā
उत्प्रवास करना

retire (v)
kārya nivṛtt honā
कार्य निवृत्त होना

die (v)
marnā
मरना

make a will (v)
vasīyat banānā
वसीयत बनाना

birth certificate
janm pramāṇpatr
जन्म प्रमाणपत्र

wedding reception
vivāh bhoj
विवाह भोज

honeymoon
hanīmūn
हनीमून

celebrations • utsav • उत्सव

birthday party
janmdin kī partī
जन्मदिन की पार्टी

card
kārḍ
कार्ड

birthday
janmdin | जन्मदिन

present
tohfā
तोहफ़ा

Christmas
krismas | क्रिसमस

New Year
nav varṣ | नव वर्ष

carnival
kārnivāl | कार्निवाल

procession
śobhāyātrā
शोभायात्रा

ribbon
riban
रिबन

Thanksgiving
thaiṅks giviṅg | थैंक्स गिविंग

Easter
īsṭar | ईस्टर

Halloween
hailovīn | हैलोवीन

festivals • tyohār • त्योहार

Passover | yahūdī parv | यहूदी पर्व

Ramadan
ramzān | रमज़ान

Diwali
dīvālī | दीवाली

appearance
veśbhūṣā
वेशभूषा

children's clothing • bāl paridhān • बाल परिधान

baby • śiśu • शिशु

snowsuit
garm sūṭ | गर्म सूट

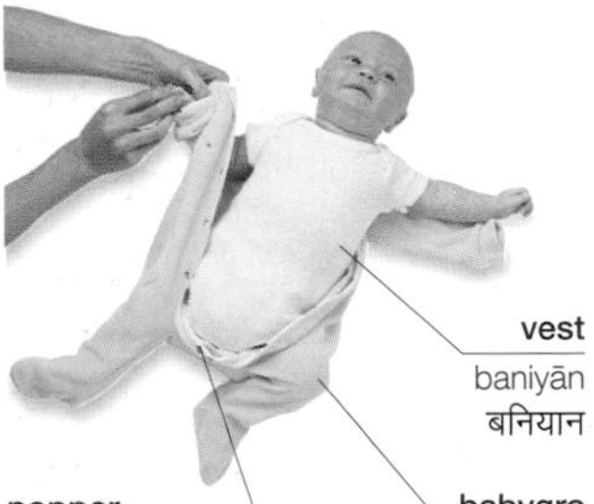

vest
baniyān
बनियान

popper
ṭich baṭan kā sūṭ
टिच बटन का सूट

babygro
bābā sūṭ
बाबा सूट

sleepsuit | slīp sūṭ | स्लीप सूट

romper suit
rompar | रोम्पर

bib
bib | बिब

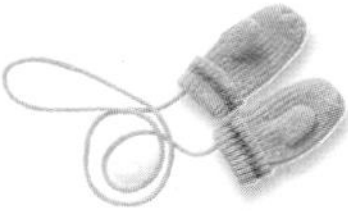

mittens
dastāne
दस्ताने

booties
bebī jūte
बेबी जूते

terry nappy
ṭairī naipī
टैरी नैपी

disposable nappy
dispozebal naipī
डिस्पोज़ेबल नैपी

plastic pants
plāsṭik kī laṇgoṭī
प्लास्टिक की लंगोटी

toddler • chhoṭā bacchā • छोटा बच्चा

sunhat
ṭop | टोप

apron
epren | एप्रेन

shorts
nekar
नेकर

dungarees
ḍaṇgarī
डंगरी

t-shirt
ṭī śarṭ
टी शर्ट

skirt
skarṭ
स्कर्ट

child • bacchā • बच्चा

dress
ḍres
ड्रेस

sandals
sainḍil
सैंडिल

summer
garmī | गर्मी

hood
ṭopī
टोपी

raincoat
barsātī | बरसाती

jeans
jīns
जीन्स

backpack
piṭṭhū baig
पिट्ठू बैग

autumn | śarad
ṛtu | शरद ऋतु

toggle
lambā
baṭan
लंबा बटन

duffel coat
garm koṭ
गर्म कोट

scarf
gulūband
गुलूबंद

anorak
barsātī
koṭ
बरसाती कोट

wellington boots
veliṅgṭan
būṭ
वेलिंगटन बूट

winter
sardī
सर्दी

dressing gown
ḍresiṅg gāun
ड्रेसिंग गाउन

nightie
nāiṭī
नाइटी

slippers
chappal
चप्पल

nightwear
rātri pośāk | रात्रि पोशाक

logo
logo
लोगो

trainers
ṭrenars
ट्रेनर्स

football strip
football sṭrip
फुटबॉल स्ट्रिप

tracksuit
ṭraik sūṭ
ट्रैक सूट

leggings
garm pajāmī
गर्म पजामी

vocabulary • śabdāvalī • शब्दावली

natural fibre
prakṛtik reśe
प्राकृतिक रेशे

synthetic
kṛtrim
कृत्रिम

Is it machine washable?
kyā yah maśīn meṃ dhul saktā hai?
क्या यह मशीन में धुल सकता है?

Will this fit a two-year-old?
kyā yah do sāl ke bacche ko ā jāegā?
क्या यह दो साल के बच्चे को आ जाएगा?

men's clothing • puruṣ paridhān • पुरुष परिधान

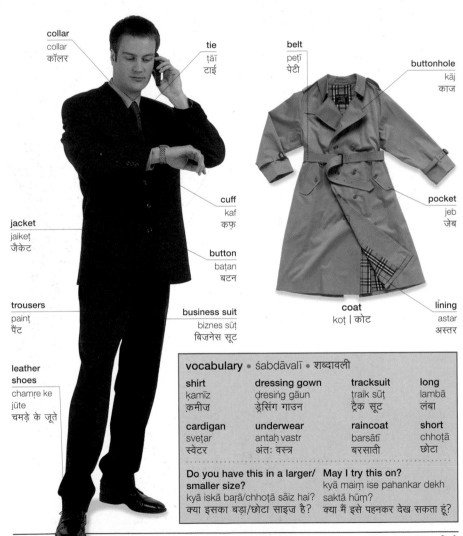

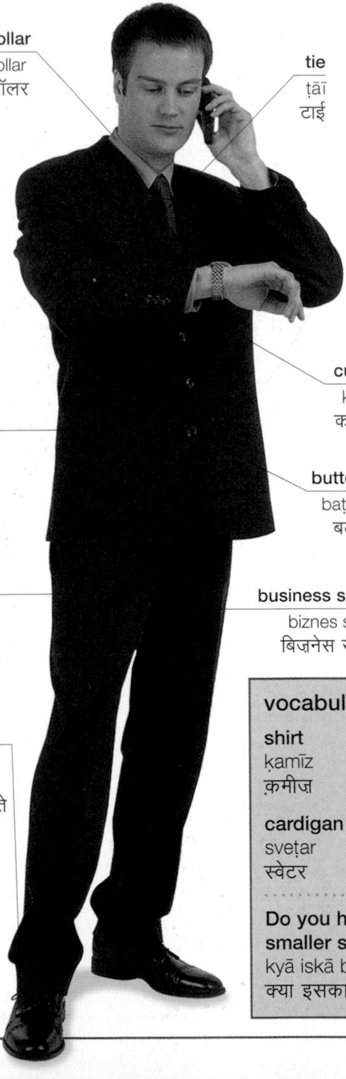
collar
collar
कॉलर
tie
ṭāī
टाई
cuff
kaf
कफ़
jacket
jaiket̤
जैकेट
button
baṭan
बटन
trousers
paiṇṭ
पैंट
business suit
biznes sūṭ
बिज़नेस सूट
leather shoes
chamṛe ke jūte
चमड़े के जूते

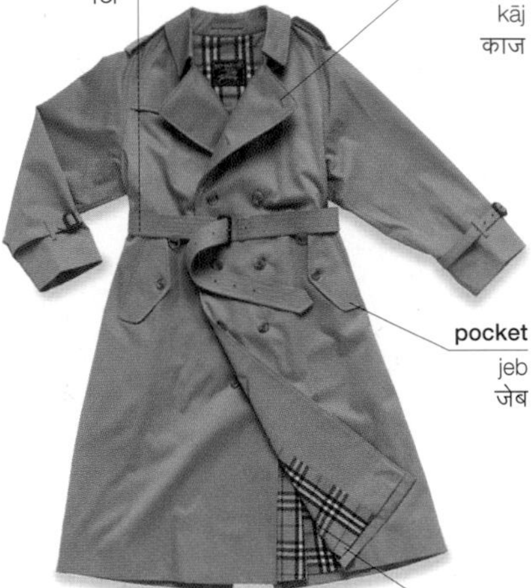
belt
peṭī
पेटी
buttonhole
kāj
काज
pocket
jeb
जेब
lining
astar
अस्तर

coat
koṭ | कोट

vocabulary • śabdāvalī • शब्दावली

shirt ḳamīz क़मीज़	**dressing gown** ḍresiṅg gāun ड्रेसिंग गाउन	**tracksuit** ṭraik sūṭ ट्रैक सूट	**long** lambā लंबा
cardigan sveṭar स्वेटर	**underwear** antaḥ vastr अंतः वस्त्र	**raincoat** barsātī बरसाती	**short** chhoṭā छोटा

Do you have this in a larger/ smaller size?
kyā iskā baṛā/chhoṭā sāiz hai?
क्या इसका बड़ा/छोटा साइज है?

May I try this on?
kyā maiṃ ise pahankar dekh saktā hūṃ?
क्या मैं इसे पहनकर देख सकता हूं?

blazer
blezar | ब्लेज़र

sports jacket | sporṭs jaikeṭ | स्पोर्ट्स जैकेट

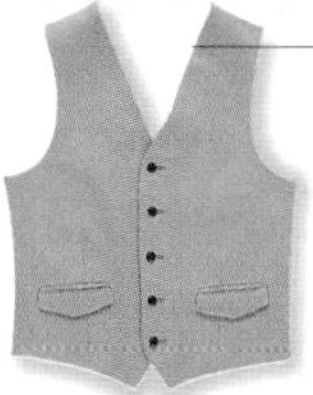

waistcoat
vāskaṭ | वास्कट

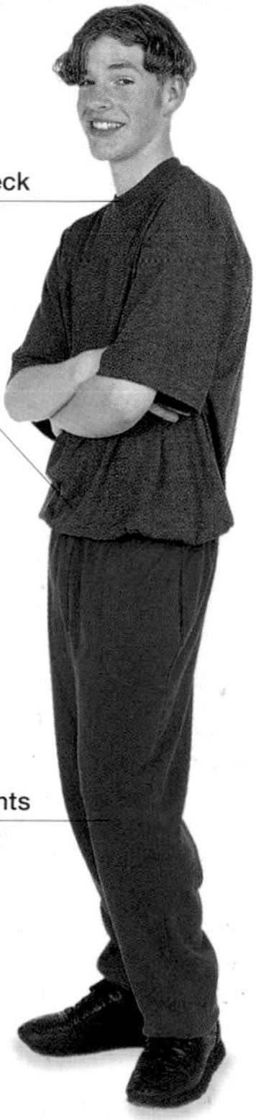
v-neck
vī galā
वी गला
round neck
gol galā
गोल गला
t-shirt
ṭī śarṭ
टी शर्ट
sweatpants
sveṭ painṭ
स्वेट पैंट

anorak
ainoraik | ऐनोरैक

sweatshirt
sveṭ śarṭ | स्वेट शर्ट

windcheater
vinḍchīṭar | विंडचीटर

sweater
sveṭar | स्वेटर

pyjamas
pajāmā sūṭ | पजामा सूट

vest
baniyān | बनियान

casual wear
rozmarrā ke vastr
रोज़मर्रा के वस्त्र

shorts
nekar | नेकर

briefs
chaḍḍī | चड्डी

boxer shorts | boxer shorts | बॉक्सर शॉर्ट्स

socks
moze | मोज़े

women's clothing • mahilā paridhān • महिला परिधान

jacket
jaikeṭ
जैकेट

neckline
galā
गला

seam
sīvan
सीवन

sleeve
āstīn
आस्तीन

skirt
skarṭ
स्कर्ट

hem
kinārī
किनारी

knee-length
ghuṭne tak lambī
घुटने तक लंबी

tights
pārdarśī moze
पारदर्शी मोज़े

shoes
jūte
जूते

ankle length
lambī pośāk
लंबी पोशाक

evening dress
gāun
गाउन

sleeveless
āstīn rahit
pośāk
आस्तीन रहित
पोशाक

dress
paridhān | परिधान

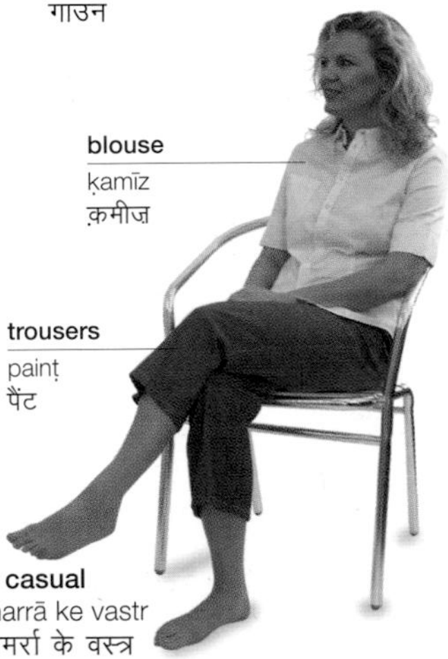

blouse
ḳamīz
क़मीज़

trousers
painṭ
पैंट

casual
rozmarrā ke vastr
रोज़मर्रा के वस्त्र

lingerie • adhovastr • अधोवस्त्र

negligée
gāun | गाउन

slip
slip | स्लिप

strap
sṭrep
स्ट्रेप

camisole
śamīz | शमीज़

suspenders
tanī
तनी

basque
aṅgiyā
अंगिया

stockings
lambī jurrāb
लंबी जुर्राब

tights
pārdarśī moze
पारदर्शी मोज़े

vest
śamīz
शमीज़

bra
brā | ब्रा

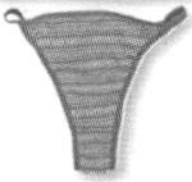

knickers
jāṅghiyā | जांघिया

nightdress
nāiṭī | नाइटी

wedding • vivāh • विवाह

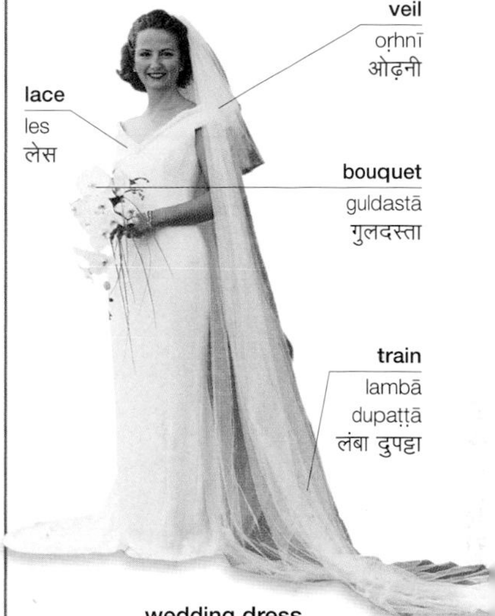
veil
oṛhnī
ओढ़नी
lace
les
लेस
bouquet
guldastā
गुलदस्ता
train
lambā
dupaṭṭā
लंबा दुपट्टा

wedding dress
vivāh kī pośāk | विवाह की पोशाक

vocabulary • śabdāvalī • शब्दावली

corset
cholī
चोली

garter
geṭis
गेटिस

shoulder pad
śolḍar paiḍ
शोल्डर पैड

waistband
kamarband
कमरबंद

tailored
sile vastr
सिले वस्त्र

halter neck
ḍorī vālā galā
डोरी वाला गला

underwired
aṅḍarvāyarḍ
अंडरवायर्ड

sports bra
sporṭs brā
स्पोर्ट्स ब्रा

accessories • sahāyak vastueṃ • सहायक वस्तुएं

cap
ṭopī | टोपी

hat
ṭop | टोप

scarf
gulūband | गुलूबंद

buckle
baksuā
बकसुआ

belt
peṭī | पेटी

handle
hatthā
हत्था
tip
nok
नोक

handkerchief
rūmāl | रूमाल

bow tie
bo-ṭāī | बो–टाई

tie-pin
ṭāī pin | टाई पिन

gloves
dastāne | दस्ताने

umbrella
chhātā | छाता

jewellery • zevar • ज़ेवर

pendant
locket | लॉकेट

brooch
jaṛāū pin | जड़ाऊ पिन

cufflink
kafliṅk | कफ़लिंक

link
kaṛī
कड़ी

bracelet
bresleṭ | ब्रेसलेट

clasp
baksuā
बकसुआ
stone
ḳīmtī patthar
क़ीमती पत्थर

chain
chen | चेन

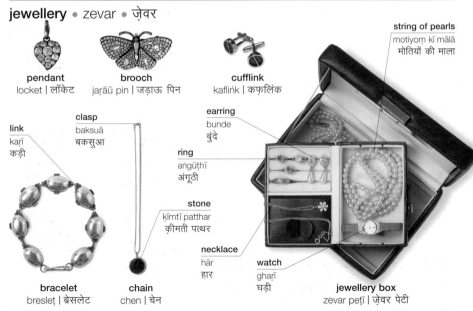

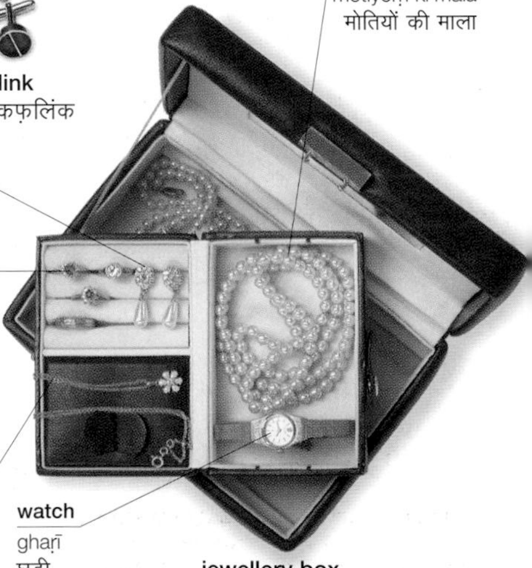
string of pearls
motiyoṃ kī mālā
मोतियों की माला
earring
bunde
बुंदे
ring
aṅgūṭhī
अंगूठी
necklace
hār
हार
watch
ghaṛī
घड़ी

jewellery box
zevar peṭī | ज़ेवर पेटी

bags • baig • बैग

wallet
wallet | वॉलेट

purse
baṭuā | बटुआ

shoulder bag
baig | बैग

holdall
bistar band | बिस्तर बंद

briefcase
brīfkes | ब्रीफ़केस

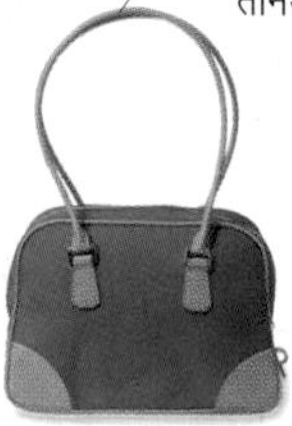
handles
taniyāṃ
तनियां

handbag
haiṇḍ baig | हैंड बैग

shoulder strap
baig kī tanī
बैग की तनी

backpack
piṭṭhū baig | पिट्ठू बैग

shoes • jūte-chappal • जूते–चप्पल

eyelet
chhed
छेद
lace
tasme/fīte
तस्मे/फ़ीते
tongue
jībh
जीभ
sole
talā
तला
heel
eṛī
एड़ी

lace-up
fīte vāle jūte | फ़ीते वाले जूते

walking boot
būṭ | बूट

trainer
ṭrenar | ट्रेनर

leather shoe
chamṛe ke jūte
चमड़े के जूते

flip-flop
chappal
चप्पल

high heel shoe
ūṃchī eṛī ke jūte
ऊंची एड़ी के जूते

platform shoe
platform chappal
प्लेटफ़ॉर्म चप्पल

sandal
saiṇḍil
सैंडिल

slip-on
jūtiyāṃ
जूतियां

brogue
brog
ब्रोग

hair • bāl • बाल

comb
kaṇghā
कंघा

comb (v)
kaṇghī karnā | कंघी करना

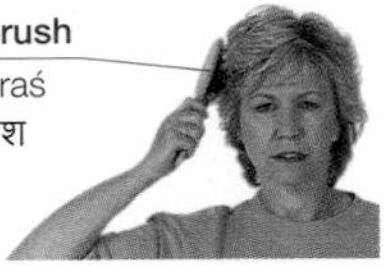

brush
braś
ब्रश

brush (v)
braś karnā | ब्रश करना

hairdresser
heyar ḍraisar
हेयर ड्रैसर

sink
besin
बेसिन

client
grāhak
ग्राहक

wash (v)
bāl dhonā | बाल धोना

rinse (v)
bāl dhonā | बाल धोना

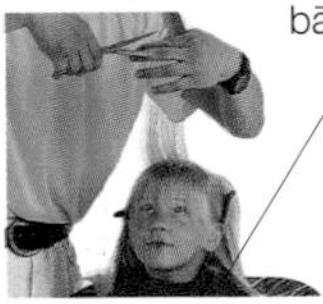

robe
vastr
वस्त्र

cut (v)
bāl kāṭnā | बाल काटना

blow dry (v)
bāl sukhānā | बाल सुखाना

set (v) | bāl seṭ karnā | बाल सेट करना

accessories • saundarya prasādhan • सौंदर्य प्रसाधन

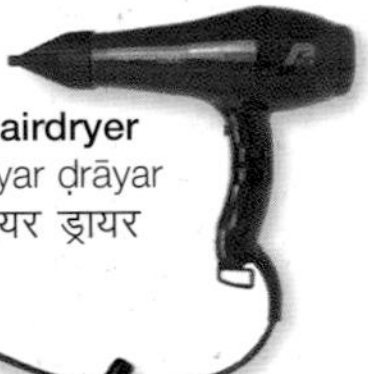

hairdryer
heyar ḍrāyar
हेयर ड्रायर

shampoo
śaimpū | शैम्पू

conditioner
kanḍiśnar | कंडीशनर

gel
jail | जैल

hairspray
heyar spre | हेयर–स्प्रे

curling tongs
karliṅg chimṭī
कर्लिंग चिमटी

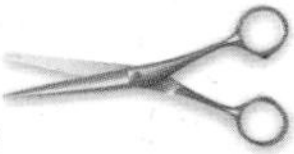

scissors
ḳaiṃchī | कैंची

hairband
heyar baiṇḍ | हेयर बैंड

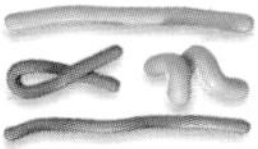

curler
karlar | कर्लर

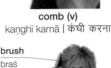

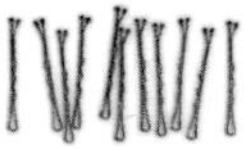

hairpin
bāl pin | बाल पिन

styles • keś sajjā • केश सज्जा

ribbon
riban
रिबन

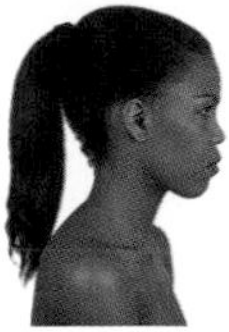

ponytail
ponī ṭel | पोनी टेल

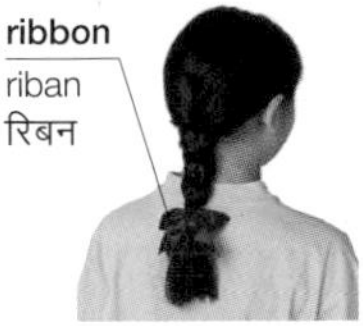

plait
choṭī | चोटी

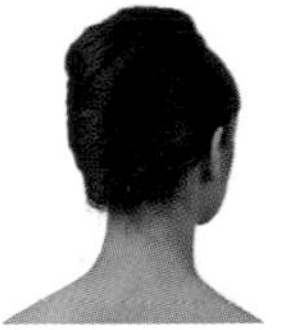

french pleat
french jūṛā | फ़्रेंच जूड़ा

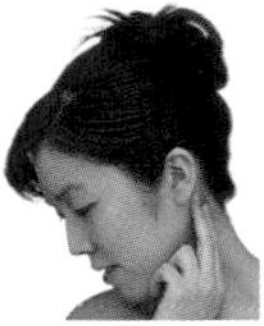

bun
jūṛā | जूड़ा

pigtails
do choṭī | दो चोटी

bob
bob | बॉब

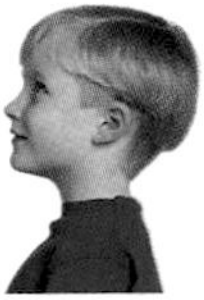

crop
crop | क्रॉप

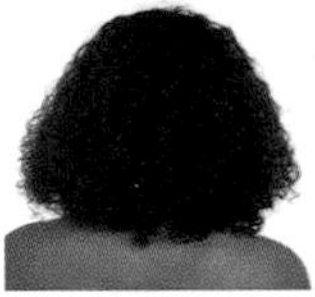

curly
ghuṅghrāle | घुंघराले

perm
parm | पर्म

straight
sidhe bāl | सीधे बाल

roots
jaṛem
जड़ें

highlights
haīlāiṭ | हाईलाइट

bald
ganjā | गंजा

wig
vig | विग

vocabulary • śabdāvalī • शब्दावली

trim (v) chhāṁṭnā छांटना	**greasy** tailīya तैलीय
straighten (v) sīdhā karnā सीधा करना	**dry** rūkhe रूखे
barber nāī नाई	**normal** sāmānya सामान्य
dandruff rūsī रूसी	**scalp** śirovalk शिरोवल्क
split ends domuṁhe bāl दोमुंहे बाल	**hairtie** bāloṁ kā fītā बालों का फ़ीता

colours • raṅg • रंग

blonde
sunahrā
सुनहरा

brunette
kālā-bhūrā
काला–भूरा

auburn
bhūrā | भूरा

ginger
lālī lie pīlā raṅg
लाली लिए पीला रंग

black
kālā | काला

grey
sleṭī | स्लेटी

white
safed | सफ़ेद

dyed | raṅge
hue | रंगे हुए

beauty • saundarya • सौंदर्य

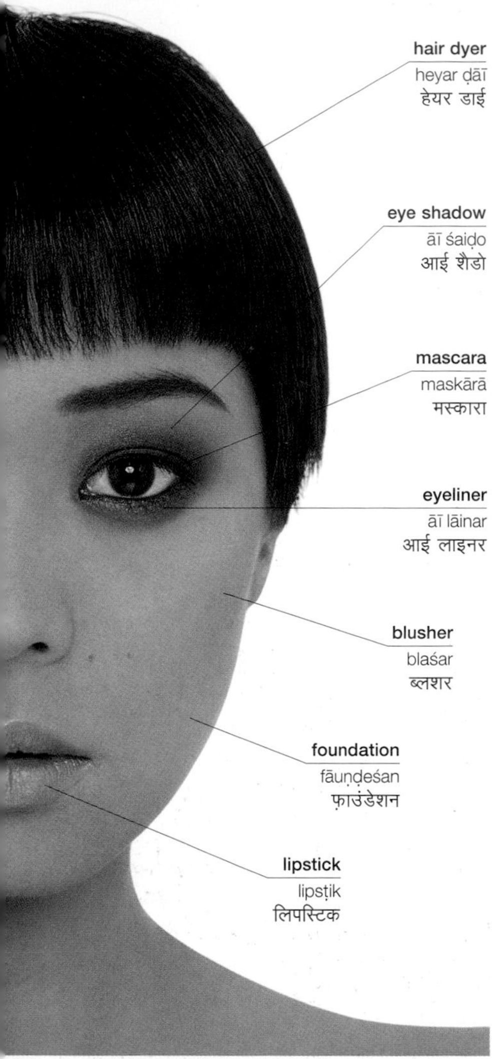
hair dyer
heyar ḍāī
हेयर डाई
eye shadow
āī śaiḍo
आई शैडो
mascara
maskārā
मस्कारा
eyeliner
āī lāinar
आई लाइनर
blusher
blaśar
ब्लशर
foundation
fāunḍeśan
फ़ाउंडेशन
lipstick
lipsṭik
लिपस्टिक

make-up • sāj-śṛṅgār • साज–शृंगार

eyebrow pencil
āī bro pensil | आई ब्रो पेंसिल

eyebrow brush
āī bro braś | आई ब्रो ब्रश

tweezers
chimṭī | चिमटी

lip gloss
lip gloss
लिप ग्लॉस

lip brush
lip braś
लिप ब्रश

lip liner
lip lāinar | लिप लाइनर

brush
braś | ब्रश

concealer
kansīlar | कंसीलर

mirror
śīśā
शीशा
face powder
fes pāuḍar
फ़ेस पाउडर
powder puff
paf
पफ़
compact | pāuḍar | पाउडर

beauty treatments • sundarya upchār • सौंदर्य उपचार

face pack
fes paik
फ़ेस पैक

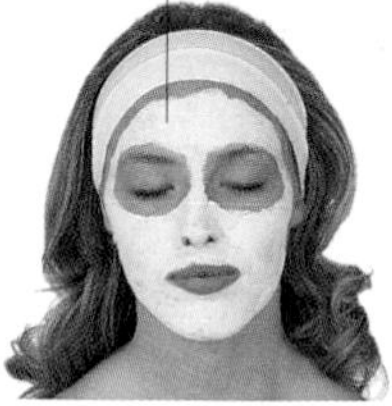

facial
feśiyal | फ़ेशियल

sunbed
san baiḍ | सन बैड

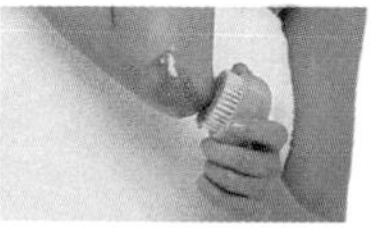

exfoliate (v)
mṛt tvachā utārnā
मृत त्वचा उतारना

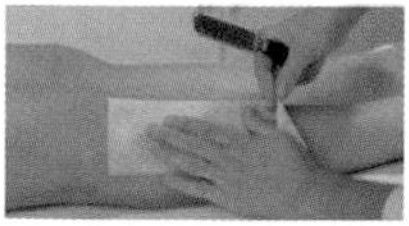

wax
vaiks | वैक्स

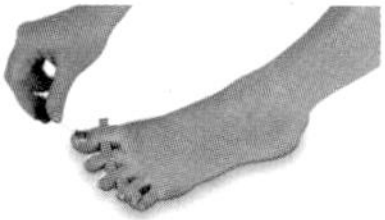

pedicure
pairoṃ kī safāī
पैरों की सफ़ाई

manicure • hāthoṃ kī safāī • हाथों की सफ़ाई

nail file
nel fāilar
नेल फ़ाइलर

nail varnish remover
nel polish rimūvar
नेल पॉलिश रिमूवर

nail varnish
nel polish
नेल पॉलिश

nail scissors
nakh kaiṃchī
नख क़ैंची

nail clippers
nel kaṭar
नेल कटर

toiletries • saundarya prasādhan • सौंदर्य प्रसाधन

cleanser
klīnzar
क्लींज़र

toner
ṭonar
टोनर

moisturizer
moisturizer
मॉइश्चराइज़र

self-tanning cream
ṭain karne kī krīm
टैन करने की क्रीम

perfume
itr
इत्र

eau de toilette
parfyūm spre
परफ़्यूम स्प्रे

vocabulary • śabdāvalī • शब्दावली

complexion raṅg rūp रंग–रूप	**oily** tailīya तैलीय	**dark** kālī काली
fair gorī गोरी	**sensitive** saṃvedanśīl संवेदनशील	**tattoo** gudnā गुदना
dry rūkhī रूखी	**shade** raṅg रंग	**cotton balls** rūī ke phāhe रूई के फाहे
anti-wrinkle jhurrī-nivārak झुर्री–निवारक	**hypoallergenic** elarjī rodhak एलर्जी रोधक	**tan** bhūre raṅg kā honā भूरे रंग का होना

health

svāsthya

स्वास्थ्य

illness • bīmārī • बीमारी

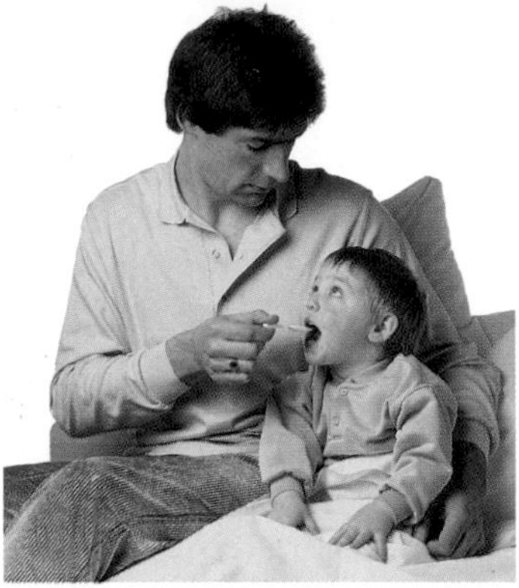

fever
bukhār | बुख़ार

headache
sirdard
सिरदर्द

nosebleed
naksīr
नकसीर

cough
khāṃsī
खांसी

sneeze
chhīṃk | छींक

cold
zukām | ज़ुकाम

flu
nazlā | नज़ला

inhaler
inhelar
इनहेलर

asthma
damā | दमा

cramps
maroṛ | मरोड़

nausea
mitlī | मितली

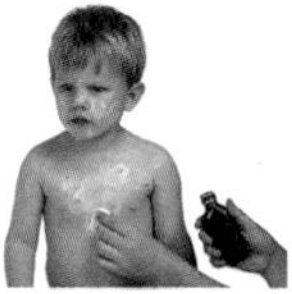

chickenpox
chhoṭī chechak | छोटी चेचक

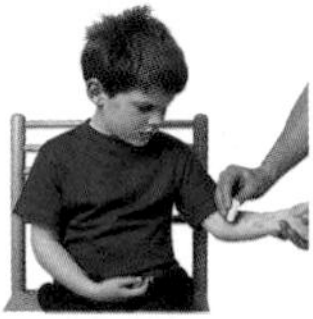

rash
funsī | फुंसी

vocabulary • śabdāvalī • शब्दावली

heart attack dil kā daurā दिल का दौरा	**diabetes** madhumeh मधुमेह	**eczema** khāj खाज	**chill** sardī सर्दी	**vomit (v)** ulṭī karnā उल्टी करना	**diarrhoea** dast दस्त
stroke pakṣāghāt पक्षाघात	**allergy** elarjī एलर्जी	**infection** saṅkramaṇ संक्रमण	**stomach ache** peṭ kā dard पेट का दर्द	**epilepsy** mirgī मिरगी	**measles** khasrā खसरा
blood pressure raktchāp रक्तचाप	**hayfever** parāg jvar पराग ज्वर	**virus** viṣāṇu विषाणु	**faint (v)** behoś honā बेहोश होना	**migraine** ādhāsīsī आधासीसी	**mumps** kanpheṛe कनफेड़े

doctor • chikitsak • चिकित्सक

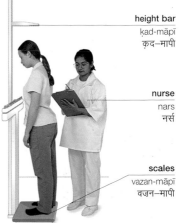

consultation • parāmarś • परामर्श

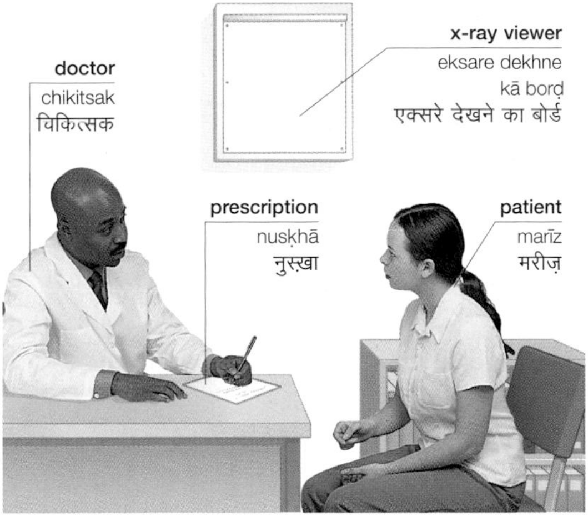
doctor
chikitsak
चिकित्सक
x-ray viewer
eksare dekhne
kā borḍ
एक्सरे देखने का बोर्ड
prescription
nusḳhā
नुस्ख़ा
patient
marīz
मरीज़

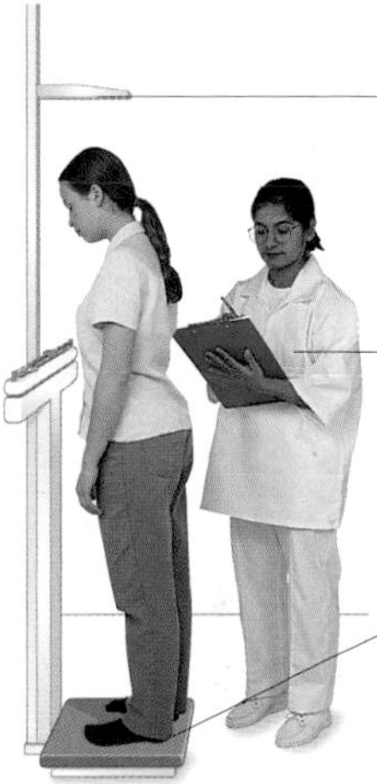
height bar
ḳad-māpī
क़द–मापी
nurse
nars
नर्स
scales
vazan-māpī
वज़न–मापी

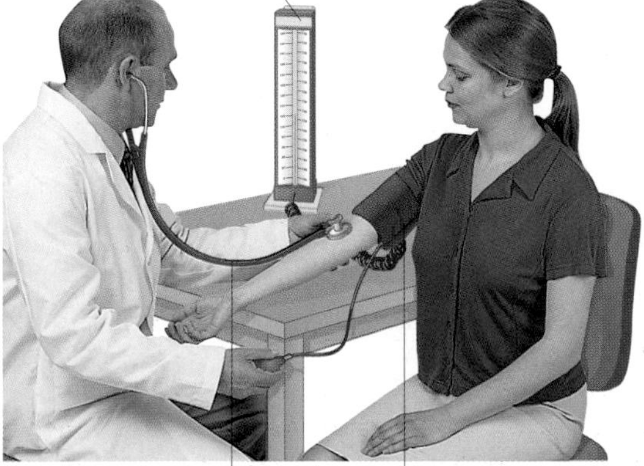
blood pressure gauge
raktchāp māpak
रक्तचाप मापक
stethoscope
sṭethoskop | स्टेथोस्कोप
cuff
kaf | कफ़

vocabulary • śabdāvalī • शब्दावली

appointment
milne kā samaya
मिलने का समय

surgery
śalya chikitsā
शल्य चिकित्सा

waiting room
pratīkṣā kakṣ
प्रतीक्षा कक्ष

inoculation
ṭīkā
टीका

thermometer
tharmāmīṭar
थर्मामीटर

medical examination
śārīrik jāṃch
शारीरिक जांच

I need to see a doctor.
mujhe doctor ko dikhānā hai
मुझे डॉक्टर को दिखाना है।

It hurts here.
yahāṃ dard ho rahā hai
यहां दर्द हो रहा है।

injury • choṭ • चोट

sprain | moch | मोच

sling
sliṅg paṭṭī
स्लिंग पट्टी

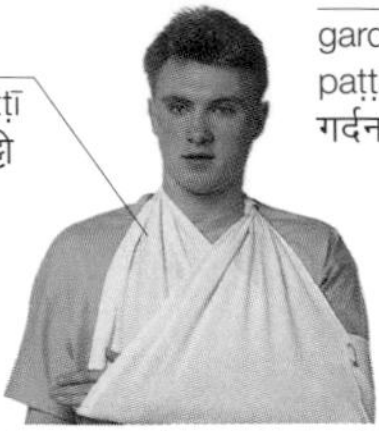

fracture | haḍḍī ṭūṭnā
हड्डी टूटना

neck brace
gardan kā
paṭṭā
गर्दन का पट्टा

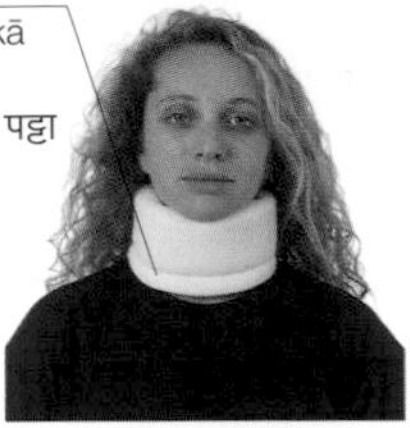

whiplash | gale kī moch
गले की मोच

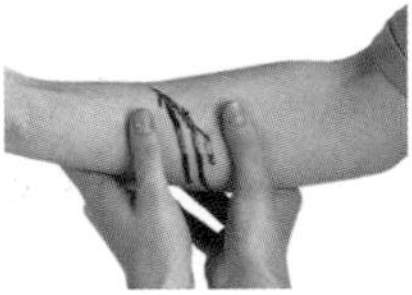

cut
kaṭnā | कटना

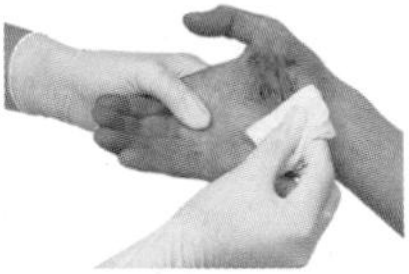

graze
ghisaṭ | घिसट

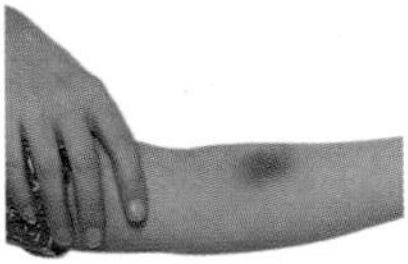

bruise
kharoṃch | खरोंच

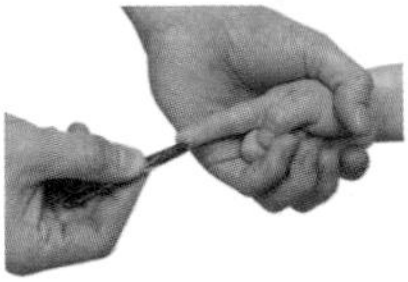

splinter
khapchī | खपची

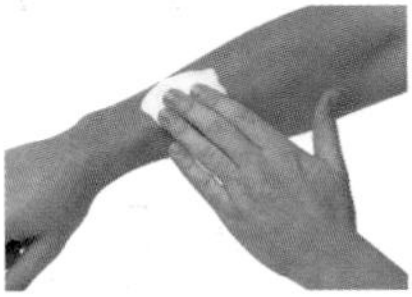

sunburn
dhūp se jalnā
धूप से जलना

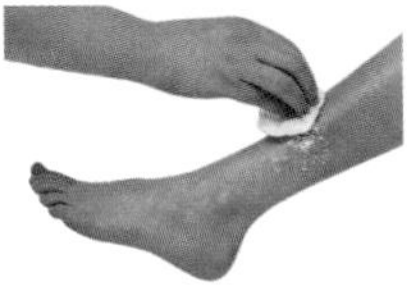

burn
jalnā
जलना

bite
kāṭā huā
काटा हुआ

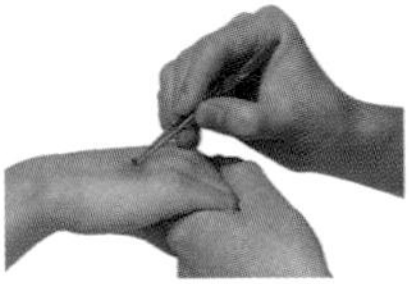

sting
ḍaṅk
डंक

vocabulary • śabdāvalī • शब्दावली

accident durghaṭnā दुर्घटना	**haemorrhage** raktsrāv रक्तस्राव	**poisoning** viṣpān विषपान	**Will he be all right?** kyā vah ṭhīk ho jāegā? क्या वह ठीक हो जाएगा?
emergency āpātkāl आपातकाल	**blister** chhālā छाला	**electric shock** bijlī ke jhaṭke बिजली के झटके	**Where does it hurt?** kahāṃ dard ho rahā hai? कहां दर्द हो रहा है?
wound ghāv घाव	**concussion** manoghāt मनोघात	**head injury** sir kī choṭ सिर की चोट	**Please call an ambulance!** kṛpyā embulens bulāie! कृपया एंबुलेंस बुलाइए!

first aid • prāthmik chikitsā • प्राथमिक चिकित्सा

ointment
marham
मरहम

plaster
plāstar
प्लास्तर

safety pin
seftī pin
सेफ़्टी पिन

bandage
paṭṭī
पट्टी

painkillers
dardnāśak davā
दर्दनाशक दवा

antiseptic wipe
kīṭāṇunāśak paṭṭī
कीटाणुनाशक पट्टी

tweezers
chimṭī
चिमटी

scissors
kaimchī
कैंची

antiseptic
kīṭāṇunāśak
कीटाणुनाशक

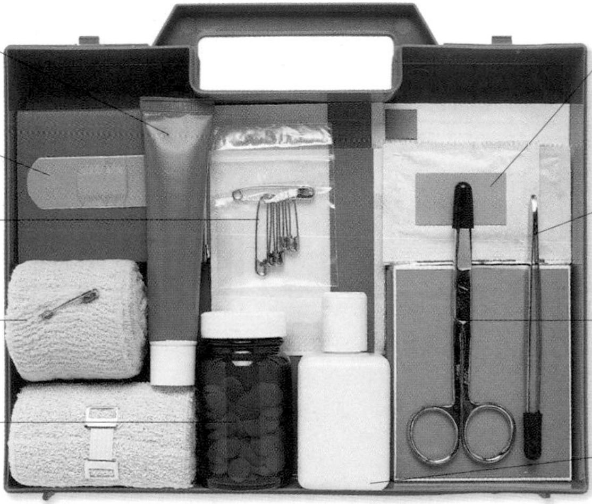

first aid box | prāthmik chikitsā peṭī | प्राथमिक चिकित्सा पेटी

gauze
gauze
गॉज़

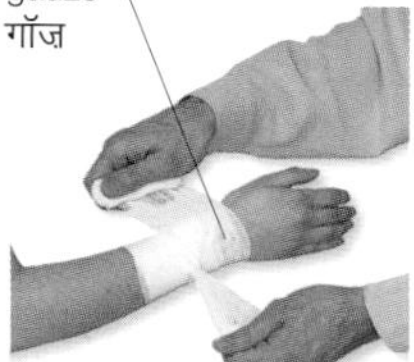

dressing
marham paṭṭī | मरहम पट्टी

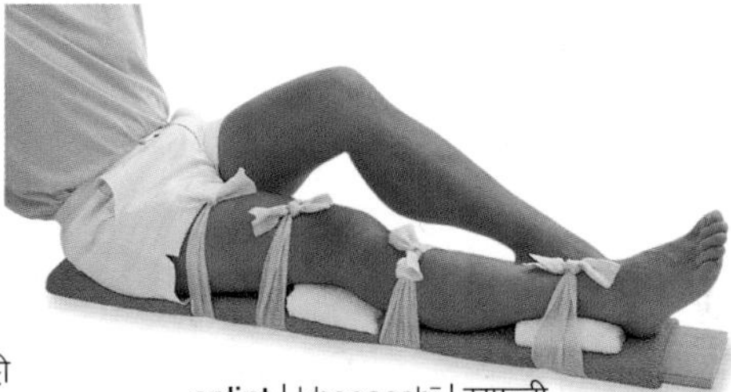

splint | khapacchī | खपच्ची

adhesive tape
chipakne vālā ṭep
चिपकने वाला टेप

resuscitation
śvasan kriyā | श्वसन क्रिया

vocabulary • śabdāvalī • शब्दावली

shock	pulse	choke (v)	Can you help?
sadmā	nāṛī	dam ghuṭnā	kyā āp madad
सदमा	नाड़ी	दम घुटना	kar sakte haiṃ?
			क्या आप मदद
unconscious	breathing	sterile	कर सकते हैं?
behoś	sāṃs	saṅkraman rahit	
बेहोश	सांस	संक्रमण रहित	

hospital • aspatāl • अस्पताल

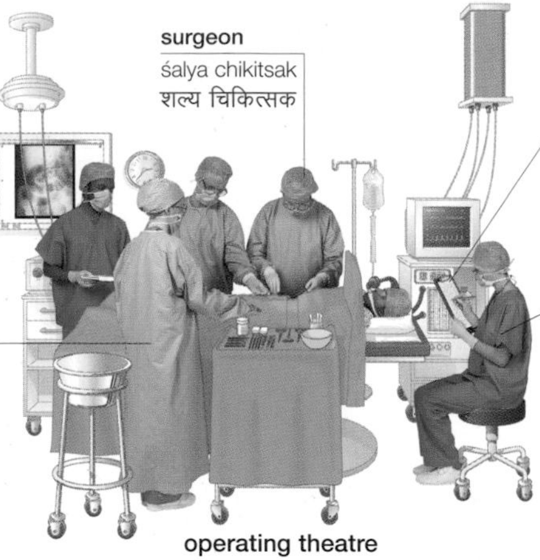
surgeon
śalya chikitsak
शल्य चिकित्सक
chart
chārṭ
चार्ट
anaesthetist
niśchetan chikitsak
निश्चेतन चिकित्सक
nurse
nars
नर्स

operating theatre
śalya kakṣ | शल्य कक्ष

blood test
ḳhūn kī jāṃch
ख़ून की जांच

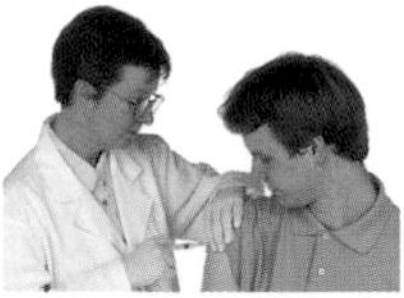

injection
ṭīkākaraṇ | टीकाकरण

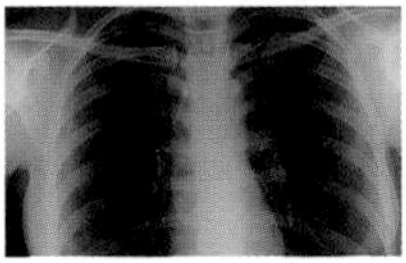

x-ray
eks-re | एक्स–रे

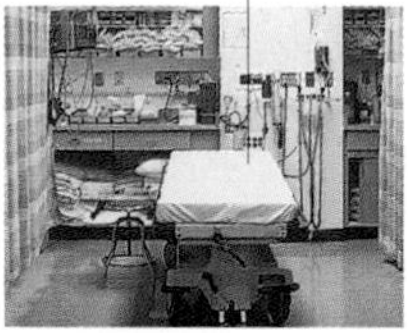
trolley
trolley
ट्रॉली

emergency room
āpātkālīn kakṣ
आपातकालीन कक्ष

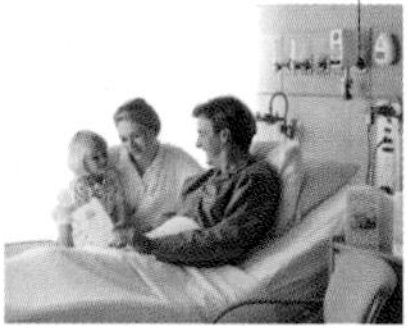
call button
call baṭan
कॉल बटन

ward
kakṣ | कक्ष

wheelchair
vhīlcheyar | व्हीलचेयर

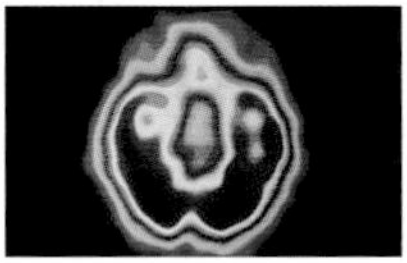

scan
skain | स्कैन

vocabulary • śabdāvalī • शब्दावली

operation śalya chikitsā शल्य चिकित्सा	**discharged** chhuṭṭī denā छुट्टी देना	**visiting hours** milne kā samaya मिलने का समय	**children's ward** bacchoṃ kā ward बच्चों का वॉर्ड	**intensive care unit** saghan chikitsā kakṣ सघन चिकित्सा कक्ष
admitted bhartī भर्ती	**clinic** chikitsālaya चिकित्सालय	**maternity ward** prasūti kakṣ प्रसूति कक्ष	**private room** nijī kamrā निजी कमरा	**outpatient** anivāsī rogī अनिवासी रोगी

departments • vibhāg • विभाग

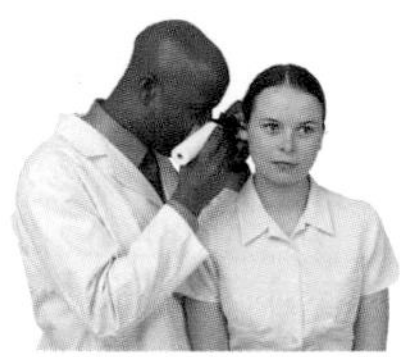

ENT | kān, nāk, evam galā chikitsā
कान, नाक एवं गला चिकित्सा

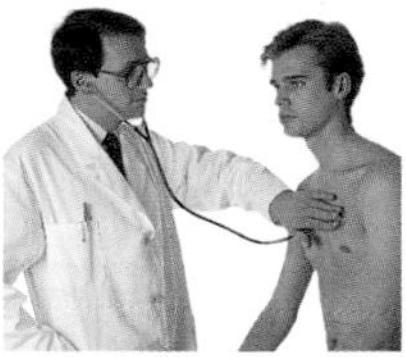

cardiology
hṛdaya chikitsā
हृदय चिकित्सा

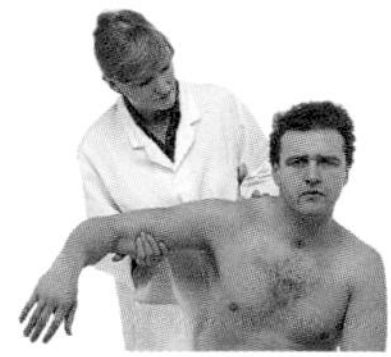

orthopaedy
asthi chikitsā
अस्थि चिकित्सा

gynaecology
strī rog chikitsā
स्त्री–रोग चिकित्सा

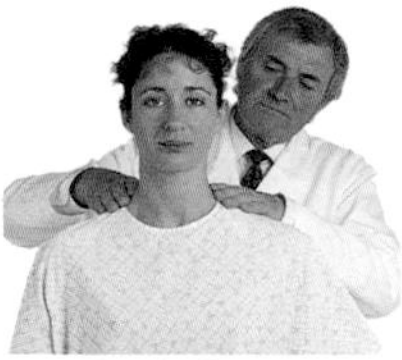

physiotherapy
vyāyām chikitsā
व्यायाम चिकित्सा

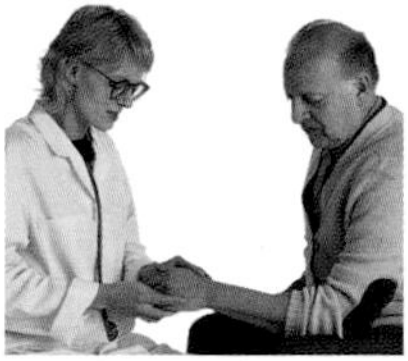

dermatology
tvachā chikitsā
त्वचा चिकित्सा

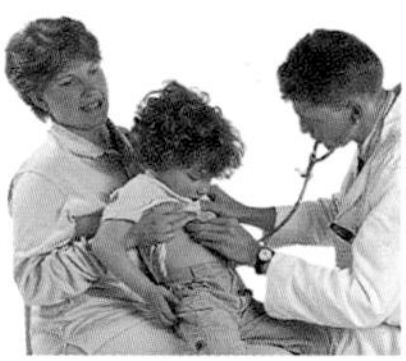

paediatrics
bāl chikitsā
बाल चिकित्सा

radiology
vikiraṇ chikitsā
विकिरण चिकित्सा

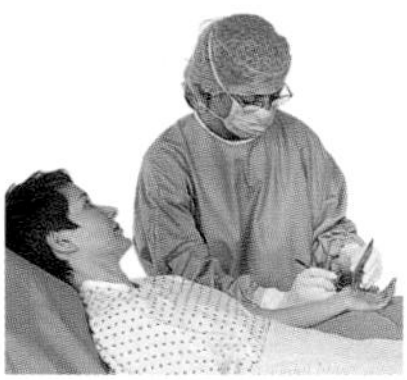

surgery
śalya chikitsā
शल्य चिकित्सा

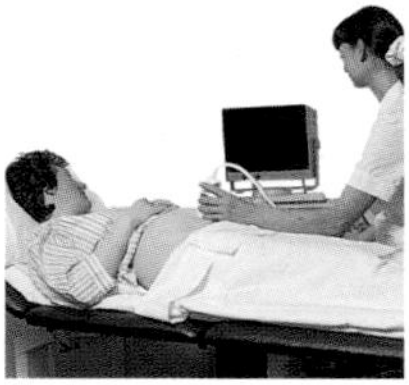

maternity
prasūti
प्रसूति

psychiatry
manochikitsā
मनोचिकित्सा

ophthalmology
netr chikitsā
नेत्र चिकित्सा

vocabulary • śabdāvalī • शब्दावली

neurology
snāyu vijñān
स्नायु विज्ञान

urology
mūtr vijñān
मूत्र विज्ञान

endocrinology
antrāsargikī
अंतरासर्गिकी

pathology
rog nidān
रोग निदान

result
pariṇām
परिणाम

oncology
kainsar vijñān
कैंसर विज्ञान

plastic surgery
plāsṭik sarjarī
प्लास्टिक सर्जरी

referral
sifāriś
सिफ़ारिश

test
jāṃch
जांच

consultant
parāmarśdātā
परामर्शदाता

dentist • dant chikitsak • दंत चिकित्सक

tooth • dāṃt • दांत

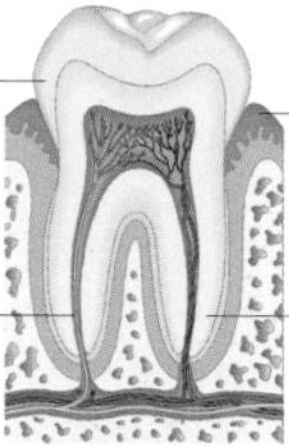

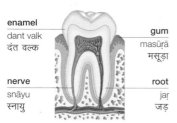

enamel
dant valk
दंत वल्क

gum
masūṛā
मसूड़ा

nerve
snāyu
स्नायु

root
jaṛ
जड़

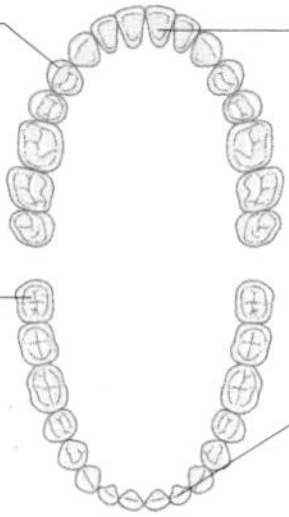

premolar
chhoṭī dāṛh
छोटी दाढ़

incisor
karttan dāṃt
कर्त्तन दांत

molar
dāṛh
दाढ़

canine
kīlā
कीला

check-up • jāṃch • जांच

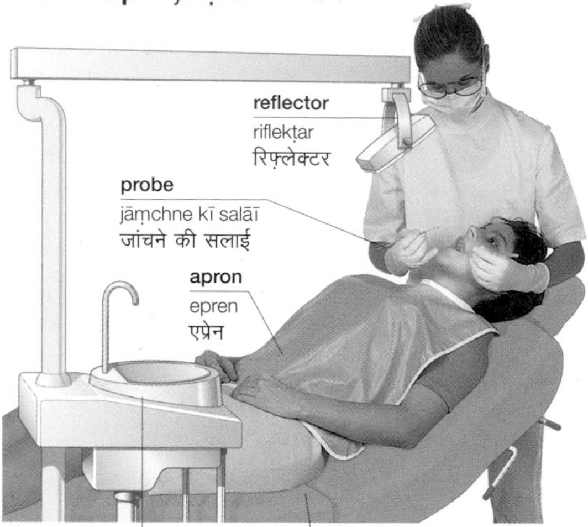

reflector
riflekṭar
रिफ़्लेक्टर

probe
jāṃchne kī salāī
जांचने की सलाई

apron
epren
एप्रेन

basin
besin
बेसिन

dentist's chair
dant chikitsā kursī
दंत चिकित्सा–कुर्सी

vocabulary • śabdāvalī • शब्दावली

toothache
dāṃt kā dard
दांत का दर्द

plaque
plāk
प्लाक

decay
saṛan
सड़न

filling
bharāvan
भरावन

drill
chhed karnā
छेद करना

extraction
dāṃt ukhāṛnā
दांत उखाड़ना

crown
upri dant
उपरि दंत

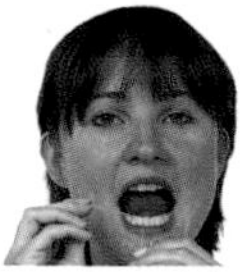

floss (v)
dhāge se safāī karnā
धागे से सफ़ाई करना

brush
braś karnā
ब्रश करना

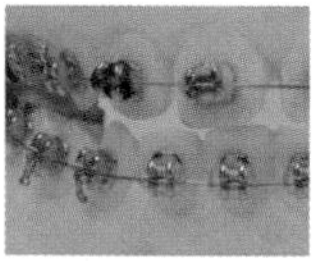

brace
tār kasnā
तार कसना

dental x-ray
dāṃtoṃ kā eksare
दांतों का एक्सरे

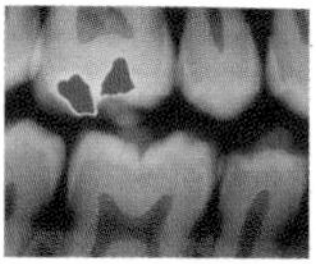

x-ray film
eksare film
एक्सरे फ़िल्म

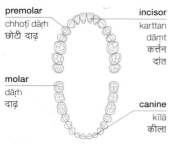

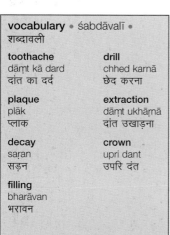

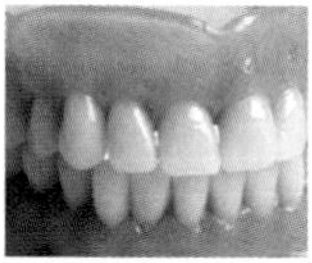

dentures
naklī battīsī
नक़ली बत्तीसी

optician • dṛṣṭi parīkṣak • दृष्टि परीक्षक

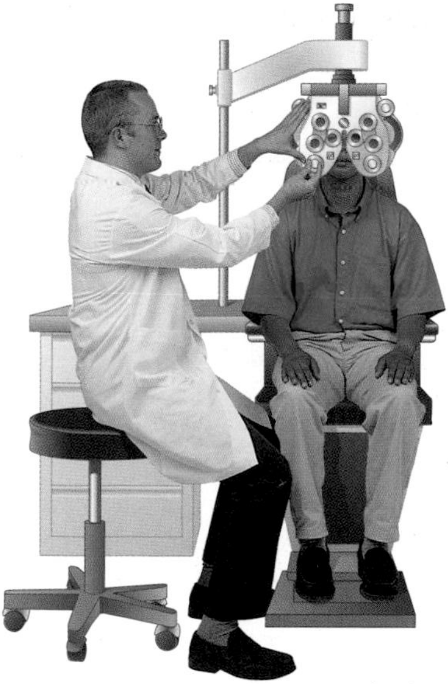

eye test | āṃkhoṃ kī jāṃch | आंखों की जांच

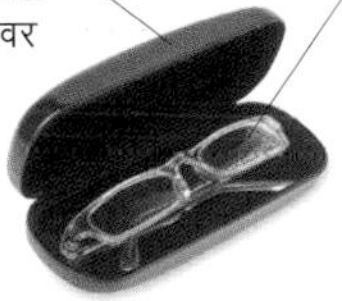
case
kavar
कवर
lens
lains
लैंस

glasses
chaśmā | चश्मा

frame
frem
फ़्रेम

sunglasses
dhūp kā chaśmā | धूप का चश्मा

cleaning fluid
lains sāf karne
kā dṛavya
लैंस साफ़ करने का द्रव्य

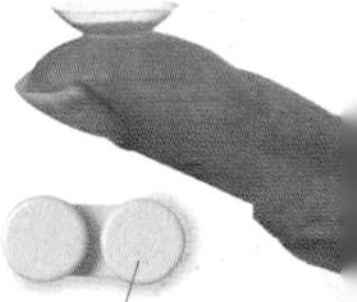
lens case
lains kavar
लैंस कवर

contact lenses | contact lains | कॉन्टेक्ट लैंस

eye • āṃkh • आंख

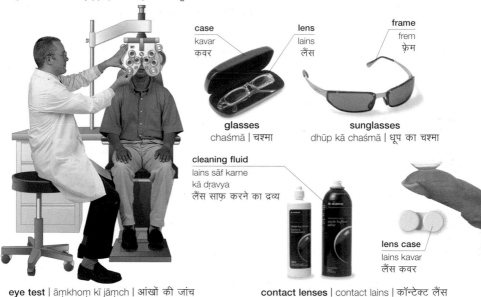

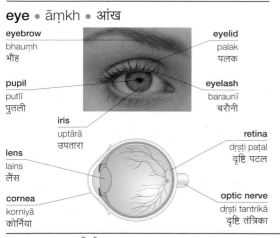

eyebrow
bhauṃh
भौंह
eyelid
palak
पलक
pupil
putlī
पुतली
eyelash
baraunī
बरौनी
iris
uptārā
उपतारा

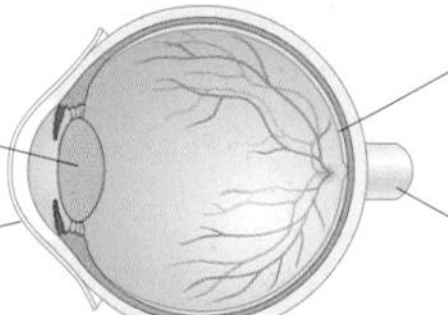
lens
lains
लैंस
retina
dṛṣṭi paṭal
दृष्टि पटल
cornea
korniyā
कोर्निया
optic nerve
dṛṣṭi tantrikā
दृष्टि तंत्रिका

vocabulary • śabdāvalī • शब्दावली

vision dṛṣṭi दृष्टि	**astigmatism** dṛṣṭi vaiṣamya दृष्टि वैषम्य
long sight dīrgh dṛṣṭi दीर्घ दृष्टि	**tear** āṃsū आंसू
cataract motiyābind मोतियाबिंद	**short sight** alp dṛṣṭi अल्प दृष्टि
diopter śīśā parakhne kī ikāī शीशा परखने की इकाई	**bifocal** bāyafokal बायफ़ोकल

pregnancy • garbhāvasthā • गर्भावस्था

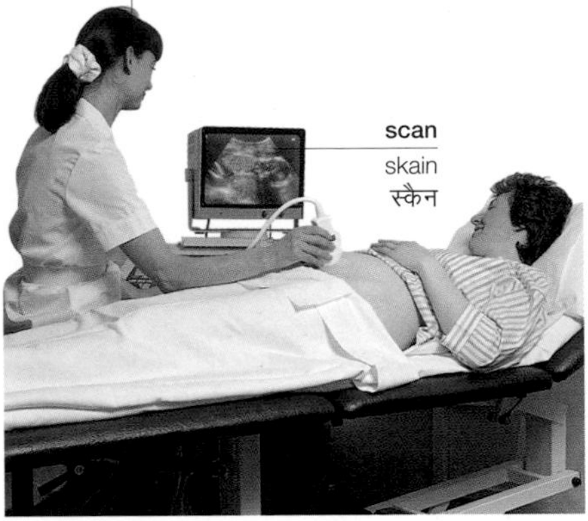

nurse
nars
नर्स

pregnancy test
garbhāvasthā jāṃch
गर्भावस्था जांच

umbilical cord
nābhi-rajju
नाभि–रज्जु

placenta
garbhnāl
गर्भनाल

cervix
garbhaśaya dvār
गर्भाशय द्वार

scan
skain
स्कैन

uterus
garbhāśaya
गर्भाशय

ultrasound
alṭrāsāuṇḍ | अल्ट्रासाउंड

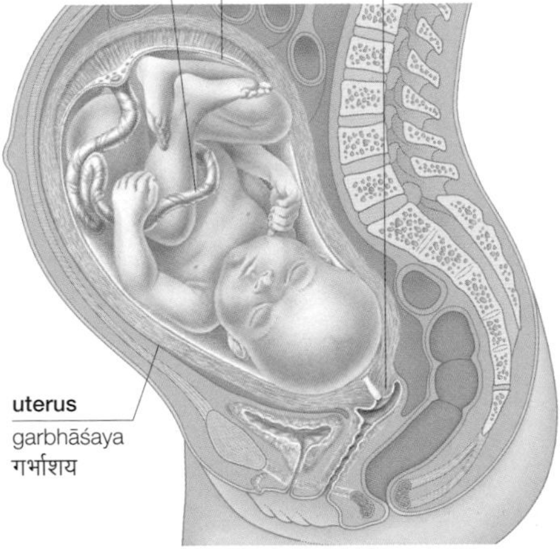

foetus
bhrūṇ | भ्रूण

vocabulary • śabdāvalī • शब्दावली

ovulation bījjanan बीजजनन	**antenatal** janm pūrv जन्म पूर्व	**contraction** saṅkuchan संकुचन	**dilation** phailāv फैलाव	**delivery** prasav प्रसव	**breech** ulṭā bhrūṇ उल्टा भ्रूण
conception garbhādhān गर्भाधान	**womb** bacchedānī बच्चेदानी	**break waters (v)** pānī jānā पानी जाना	**epidural** epiḍyūral एपिड्यूरल	**birth** janm जन्म	**premature** samaya pūrv समय पूर्व
pregnant garbhvatī गर्भवती	**trimester** trimās त्रिमास	**amniotic fluid** ulv drav उल्व द्रव	**episiotomy** bhagacchhedan भगच्छेदन	**miscarriage** garbhpāt गर्भपात	**gynaecologist** strī rog viśeṣajñ स्त्री–रोग विशेषज्ञ
expectant garbhvatī गर्भवती	**embryo** aviksit bhrūṇ अविकसित भ्रूण	**amniocentesis** sīrinj se ulv drav nikālnā सीरिंज से उल्व–द्रव निकालना	**caesarean section** operation prasav ऑपरेशन प्रसव	**stitches** ṭāṃke टांके	**obstetrician** prasav viśeṣajñ प्रसव विशेषज्ञ

childbirth • śiśu janm • शिशु जन्म

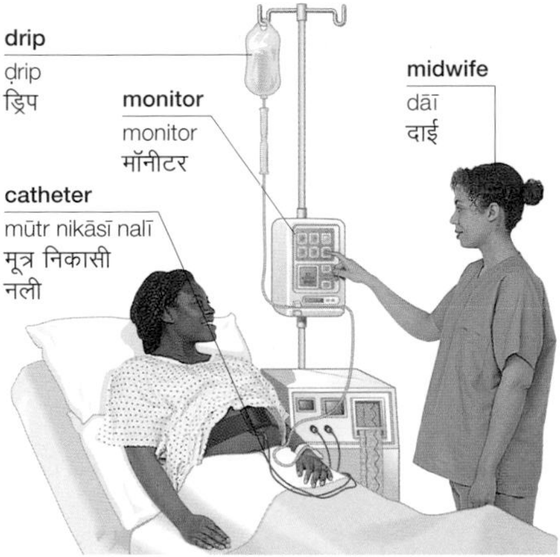
drip
ḍrip
ड्रिप
monitor
monitor
मॉनीटर
catheter
mūtr nikāsī nalī
मूत्र निकासी नली
midwife
dāī
दाई

induce labour (v)
kṛtrim prasav karānā | कृत्रिम प्रसव कराना

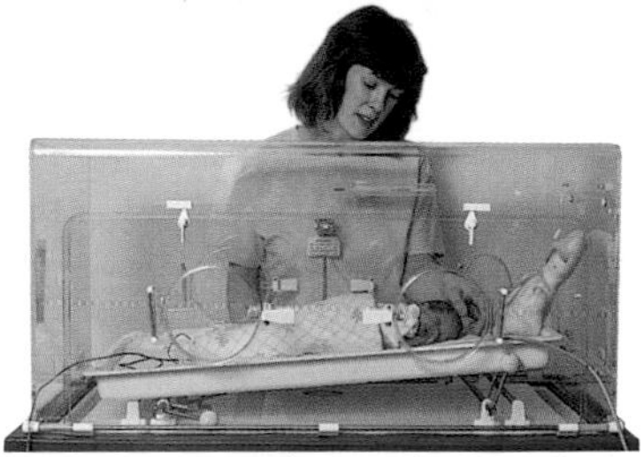

incubator | ūṣmak | ऊष्मक

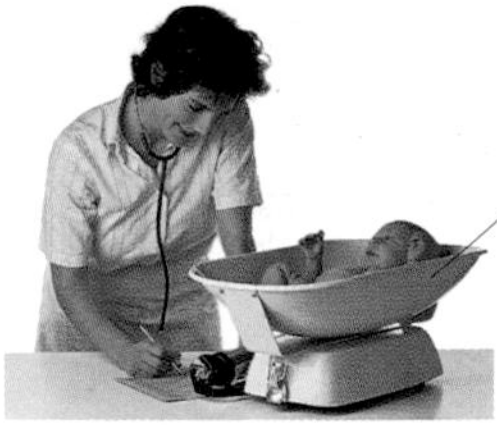
scales
tarāzū
तराज़ू

birth weight
janm bhār | जन्म भार

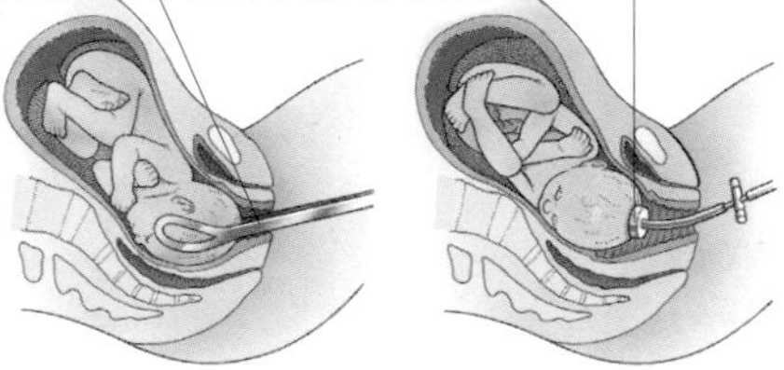
forceps
chimṭī
चिमटी
ventouse cup
prasav meṃ sahāyak upkaraṇ
प्रसव में सहायक उपकरण

assisted delivery
upkaraṇ dvārā prasav | उपकरण द्वारा प्रसव

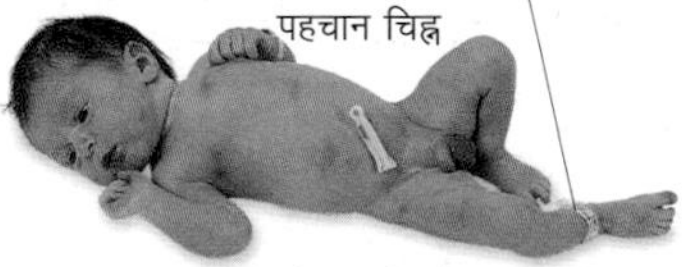
identity tag
pahchān chihn
पहचान चिह्न

newborn baby
navjāt śiśu | नवजात शिशु

nursing • stanpān • स्तनपान

breast pump
stan pamp
स्तन पंप

nursing bra
narsiṅg brā
नर्सिंग ब्रा

breastfeed (v)
stanpān karānā
स्तनपान कराना

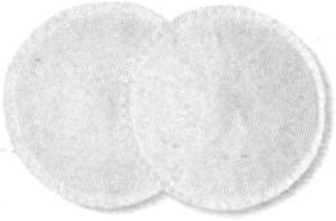

pads
paid
पैड

alternative therapy • vaikalpik chikitsā • वैकल्पिक चिकित्सा

yoga
yog | योग

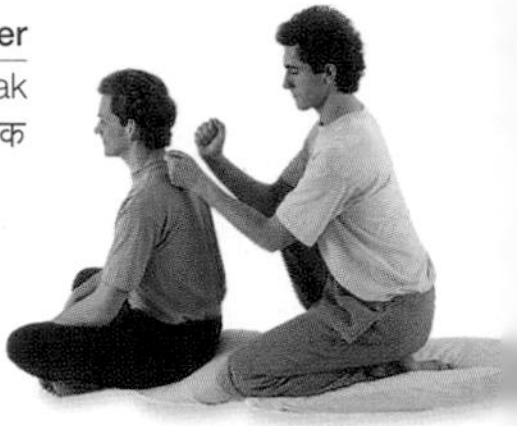

massage
māliś | मालिश

shiatsu
śiyātsu | शियात्सु

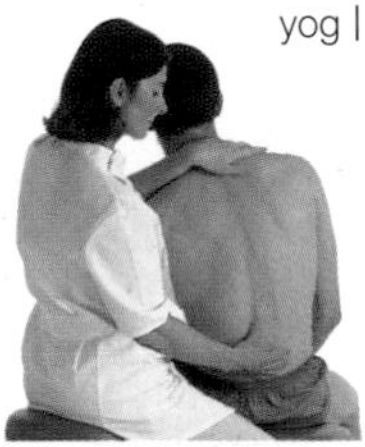

chiropractic
merudaṇḍ upchār
मेरुदंड उपचार

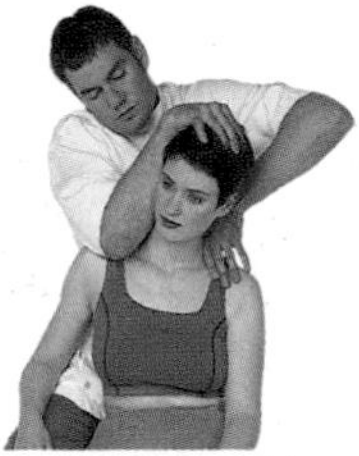

osteopathy | asthi chikitsā | अस्थि चिकित्सा

reflexology | riflaiksolojī
रिफ़्लैक्सोलोजी

meditation
dhyān | ध्यान

counsellor
parāmarśdātā
परामर्शदाता

group therapy
samūh chikitsā | समूह चिकित्सा

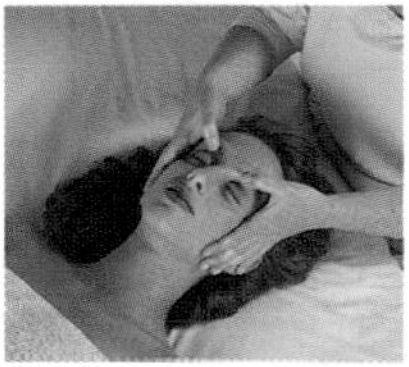

reiki
rekī | रेकी

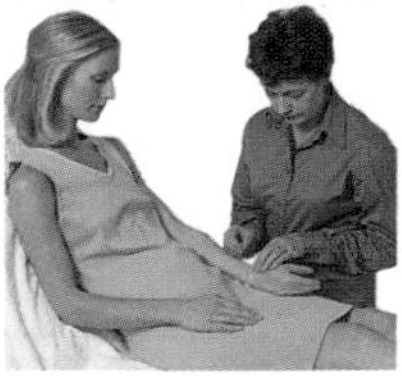

acupuncture
ekyūpaṅkchar
एक्यूपंक्चर

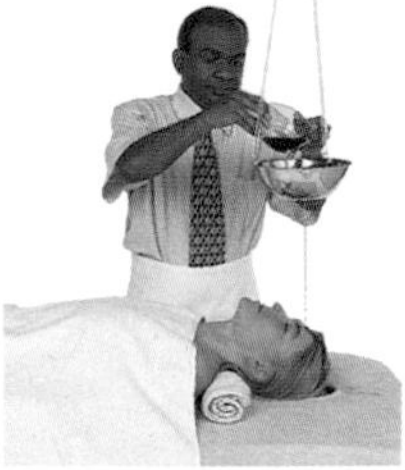

ayurveda
āyurved | आयुर्वेद

hypnotherapy
sammohan chikitsā
सम्मोहन चिकित्सा

herbalism | jaṛī-būṭī
sevan | जड़ी–बूटी सेवन

essential oils
sugandhit tel
सुगंधित तेल

aromatherapy
sugandh chikitsā
सुगंध चिकित्सा

homeopathy
homyopaithī
होम्योपैथी

acupressure
ekyūpraiśar
एक्यूप्रैशर

therapist
chikitsak
चिकित्सक

psychotherapy
manochikitsā | मनोचिकित्सा

vocabulary • śabdāvalī • शब्दावली

supplement pūrak पूरक	**feng shui** feṅg śuī फ़ेंग शुई	**relaxation** tanāv mukti तनाव मुक्ति	**naturopathy** prākṛtik chikitsā प्राकृतिक चिकित्सा
hydrotherapy jal chikitsā जल चिकित्सा	**herb** jaṛī-būṭī जड़ी–बूटी	**stress** tanāv तनाव	**crystal healing** krisṭal chikitsā क्रिस्टल चिकित्सा

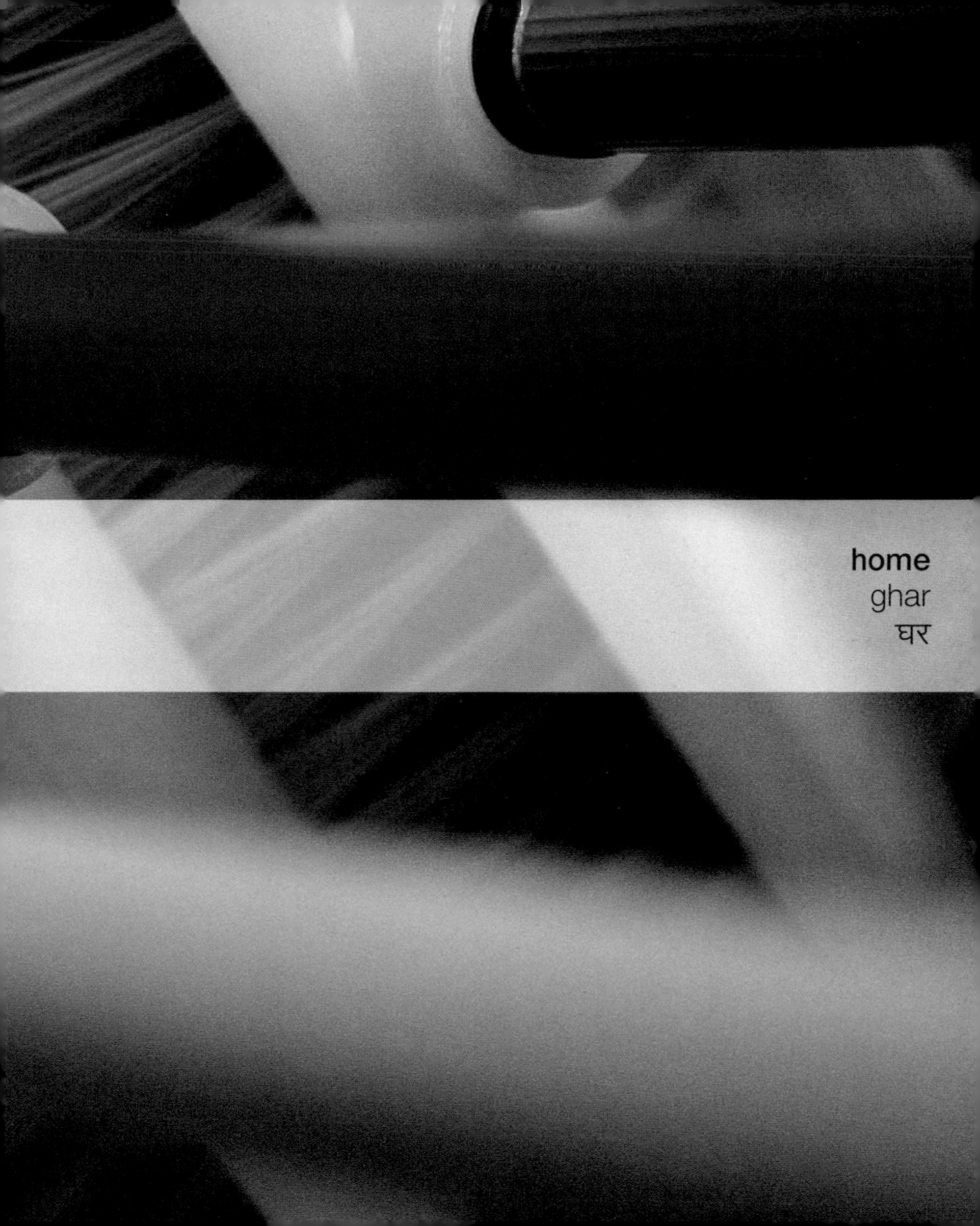

home
ghar
घर

house • makān • मकान

gutter
gaṭar
गटर
roof
chhat
छत
chimney
chimnī
चिमनी
wall
dīvār
दीवार
tile
ṭāil
टाइल
eaves
chhajjā
छज्जा
shutter
kapāṭ
कपाट
porch
dvārmaṇḍap
द्वारमंडप
window
khiṛkī
खिड़की
extension
atirikt bhāg
अतिरिक्त भाग
path
rāstā
रास्ता
front door
mukhyadvār
मुख्यद्वार

vocabulary • śabdāvalī • शब्दावली

detached ekal ghar एकल घर	**tenant** kirāedār किराएदार	**garage** gairej गैरेज	**letterbox** laiṭar box लैटर बॉक्स	**burglar alarm** chor ghaṇṭī चोर घंटी	**rent (v)** kirāe par lenā किराए पर लेना
townhouse śahrī makān शहरी मकान	**bungalow** baṅglā बंगला	**attic** aṭārī अटारी	**landlord** makān mālik मकान मालिक	**courtyard** āṅgan आंगन	**rent** kirāyā किराया
semidetached saṭā huā ghar सटा हुआ घर	**basement** tahk̲hānā तहख़ाना	**room** kamrā कमरा	**porch light** dvārmaṇḍap battī द्वारमंडप बत्ती	**floor** manzil मंज़िल	**terraced** chhat vālā छत वाला

entrance • praveś dvār • प्रवेश द्वार

hand rail
reliṅg
रेलिंग

staircase
zīnā
ज़ीना

landing
chauṛī sīṛhī
चौड़ी सीढ़ी

banister
sīṛhiyoṃ
kā jaṅglā
सीढ़ियों
का जंगला

hallway
galiyārā | गलियारा

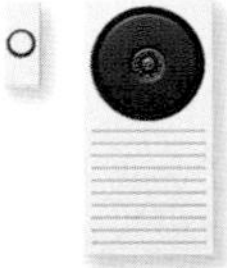

doorbell
darvāze kī ghaṇṭī
दरवाज़े की घंटी

doormat
pāyadān
पायदान

door knocker
kuṇḍā
कुंडा

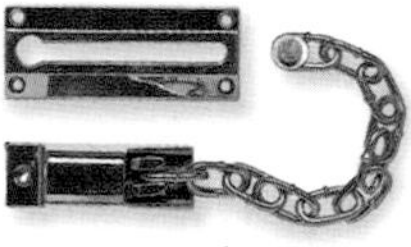

door chain | darvāze kī kaṛī | दरवाज़े की कड़ी

key
chābī
चाबी

lock
tālā | ताला

bolt
chaṭkhanī | चटख़नी

flat • flaiṭ • फ़्लैट

balcony
bālkanī
बालकनी

block of flats
apārṭmenṭ | अपार्टमेंट

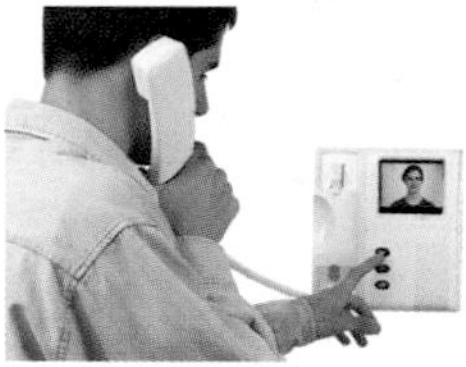

intercom
antaḥ sanchār | अंतः संचार

lift
lifṭ | लिफ़्ट

internal systems • gharelū upkaraṇ • घरेलू उपकरण

radiator | reḍieṭar | रेडिएटर

heater | hīṭar | हीटर

blade
paṅkhṛī | पंखड़ी

fan | paṅkhā | पंखा

convector heater
bloar | ब्लोअर

electricity • bijlī • बिजली

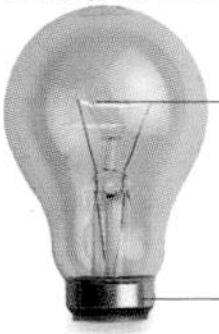

filament
filāmenṭ
फ़िलामेंट

bayonet fitting
beyoneṭ fiṭiṅg
बेयोनेट फ़िटिंग

light bulb
balb | बल्ब

earthing
arthiṅg
अर्थिंग

plug
plag | प्लग

pin
pin
पिन

neutral
nyūṭral | न्यूट्रल

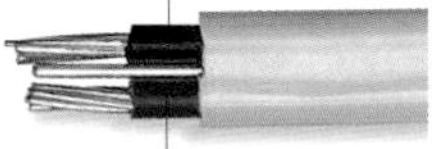

live
lāiv
लाइव

wires
tār | तार

vocabulary • śabdāvalī • शब्दावली

voltage
volṭej
वोल्टेज

amp
ampīyar
अंपीयर

power
ūrjā
ऊर्जा

fuse
fyūz
फ़्यूज़

fuse box
fyūz box
फ़्यूज़ बॉक्स

generator
jenreṭar
जेनरेटर

socket
socket
सॉकेट

switch
svich
स्विच

power cut
bijlī kaṭautī
बिजली कटौती

mains supply
men saplāī
मेन सप्लाई

transformer
transformer
ट्रांसफ़ॉर्मर

electricity meter
bijlī kā mīṭar
बिजली का मीटर

direct current
ḍāyarekṭ
karanṭ
डायरेक्ट करंट

alternating current
alternating
karanṭ
ऑल्टरनेटिंग
करंट

plumbing • nalsāzī • नलसाज़ी

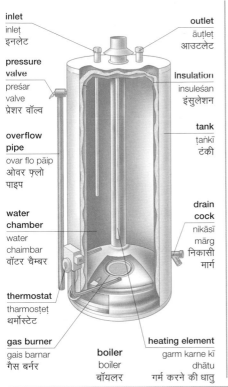

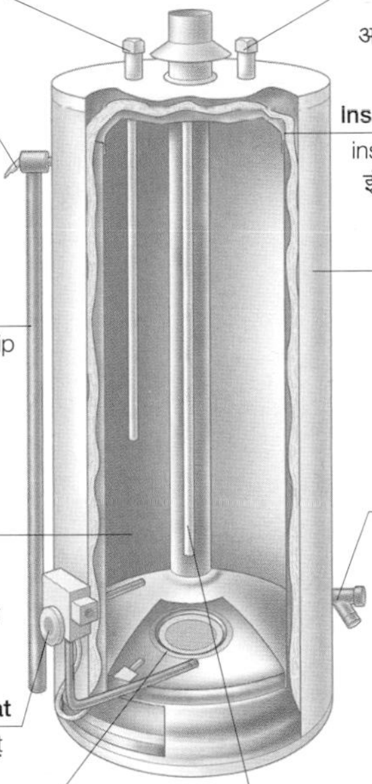
inlet
inleṭ
इनलेट
outlet
āuṭleṭ
आउटलेट
pressure valve
preśar valve
प्रेशर वॉल्व
insulation
insuleśan
इंसुलेशन
tank
ṭaṅkī
टंकी
overflow pipe
ovar flo pāip
ओवर फ़्लो पाइप
water chamber
water chaimbar
वॉटर चैम्बर
drain cock
nikāsī mārg
निकासी मार्ग
thermostat
tharmosṭeṭ
थर्मोस्टेट
gas burner
gais barnar
गैस बर्नर
boiler
boiler
बॉयलर
heating element
garm karne kī dhātu
गर्म करने की धातु

sink • siṅk • सिंक

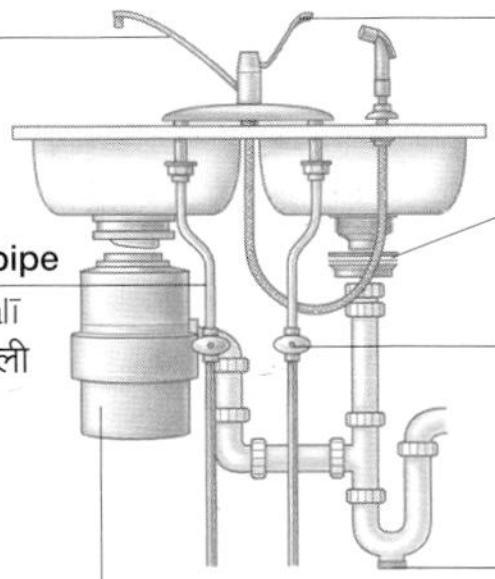
tap
nal
नल
lever
uttolak
उत्तोलक
gasket
gāskeṭ
गास्केट
supply pipe
āpūrti nalī
आपूर्ति नली
shutoff valve
shutoff valve
शटऑफ़ वॉल्व
drain
nikās
निकास
waste disposal unit
kūṛā nikās ikāī
कूड़ा निकास इकाई

water closet • śauchālaya • शौचालय

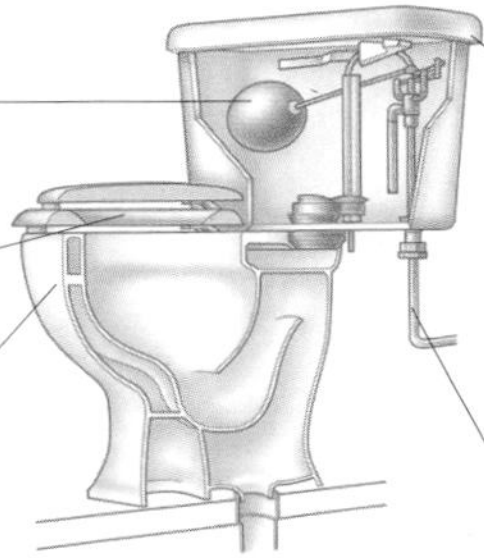
float ball
floṭ ball
फ़्लोट बॉल
cistern
ṭaṅkī
टंकी
seat
sīṭ
सीट
bowl
bāul
बाउल
waste pipe
nikās pāip
निकास पाइप

waste disposal • kūṛe kā nipṭārā • कूड़े का निपटारा

bottle
botal
बोतल

recycling bin
punarchakravat pātr
पुनर्चक्रवत पात्र

lid
ḍhakkan
ढक्कन
pedal
paiḍal
पैडल

rubbish bin
kūṛedān
कूड़ेदान

sorting unit
chhaṃṭāī yūniṭ
छंटाई यूनिट

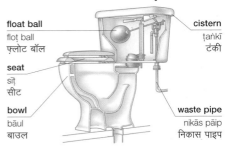

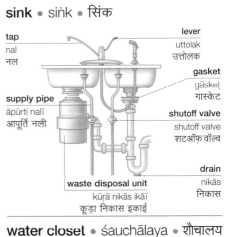

organic waste
jaivik kūṛā
जैविक कूड़ा

living room • baiṭhak • बैठक

painting
chitr
चित्र

frame
frem
फ़्रेम

lamp
laimp
लैंप

wall light
lāiṭ
लाइट

clock
ghaṛī
घड़ी

ceiling
chhat
छत

cabinet
almārī
अलमारी

sofa
sofā
सोफ़ा

cushion
gaddī
गद्दी

coffee table
coffee ṭebal
कॉफ़ी टेबल

floor
zamīn
ज़मीन

mirror
śīśā
शीशा

vase
guldān
गुलदान

mantelpiece
ātiśdān
आतिशदान

fireplace
alāv
अलाव

screen
skrīn
स्क्रीन

candle
mombattī
मोमबत्ती

sofabed
sofā-kam-beḍ
सोफ़ा–कम–बेड

curtain
pardā | पर्दा

net curtain
jālīdār pardā
जालीदार पर्दा

venetian blind
veneśiyan blāiṇḍ
वेनेशियन ब्लाइंड

roller blind | rolar blāiṇḍ | रोलर ब्लाइंड

moulding
paṭṭī | पट्टी

armchair
kursī
कुर्सी

bookshelf
kitābom̐ kī almārī
किताबों की अलमारी

rug
darī
दरी

study | paṛhne kā kamrā | पढ़ने का कमरा

dining room • bhojan kakṣ • भोजन कक्ष

table
mez
मेज़
pepper
kālī mirch
काली मिर्च
salt
namak
नमक
crockery
chīnī miṭṭī ke bartan
चीनी मिट्टी के बर्तन
cutlery
chhurī-kāṃṭe
छुरी–कांटे
chair
kursī
कुर्सी
back
pīṭh
पीठ
seat
sīṭ
सीट
leg
pāyā
पाया

vocabulary • śabdāvalī • शब्दावली

serve (v)
parosnā
परोसना

eat (v)
khānā
खाना

lay the table (v)
mez lagānā
मेज़ लगाना

hungry
bhūkhā
भूखा

tablecloth
mezpoś
मेज़पोश

breakfast
nāśtā
नाश्ता

dinner
rāt kā bhojan
रात का भोजन

hostess
mahilā mezbān
महिला मेज़बान

lunch
dopahar kā bhojan
दोपहर का भोजन

full
bharā huā
भरा हुआ

portion
hissā
हिस्सा

meal
bhojan
भोजन

host
mezbān
मेज़बान

guest
mehmān
मेहमान

place mat
ṭebal maiṭ
टेबल मैट

Can I have some more, please?
kyā maiṃ aur le saktā hūṃ?
क्या मैं और ले सकता हूं?

I've had enough, thank you.
aur nahīṃ chāhie, dhanyavād.
और नहीं चाहिए धन्यवाद।

That was delicious.
khānā svādiṣṭ thā.
खाना स्वादिष्ट था।

crockery and cutlery • bartan aur chhurī-kāṃṭe • बर्तन और छुरी–कांटे

teaspoon
chhoṭā chammach
छोटा चम्मच

mug
mag
मग

coffee cup
coffee kā pyālā
कॉफ़ी का प्याला

teacup
chāya kā pyālā
चाय का प्याला

plate
pleṭ
प्लेट

bowl
kaṭorā
कटोरा

wine glass
vāin gilās
वाइन गिलास

tumbler
gilās
गिलास

cafetière
coffee kī ketlī
कॉफ़ी की केतली

teapot
ketlī
केतली

jug
jag
जग

egg cup
aṇḍe kā kap
अंडे का कप

glassware
kāṃch ke gilās
कांच के गिलास

napkin ring
naipkin riṅg
नैपकिन रिंग

side plate
chhoṭī pleṭ
छोटी प्लेट

dinner plate
baṛī pleṭ
बड़ी प्लेट

soup bowl
sūp kī pleṭ
सूप की प्लेट

soup spoon
sūp kā chammach
सूप का चम्मच

napkin
naipkin
नैपकिन

fork
kāṃṭā
कांटा

place setting
bartan lagāne kā tarīḳā
बर्तन लगाने का तरीक़ा

spoon
chammach
चम्मच

knife
chhurī
छुरी

kitchen • rasoī • रसोई

shelves
k̤hāne
ख़ाने
tap
nal
नल
sink
siṅk
सिंक
drawer
darāz
दराज़
extractor
chimnī
चिमनी
ceramic hob
sṭov
स्टोव
worktop
khānā banāne kī jagah
खाना बनाने की जगह
oven
ovan
ओवन
cabinet
almārī
अलमारी

appliances • upkaraṇ • उपकरण

microwave oven
māikrovev ovan | माइक्रोवेव ओवन

kettle
ketlī
केतली

toaster
ṭosṭar
टोस्टर

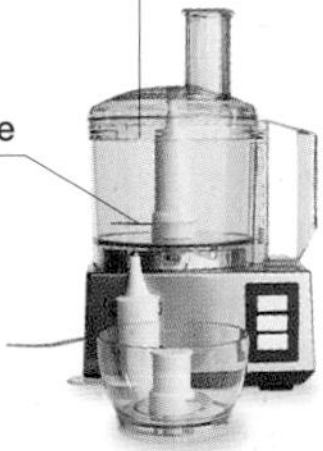
mixing bowl
miksiṅg bāul
मिक्सिंग बाउल
blade
bleḍ
ब्लेड

food processor
fūḍ prosesar
फ़ूड प्रोसेसर

lid
ḍhakkan
ढक्कन

blender
blenḍar
ब्लेंडर

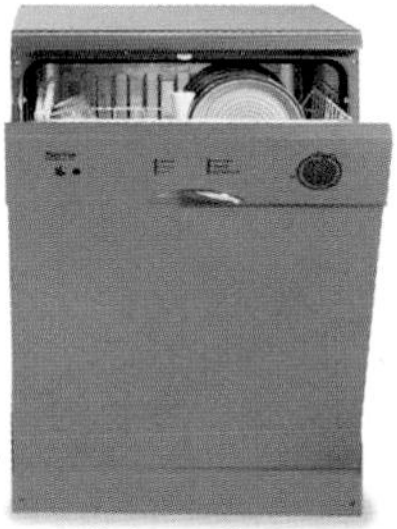

dishwasher
bartan dhone kī maśīn
बर्तन धोने की मशीन

ice maker
baraf jamāne kī jagah
बर्फ़ जमाने की जगह

freezer
frīzar
फ़्रीज़र

refrigerator
refrījareṭar
रेफ़्रीजरेटर

shelf
ḳhānā
ख़ाना

crisper
krispar
क्रिस्पर

fridge-freezer
frij | फ़्रिज

vocabulary • śabdāvalī • शब्दावली

burner
barnar
बर्नर

hob
sṭov
स्टोव

rubbish bin
kūṛedān
कूड़ेदान

draining board
ḍreniṅg borḍ
ड्रेनिंग बोर्ड

freeze (v)
jamānā
जमाना

defrost (v)
pighlānā
पिघलाना

sauté (v)
halkā bhūnnā
हल्का भूनना

steam (v)
bhāp se pakānā
भाप से पकाना

cooking • khānā pakānā • खाना पकाना

peel (v)
chhīlnā | छीलना

slice (v)
kāṭnā | काटना

grate (v)
ghisnā | घिसना

pour (v)
uṛelnā | उड़ेलना

mix (v)
milānā | मिलाना

whisk (v)
pheṃṭnā | फेंटना

boil (v)
ubālnā | उबालना

fry (v)
talnā | तलना

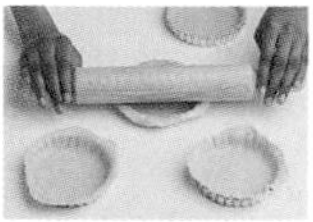

roll (v)
belnā | बेलना

stir (v)
chalānā | चलाना

simmer (v)
khadaknā
खदकना

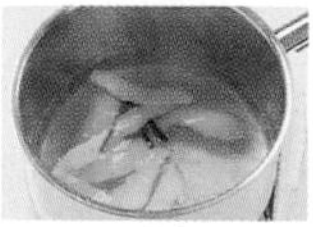

poach (v)
pānī meṃ pakānā
पानी में पकाना

bake (v)
bek karnā
बेक करना

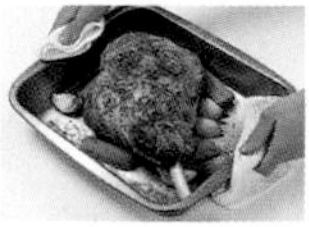

roast (v)
bhūnnā
भूनना

grill (v) | tandūr meṃ bhūnnā
तंदूर में भूनना

kitchenware • rasoī upkaraṇ • रसोई उपकरण

chopping board
sabzī kāṭne kā takhtā | सब्ज़ी काटने का तख़्ता

bread knife
breḍ kāṭne kī chhurī
ब्रेड काटने की छुरी

kitchen knife
chākū
चाक़ू

cleaver
chāpaṛ
चापड़

knife sharpener
chākū tez karne vālā
चाक़ू तेज़ करने वाला

meat tenderizer
māṃs kūṭne kā auzār | मांस कूटने का औज़ार

skewer
sīkh | सीख

peeler | chhīlne vālā chākū
छीलने वाला चाक़ू

apple corer | bīj nikālne kī salāī
बीज निकालने की सलाई

grater
kaddūkas
कद्दूकस

pestle
mūsal
मूसल

mortar
kharal | खरल

masher
meśar | मेशर

can opener
kain opnar
कैन ओपनर

bottle opener
botal opnar
बोतल ओपनर

garlic press
lahsun kūṭne vālā
लहसुन कूटने वाला

serving spoon
parosne kā chammach
परोसने का चम्मच

fish slice
palṭā | पलटा

colander
chhalnā | छलना

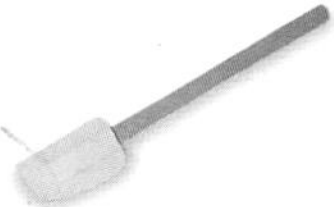

spatula
speṭulā | स्पेटुला

wooden spoon
lakṛī kā chammach
लकड़ी का चम्मच

slotted spoon
kalchhī | कलछी

ladle
chamchā | चमचा

carving fork | ghumāvdār kāṃṭā | घुमावदार कांटा

scoop
chammach | चम्मच

whisk
phemṭnī | फेंटनी

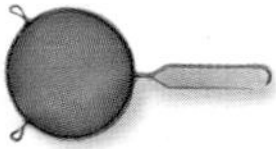

sieve
chhannī | छन्नी

lid
ḍhakkan | ढक्कन

non-stick
non stick | नॉनस्टिक

frying pan
frāiṅg pain
फ़्राइंग पैन

saucepan
ḍegchī
डेगची

grill pan
gril pain
ग्रिल पैन

wok
kaṛāhī
कड़ाही

earthenware dish
miṭṭī kā bartan
मिट्टी का बर्तन

glass
kāṃch
कांच

ovenproof
ovan rodhī | ओवन रोधी

mixing bowl
miksiṅg bāul
मिक्सिंग बाउल

soufflé dish
sūfle bartan
सूफ़ले बर्तन

gratin dish
grāṭin ḍiś
ग्राटिन डिश

ramekin
remikīn
रेमिकीन

casserole dish
kaisrol
कैसरोल

baking cakes • kek banānā • केक बनाना

scales
tarāzū
तराज़ू

measuring jug
māpak jag
मापक जग

cake tin | kek banāne kā sāṃchā | केक बनाने का सांचा

pie tin | pāī banāne kā sāṃchā | पाई बनाने का सांचा

flan tin | flain banāne kā sāṃchā | फ़्लैन बनाने का सांचा

pastry brush
pesṭrī braś | पेस्ट्री ब्रश

rolling pin
belan | बेलन

piping bag | pāipiṅg baig | पाइपिंग बैग

muffin tray
muffin ṭre
मॅफ़िन ट्रे

baking tray
bekiṅg ṭre
बेकिंग ट्रे

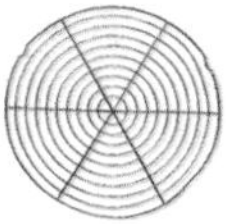

cooling rack
kūliṅg raik
कूलिंग रैक

oven glove
ovan ke dastāne
ओवन के दस्ताने

apron
epren
एप्रेन

bedroom • śayan kakṣ • शयन कक्ष

wardrobe
almārī
अलमारी

bedside lamp
sāiḍ laimp
साइड लैम्प

headboard
palaṅg kā sirhānā
पलंग का सिरहाना

bedside table
sāiḍ ṭebal
साइड टेबल

chest of drawers
darāzoṃ kī almārī
दराज़ों की अलमारी

drawer
darāz
दराज़

bed
palaṅg
पलंग

mattress
gaddā
गद्दा

bedspread
palaṅgpoś
पलंगपोश

pillow
takiyā
तकिया

hot-water bottle | garm panī kī thailī | गर्म पानी की थैली

clock radio
reḍiyo ghaṛī
रेडियो घड़ी

alarm clock
alārm ghaṛī
अलार्म घड़ी

box of tissues
ṭiśyū box
टिश्यू बॉक्स

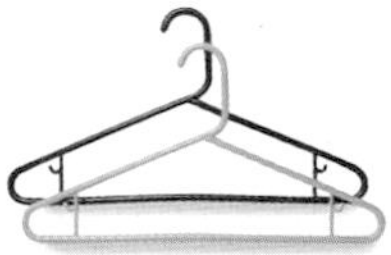

coat hanger
koṭ kā haiṅgar
कोट का हैंगर

bed linen • chādar va takiyā gilāf ādi • चादर व तकिया गिलाफ़ आदि

mirror
śīśā
शीशा

dressing table
śṛaṅgār mez
श्रृंगार मेज़

floor
farś
फ़र्श

pillowcase
gilāf
गिलाफ़

sheet
chādar
चादर

valance
jhālar
झालर

duvet
roeṃ se banī razāī
रोएं से बनी रज़ाई

quilt
razāī
रज़ाई

blanket
kambal
कंबल

vocabulary • śabdāvalī • शब्दावली

single bed
siṅgal palaṅg
सिंगल पलंग

double bed
ḍabal palaṅg
डबल पलंग

electric blanket
vidyut kambal
विद्युत कंबल

footboard
pāyadān
पायदान

spring
spriṅg
स्प्रिंग

carpet
ḳālīn
क़ालीन

insomnia
anidrā
अनिद्रा

go to bed (v)
sone jānā
सोने जाना

go to sleep (v)
sonā
सोना

wake up (v)
jāgnā
जागना

get up (v)
uṭhnā
उठना

set the alarm (v)
alārm lagānā
अलार्म लगाना

make the bed (v)
bistar lagānā
बिस्तर लगाना

snore (v)
ḳharrāṭe lenā
ख़र्राटे लेना

built-in wardrobe
kapṛoṃ kī almārī
कपड़ों की अलमारी

bathroom • snānghar • स्नानघर

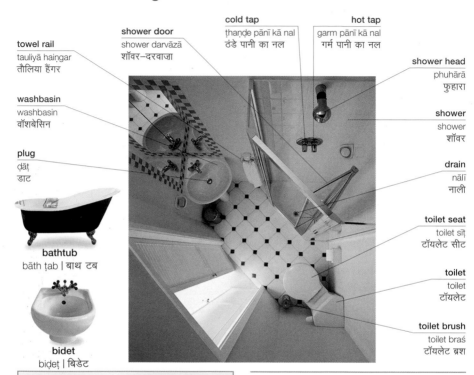

towel rail
tauliyā haiṇgar
तौलिया हैंगर
shower door
shower darvāzā
शॉवर–दरवाज़ा
cold tap
ṭhaṇḍe pānī kā nal
ठंडे पानी का नल
hot tap
garm pānī kā nal
गर्म पानी का नल
shower head
phuhārā
फुहारा
washbasin
washbasin
वॉशबेसिन
shower
shower
शॉवर
plug
ḍāṭ
डाट
drain
nālī
नाली
toilet seat
toilet sīṭ
टॉयलेट सीट
toilet
toilet
टॉयलेट
toilet brush
toilet braś
टॉयलेट ब्रश

bathtub
bāth ṭab | बाथ टब

bidet
biḍeṭ | बिडेट

vocabulary • śabdāvalī • शब्दावली

medicine cabinet davāī kī almārī दवाई की अलमारी	**bath mat** snānghar kī chaṭāī स्नानघर की चटाई
toilet roll toilet rol टॉयलेट रोल	**shower curtain** shower kā pardā शॉवर का पर्दा
take a shower (v) phuhāre meṃ nahānā फुहारे में नहाना	**take a bath (v)** ṭab meṃ nahānā टब में नहाना

dental hygiene • dāṃtoṃ kī safāī • दांतों की सफ़ाई

toothbrush
ṭūthbraś | टूथब्रश

dental floss
ḍenṭal floss
डेंटल फ़्लॉस

toothpaste
ṭūthpesṭ | टूथपेस्ट

mouthwash
mouthwash | माउथवॉश

loofah
jhāvāṃ
झावां

sponge
spañj | स्पंज

pumice stone
jhāmak | झामक

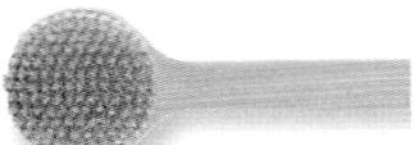

back brush | pīṭh ragaṛne kā braś | पीठ रगड़ने का ब्रश

deodorant
ḍiyoḍrenṭ | डियोडरेंट

soap dish
sābundānī
साबुनदानी

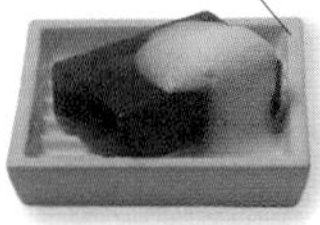

soap
sābun
साबुन

face cream
krīm
क्रीम

shower gel
shower jail
शॉवर जैल

bubble bath
babbal bāth
बब्बल बाथ

bathrobe | ḍresiṅg gāun | ड्रेसिंग गाउन

hand towel
chhoṭā tauliyā
छोटा तौलिया

bath towel
baṛā tauliyā
बड़ा तौलिया

towels
taulie | तौलिए

body lotion
body lośan | बॉडी लोशन

talcum powder
ṭelkam pāuḍar
टेल्कम पाउडर

shaving • hajāmat • हजामत

electric razor
ilekṭrik rezar
इलेक्ट्रिक रेज़र

shaving foam
śeviṅg fom
शेविंग फ़ोम

disposable razor
ḍispozebal rezar
डिस्पोज़ेबल रेज़र

razor blade
rezar bleḍ
रेज़र ब्लेड

aftershave
āfṭar śev
आफ़्टर शेव

nursery • śiśugṛh • शिशुगृह

baby care • śiśu dekhbhāl • शिशु देखभाल

sponge
spañj
स्पंज

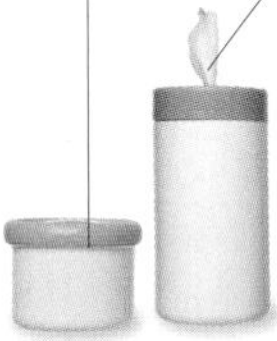

nappy rash cream
naipī reś krīm
नैपी रेश क्रीम

wet wipe
nam ṭiśyu
नम टिश्यु

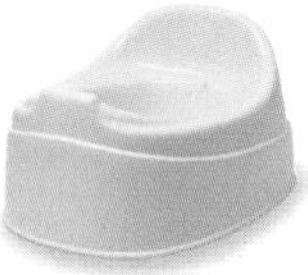

baby bath
śiśu snān | शिशु स्नान

potty
potty | पॉटी

changing mat | kapṛe badalne kī gaddī | कपड़े बदलने की गद्दी

sleeping • sonā • सोना

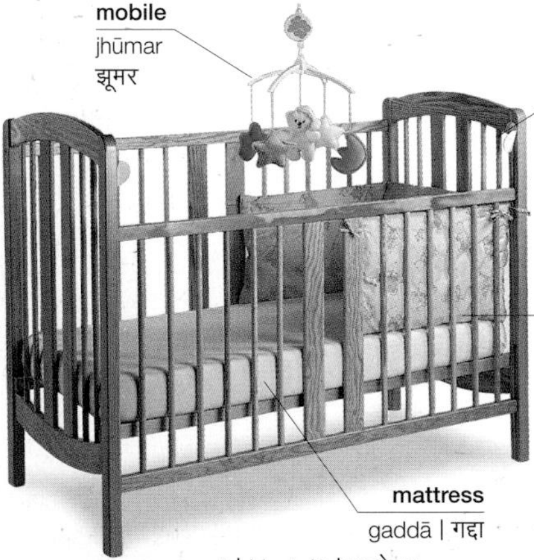

mobile
jhūmar
झूमर

bars
sīṃkhche
सींखचे

bumper
bampar
बम्पर

mattress
gaddā | गद्दा

cot | khaṭolā | खटोला

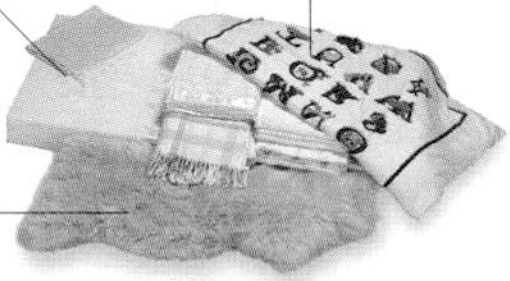

sheet
chādar
चादर

blanket
kambal
कंबल

fleece
ūnī chādar
ऊनी चादर

bedding
bichhaunā | बिछौना

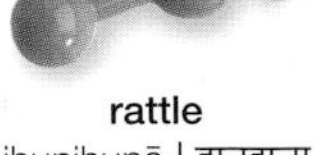

rattle
jhunjhunā | झुनझुना

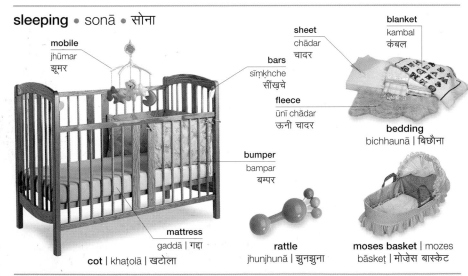

moses basket | mozes bāskeṭ | मोज़ेस बास्केट

playing • khelnā • खेलना

doll
guṛiyā
गुड़िया

soft toy
mulāyam khilaune
मुलायम खिलौने

doll's house
guṛiyā ghar
गुड़िया घर

playhouse
khel ghar | खेल घर

toy
khilaunā
खिलौना

toy basket | khilaune kī ṭokrī | खिलौने की टोकरी

ball
gend
गेंद

playpen
khel bāṛā | खेल बाड़ा

safety • surakṣā • सुरक्षा

child lock
bacchoṃ kā tālā
बच्चों का ताला

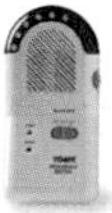

baby monitor
bebī monitor
बेबी मॉनीटर

stair gate
siṛhiyoṃ kā geṭ
सीढ़ियों का गेट

eating • khānā • खाना

high chair
ūṃchī kursī | ऊंची कुर्सी

teat
nippal
निप्पल

drinking cup
pīne kā kap
पीने का कप

bottle
botal | बोतल

going out • bāhar jānā • बाहर जाना

pushchair | hāth gāṛī | हाथ गाड़ी

hood
chhatrī
छतरी

pram
bagghī | बग्घी

carrycot
pālnā | पालना

nappy
laṅgoṭī
लंगोटी

changing bag | bacchoṃ kā thailā | बच्चों का थैला

baby sling | śiśu paṭṭā
शिशु पट्टा

utility room • gharelū kārya kakṣ • घरेलू कार्य कक्ष

laundry • laundry • लॉन्ड्री

clean clothes
dhule kapṛe
धुले कपड़े

dirty washing
gande kapṛe
गंदे कपड़े

laundry basket
gande kapṛoṃ kī ṭokrī | गंदे कपड़ों की टोकरी

washing machine |
kapṛe dhone kī maśīn | कपड़े धोने की मशीन

washer-dryer
washer ḍrāyar
वॉशर–ड्रायर

tumble dryer
ḍrāyar
ड्रायर

linen basket
kapṛoṃ kī ṭokrī
कपड़ों की टोकरी

clothes line
alganī
अलगनी

clothes peg
chimṭī
चिमटी

dry (v)
sukhānā | सुखाना

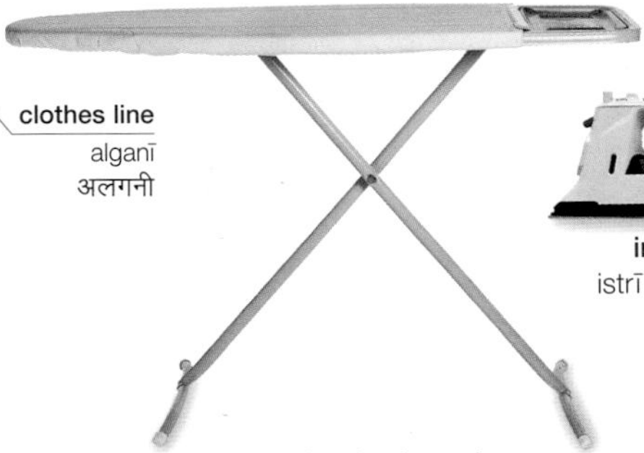

ironing board
istrī kā taḳhtā | इस्त्री का तख़्ता

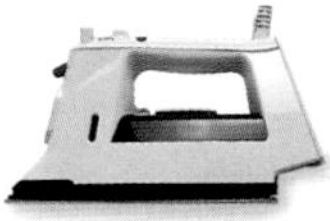

iron
istrī | इस्त्री

vocabulary • śabdāvalī • शब्दावली

rinse (v)
khaṅgālnā
खंगालना

load (v)
kapṛe maśīn meṃ ḍālnā
कपड़े मशीन में डालना

spin (v)
kapṛe nichoṛnā
कपड़े निचोड़ना

spin dryer
kapṛe nichoṛne vālā
कपड़े निचोड़ने वाला

iron (v)
istrī karnā
इस्त्री करना

conditioner
kanḍīśnar
कंडीशनर

How do I operate the washing machine?
washing maśīn kaise chalānī hai?
वॉशिंग मशीन कैसे चलानी है?

cleaning equipment • safāī upkaraṇ • सफ़ाई उपकरण

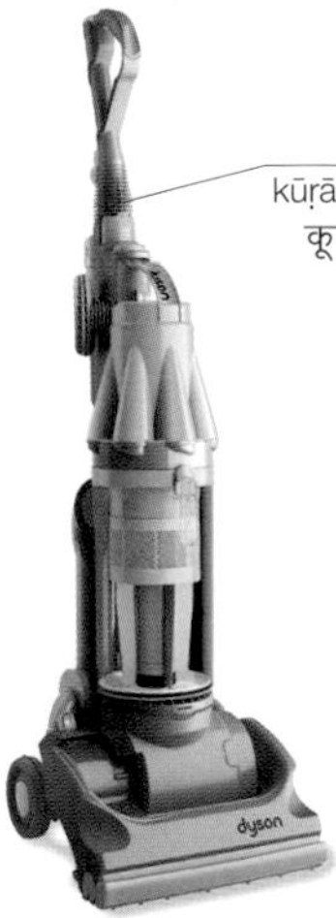

suction hose
kūṛā khīṃchne kī nalī
कूड़ा खींचने की नली

vacuum cleaner | vekyūm klīnar | वेक्यूम क्लीनर

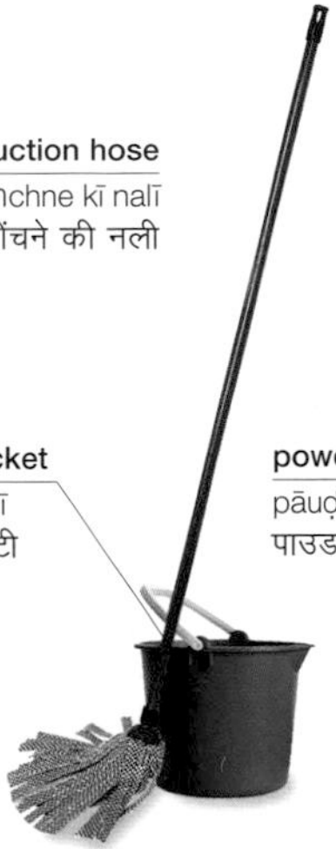

bucket
bālṭī
बाल्टी

mop
pochhā | पोछा

brush
braś
ब्रश

dust pan | kūṛe kā paṅjā | कूड़े का पंजा

bleach
blīch | ब्लीच

powder
pāuḍar
पाउडर

liquid
dravya
द्रव्य

detergent
ḍiṭarjenṭ | डिटर्जेंट

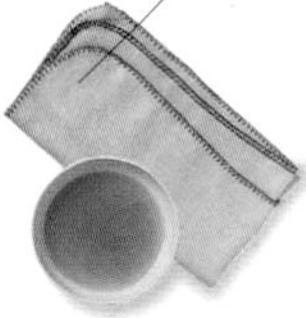

duster
jhāṛan
झाड़न

polish
polish | पॉलिश

activities • gatividhiyāṃ • गतिविधियां

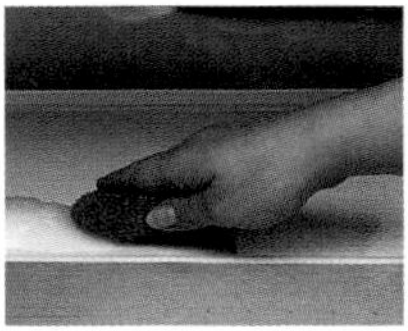

clean (v)
safāī karnā | सफ़ाई करना

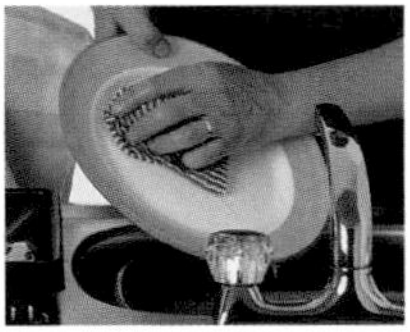

wash (v)
dhonā | धोना

wipe (v)
poṃchhnā | पोंछना

scrub (v)
ghisnā | घिसना

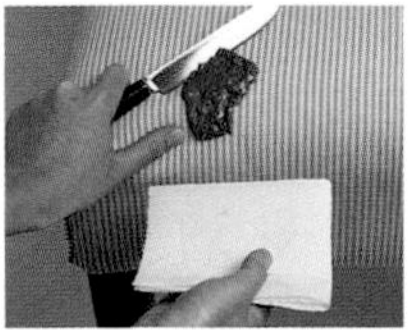

scrape (v)
khurachnā | खुरचना

broom
jhāṛū
झाड़ू

sweep (v)
jhāṛū lagānā | झाड़ू लगाना

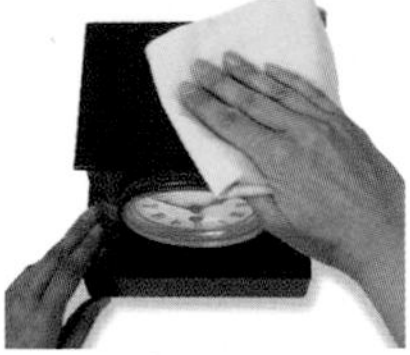

dust (v)
dhūl jhāṛnā | धूल झाड़ना

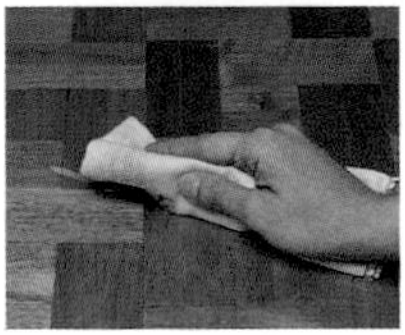

polish (v)
chamkānā | चमकाना

workshop • kārḳhānā • कारख़ाना

chuck
chakkā
चक्का

drill bit
chhed karne kī sūī
छेद करने की सूई

battery pack
baiṭarī paik
बैटरी पैक

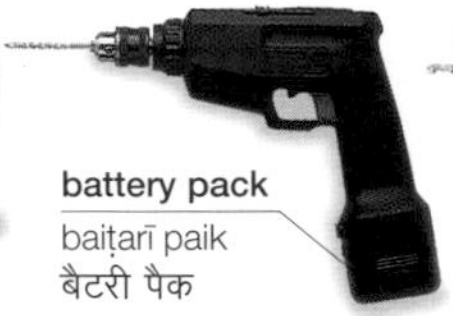

jigsaw
chhoṭā ārā
छोटा आरा

rechargeable drill
richārjebal ḍril
रिचार्जेबल ड्रिल

electric drill
vidyut ḍril/vedhnī
विद्युत ड्रिल/वेधनी

glue gun
gond gan | गोंद गन

clamp
śikanjā/paṭṭī
शिकंजा/पट्टी

blade
bleḍ
ब्लेड

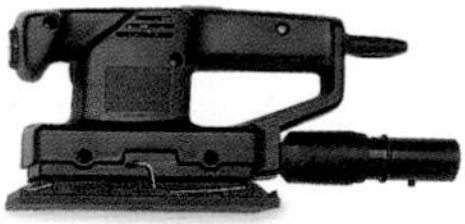

vice
śikanjā | शिकंजा

sander
senḍar | सेंडर

circular saw
vṛttākār ārī | वृत्ताकार आरी

workbench
kām karne kī mez
काम करने की मेज़

wood glue
lakṛī kā gond
लकड़ी का गोंद

router
rūṭar
रूटर

wood shavings
lakṛī kī chhīlan
लकड़ी की छीलन

tool rack
auzār raik
औज़ार रैक

bit brace
biṭ bres
बिट ब्रेस

extension lead
atirikt tār
अतिरिक्त तार

techniques • vidhiyāṃ • विधियां

cut (v)
kāṭnā | काटना

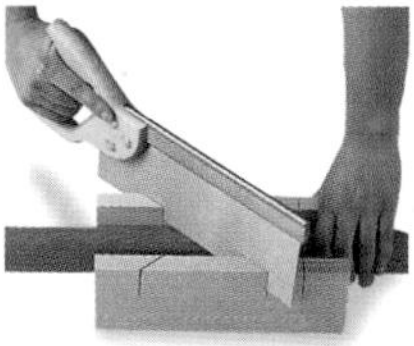

saw (v)
chīrnā | चीरना

drill (v)
chhed karnā | छेद करना

hammer (v)
ṭhoknā | ठोकना

plane (v) | randā karnā | रंदा करना

turn (v)
kharādnā | खरादना

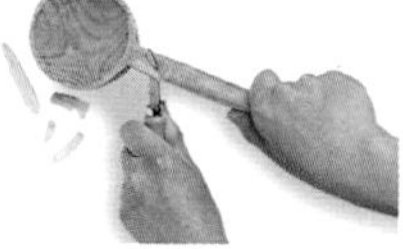

carve (v)
nakķāśī karnā | नक़्क़ाशी करना

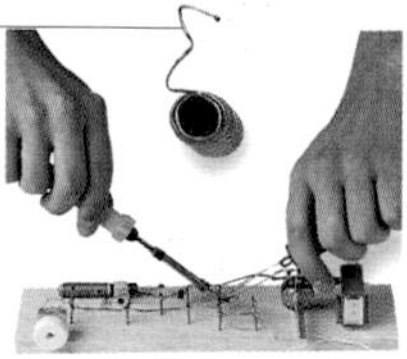
solder
soldar karne kā tār
सोल्डर करने का तार

solder (v) | ṭāṃkā lagānā | टांका लगाना

materials • sāmān • सामान

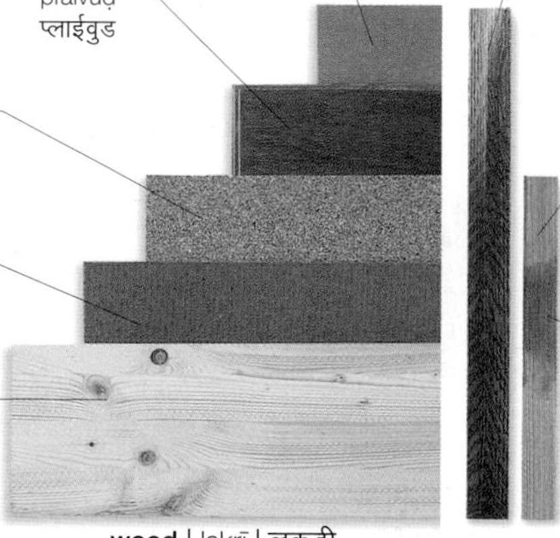
MDF
em ḍī ef
एम डी एफ़
plywood
plāīvuḍ
प्लाईवुड
chipboard
chip borḍ
चिप बोर्ड
hardboard
hārḍ borḍ
हार्ड बोर्ड
softwood
mulāyam lakṛī
मुलायम लकड़ी
hardwood
kaṭhor lakṛī
कठोर लकड़ी
varnish
rogan
रोग़न
woodstain
lakṛī ke dāg
लकड़ी के दाग़

wood | lakṛī | लकड़ी

wire
tār
तार

cable
kebal | केबल

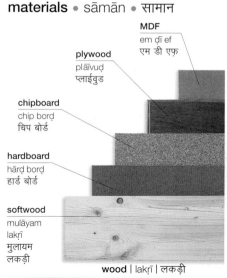

stainless steel
ispāt
इस्पात
galvanised
ķalaīdār
क़लईदार

metal | dhātu | धातु

toolbox • auzār peṭī • औज़ार पेटी

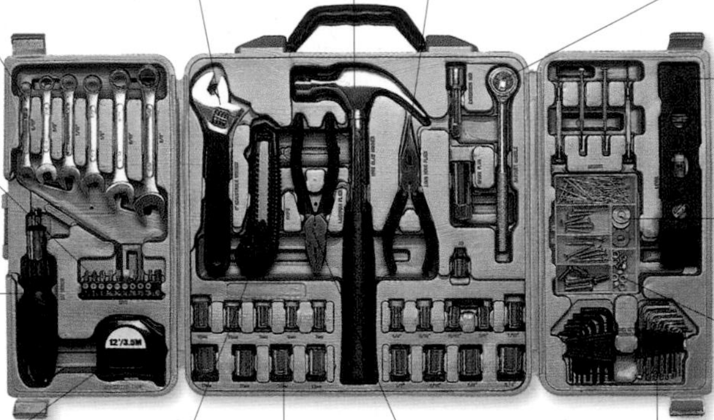

spanner
pānā
पाना

adjustable spanner
parivartnīya pānā
परिवर्तनीय पाना

hammer
hathauṛā
हथौड़ा

needle-nose pliers
bārīk plās
बारीक प्लास

socket wrench
socket rinch
सॉकेट रिंच

screwdriver bits
pechkas vajr
पेचकस वज्र

spirit level
leval
लेवल

washer
wāśar
वाशर

screwdriver
pechkas
पेचकस

nut
purzā
पुर्ज़ा

tape measure
inch ṭep
इंच टेप

knife
chākū
चाक़ू

socket
socket
सॉकेट

bull-nose pliers
moṭā plās
मोटा प्लास

key
chābī
चाबी

drill bits • ḍriliṅg maśīn ke vajr • ड्रिलिंग मशीन के वज्र

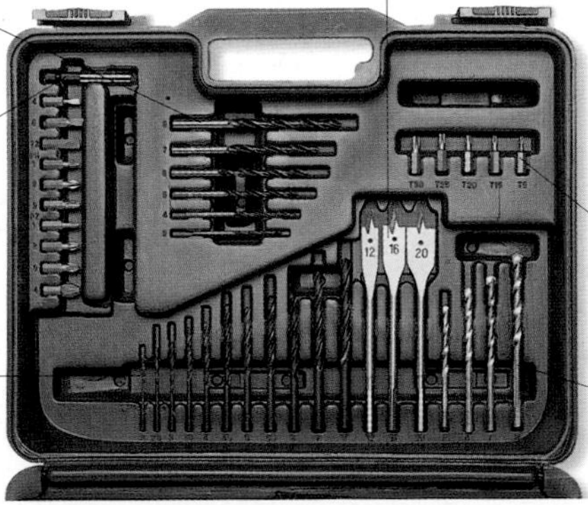

flat wood bit
samtal taḳhtā vajr | समतल तख़्ता वज्र

metal bit
dhātu vajr
धातु वज्र

reamer
barmā
बरमा

carpentry bits
baṛhaīgirī ke vajr
बढ़ईगिरी के वज्र

security bit
surakṣā vajr
सुरक्षा वज्र

masonry bit
rājgirī ke vajr
राजगिरी के वज्र

phillips screwdriver
filips pechkas
फ़िलिप्स पेचकस

head
sirā
सिरा

nail
kīl | कील

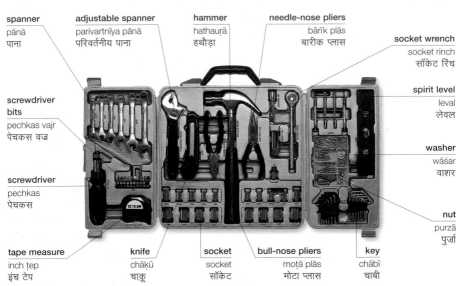

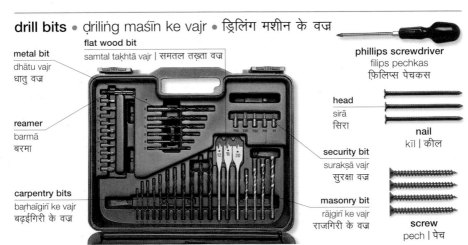

screw
pech | पेच

wire strippers
tār chhīlne kā plās
तार छीलने का प्लास

wire cutters
tār kāṭne kā yantr
तार काटने का यंत्र

soldering iron
ṭāṃke kā upkaraṇ
टांके का उपकरण

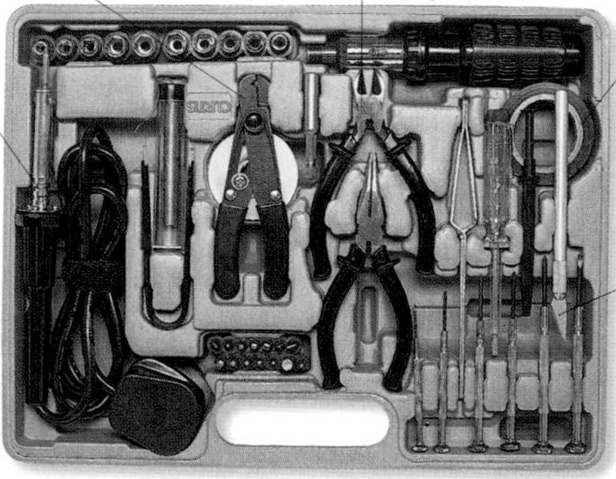

insulating tape
bijlī kā ṭep
बिजली का टेप

scalpel
chhurī
छुरी

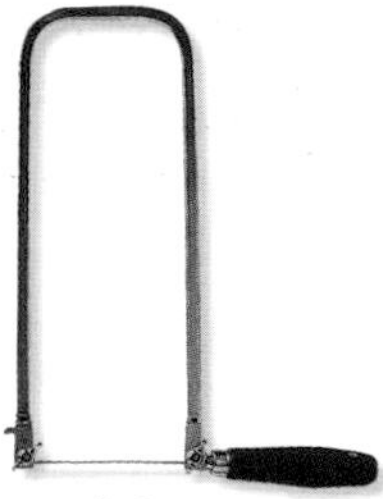

fretsaw
patlī ārī
पतली आरी

solder
ṭāṃkā lagāne kā tār
टांका लगाने का तार

tenon saw | chul ārā | चुल आरा

safety goggles
surakṣā chaśmā
सुरक्षा–चश्मा

plane
randā | रंदा

handsaw | ārī | आरी

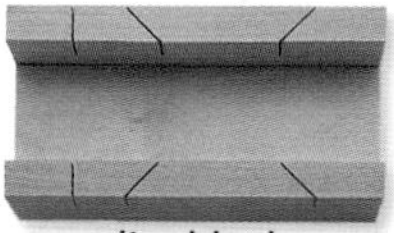

mitre block
mīṭar block
मीटर ब्लॉक

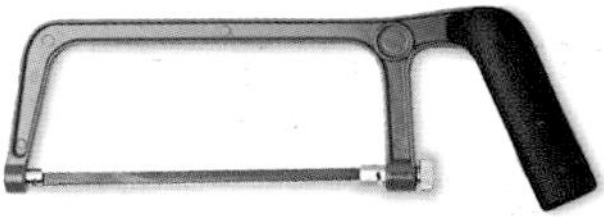

hacksaw
dāṃtedār ārī | दांतेदार आरी

hand drill
haiṇḍ ḍril
हैंड ड्रिल

wire wool
tār
तार

sandpaper
regmāl
रेगमाल

wrench
rinch
रिंच

chisel
chhenī | छेनी

file
retī | रेती

sharpening stone
sān | सान

pipe cutter | pāip kaṭar | पाइप कटर

plunger
ḍaṭṭā
डट्टा

decorating • gṛh sajjā • गृह सज्जा

scissors
ḳaiṃchī | कैंची

craft knife
chhurī | छुरी

plumb line
sāhul ḍorī | साहुल डोरी

scraper
khurachnī | खुरचनी

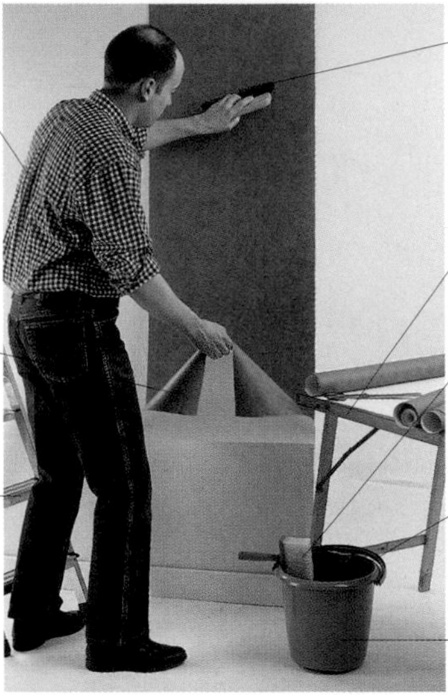
decorator
prasādhak
प्रसाधक
wallpaper
wallpaper
वॉलपेपर
stepladder
sīṛhī
सीढ़ी
wallpaper brush
wallpaper
braś
वॉलपेपर ब्रश
pasting table
pesṭiṅg ṭebal
पेस्टिंग टेबल
pasting brush
pesṭiṅg braś
पेस्टिंग ब्रश
wallpaper paste
wallpaper pesṭ
वॉलपेपर पेस्ट
bucket
ṭokrī
टोकरी

wallpaper (v) | wallpaper lagānā | वॉलपेपर लगाना

strip (v) | khurachnā | खुरचना

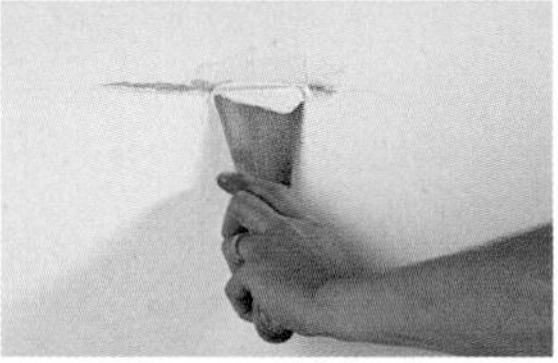

fill (v) | bharnā | भरना

sand (v)
ghisāī karnā | घिसाई करना

plaster (v)
plastar karnā | प्लस्तर करना

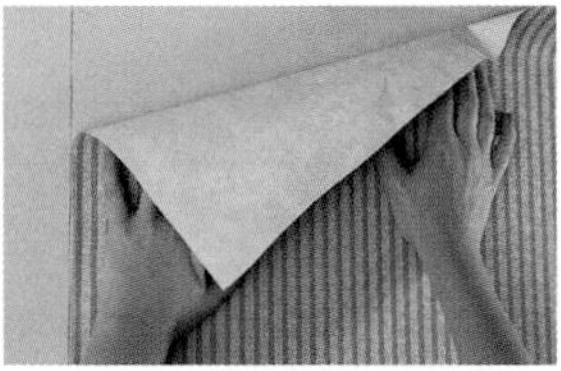

hang (v)
laṭkānā | लटकाना

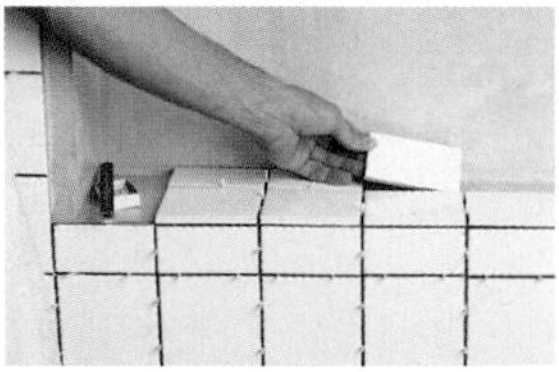

tile (v)
ṭāil lagānā | टाइल लगाना

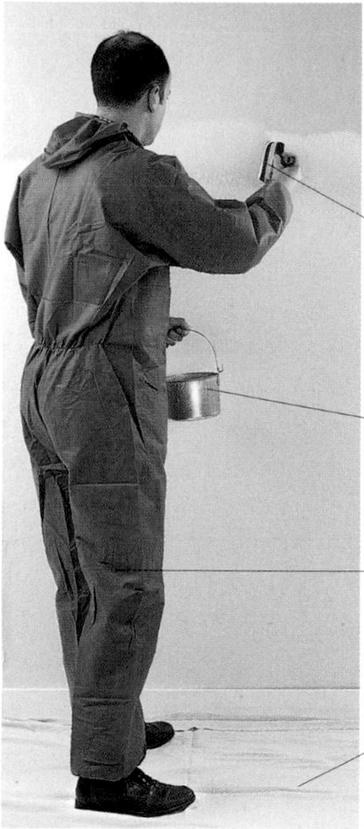

roller
rolar
रोलर

brush
braś
ब्रश

paint tin
penṭ kā ḍibbā
पेंट का डिब्बा

overalls
ūprī vastr
ऊपरी वस्त्र

dustsheet
gandī darī
गंदी दरी

paint (v)
raṅgnā | रंगना

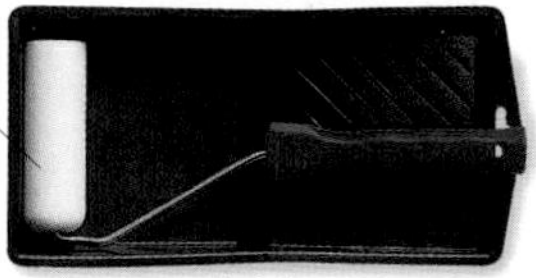

paint tray
penṭ ṭre | पेंट ट्रे

paint
penṭ | पेंट

sponge
spañj
स्पंज

masking tape
apārdarśī ṭep
अपारदर्शी टेप

sandpaper
regmāl
रेगमाल

filler
filar | फ़िलर

turpentine
tārpīn
तारपीन

white spirit
safed spriṭ | सफ़ेद स्प्रिट

vocabulary • śabdāvalī • शब्दावली

plaster plastar प्लस्तर	**gloss** lep लेप	**embossed paper** embosḍ pepar एम्बोस्ड पेपर	**undercoat** bhītrī parat भीतरी परत	**sealant** sīlanṭ सीलंट
varnish rogan रोग़न	**mat** chaṭāī चटाई	**lining paper** astar अस्तर	**top coat** ūprī parat ऊपरी परत	**preservative** parirakṣak परिरक्षक
emulsion imalśan इमल्शन	**stencil** sṭensil स्टेंसिल	**primer** prāimar प्राइमर	**solvent** solvent सॉलवेंट	**grout** masālā मसाला

garden • bagīchā • बग़ीचा

garden styles • bagīche kī śailiyāṃ • बग़ीचे की शैलियां

patio garden | upvan/bagīchī | उपवन/बग़ीची

roof garden
chhat bagīchī
छत बग़ीची

rock garden
pathrīlā bāg | पथरीला बाग़

formal garden | bagīchā | बग़ीचा

courtyard | āṅgan | आंगन

cottage garden
kuṭīr udyān
कुटीर उद्यान

herb garden
auṣadhi udyān
औषधि उद्यान

water garden
jal udyān
जल उद्यान

garden features • bagīche kī rūp sajjā • बग़ीचे की रूप सज्जा

hanging basket
jhūltī ṭokrī | झूलती टोकरी

trellis
bāṛā/jālī | बाड़ा/जाली

pergola
latāmaṇḍap
लतामंडप

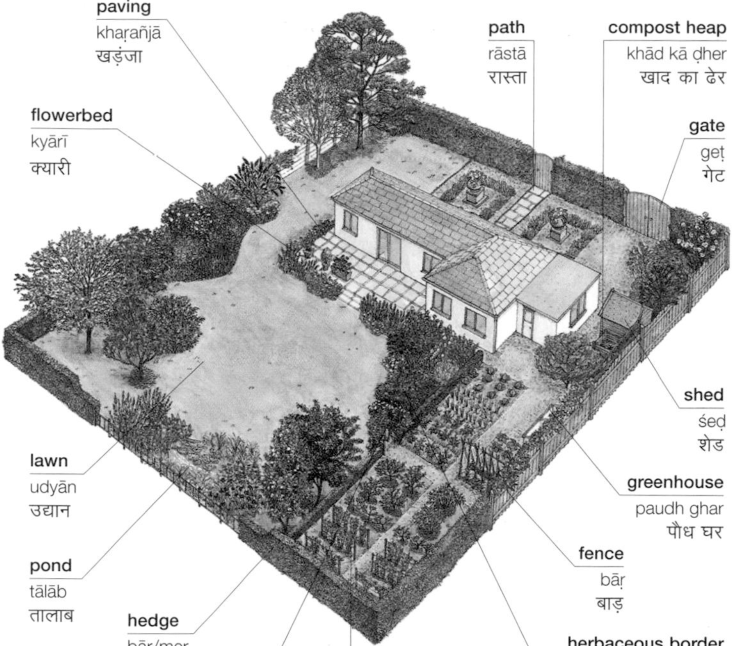
paving
kharañjā
खड़ंजा
path
rāstā
रास्ता
compost heap
khād kā ḍher
खाद का ढेर
flowerbed
kyārī
क्यारी
gate
geṭ
गेट
shed
śeḍ
शेड
lawn
udyān
उद्यान
greenhouse
paudh ghar
पौध घर
pond
tālāb
तालाब
fence
bāṛ
बाड़
hedge
bāṛ/meṛ
बाड़/मेड़
arch
ārch
आर्च
vegetable garden
sabziyoṃ kā bagīchā
सब्ज़ियों का बग़ीचा
herbaceous border
hare-bhare paudhoṃ se banā gherā
हरे-भरे पौधों से बना घेरा

decking
chabūtrā | चबूतरा

fountain | favvārā | फ़व्वारा

soil • miṭṭī • मिट्टी

topsoil
ūprī miṭṭī | ऊपरी मिट्टी

sand
ret | रेत

chalk
khaṛiyā | खड़िया

silt
gād | गाद

clay | miṭṭī | मिट्टी

garden plants • bagīche ke paudhe • बग़ीचे के पौधे

types of plants • paudhoṃ ke prakār • पौधों के प्रकार

annual | vārṣikī paudh | वार्षिकी पौध

biennial | dvivārṣik paudh | द्विवार्षिक पौध

perennial
bārahmāsī | बारहमासी

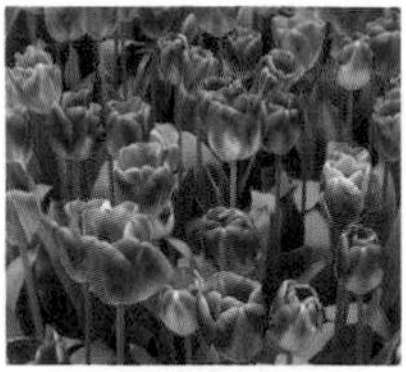
bulb
balb | बल्ब

fern
parṇāṅg | पर्णाङ्ग

rush
jalbeṃt | जलबेंत

bamboo
bāṃs | बांस

weeds
ghās-pāt | घास–पात

herb
jaṛī-būṭī | जड़ी–बूटी

water plant
jalīya paudh | जलीय पौध

tree
peṛ | पेड़

palm
tāṛ | ताड़

conifer
śaṅku vṛkṣ | शंकु वृक्ष

evergreen
sadābahār | सदाबहार

deciduous
parṇpātī | पर्णपाती

topiary
kaṭāī-chhaṃṭāī
कटाई–छंटाई

alpine
parvatīya paudhe
पर्वतीय पौधे

succulent
ārdr paudh
आर्द्र पौध

cactus
kaikṭas
कैक्टस

potted plant
gamle ke paudhe
गमले के पौधे
shade plant
chhāyādār paudhe
छायादार पौधे
climber
latā
लता
flowering shrub
phūloṃ kī jhāṛī
फूलों की झाड़ी
ground cover
grāuṇḍ kavar
ग्राउंड कवर
creeper
bel
बेल
ornamental
sajāvaṭī
सजावटी
grass
ghās
घास

garden tools • bagīche ke upkaraṇ • बग़ीचे के उपकरण

spade
phāvṛā
फावड़ा

fork
kāṃṭā auzār
कांटा औज़ार

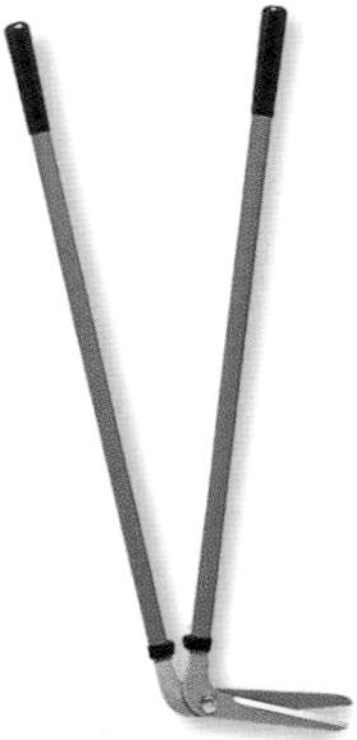

long-handled shears
lambe hatthe kī ḳaiṃchī
लंबे हत्थे की क़ैंची

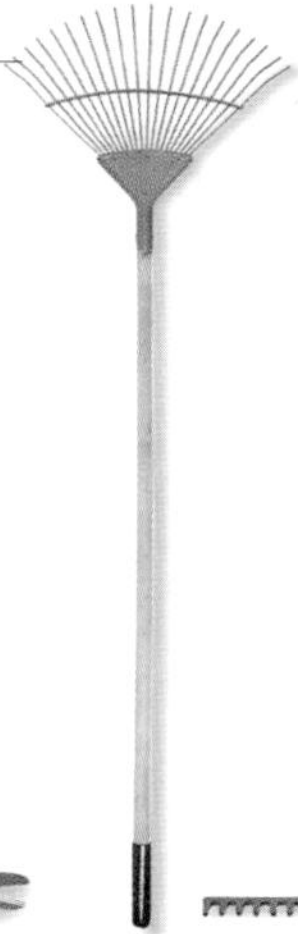

lawn rake
jhāṛū
झाड़ू

rake
pāñchā
पांचा

hoe
khurpā | खुरपा

compost
khād | खाद

seeds
bīj | बीज

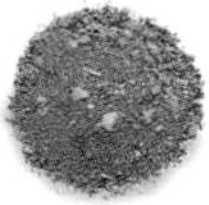

bone meal
asthi chūrṇ | अस्थि चूर्ण

gravel
bajrī | बजरी

trug | ṭre/ṭokrī | ट्रे/टोकरी

shield
pleṭ
प्लेट

trimmer | katarne kā auzār
कतरने का औज़ार

grass bag
ghās kā thailā
घास का थैला

motor
moṭar
मोटर

lawnmower | ghās kāṭne kī maśīn | घास काटने की मशीन

handle
hatthā
हत्था

stand
staiṇḍ
स्टैंड

wheelbarrow
ṭhelā gāṛī | ठेला गाड़ी

hand fork
kurednī | कुरेदनी
secateurs
kaṭar | कटर
gardening gloves
bāgbānī ke dastāne
बाग़बानी के दस्ताने
trowel
khurpī | खुरपी
twine
ḍorī
डोरी
labels
lebal
लेबल
twist ties
chimṭiyāṃ
चिमटियां
blade
phal
फल
seed tray
bīj ṭre | बीज ट्रे
ring ties
chhalle
छल्ले
canes
beṃt | बेंत
shears
baṛī ḳaiṃchī
बड़ी क़ैंची
sieve
chhalnī
छलनी
hand saw
ārī | आरी
pesticide
kīṭnāśak
कीटनाशक
plant pot
gamlā
गमला
rubber boots | rabaṛ ke jūte | रबड़ के जूते

watering • sīṃchnā • सींचना

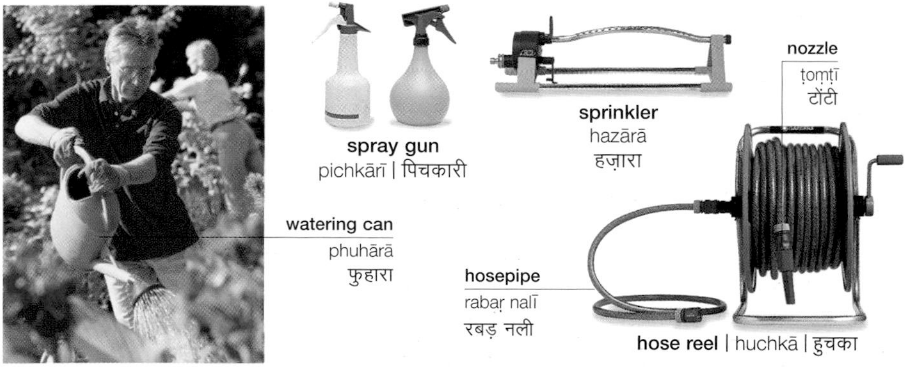
spray gun
pichkārī | पिचकारी
sprinkler
hazārā
हज़ारा
nozzle
ṭomṭī
टोंटी
watering can
phuhārā
फुहारा
hosepipe
rabaṛ nalī
रबड़ नली
hose reel | huchkā | हुचका

gardening • bāgbānī • बाग़बानी

lawn
udyān
उद्यान

flowerbed
kyārī | क्यारी

lawnmower
ghās kāṭne
kī maśīn
घास काटने
की मशीन

hedge
bāṛ
बाड़

stake
khūṃṭā
खूंटा

mow (v) | ghās kāṭnā | घास काटना

turf (v)
ghās bichhānā
घास बिछाना

spike (v)
khūṃṭā ṭhoknā
खूंटा ठोकना

rake (v)
buhārnā
बुहारना

trim (v)
chhāṃṭnā | छांटना

dig (v)
khodnā | खोदना

sow (v)
bonā | बोना

top dress (v)
khād ḍālnā | खाद डालना

water (v)
sīṃchnā | सींचना

train (v) | ākār denā | आकार देना

deadhead (v) | sūkhe patte nikālnā | सूखे पत्ते निकालना

spray (v) chhiṛaknā | छिड़कना

graft (v) | ḳalam bāṃdhnā | क़लम बांधना

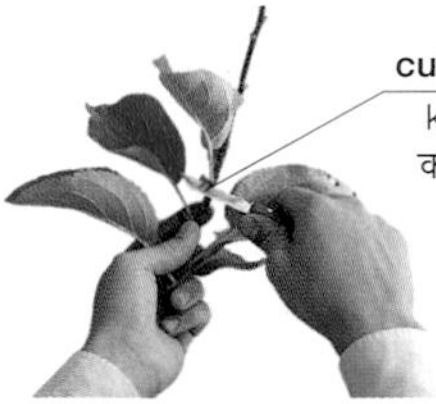

propagate (v) baṛhānā | बढ़ाना

prune (v) chhāṃṭnā | छांटना

stake (v) | khūṃṭī se bāṃdhnā | खूंटी से बांधना

transplant (v)
pratiropit karnā
प्रतिरोपित करना

weed (v)
nirānā
निराना

mulch (v)
ghās-pāt se ḍhaknā
घास–पात से ढकना

harvest (v)
fasal kāṭnā
फ़सल काटना

vocabulary • śabdāvalī • शब्दावली

cultivate (v)
khetī karnā
खेती करना

fertilize (v)
urvar banānā
उर्वर बनाना

sieve (v)
chhānnā
छानना

organic
jaiv
जैव

seedling
paud
पौद

pot up (v)
gamle meṃ ḍālnā
गमले में डालना

subsoil
avmṛdā
अवमृदा

tend (v)
dekhbhāl karnā
देखभाल करना

pick (v)
chunnā/toṛnā
चुनना/तोड़ना

aerate (v)
havā lagānā
हवा लगाना

drainage
morī
मोरी

fertilizer
urvarak
उर्वरक

weedkiller
kharpatvār nāśak
खरपतवार नाशक

JKL
5
TUV
8
0

services

sevāeṃ

सेवाएं

emergency services • āpātkālīn sevāeṃ • आपातकालीन सेवाएं

ambulance • embulens • एंबुलेंस

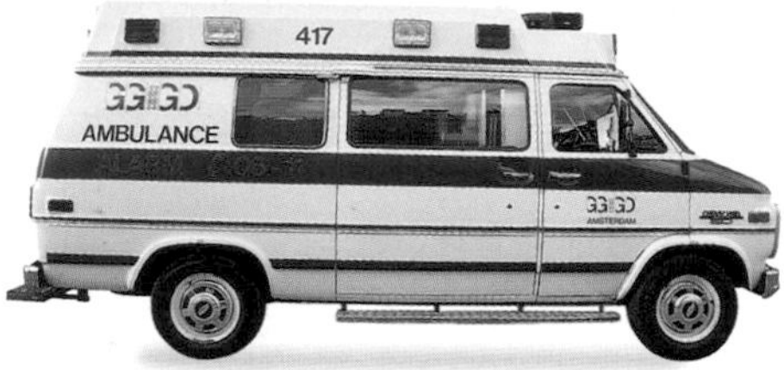

ambulance | embulens | एंबुलेंस

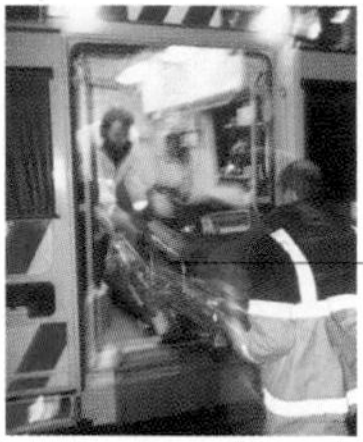

stretcher
sṭrechar
स्ट्रेचर

paramedic
chikitsakīya sahāyak | चिकित्सकीय सहायक

police • pulis • पुलिस

badge
billā
बिल्ला

uniform
vardī
वर्दी

truncheon
beṃt
बेंत

gun
bandūḳ
बंदूक़

handcuffs
hathkaṛī
हथकड़ी

police officer
pulis adhikārī | पुलिस अधिकारी

siren
sāyaran
सायरन

lights
battī
बत्ती

police car
pulis kār | पुलिस कार

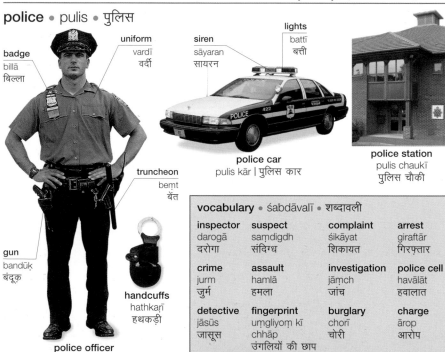

police station
pulis chaukī
पुलिस चौकी

vocabulary • śabdāvalī • शब्दावली

inspector darogā दरोगा	**suspect** saṃdigdh संदिग्ध	**complaint** śikāyat शिकायत	**arrest** giraftār गिरफ़्तार
crime jurm जुर्म	**assault** hamlā हमला	**investigation** jāṃch जांच	**police cell** havālāt हवालात
detective jāsūs जासूस	**fingerprint** uṃgliyoṃ kī chhāp उंगलियों की छाप	**burglary** chorī चोरी	**charge** ārop आरोप

fire brigade • damkal dastā • दमकल दस्ता

smoke
dhuāṃ
धुआं
cradle
kraiḍal
क्रैडल
boom
pāl daṇḍ
पाल दंड

fire | āg | आग

helmet
hailmeṭ
हैलमेट
hose
pānī kī nalī
पानी की
नली
water jet
pānī kī dhār
पानी की धार

fire fighters
agniśāmak karmī
अग्निशामक कर्मी

fire station
damkal kendr
दमकल केंद्र

fire escape
āpātkālīn rakṣā mārg
आपातकालीन रक्षा मार्ग

ladder
sīṛhī
सीढ़ी
cab
gāṛī
गाड़ी

fire engine
damkal | दमकल

smoke alarm
smok alārm
स्मोक अलार्म

fire alarm
fāyar alārm
फ़ायर अलार्म

axe
kulhāṛī
कुल्हाड़ी

fire extinguisher
agniśāmak upkaraṇ
अग्निशामक उपकरण

hydrant
nal kī ṭoṃṭī
नल की टोंटी

I need the ambulance.
mujhe embulens bulānī hai.
मुझे एंबुलेंस बुलानी है।

There's a fire at...
...meṃ āg lagī hai.
... में आग लगी है।

There's been an accident.
ek durghaṭnā huī hai.
एक दुर्घटना हुई है।

Call the police!
pulis ko bulāo!
पुलिस को बुलाओ!

bank • baink • बैंक

customer
grāhak
ग्राहक

window
khiṛkī
खिड़की

cashier
ḳhazānchī
ख़ज़ांची

leaflets
parchī
पर्ची

counter
kāunṭar
काउंटर

paying-in slips
jamā parchī
जमा पर्ची

bank manager
baink prabandhak
बैंक प्रबंधक

debit card
ḍebiṭ kārḍ
डेबिट कार्ड

credit card
kreḍiṭ kārḍ
क्रेडिट कार्ड

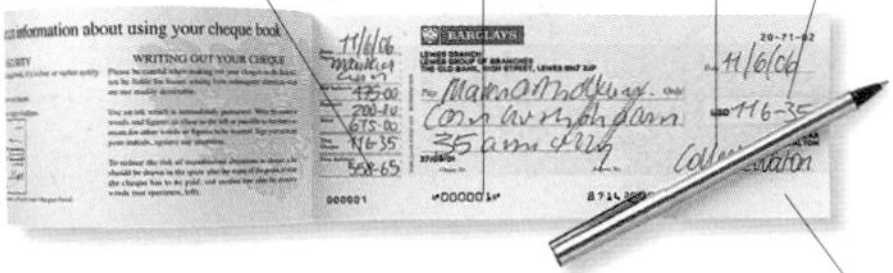

stub
parchī
पर्ची

account number
khātā sankhyā
खाता संख्या

signature
hastākṣar
हस्ताक्षर

amount
raḳam
रक़म

chequebook
chek buk
चेक बुक

cheque
chek
चेक

vocabulary • śabdāvalī • शब्दावली

savings
bachat
बचत

tax
kar
कर

loan
ṛiṇ
ऋण

mortgage
rehan
रेहन

overdraft
ovar ḍrāfṭ
ओवर ड्राफ़्ट

interest rate
byāj dar
ब्याज दर

payment
bhugtān
भुगतान

direct debit
pratyakṣ bhugtān
प्रत्यक्ष भुगतान

withdrawal slip
pratyāharaṇ parchī
प्रत्याहरण पर्ची

pay in (v)
jamā karnā
जमा करना

bank charge
baink prabhār
बैंक प्रभार

bank transfer
baink dvārā antraṇ
बैंक द्वारा अंतरण

current account
chālū khātā
चालू खाता

savings account
bachat khātā
बचत खाता

pin number
pin nambar
पिन नंबर

coin
sikkā
सिक्का

note
noṭ
नोट

money
dhan | धन

screen
skrīn
स्क्रीन

key pad
kuñjī paṭal
कुंजी पटल

card slot
kārḍ ḍālne kī jagah
कार्ड डालने की जगह

cash machine
paise kī maśīn | पैसे की मशीन

currency • mudrā • मुद्रा

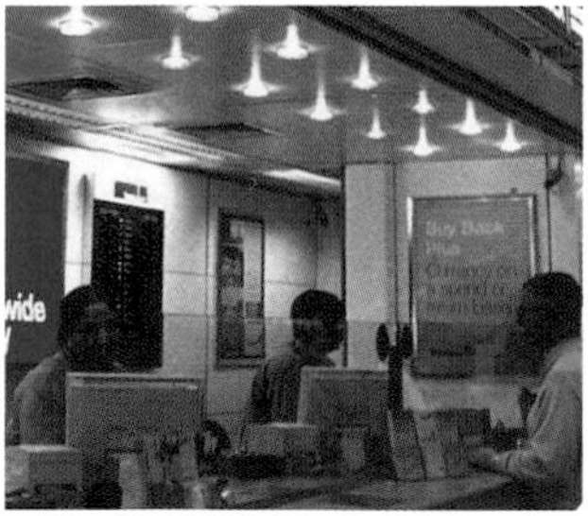

bureau de change
videśī mudrā vinimaya kendr
विदेशी मुद्रा विनिमय केंद्र

traveller's cheque
yātrī chek | यात्री चेक

exchange rate
vinimaya dar
विनिमय दर

vocabulary • śabdāvalī • शब्दावली

cash (v)
nakad nikālnā
नक़द निकालना

denomination
abhidhān
अभिधान

commission
dalālī
दलाली

investment
niveś
निवेश

stocks
stock
स्टॉक

shares
śeyar
शेयर

dividends
lābhānś
लाभांश

accountant
lekhākār
लेखाकार

portfolio
niveś vivaraṇikā
निवेश विवरणिका

equity
śeyar pūñjī
शेयर पूंजी

Can I change this please?
kyā maiṃ inheṃ badal saktā hūṃ?
क्या मैं इन्हें बदल सकता हूं?

What's today's exchange rate?
vartmān vinimaya dar kyā hai?
वर्तमान विनिमय दर क्या है?

finance • vitt • वित्त

financial advisor
vittīya salāhkār
वित्तीय सलाहकार

share price
śeyar mūlya
शेयर मूल्य

stockbroker
śeyar dalāl
शेयर दलाल

stock exchange
śeyar bāzār | शेयर बाज़ार

communications • sañchār • संचार

postal worker
ḍāk karmī
डाक कर्मी

window
khiṛkī
खिड़की

scales
tarāzū
तराज़ू

counter
kāunṭar
काउंटर

post office
ḍākghar | डाकघर

postman
ḍākiyā | डाकिया

postmark
mohar
मोहर

stamp
ḍāk ṭikaṭ
डाक टिकट

address
patā
पता

postal code
ḍāk koḍ
डाक कोड

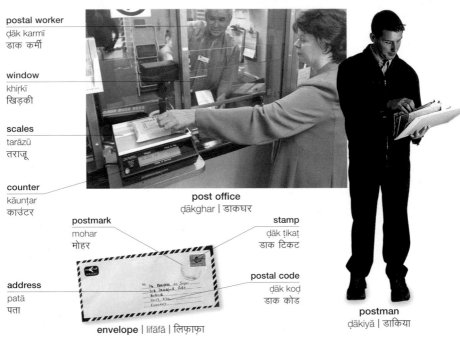

envelope | lifāfā | लिफ़ाफ़ा

vocabulary • śabdāvalī • शब्दावली

letter patr पत्र	**return address** vāpsī kā patā वापसी का पता	**delivery** vitraṇ वितरण	**fragile** nāzuk vastu नाज़ुक वस्तु	**do not bend (v)** kṛpyā moṛeṃ nahīṃ कृपया मोड़ें नहीं
by airmail havāī ḍāk dvārā हवाई डाक द्वारा	**signature** hastākṣar हस्ताक्षर	**postal order** posṭal order पोस्टल ऑर्डर	**mailbag** ḍāk thailā डाक थैला	**this way up** is prakār rakheṃ इस प्रकार रखें।
registered post rajisṭarḍ ḍāk रजिस्टर्ड डाक	**collection** saṅgrah संग्रह	**postage** ḍāk vyaya डाक व्यय	**telegram** tār तार	**fax** faiks फ़ैक्स

postbox
ḍākpeṭī | डाकपेटी

letterbox
patrpeṭī | पत्रपेटी

parcel
pārsal | पार्सल

courier
kūriyar | कूरियर

telephone • dūrbhāṣ • दूरभाष

handset
haiṇḍ set
हैंडसेट

base station
fon sṭaiṇḍ
फ़ोन स्टैंड

answering machine
āṇsariṅg maśīn
आंसरिंग मशीन

cordless phone
betār dūrbhāṣ
बेतार दूरभाष

video phone
vīḍiyo fon
वीडियो फ़ोन

telephone box
ṭelifon box
टेलिफ़ोन बॉक्स

keypad
kī paiḍ
की–पैड

mobile phone
mobāil fon
मोबाइल फ़ोन

receiver
risīvar
रिसीवर

coin return
sikkā vāpsī
सिक्का वापसी

coin phone
sikke vālā fon
सिक्के वाला फ़ोन

card phone
kārḍ fon
कार्ड फ़ोन

vocabulary • śabdāvalī • शब्दावली

dial (v)
nambar milānā
नंबर मिलाना

reverse charge call
revars chārj call
रिवर्स चार्ज कॉल

directory enquiries
ḍāyarekṭarī pūchhtāchh
डायरेक्टरी पूछताछ

answer (v)
uttar denā
उत्तर देना

text message
pāṭhya sandeś
पाठ्य संदेश

voice message
dhvani sandeś
ध्वनि संदेश

operator
prachālak
प्रचालक

engaged/busy
vyast
व्यस्त

disconnected
sampark ṭūṭnā
संपर्क टूटना

Can you give me the number for...?
kyā āp mujhe … kā nambar de sakte haiṃ?
क्या आप मुझे... का नंबर दे सकते हैं?

What is the dialling code for...?
… ke lie ḍāyaliṅg koḍ kyā hai?
... के लिए डायलिंग कोड क्या है?

hotel • hoṭal • होटल

lobby • lobby • लॉबी

guest
mehmān
मेहमान

room key
kamre kī chābī
कमरे की चाबी

messages
sandeś
संदेश

pigeonhole
koṣṭh
कोष्ठ

receptionist
svāgat adhikārī
स्वागत अधिकारी

register
rajisṭar
रजिस्टर

counter
kāunṭar
काउंटर

reception | svāgat | स्वागत

luggage
sāmān
सामान

trolley
trolley
ट्रॉली

porter | darbān | दरबान

lift | lifṭ | लिफ़्ट

room number
kamrā nambar
कमरा नंबर

rooms • kamre • कमरे

single room
siṅgal kamrā
सिंगल कमरा

double room
ḍabal kamrā
डबल कमरा

twin room
ṭvin kamrā
ट्विन कमरा

private bathroom
nijī snānghar
निजी स्नानघर

services • sevāeṃ • सेवाएं

maid service
parichārikā sevā
परिचारिका सेवा

laundry service
laundry sevā
लॉन्ड्री सेवा

breakfast tray
nāśte kī ṭre | नाश्ते की ट्रे

room service | rūm sarvis | रूम सर्विस

mini bar
minī bār | मिनी बार

restaurant
restrāṃ
रेस्तरां

gym
vyāyāmśālā
व्यायामशाला

swimming pool
taranṭāl
तरणताल

vocabulary • śabdāvalī • शब्दावली

bed and breakfast
rahnā aur nāśtā
रहना और नाश्ता

full board
ful borḍ
फ़ुल बोर्ड

half board
hāf borḍ
हाफ़ बोर्ड

Do you have any vacancies?
kyā āpke yahāṃ kamrā ḳhālī hai?
क्या आपके यहां कमरा ख़ाली है?

I have a reservation.
maiṃne kamrā ārakṣit karāyā huā hai
मैंने कमरा आरक्षित कराया हुआ है।

I'd like a single room.
mujhe ek siṅgal kamrā chāhie
मुझे एक सिंगल कमरा चाहिए।

I'd like a room for three nights.
mujhe tīn rātoṃ ke lie ek kamrā chāhie
मुझे तीन रातों के लिए एक कमरा चाहिए।

What is the charge per night?
ek rāt kā kirāyā kitnā hai?
एक रात का किराया कितना है?

When do I have to vacate the room?
mujhe kab kamrā ḳhālī karnā hai?
मुझे कब कमरा ख़ाली करना है?

shopping
ḳharīdārī
ख़रीदारी

shopping centre • ḳharīdārī kendr • ख़रीदारी केंद्र

atrium
parisar
परिसर

sign
nām
नाम

lift
lifṭ
लिफ़्ट

second floor
dūsrī mañzil
दूसरी मंज़िल

first floor
pahlī mañzil
पहली मंज़िल

escalator
svachālit sīṛhiyāṃ
स्वचालित सीढ़ियां

ground floor
bhūtal
भूतल

customer
grāhak
ग्राहक

vocabulary • śabdāvalī • शब्दावली

luggage department
sāmān vibhāg
सामान विभाग

shoe department
jūtā chappal khaṇḍ
जूता चप्पल खंड

children's department
bāl vibhāg
बाल विभाग

store directory
sṭor nirdeśikā
स्टोर निर्देशिका

sales assistant
bikrī sahāyak
बिक्री सहायक

customer services
grāhak sevāeṃ
ग्राहक सेवाएं

changing rooms
chenjiṅg rūm
चेंजिंग रूम

toilets
prasādhan
प्रसाधन

baby changing facilities
bāl suvidhā kendr
बाल–सुविधा केंद्र

How much is this?
iskī kyā ḳīmat hai?
इसकी क्या क़ीमत है?

May I exchange this?
kyā maiṃ ise badal saktā hūṃ?
क्या मैं इसे बदल सकता हूं?

department store • ḍepārṭmenṭal sṭor • डिपार्टमेंटल स्टोर

men's wear
puruṣ paridhān
पुरुष परिधान

women's wear
mahilā paridhān
महिला परिधान

lingerie
adhovastr
अधोवस्त्र

perfumery
itr ityādi
इत्र इत्यादि

beauty
saundarya
सौंदर्य

linen
chādar takiyā ādi
चादर तकिया आदि

home furnishings
gṛh sāj-sajjā
गृह साज–सज्जा

haberdashery
janral sṭor
जनरल स्टोर

kitchenware
rasoī ke bartan
रसोई के बर्तन

china
chīnī miṭṭī ke bartan
चीनी मिट्टी के बर्तन

electrical goods
bijlī kā sāman
बिजली का सामान

lighting
lāiṭiṅg
लाइटिंग

sports
sporṭs | स्पोर्ट्स

toys
khilaune | खिलौने

stationery | lekhan sāmagrī | लेखन सामग्री

food hall
fūḍ hall | फ़ूड हॉल

supermarket • supar bāzār • सुपर बाज़ार

aisle
galiyārā
गलियारा

shelf
tāk
ताक़

conveyer belt
chal paṭṭī
चल पट्टी

cashier
khazānchī
ख़ज़ांची

offers
chhūṭ
छूट

checkout | ādāyagī paṭal | अदायगी पटल

customer
grāhak
ग्राहक

till
tijorī
तिजोरी

shopping bag
kharīdārī kā thailā
ख़रीदारी का थैला

groceries
kirānā vastueṃ
किराना वस्तुएं

trolley | trolley | ट्रॉली

handle
haiṇḍil
हैंडिल

basket | ṭokrī | टोकरी

780863 185779
bar code
bār koḍ | बार कोड

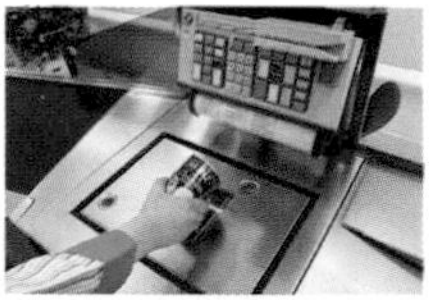

scanner | skainar | स्कैनर

bakery
bekrī
बेकरी

dairy
dugdh utpād
दुग्ध उत्पाद

cereals
nāśtā sīriyal
नाश्ता सीरियल

tinned food
ḍibbāband khādya padārth
डिब्बाबंद खाद्य पदार्थ

confectionery
mīṭhe khādya
मीठे खाद्य

vegetables
sāg-sabzī
साग–सब्ज़ी

fruit
phal
फल

meat and poultry
māṃsāhārī khādya padārth
मांसाहारी खाद्य पदार्थ

fish
machhlī
मछली

deli
viśiṣṭ khādya
विशिष्ट खाद्य

frozen food
frozan āhār
फ़्रोज़न आहार

convenience food
ḍibbāband āhār
डिब्बाबंद आहार

drinks
peya padārth
पेय पदार्थ

household products
gharelū vastueṃ
घरेलू वस्तुएं

toiletries
saundarya prasādhan
सौंदर्य प्रसाधन

baby products
śiśu utpād
शिशु उत्पाद

electrical goods
bijlī kī vastueṃ
बिजली की वस्तुएं

pet food
paśu āhār
पशु आहार

magazines | patrikāeṃ | पत्रिकाएं

chemist • davāī vikretā • दवाई विक्रेता

dental care
dant surakṣā
दंत सुरक्षा
feminine hygiene
strī svacchhatā sāmān
स्त्री–स्वच्छता सामान
vitamins
viṭāmin
विटामिन
dispensary
davāḳhānā
दवाख़ाना
pharmacist
auṣadh vitrak
औषध वितरक
cough medicine
khāṃsī kī davāī
खांसी की दवाई
herbal remedies
jaṛī-būṭī auṣadh
जड़ी–बूटी औषध
skin care
tvachā surakṣā
त्वचा सुरक्षा

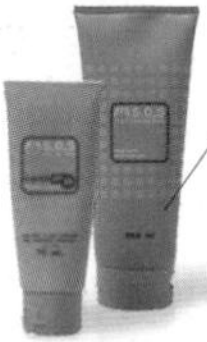
aftersun
āfṭarsan
आफ़्टरसन

sunscreen
sanskrīn | सनस्क्रीन

sunblock
sunblock
सनब्लॉक

insect repellent
macchhar avrodhak
मच्छर अवरोधक

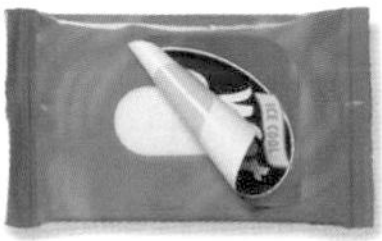

wet wipe
namīyukt ṭiśyū
नमीयुक्त टिश्यू

tissue
ṭiśyū | टिश्यू

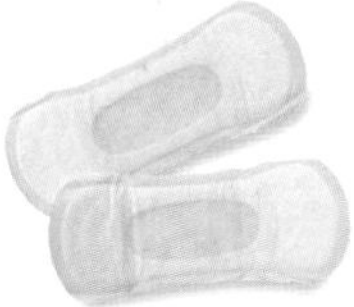

sanitary towel | sainiṭarī paid | सैनिटरी पैड

tampon
ṭempon | टेम्पोन

panty liner | painṭī lāinar | पैंटी लाइनर

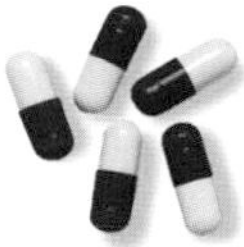

capsule
kaipsūl | कैप्सूल

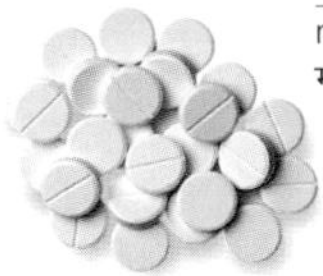

plll
goliyāṃ | गोलियां

measuring spoon
māpak chammach
मापक चम्मच

syrup
sirap | सिरप

instructions
nirdeś
निर्देश

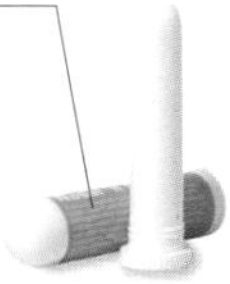

inhaler | śvās yantr |
श्वास यंत्र

cream
krīm | क्रीम

ointment
marham | मरहम

gel
jail | जैल

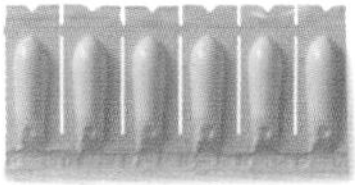

suppository
guhyavarti | गुह्यवर्ति

dropper
dropper
ड्रॉपर

drops | drops | ड्रॉप्स

needle
sūī
सूई

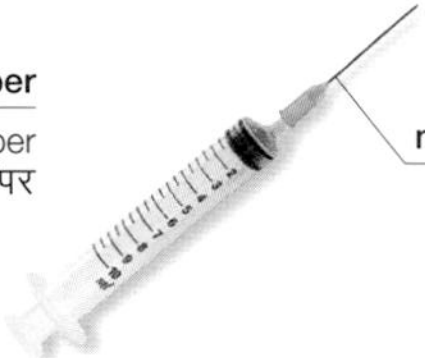

syringe
siriṅj | सिरिंज

spray
spre | स्प्रे

powder
pāuḍar | पाउडर

vocabulary • śabdāvalī • शब्दावली

iron
āyaran
आयरन

calcium
kailśiyam
कैल्शियम

magnesium
maignīśiyam
मैग्नीशियम

multivitamins
bahu viṭāmin
बहु विटामिन

insulin
insulin
इंसुलिन

side-effects
viprīt prabhāv
विपरीत प्रभाव

expiry date
samāpti tithi
समाप्ति तिथि

travel sickness pills
mitlī kī davā
मितली की दवा

disposable
ḍispozebal
डिस्पोज़ेबल

soluble
ghulanśīl
घुलनशील

dosage
ḳhurāk
ख़ुराक

medication
upchār
उपचार

medicine
davāī
दवाई

laxative
ḳabzḳuśā
क़ब्ज़कुशा

diarrhoea
dast
दस्त

throat lozenge
ḳharāś kī davā
ख़राश की दवा

painkiller
dardnāśak
दर्दनाशक

sedative
praśāmak
प्रशामक

sleeping pill
nīṃd kī golīyāṃ
नींद की गोलियां

anti-inflammatory
sūjan rodhī
सूजन रोधी

florist • phūl vikretā • फूल विक्रेता

flowers
phūl
फूल

lily
lilī
लिली

acacia
babūl
बबूल

carnation
kārneśan
कार्नेशन

pot plant
gamle kā
paudhā
गमले का पौधा

gladiolus
gleḍiyolas
ग्लेडियोलस

iris
āyaris
आयरिस

daisy
ḍezī
डेज़ी

chrysanthemum
guldāūdī
गुलदाऊदी

gypsophila
jipsofilā
जिप्सोफ़िला

stocks
stocks | स्टॉक्स

gerbera
jarberā | जरबेरा

foliage
phūl-patte | फूल–पत्ते

rose
gulāb | गुलाब

freesia
frīziyā | फ़्रीज़िया

vase
phūldān
फूलदान

orchid
orchid | ऑरकिड

peony
piyoni | पियोनि

bunch
gucchhā
गुच्छा

stem
ḍaṇḍī
डंडी

daffodil
ḍaifoḍil
डैफ़ोडिल

bud
kalī
कली

wrapping
gift pepar
गिफ़्ट पेपर

tulip | ṭyūlip | ट्यूलिप

arrangements • sajāvaṭ • सजावट

ribbon
riban
रिबन

bouquet
guldastā | गुलदस्ता

dried flowers | sūkhe phūl | सूखे फूल

pot-pourri
sūkhe phūl | सूखे फूल

wreath
puṣp chakr | पुष्प चक्र

garland
phūlmālā
फूलमाला

vocabulary • śabdāvalī • शब्दावली

Can I have them wrapped?
āp inheṃ kagaz meṃ lapeṭ deṇge?
आप इन्हें काग़ज़ में लपेट देंगे?

Can I attach a message?
kyā maiṃ ek sandeś lagā saktā hūṃ?
क्या मैं एक संदेश लगा सकता हूं?

Can I have a bunch of... please.
kyā mujhe ... kā gucchhā mil saktā hai?
क्या मुझे... का गुच्छा मिल सकता है?

Can you send them to...?
kyā āp unheṃ ... ko bhej sakte haiṃ?
क्या आप उन्हें... को भेज सकते हैं?

newsagent • samāchār patr vikretā • समाचार पत्र विक्रेता

cigarettes
sigreṭ
सिगरेट

packet of cigarettes
sigreṭ kī ḍibbī
सिगरेट की डिब्बी

matches
māchis
माचिस

lottery tickets
lottery ṭikṭeṃ
लॉटरी टिकटें

stamps
ḍāk ṭikaṭ
डाक टिकट

postcard
posṭ kārḍ | पोस्ट कार्ड

comic
chitrkathā | चित्रकथा

magazine
patrikā | पत्रिका

newspaper
aḳhbār | अख़बार

smoking • dhūmrpān • धूम्रपान

tobacco
tambāḳū | तंबाक़ू

lighter
lāiṭar | लाइटर

stem
nalī
नली

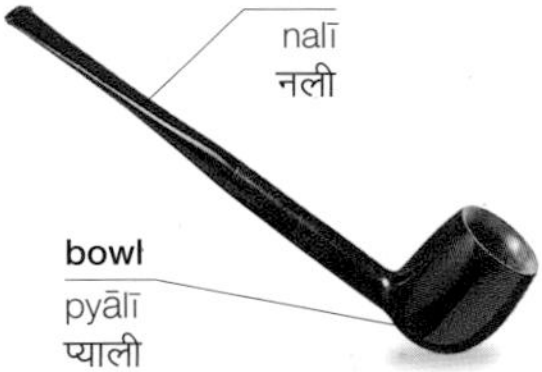

bowl
pyālī
प्याली

pipe
pāip | पाइप

cigar
sigār | सिगार

confectioner • kanfekśnar • कनफ़ेक्शनर

box of chocolates
chocolate box
चॉकलेट बॉक्स

snack bar
snaiks bār
स्नैक्स बार

crisps
krisps
क्रिस्प्स

sweet shop | toffee kī dukān | टॉफ़ी की दुकान

vocabulary • śabdāvalī • शब्दावली

milk chocolate
dūdh kī chocolate
दूध की चॉकलेट

plain chocolate
sādī chocolate
सादी चॉकलेट

white chocolate
safed chocolate
सफ़ेद चॉकलेट

pick and mix
manpasand goliyāṃ
मनपसंद गोलियां

caramel
toffee
टॉफ़ी

truffle
ṭrafal
ट्रफ़ल

biscuit
biskuṭ
बिस्कुट

boiled sweets
mīṭhī goliyāṃ
मीठी गोलियां

confectionery • kanfekśnarī • कनफ़ेक्शरी

chocolate
chocolate | चॉकलेट

chocolate bar
chocolate kī paṭṭī
चॉकलेट की पट्टी

sweets
kaiṇḍī | कैंडी

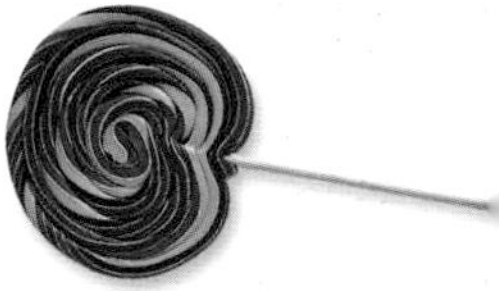

lollipop
lollipop | लॉलीपॉप

toffee | toffee | टॉफ़ी

nougat | girī kī chocolate |
गिरी की चॉकलेट

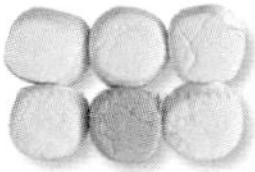

marshmallow
mārśmailo
मार्शमैलो

mint
minṭ toffee | मिंट टॉफ़ी

chewing gum
chuingam | चुइंगम

jellybean
jailībīn | जैलीबीन

fruit gum
frūṭ gam | फ़्रूट गम

licquorice
mulethī kaiṇḍī
मुलेठी कैंडी

other shops • anya dukānem̩ • अन्य दुकानें

baker's
bekrī
बेकरी

cake shop
kek kī dukān
केक की दुकान

butcher's
ḳasāī kī dukān
क़साई की दुकान

fishmonger's
machhlī kī dukān
मछली की दुकान

greengrocer's | phal evam sabziyom̩ kī dukān | फल एवं सब्ज़ियों की दुकान

grocer's
pansārī kī dukān
पंसारी की दुकान

shoe shop
jūte kī dukān
जूते की दुकान

hardware shop
hārḍveyar shop
हार्डवेयर शॉप

antiques shop | prāchīn vastuom̩ kī dukān
प्राचीन वस्तुओं की दुकान

gift shop
uphārom̩ kī dukān
उपहारों की दुकान

travel agent's
ṭreval ejensī
ट्रेवल एजेंसी

jeweller's
sunār kī dukān
सुनार की दुकान

book shop
kitāboṃ kī dukān
किताबों की दुकान

record shop
record kī dukān
रिकॉर्ड की दुकान

off licence
śarāb kī dukān
शराब की दुकान

pet shop
pāltū jānvaroṃ kī dukān
पालतू जानवरों की दुकान

furniture shop
farnīchar kī dukān
फ़र्नीचर की दुकान

boutique
buṭīk
बुटीक

vocabulary • śabdāvalī • शब्दावली

estate agent's
property ḍīlar
प्रॉपर्टी डीलर

garden centre
bagbānī kī dukān
बाग़बानी की दुकान

dry cleaner's
ḍraī klīnar
ड्राई क्लीनर

launderette
laundry
लॉन्ड्री

camera shop
kaimre kī dukān
कैमरे की दुकान

art shop
ārṭ shop
आर्ट शॉप

second-hand shop
saikaṇḍ haiṇḍ shop
सैकंड हैंड शॉप

health food shop
svāsthya āhār
kī dukān
स्वास्थ्य आहार
की दुकान

tailor's | darzī kī dukān | दर्ज़ी की दुकान

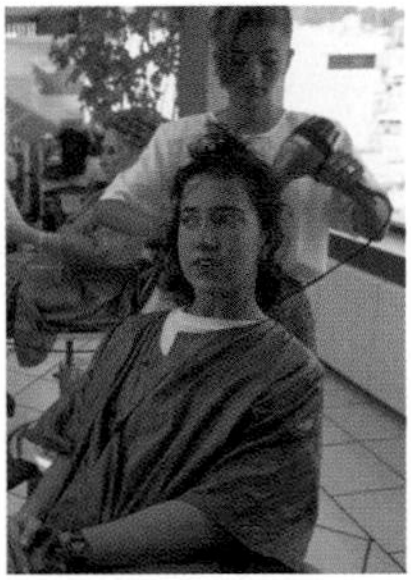

hairdresser's | nāī kī dukān | नाई की दुकान

market | bāzār | बाज़ार

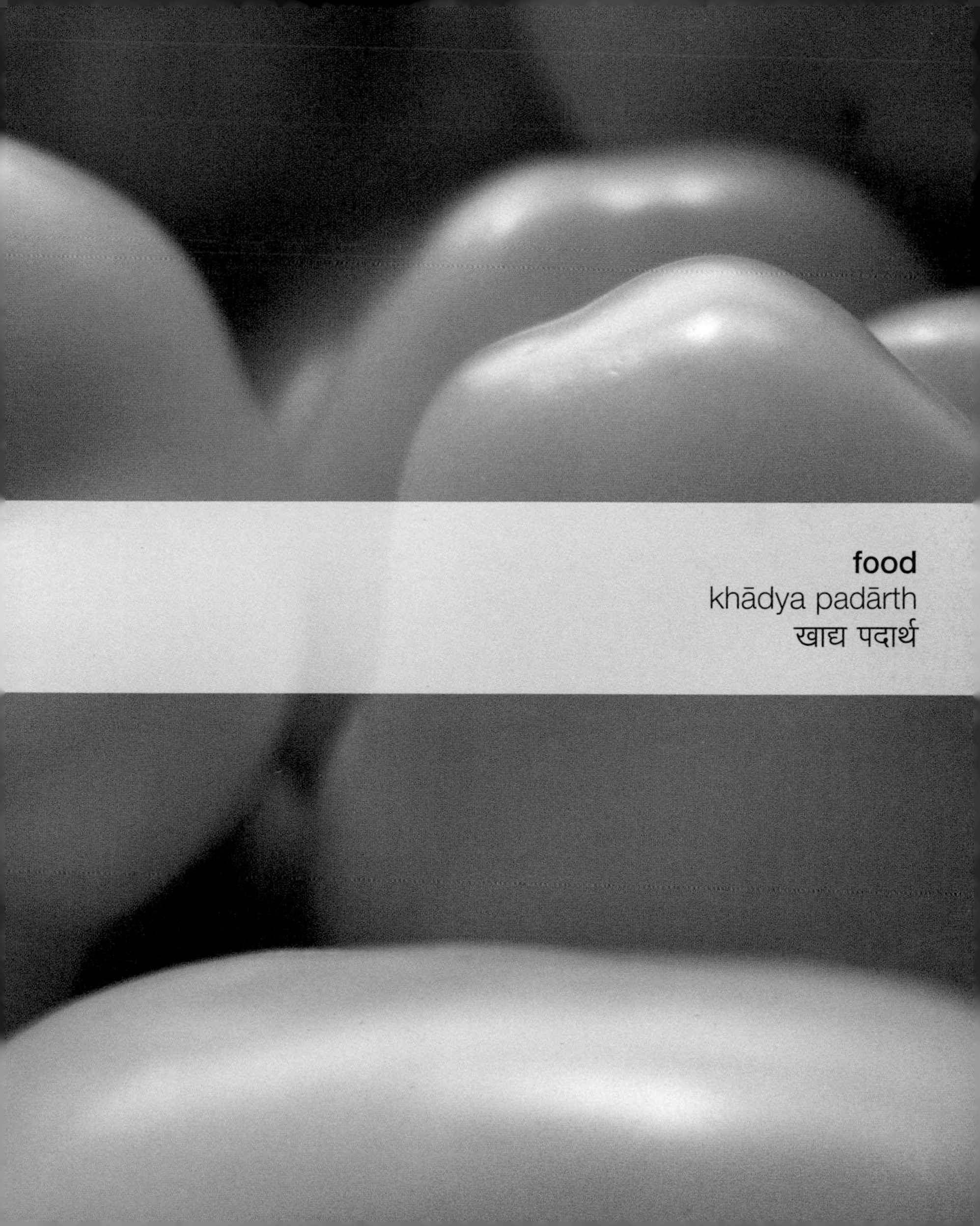

food
khādya padārth
खाद्य पदार्थ

meat • māṃs • मांस

butcher
ḳasāī
क़साई

knife sharpener
chāḳū/chhurī tez
karne kā upkaraṇ
चाकू/छुरी तेज़
करने का उपकरण

meat hook
mīṭ huk
मीट हुक

scales
tarāzū
तराजू

lamb
maṭan | मटन

bacon
bekan | बेकन

sausages
sausages | सॉसेजेस

liver
kalejī | कलेजी

vocabulary • śabdāvalī • शब्दावली

pork
sūar kā māṃs
सूअर का मांस

venison
mṛg māṃs
मृग मांस

offal
chhīchhṛe
छीछड़े

free range
jaṅglī
जंगली

red meat
lāl māṃs
लाल मांस

beef
go māṃs
गो मांस

rabbit
ḳhargoś
ख़रगोश

cured
sanrakṣit
संरक्षित

organic
jaivik
जैविक

lean meat
binā charbī kā
māṃs
बिना चर्बी का मांस

veal
bachhṛe kā
māṃs
बछड़े का मांस

tongue
jībh
जीभ

smoked
dhūmrit
धूम्रित

white meat
safed māṃs
सफ़ेद मांस

cooked meat
pakā huā māṃs
पका हुआ मांस

cuts • māṃs ke ṭukṛe • मांस के टुकड़े

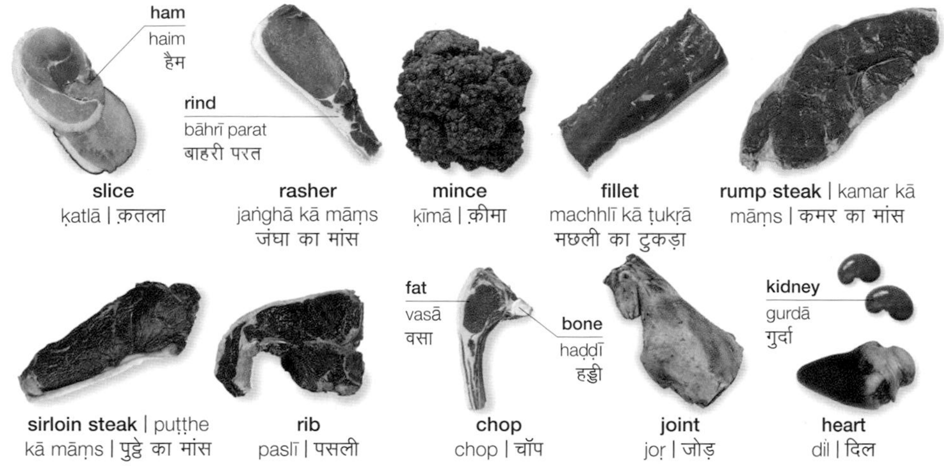
ham
haim
हैम
rind
bāhrī parat
बाहरी परत
slice
ḳatlā | क़तला
rasher
jaṅghā kā māṃs
जंघा का मांस
mince
ḳīmā | क़ीमा
fillet
machhlī kā ṭukṛā
मछली का टुकड़ा
rump steak | kamar kā
māṃs | कमर का मांस
fat
vasā
वसा
bone
haḍḍī
हड्डी
kidney
gurdā
गुर्दा
sirloin steak | puṭṭhe
kā māṃs | पुट्ठे का मांस
rib
paslī | पसली
chop
chop | चॉप
joint
joṛ | जोड़
heart
dil | दिल

poultry • pakṣī-māṃs • पक्षी–मांस

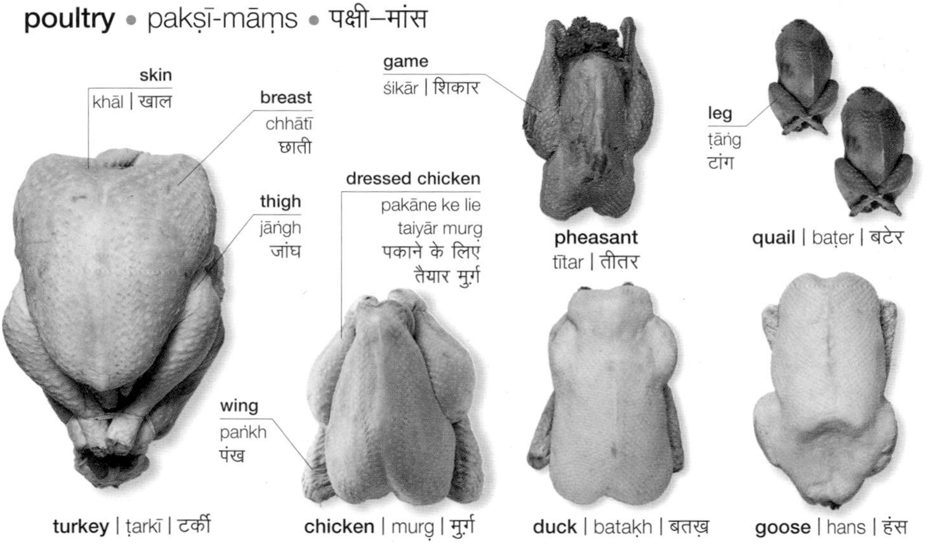
skin
khāl | खाल
breast
chhātī
छाती
thigh
jāṅgh
जांघ
wing
paṅkh
पंख
game
śikār | शिकार
dressed chicken
pakāne ke lie
taiyār murg
पकाने के लिए
तैयार मुर्ग
leg
ṭāṅg
टांग
pheasant
tītar | तीतर
quail | baṭer | बटेर
turkey | ṭarkī | टर्की
chicken | murg | मुर्ग़
duck | bataḳh | बतख़
goose | hans | हंस

fish • machhlī • मछली

peeled prawns
chhile hue jhīṅge
छिले हुए झींगे

ice
baraf
बर्फ़

red mullet
chhoṭī machhlī
छोटी मछली

halibut fillets
hailibaṭ ḳatlī
हैलिबट क़तली

rainbow trout
renbo ṭrāuṭ machhlī
रेनबो ट्राउट मछली

skate wings
skeṭ machhlī
स्केट मछली

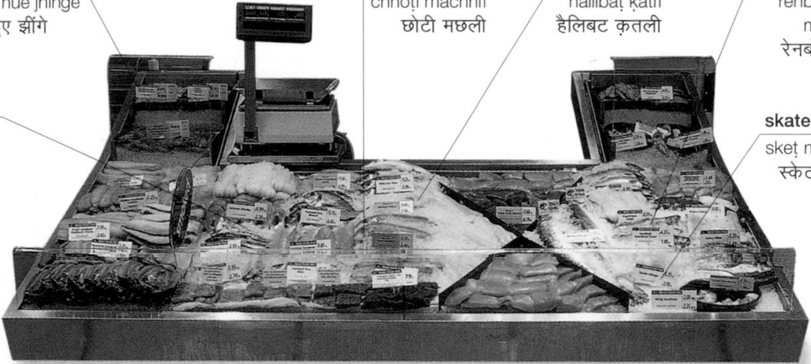

fishmonger's
machhlī kī dukān | मछली की दुकान

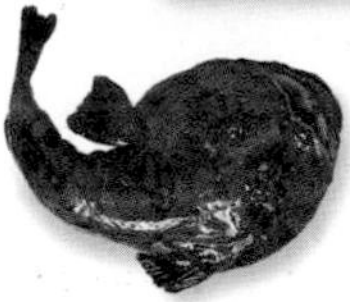

monkfish
maṅk fiś | मंक फ़िश

mackerel | maikral machhlī | मैकरल मछली

trout | ṭrāuṭ machhlī
ट्राउट मछली

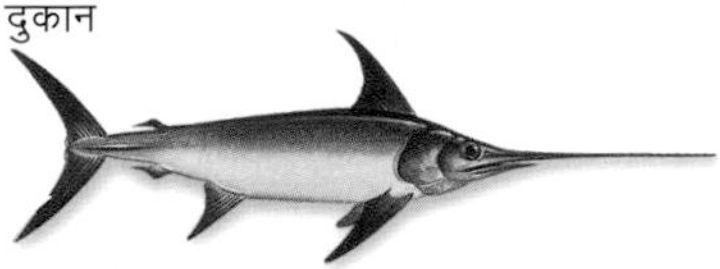

swordfish
khaṅg mīn
खंग मीन

Dover sole
sol machhlī
सोल मछली

lemon sole
laiman sol
लैमन सोल

haddock
haddock | हैडॉक

sardine
sārḍin | सार्डिन

skate | śaṅkuchi machhlī | शंकुचि मछली

whiting | viṭiṅg | विटींग

sea bass | sī bās | सी बास

salmon | sāman machhlī | सामन मछली

cod | cod machhlī | कॉड मछली

sea bream
sī brīm | सी ब्रीम

tuna | ṭyūnā machhlī | ट्यूना मछली

seafood • samudrī bhojan • समुद्री भोजन

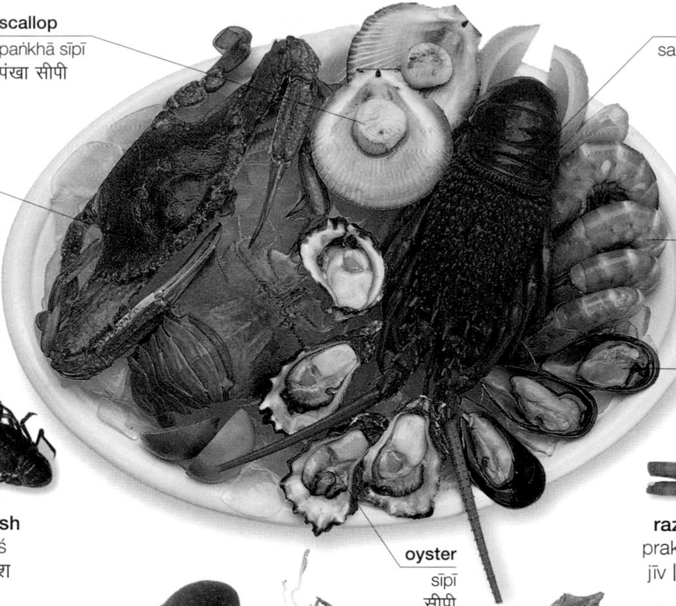

scallop
paṅkhā sīpī
पंखा सीपी

lobster
samudrī jhīṅgā
समुद्री झींगा

crab
kekṛā
केकड़ा

king prawn
jhīṅgā
झींगा

mussel
śambūk
शंबूक

crayfish
krefiś
क्रेफ़िश

oyster
sīpī
सीपी

razor-shell | ek prakār kā samudrī jīv | एक प्रकार का समुद्री जीव

cockle | cockle
sīpī | कॉकल सीपी

octopus
aṣṭbhuj | अष्टभुज

cuttlefish
kaṭal fiś | कटल फ़िश

squid
sklvaḍ | स्क्विड

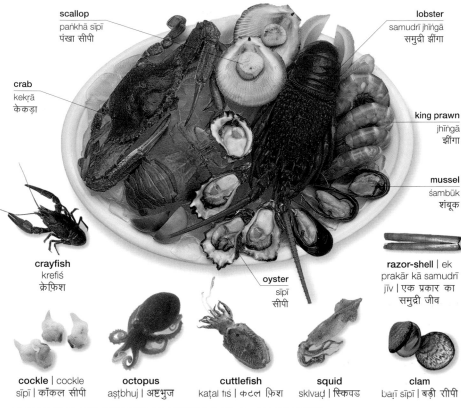

clam
baṛī sīpī | बड़ी सीपी

vocabulary • śabdāvalī • शब्दावली

fresh tāzā ताज़ा	**cleaned** svacchh स्वच्छ	**smoked** dhūmrit धूम्रित	**tail** pūñchh पूंछ	**fillet** ḳatlā क़तला	**salted** lavaṇit लवणित	**loin** śroṇik māṃs श्रोणिक मांस
frozen saṃśītit संशीतित	**filleted** ḳatle kiyā huā क़तले किया हुआ	**skinned** khāl rahit खाल रहित	**bone** kāṃṭe कांटे	**scale** mīn śalk मीन शल्क		

Will you clean it for me?
kyā āp ise sāf kar deṅge?
क्या आप इसे साफ़ कर देंगे?

vegetables 1 • sabziyāṃ • सब्ज़ियां

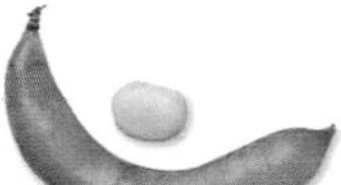

broad bean
bāklā
बाकला

runner bean
guār kī phalī
गुआर की फली

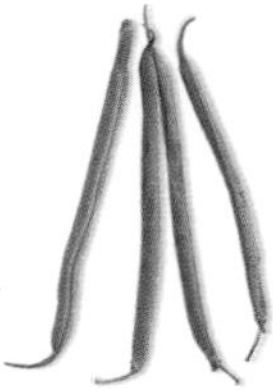

french bean
frānsbīn
फ़्रांसबीन

garden pea
maṭar
मटर

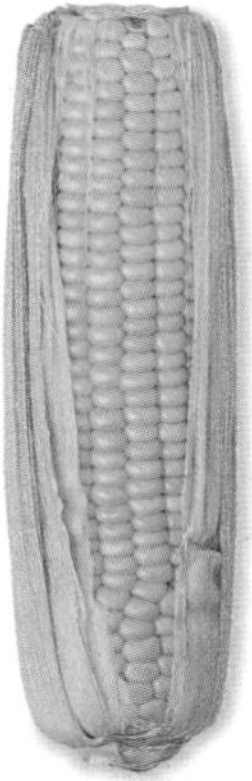

sweetcorn
makaī
मकई

bean sprout
aṅkurit phalī
अंकुरित फली

bamboo
bāṃs
बांस

okra
bhiṇḍī
भिंडी

celery
selerī
सेलेरी

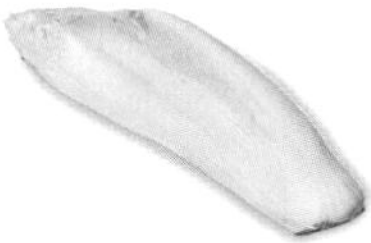

chicory
chikorī
चिकोरी

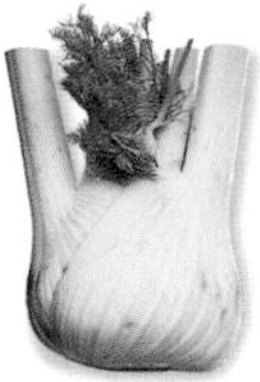

fennel
soā
सोआ

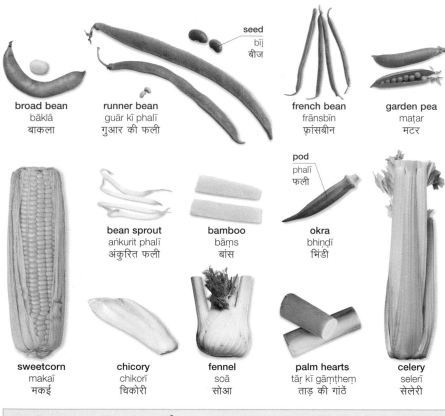

palm hearts
tāṛ kī gāṃṭheṃ
ताड़ की गांठें

vocabulary • śabdāvalī • शब्दावली

leaf pattī पत्ती	**floret** chhoṭā phūl छोटा फूल	**tip** nok नोक	**organic** jaivik जैविक
stalk ḍanṭhal डंठल	**kernel** girī गिरी	**heart** bhītrī gāṃṭh भीतरी गांठ	**plastic bag** plāsṭik baig प्लास्टिक बैग

Do you sell organic vegetables?
āp jaivik sabziyāṃ bechte haiṃ?
आप जैविक सब्ज़ियां बेचते हैं?

Are these grown locally?
kyā ye āspās ugāī jātī haiṃ?
क्या ये आसपास उगाई जाती हैं?

rocket
rocket salād
रॉकेट सलाद

watercress
watercress
वॉटरक्रेस

radicchio
lāl pattāgobhī
लाल पत्तागोभी

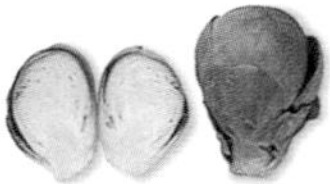

brussel sprout
gāṃṭh gobhī
गांठ गोभी

swiss chard
svis chārḍ | स्विस चार्ड

kale
kel pattī | केल पत्ती

sorrel
sorrel pattī | सॉरेल पत्ती

endive | enḍāiv
pattī | एनडाइव पत्ती

dandelion
ḍenḍiliyan
डेंडिलियन

spinach
pālak
पालक

kohlrabi
śalgam
शलंगम

pak-choi
pāk-choī
पाक–चोई

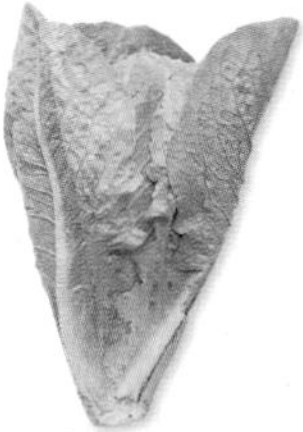

lettuce
salād pattā | सलाद पत्ता

broccoli
broklī | ब्रोकली

cabbage
bandgobhī | बंदगोभी

spring greens
harā salād pattā | हरा सलाद पत्ता

vegetables 2 • sabziyāṃ • सब्ज़ियां

artichoke
artichoke
आर्टीचॉक
radish
chhoṭī mūlī
छोटी मूली
cauliflower
phūlgobhī
फूलगोभी
turnip
śalgam
शलग़म
potato
ālū
आलू
onion
pyāz
प्याज़
pepper
śimlā mirch
शिमला मिर्च
chilli
harī mirch
हरी मिर्च
marrow
harā kaddū
हरा कद्दू

vocabulary • śabdāvalī • शब्दावली

cherry tomato bebī ṭamāṭar बेबी टमाटर	**taro root** kachālū कचालू	**frozen** saṃśītit संशीतित	**bitter** kaṛvā कड़वा
carrot gājar गाजर	**cassava** kasāvā कसावा	**raw** kacchā कच्चा	**firm** saḳht सख़्त
breadfruit breḍfrūṭ ब्रेडफ्रूट	**water chestnut** siṅghāṛā सिंघाड़ा	**hot (spicy)** tīkhā तीखा	**flesh** gūdā गूदा
new potato nayā ālū नया आलू	**celeriac** ek prakār kā kand एक प्रकार का कंद	**sweet** mīṭhā मीठा	**root** jaṛ जड़

What's the price per kilo?
ek kilo kitne kā hai?
एक किलो कितने का है?

What are those called?
inheṃ kyā kahte haiṃ?
इन्हें क्या कहते हैं?

Can I have one kilo of potatoes please?
kyā mujhe ek kilo ālū deṅge?
क्या मुझे एक किलो आलू देंगे?

sweet potato
śakarkandī
शकरकंदी

yam
jimīkand
जिमीकंद

beetroot
chukandar
चुकंदर

swede
svīḍan kā śalgam
स्वीडन का शलग़म

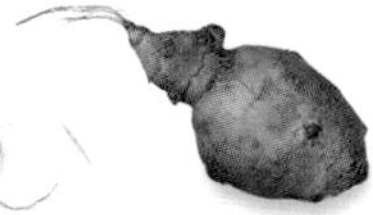
jerusalem artichoke
yerūśalam artichoke
येरूशलम आर्टीचॉक

horseradish
tīkhī mūlī
तीखी मूली

parsnip
pīlī gājar
पीली गाजर

ginger
adrak
अदरक

aubergine
baiṅgan
बैंगन

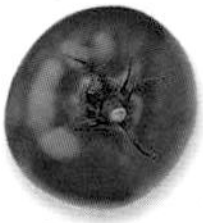
tomato
ṭamāṭar
टमाटर

spring onion
harā pyāz
हरा प्याज़

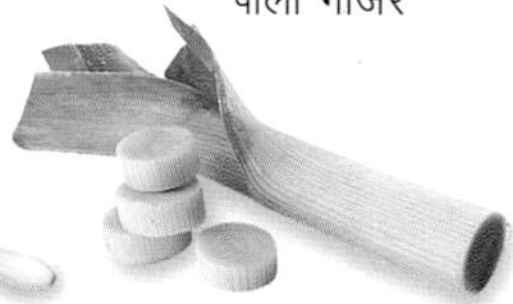
leek
līk
लीक

shallot
pyāz
प्याज़

clove
kalī
कली

garlic
lahsun
लहसुन

truffle
gucchhī
गुच्छी

mushroom
maśrūm
मशरूम

cucumber
khīrā
खीरा

courgette
toraī
तोरई

butternut squash
peṭhā
पेठा

acorn squash
banjuphal
बंजुफल

pumpkin
kaddū
कद्दू

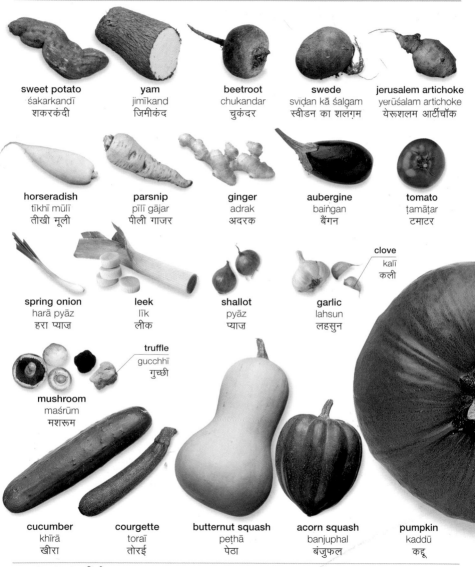

fruit 1 • phal • फल

citrus fruit • khaṭṭe phal • खट्टे फल

orange
santrā | संतरा

clementine
māltā | माल्टा

ugli fruit
aglī frūṭ | अगली फ़्रूट

pith
bhītrī
chhilkā
भीतरी
छिलका

grapefruit
chakotrā | चकोतरा

tangerine
nāraṅgī | नारंगी

segment
phāṃk
फांक

satsuma
jāpānī santrā
जापानी संतरा

zest
chhilkā
छिलका

lime
nībū | नीबू

lemon
khaṭṭā | खट्टा

kumquat
kummkāṭ | कुम्मकाट

stoned fruit • guṭhlīdār phal • गुठलीदार फल

peach
āṛū | आड़ू

nectarine
śaftālū | शफ़तालू

apricot
ḳhubānī
ख़ुबानी

plum
ālū buḳhārā
आलू बुख़ारा

cherry
cherī
चेरी

pear
nāśpātī
नाशपाती

apple
seb | सेब

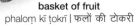

basket of fruit
phaloṃ kī ṭokrī | फलों की टोकरी

berries and melons • ber aur sardā • बेर और सर्दा

strawberry
strawberry | स्ट्रॉबेरी

raspberry
rasbharī | रसभरी

melon
sardā
सर्दा

grapes
āṃgūr | अंगूर

blackberry
blaikberī | ब्लैकबेरी

redcurrant
reḍ karanṭ | रेड करंट

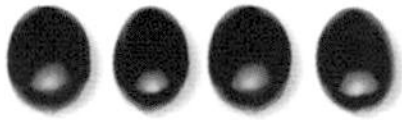

cranberry
krainberī
क्रैनबेरी

blackcurrant
blaik karanṭ
ब्लैक करंट

blueberry
jāmun | जामुन

white currant
vhāiṭ karanṭ
व्हाइट करंट

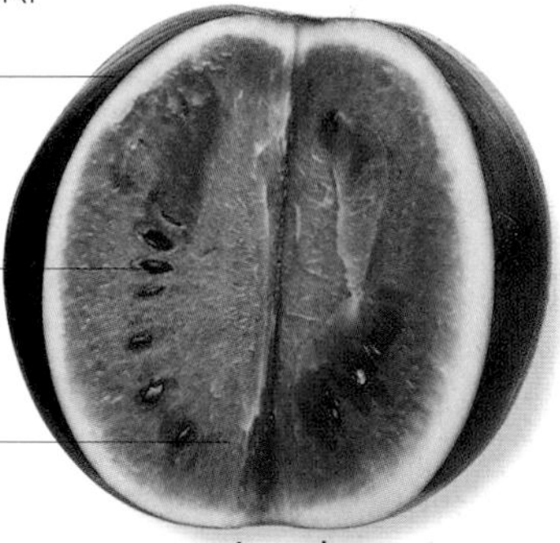
rind
chhilkā
छिलका
seed
bīj
बीज
flesh
gūdā'
गूदा

watermelon
tarbūz
तरबूज़

loganberry
loganberī
लोगन्‍बेरी

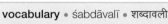

gooseberry
jharberī
झरबेरी

vocabulary • śabdāvalī • शब्दावली

rhubarb revāchīnī रेवाचीनी	**sour** khaṭṭā खट्टा	**crisp** kurkurā कुरकुरा	**juice** jūs जूस	**Are they ripe?** kyā ye pake hue haiṃ? क्या ये पके हुए हैं?
fibre reśedār रेशेदार	**fresh** tāzā ताज़ा	**rotten** saṛā huā सड़ा हुआ	**core** bīj बीज	**Can I try one?** kyā maiṃ ek chakh lūṃ? क्या मैं एक चख लूं?
sweet mīṭhā मीठा	**juicy** rasīlā रसीला	**pulp** gūdā गूदा	**seedless** bīj rahit बीज रहित	**How long will they keep?** ye kab tak ṭhīk raheṅge? ये कब तक ठीक रहेंगे?

fruit 2 • phal 2 • फल 2

mango
ām | आम
pineapple
anannās
अनन्नास
avocado
avokāḍo
अवोकाडो
papaya
papītā
पपीता
peach
āṛū
आड़ू
lychee
līchī
लीची
kiwifruit
kīvī | कीवी
cape gooseberry
rasbharī
रसभरी

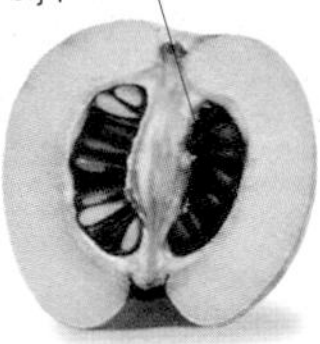
pip
bīj | बीज

quince
kīns | कीन्स

passion fruit
paiśan frūṭ
पैशन फ़्रूट

skin
chhilkā
छिलका

banana
kelā | केला

guava
amrūd | अमरूद

pomegranate
anār | अनार

persimmon
tendū phal
तेंदू फल

feijoa
fehoā | फ़ेहोआ

prickly pear
nākh | नाख

starfruit
kamrakh
कमरख

mangosteen
maṅgusṭh
मंगुष्ठ

nuts and dried fruit • meve aur girī • मेवे और गिरी

pine nut
chilgoza | चिलगोज़ा

pistachio
pistā | पिस्ता

cashewnut
kājū | काजू

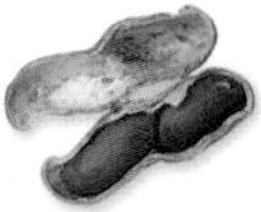

peanut
mūṅgphalī | मूंगफली

hazelnut
pahāṛī bādām
पहाड़ी बादाम

brazilnut
brāzīlnaṭ | ब्राज़ीलनट

pecan
pīkan | पीकन

almond
bādām | बादाम

walnut
akhroṭ | अख़रोट

chestnut
chesṭnaṭ | चेस्टनट

macadamia
maikāḍemiyā
मैकाडेमिया

fig
añjīr | अंजीर

date
khajūr | खजूर

prune
sūkhā alūchā
सूखा अलूचा

sultana
bījrahit kiśmiś
बीजरहित किशमिश

raisin
kiśmiś
किशमिश

currant
munakkā
मुनक्का

coconut
nāriyal | नारियल

vocabulary • śabdāvalī • शब्दावली

green harā हरा	**hard** sakht सख़्त	**kernel** girī गिरी	**salted** lavaṇit लवणित	**roasted** bhunā भुना	**tropical fruit** uṣṇdeśīya phal उष्णदेशीय फल	**shelled** chhilkā rahit छिलका रहित
ripe pakā पका	**soft** narm नर्म	**desiccated** sukhāyā huā सुखाया हुआ	**raw** kacchā कच्चा	**seasonal** mausmī मौसमी	**candied fruit** page phal पगे फल	**whole** sābut साबुत

grains and pulses • anāj evam dāleṃ • अनाज एवं दालें

grains • anāj • अनाज

wheat
gehūṃ | गेहूं

oats
jaī | जई

barley
jau | जौ

millet
jvār | ज्वार

corn
makkā | मक्का

quinoa
kinoyā | किनोया

vocabulary • śabdāvalī • शब्दावली

seed bīj बीज	**fragranced** k̤husbūdār ख़ुशबूदार	**long-grain** baṛā dānā बड़ा दाना
husk bhūsī भूसी	**cereal** khādyānn खाद्यान्न	**short-grain** chhoṭā dānā छोटा दाना
kernel girī गिरी	**wholegrain** sābut साबुत	**fresh** tāzā ताज़ा
dry sukhā सूखा	**soak (v)** bhigonā भिगोना	**easy cook** jaldī pakne vālā जल्दी पकने वाला

rice • chāval • चावल

white rice | safed chāval | सफ़ेद चावल

brown rice | brāun rāis | ब्राउन राइस

wild rice | jaṅglī chāval | जंगली चावल

pudding rice | puḍiṅg rāis | पुडिंग राइस

processed grains • saṅsādhit anāj • संसाधित अनाज

couscous
khaskhas | खसखस

cracked wheat
daliyā | दलिया

semolina
sūjī | सूजी

bran
chokar | चोकर

beans and peas • dālem̩ • दालें

butter beans
sem
सेम

haricot beans
safed rājmā
सफ़ेद राजमा

red kidney beans
rājmā
राजमा

aduki beans
aḍukī bīn
अडुकी बीन

broad beans
bāklā
बाकला

soya beans
soyābīn
सोयाबीन

black-eyed beans
lobiyā
लोबिया

pinto beans
chitrā rājmā
चितरा राजमा

mung beans
sābut mūṅg
साबुत मूंग

flageolet beans
sūkhī frānsbīn
सूखी फ़्रांसबीन

brown lentils
kālī masūr
काली मसूर

red lentils
lāl masūr
लाल मसूर

green peas
maṭar
मटर

chick peas
kābulī chane
काबुली चने

split peas
maṭrā
मटरा

seeds • bīj • बीज

pumpkin seed
kaddū ke bīj
कद्दू के बीज

mustard seed
rāī | राई

caraway
safed zīrā
सफ़ेद ज़ीरा

sesame seed
til | तिल

sunflower seed
sūrajmukhī ke bīj | सूरजमुखी के बीज

herbs and spices • auṣadhi evam masāle • औषधि एवं मसाले

spices • masāle • मसाले

vanilla | vainilā (paudhā) | वैनिला (पौधा)

nutmeg
jāyaphal
जायफल

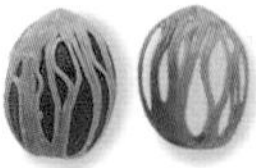
mace
jāvitrī | जावित्री

turmeric
haldī | हल्दी

cumin
zīrā | ज़ीरा

bouquet garni
masāloṃ kī poṭlī
मसालों की पोटली

allspice
lavaṅg badar
लवंग बदर

peppercorn | kālī mirch | काली मिर्च

fenugreek
methī | मेथी

chilli
mirch | मिर्च

saffron
kesar | केसर

cardamom
ilāyachī | इलायची

curry powder
śorbe kā masālā
शोरबे का मसाला

whole
sābut
साबुत
crushed
kuṭā
कुटा
ground
pisā
पिसा
flakes
dardarā
दरदरा

paprika
pisī mirch
पिसी मिर्च

garlic
lahsun | लहसुन

sticks
chhāl
छाल

cinnamon
dālchīnī | दालचीनी

lemon grass
leman grās
लेमन ग्रास

cloves
lauṅg
लौंग

star anise
sṭār enīs
स्टार एनीस

ginger
adrak
अदरक

herbs • auṣadhi • औषधि

fennel | soā | सोआ

fennel seeds
moṭī sauṃf
मोटी सौंफ़

bay leaf
tezpattā | तेज़पत्ता

parsley
pārsli | पारस्लि

chives
jambū | जंबू

mint
pudīnā | पुदीना

thyme
ajvāyan | अजवायन

sage | kapūr kā
pattā | कपूर का पत्ता

tarragon
ṭairāgan | टैरागन

marjoram
marūvā | मरूवा

basil
tulsī | तुलसी

oregano
oregano | ऑरिगानो

coriander
dhaniyā | धनिया

dill
śatpuṣpikā
शतपुष्पिका

rosemary
rozmerī | रोज़मेरी

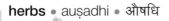

bottled foods • botalband khādya padārth • बोतलबंद खाद्य पदार्थ

cork
ḍhakkan
ढक्कन
sunflower oil
sūrajmukhī kā tel
सूरजमुखी का तेल
walnut oil
akhroṭ kā tel
अख़रोट का तेल
grapeseed oil
aṃgūr ke bīj kā tel
अंगूर के बीज का तेल
almond oil
bādām kā tel
बादाम का तेल
sesame seed oil
til kā tel
तिल का तेल
hazelnut oil
hezalnaṭ tel
हेज़लनट तेल
olive oil
zaitūn kā tel
ज़ैतून का तेल
herbs
jaṛī-būṭī
जड़ी–बूटी
flavoured oil
sugandhit tel
सुगंधित तेल

oils | tel | तेल

sweet spreads • jaim, śahad ityādi • जैम, शहद इत्यादि

jar
jār | जार
honeycomb
chhattā | छत्ता
set honey
kārtik śahad
कार्तिक शहद
lemon curd
leman karḍ
लेमन कर्ड
raspberry jam
rasbharī jaim
रसभरी जैम
marmalade
mārmleḍ
मार्मलेड
clear honey
śahad
शहद
maple syrup
mepal sirap
मेपल सिरप

condiments and spreads • chaṭnī sauce ityādi • चटनी, सॉस इत्यादि

mayonnaise
myonīz
म्योनीज़

cider vinegar
seb sirkā
सेब सिरका

balsamic vinegar
bolsam sirkā
बॉल्सम सिरका

malt vinegar
mālṭ kā sirkā
माल्ट का सिरका

wine vinegar
vāin sirkā
वाइन सिरका

vinegar | sirkā | सिरका

bottle
botal
बोतल

ketchup
ṭamāṭar sauce
टमाटर सॉस

english mustard
iṅgliś masṭarḍ
इंगलिश मस्टर्ड

french mustard
french masṭarḍ
फ्रेंच मस्टर्ड

chutney
chaṭnī
चटनी

sauce
sauce
सॉस

wholegrain mustard
sābut sarsoṃ
साबुत सरसों

peanut butter
pīnaṭ baṭar
पीनट बटर

chocolate spread
chocolate spraiḍ
चॉकलेट स्प्रैड

sealed jar
sīlband jār
सीलबंद जार

preserved fruit
sanrakṣit phal
संरक्षित फल

vocabulary • śabdāvalī • शब्दावली

corn oil
makaī kā tel
मकई का तेल

groundnut oil
mūṅgphalī kā tel
मूंगफली का तेल

vegetable oil
vanaspati tel
वनस्पति तेल

rapeseed oil
tilhan kā tel
तिलहन का तेल

cold-pressed oil
kolḍ-praisḍ tel
कोल्ड–प्रैस्ड तेल

dairy produce • ḍeyarī utpād • डेयरी उत्पाद

cheese • chīz • चीज़

rind
paprī
पपड़ी

semi-hard cheese
ardh sakht chīz
अर्ध सख़्त चीज़

blue cheese
nīlī chīz
नीली चीज़

soft cheese
mulāyam chīz
मुलायम चीज़

semi-soft cheese
ardh mulāyam chīz
अर्ध मुलायम चीज़

grated cheese
kaddūkas kiyā chīz
कद्दूकस किया चीज़

hard cheese
ṭhos chīz | ठोस चीज़

cream cheese
krīm chīz
क्रीम चीज़

cottage cheese
panīr
पनीर

fresh cheese | tāzī chīz | ताज़ी चीज़

milk • dūdh • दूध

whole milk
ful krīm dūdh
फुल क्रीम दूध

semi-skimmed milk
krīmyukt dūdh
क्रीमयुक्त दूध

skimmed milk
krīm rahit dūdh
क्रीम रहित दूध

cow's milk | gāya kā dūdh | गाय का दूध

milk carton
dūdh kā ḍibbā
दूध का डिब्बा

goat's milk
bakrī kā dūdh
बकरी का दूध

condensed milk
kanḍensḍ milk
कंडेंस्ड मिल्क

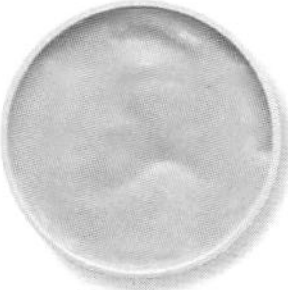
butter
makkhan | मक्खन

margarine
kṛtrim makkhan
कृत्रिम मक्खन

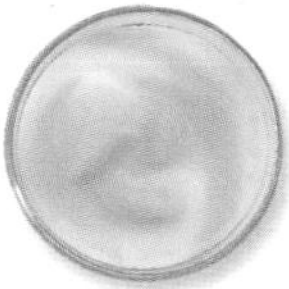
cream
krīm | क्रीम

single cream
patlī krīm | पतली क्रीम

double cream
gaṛhī krīm
गाढ़ी क्रीम

whipped cream
phemṭī huī krīm
फेंटी हुई क्रीम

sour cream
sār krīm | सार क्रीम

yoghurt
dahī | दही

ice-cream
āiskrīm |आइसक्रीम

eggs • aṇḍe • अंडे

yolk
zardī
ज़र्दी

egg white
safed bhāg
सफ़ेद भाग

shell
chhilkā
छिलका

egg cup
aṇḍe rakhne kā kap
अंडे रखने का कप

boiled egg | ublā aṇḍā | उबला अंडा

goose egg
hans kā aṇḍā
हंस का अंडा

hen's egg
murgī kā aṇḍā
मुर्ग़ी का अंडा

duck egg
batakh kā aṇḍā
बतख़ का अंडा

quail egg
baṭer kā aṇḍā
बटेर का अंडा

vocabulary • śabdāvalī • शब्दावली

pasteurized
pāscharīkṛt
पास्चरीकृत

unpasteurized
apāscharīkṛt
अपास्चरीकृत

milkshake
milkśek
मिल्कशेक

frozen yoghurt
dahī kī āiskrīm
दही की आइसक्रीम

salted
lavaṇit
लवणित

unsalted
lavaṇ rahit
लवण रहित

sheep's milk
bheṛ kā dūdh
भेड़ का दूध

buttermilk
chhāchh
छाछ

lactose
dugdh śarkarā
दुग्ध शर्करा

fat free
vasā rahit
वसा रहित

homogenised
samāṅgīkṛt dūdh
समांगीकृत दूध

powdered milk
pāuḍar dūdh
पाउडर दूध

breads and flours • bread evam āṭā • ब्रेड एवं आटा

sliced bread
breḍ slāis
ब्रेड स्लाइस
poppy seeds
khaskhas
खसखस
rye bread
rāī breḍ
राई ब्रेड
baguette
french breḍ
फ्रेंच ब्रेड

bakery | bekrī | बेकरी

making bread • breḍ banānā • ब्रेड बनाना

white flour
maidā | मैदा

brown flour
gehūṃ kā āṭā | गेहूं का आटा

wholemeal flour
āṭā | आटा

yeast
khamīr | खमीर

sift (v)
chhānnā | छानना

mix (v)
milānā | मिलाना

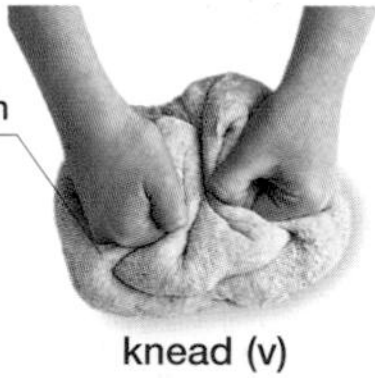
dough
loī
लोई

knead (v)
gūṃdhnā | गूंधना

bake (v)
bek karnā | बेक करना

crust
kinārā
किनारा
white bread
maidā breḍ | मैदा ब्रेड

loaf
sābut
breḍ
साबुत ब्रेड
brown bread
brāun breḍ | ब्राउन ब्रेड

wholemeal bread
āṭe kī breḍ | आटे की ब्रेड

slice
ṭukṛā
टुकड़ा
granary bread
miśrit anāj breḍ
मिश्रित अनाज ब्रेड

corn bread
makaī breḍ | मकई ब्रेड

soda bread
soḍā breḍ | सोडा ब्रेड

sourdough bread
khamīrī breḍ
खमीरी ब्रेड

flatbread
chapṭī breḍ | चपटी ब्रेड

bagel
begal ban | बेगल बन

bap
safed ban | सफ़ेद बन

roll
rol | रोल

fruit bread
frūṭ breḍ | फ्रूट ब्रेड

seeded bread
bījyukt breḍ | बीजयुक्त ब्रेड

naan bread
nān | नान

pitta bread
piṭā breḍ | पीटा ब्रेड

crispbread
kurkurī breḍ | कुरकुरी ब्रेड

vocabulary • śabdāvalī • शब्दावली

strong flour
moṭā āṭā
मोटा आटा

rise (v)
phūlnā
फूलना

prove (v)
ūpar uṭhnā
ऊपर उठना

breadcrumbs
breḍ kā chūrā
ब्रेड का चूरा

slicer
slāisar
स्लाइसर

self-raising flour
mahīn āṭā
महीन आटा

plain flour
āṭā
आटा

glaze (v)
chamak ānā
चमक आना

flute
flūṭ
फ़्लूट

baker
bekar
बेकर

cakes and desserts • kek aur miṣṭānn • केक और मिष्टान्न

éclair
ekleyar
एक्लेयर

cream
krīm
क्रीम

filling
bharāv
भराव

choux pastry
śūz pesṭrī
शूज़ पेस्ट्री

puff pastry
paf pesṭrī
पफ़ पेस्ट्री

filo pastry
filo pesṭrī
फ़िलो पेस्ट्री

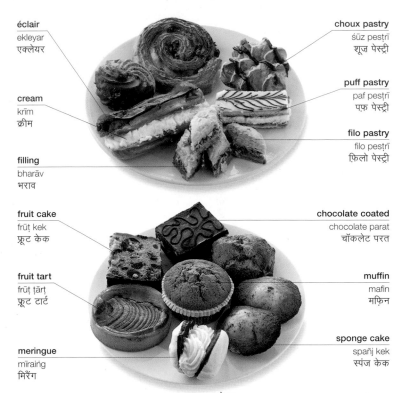

fruit cake
frūṭ kek
फ़्रूट केक

fruit tart
frūṭ ṭārṭ
फ़्रूट टार्ट

meringue
mīraiṅg
मिरैंग

chocolate coated
chocolate parat
चॉकलेट परत

muffin
mafin
मफ़िन

sponge cake
spañj kek
स्पंज केक

cakes | kek | केक

vocabulary • śabdāvalī • शब्दावली

rice pudding
khīr
खीर

celebration
samāroh
समारोह

bun
ban
बन

custard
kasṭarḍ
कस्टर्ड

pastry
pesṭrī
पेस्ट्री

slice
ṭukṛā
टुकड़ा

crème patisserie
krīm pesṭrī
क्रीम पेस्ट्री

chocolate cake
chocolate kek
चॉकलेट केक

May I have a slice please?
kyā maiṃ ek ṭukṛā le saktā hūṃ?
क्या मैं एक टुकड़ा ले सकता हूं?

chocolate chip
chocolate chip biskuṭ
चॉकलेट चिप बिस्कुट

florentine
florenṭāin
फ़्लोरेन्टाइन

sponge fingers
spañj fiṅgar
स्पंज फ़िंगर

trifle
ṭrāifal
ट्राइ.फ़ल

biscuits | biskuṭ | बिस्कुट

mousse
mūs puḍiṅg | मूस पुडिंग

sorbet
sorbet | सॉर्बेट

cream pie
krīm pāī | क्रीम पाई

crème caramel | krīm kairāmal | क्रीम कैरामल

celebration cakes • samāroh kek • समारोह केक

top tier
ūprī chakr
ऊपरी चक्र

decoration
sajāvaṭ
सजावट

ribbon
riban
रिबन

bottom tier
nichlā chakr
निचला चक्र

icing
āisiṅg
आइसिंग

marzipan
bādām parat
बादाम परत

wedding cake | śādī kā kek | शादी का केक

birthday candles
mombattī
मोमबत्ती

blow out (v)
phūṃk se bujhānā
फूंक से बुझाना

birthday cake | janmdin kā kek | जन्मदिन का केक

delicatessen • kek pesṭrī dukān • केक पेस्ट्री दुकान

spicy sausage
masāledār sausage
मसालेदार सॉसेज

oil
tel
तेल

vinegar
sirkā
सिरका

salami
salāmī
सलामी

pepperoni
tīkhī sausages
तीखी सॉसेजेस

flan
flen
फ़्लेन

uncooked meat
kacchā māṃs
कच्चा मांस

counter
kāunṭar
काउंटर

pâté
paiṭī
पैटी

mozzarella
mozerelā | मोज़ेरेला

brie
brī chīz | ब्री चीज़

goat's cheese | bakrī ke dūdh kā panīr | बकरी के दूध का पनीर

cheddar
cheḍar chīz | चेडर चीज़

parmesan | pārmā meṃ banā panīr | पारमा में बना पनीर

camembert
panīr | पनीर

rind
papṛī
पपड़ी

edam | eḍām chīz | एडाम चीज़

manchego | manchego chīz | मनचेगो चीज़

pies
pāī
पाई

black olive
kālā zaitūn
काला जैतून

chili
mirch
मिर्च

sauce
chaṭnī
चटनी

bread roll
bred rol
ब्रेड रोल

cooked meat
pakā huā māṃs
पका हुआ मांस

green olive
harā zaitūn
हरा जैतून

sandwich counter
saiṇḍvich kāuṇṭar | सैंडविच काउंटर

ham
haim
हैम

smoked fish
parirakṣit maçhhlī
परिरक्षित मछली

capers
kaipars
कैपर्स

chorizo
speniś
sausage
स्पेनिश सॉसेज

prosciutto | iṭeliyan
haim | इटेलियन हैम

stuffed olive | bharvāṃ
zaitūn | भरवां जैतून

---

vocabulary • śabdāvalī • शब्दावली

in oil	**marinated**	**in brine**
tel meṃ	masāle meṃ	namkīn pānī meṃ
pakā	liptā	rakhā
तेल में पका	मसाले में लिपटा	नमकीन पानी में रखा

smoked	**salted**	**cured**
dhūmrit	lavaṇit	sanrakṣit
धूम्रित	लवणित	संरक्षित

Take a number please.
krpyā nambar le leṃ
कृपया नंबर ले लें।

Can I try some of that please?
kyā maiṃ chakh saktā hūṃ?
क्या मैं चख सकता हूं?

May I have six slices of that please?
kyā mujhe iske chhah pīs deṇge?
क्या मुझे इसके छह पीस देंगे?

---

drinks • peya • पेय

water • pānī • पानी

bottled water
botalband pānī
बोतलबंद पानी

sparkling
gaisvālā pānī
गैसवाला पानी

still
gaisrahit pānī
गैसरहित पानी

mineral water
minral water | मिनरल वॉटर

tap water | nal kā pānī | नल का पानी

tonic water
tonic water
टॉनिक वॉटर

soda water
soḍā | सोडा

hot drinks • garm peya • गर्म पेय

teabag
ṭī baig
टी बैग

loose leaf tea
khulī chāya pattī
खुली चाय पत्ती

tea | chāya | चाय

beans
coffee ke bīj
कॉफ़ी के बीज

ground coffee
pisī coffee
पिसी कॉफ़ी

coffee | coffee | कॉफ़ी

hot chocolate
hot chocolate
हॉट चॉकलेट

malted drink
mālṭ vāle peya
माल्ट वाले पेय

soft drinks • śītal peya • शीतल पेय

straw
straw
स्ट्रॉ

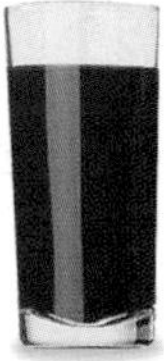

tomato juice
ṭamāṭar kā jūs
टमाटर का जूस

grape juice
aṃgūr kā jūs
अंगूर का जूस

lemonade
śikanjī
शिकंजी

orangeade
santare kā jūs
संतरे का जूस

cola
kolā
कोला

alcoholic drinks • madya peya • मद्य पेय

gin
jin | जिन

can
kain
कैन

beer
bīyar | बीयर

cider | eppal
vāin | एप्पल वाइन

bitter | ḍārk
bīyar | डार्क बीयर

stout
sṭāuṭ | स्टाउट

vodka
vodkā | वोदका

whisky
vhiskī | व्हिस्की

rum
ram | रम

brandy
brānḍī | ब्रांडी

port
porṭ | पोर्ट

dry
sādī
सादी

sherry
śerī | शेरी

campari
kampārī | कमपारी

liqueur
likar | लिकर

tequila
ṭakīlā | टकीला

champagne
śaimpen | शैम्पेन

rosé
gulābī
गुलाबी

white
safed
सफ़ेद

red
lāl
लाल

wine
vāin | वाइन

eating out
bāhar khānā
बाहर खाना

café • kaife • कैफ़े

awning
sāyabān
सायबान

menu
vyañjan sūchī
व्यंजन सूची

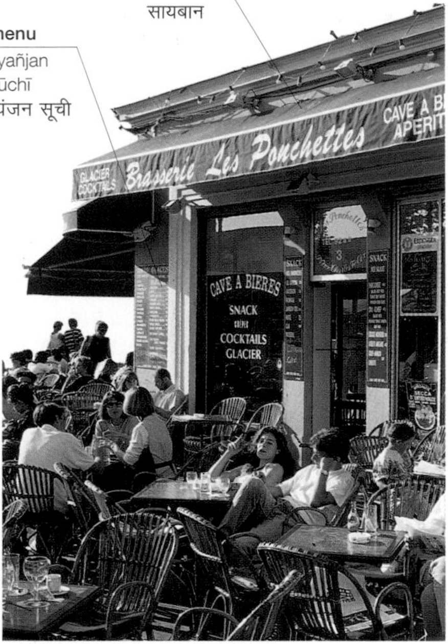

pavement café | roḍ sāiḍ kaife | रोड साइड कैफ़े

umbrella
chhātā
छाता

terrace café | khulā kaife | खुला कैफ़े

waiter
bairā
बैरा

coffee machine
coffee maśīn
कॉफ़ी मशीन

table
mez
मेज़

snack bar | snaik bār | स्नैक बार

coffee • coffee • कॉफ़ी

white coffee
coffee
कॉफ़ी

black coffee
blaik coffee
ब्लैक कॉफ़ी

filter coffee
filṭar coffee | फ़िल्टर कॉफ़ी

espresso
espraiso | एस्प्रैसो

cocoa powder
koko pāuḍar
कोको पाउडर

froth
jhāg
झाग

cappuccino
kepyūchino | केप्यूचिनो

iced coffee
āisḍ coffee | आइस्ड कॉफ़ी

tea • chāya • चाय

herbal tea
auṣadhīya chāya
औषधीय चाय

camomile tea | babūnā kī chāya | बबूना की चाय

green tea | harī chāya | हरी चाय

tea with milk
dūdh vālī chāya
दूध वाली चाय

black tea
kālī chāya
काली चाय

tea with lemon
nībū vālī chāya
नीबू वाली चाय

mint tea
pudīne kī chāya
पुदीने की चाय

iced tea
ṭhaṇḍī chāya
ठंडी चाय

juices and milkshakes • jūs evam milkśek • जूस एवं मिल्कशेक

orange juice
santare kā jūs
संतरे का जूस

apple juice
seb kā jūs
सेब का जूस

pineapple juice
anannās kā jūs
अनन्नास का जूस

tomato juice
ṭamāṭar kā jūs
टमाटर का जूस

chocolate milkshake
chocolate milkśek
चॉकलेट मिल्कशेक

strawberry milkshake
strawberry milkśek
स्ट्रॉबेरी मिल्कशेक

coffee milkshake
coffee milkśek
कॉफ़ी मिल्कशेक

food • khādya padārth • खाद्य पदार्थ

brown bread
brāun breḍ
ब्राउन ब्रेड

toasted sandwich | ṭosṭeḍ saiṇḍvich | टोस्टेड सैंडविच

salad
salād | सलाद

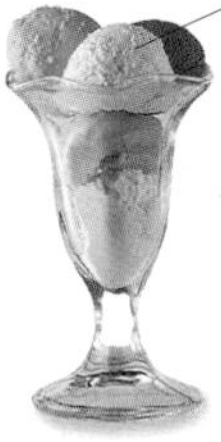

scoop
skūp
स्कूप

ice cream
āiskrīm | आइसक्रीम

pastry
pesṭrī | पेस्ट्री

bar • bār • बार

glasses
gilās
गिलास
optic
optic
ऑपटिक
till
tijorī
तिजोरी
bartender
bār ṭeṇḍar
बार टेंडर
beer tap
bīyar ṭaip
बीयर टैप
coffee machine
coffee maśīn
कॉफ़ी मशीन
ice bucket
āis box
आइस बॉक्स
bar stool
kursī
कुर्सी
ashtray
aiśṭre
ऐशट्रे
coaster
kosṭar
कोस्टर
bar counter
bār kāunṭar
बार काउंटर

bottle opener
botal opnar
बोतल ओपनर
lever
līvar
लीवर

corkscrew | corkscrew | कॉर्कस्क्रू

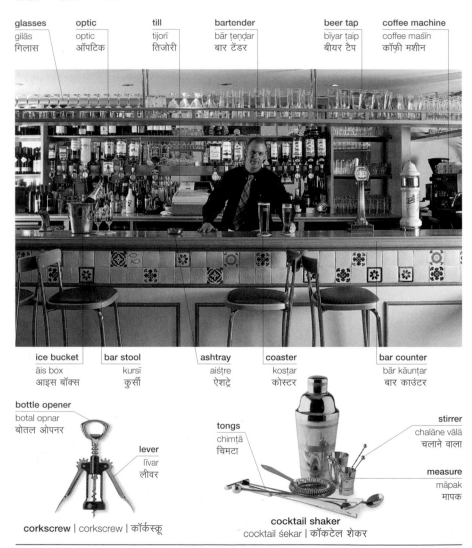

tongs
chimṭā
चिमटा
stirrer
chalāne vālā
चलाने वाला
measure
māpak
मापक

cocktail shaker
cocktail śekar | कॉकटेल शेकर

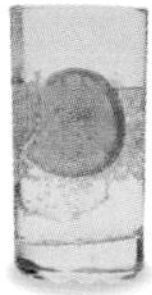

gin and tonic
jin aur tonic
जिन और टॉनिक

pitcher
jag
जग

scotch and water
scotch aur pānī
स्कॉच और पानी

ice cube
baraf
बर्फ़

rum and coke
ram aur kok
रम और कोक

vodka and orange
vodkā aur santrā
वोदका और संतरा

martini
mārṭinī | मार्टिनी

cocktail
cocktail | कॉकटेल

wine
vāin | वाइन

beer
bīyar | बीयर

a shot
ek shot | एक शॉट

single
siṅgal
सिंगल

double
ḍabal
डबल

measure
māp | माप

without ice | baraf rahit | बर्फ़ रहित

ice and lemon
baraf va śikañjī
बर्फ़ व शिकंजी

with ice | baraf ke sāth | बर्फ़ के साथ

bar snacks • bār snaiks • बार स्नैक्स

crisps | kurkurā | कुरकुरा

cashewnuts
kājū
काजू

peanuts
chīnā bādām
चीना बादाम

almonds
bādām
बादाम

nuts | meve | मेवे

olives | zaitūn | ज़ैतून

restaurant • restrāṃ • रेस्तरां

non-smoking section
dhūmrapān niṣedh sthān
धूम्रपान निषेध स्थान

napkin
naipkin
नैपकिन

commis chef
sahāyak rasoiyā
सहायक रसोइया

table setting
mez sajjā
मेज़ सज्जा

chef
rasoiyā
रसोइया

kitchen
rasoī | रसोई

glass
gilās
गिलास

tray
ṭre
ट्रे

waiter
bairā | बैरा

vocabulary • śabdāvalī • शब्दावली

receipt rasīd रसीद	**specials** viśeṣ विशेष	**price** mūlya मूल्य	**customer** grāhak ग्राहक	**service included** sevā sammilit सेवा सम्मिलित	**à la carte** menyu ke mutābik मेन्यु के मुताबिक
wine list vāin sūchī वाइन सूची	**sweet trolley** pesṭrī trolley पेस्ट्री ट्रॉली	**bill** bil बिल	**salt** namak नमक	**service not included** sevā sammilit nahīṃ सेवा सम्मिलित नहीं	**smoking section** dhūmrapān kṣetr धूम्रपान क्षेत्र
tip bakhśīś बख़्शीश	**pepper** kālī mirch काली मिर्च	**bar** bār बार	**buffet** bufe बुफ़े	**evening menu** saṅdhyākālīn vyañjan sūchī संध्याकालीन व्यंजन सूची	**lunch menu** dopahar kī vyañjan sūchī दोपहर की व्यंजन सूची

menu
vyañjan sūchī
व्यंजन सूची

child's meal
bāl āhār | बाल–आहार

order (v)
order denā | ऑर्डर देना

pay (v)
dām chukānā | दाम चुकाना

courses • bhojan kā daur • भोजन का दौर

apéritif
ārambh peya | आरंभ पेय

starter
sṭārṭar | स्टार्टर

soup
sūp | सूप

main course
men kors | मेन कोर्स

side order
sāiḍ order | साइड ऑर्डर

fork
kāṃṭā
कांटा

dessert
misṭānn | मिष्टान्न

coffee spoon
coffee kā
chammach
कॉफ़ी का चम्मच

coffee
coffee | कॉफ़ी

vocabulary • śabdāvalī • शब्दावली

A table for two please.
kṛpyā do logoṃ ke lie ṭebal batāeṃ.
कृपया दो लोगों के लिए टेबल बताएं।

Can I see the menu/winelist please?
kyā menyu/vāin lisṭ dikhāeṅge?
क्या मेन्यु/वाइन लिस्ट दिखाएंगे?

Is there a fixed price menu?
kyā yah ekdām menyu hai?
क्या यह एकदाम मेन्यु है?

Do you have any vegetarian dishes?
kyā yahāṃ śākāhārī khānā hai?
क्या यहां शाकाहारी खाना है?

Could I have the bill/a receipt please?
kyā mujhe bil/rasīd mil saktī hai?
क्या मुझे बिल/रसीद मिल सकती है?

Can we pay separately?
kyā ham alag-alag bil de sakte haiṃ?
क्या हम अलग–अलग बिल दे सकते हैं?

Where are the toilets, please?
śauchālaya kahāṃ hai?
शौचालय कहां है?

fast food • fāsṭ fūḍ • फ़ास्ट फ़ूड

burger meal | bargar mīl | बर्गर मील

home delivery
hom ḍilīvarī | होम डिलीवरी

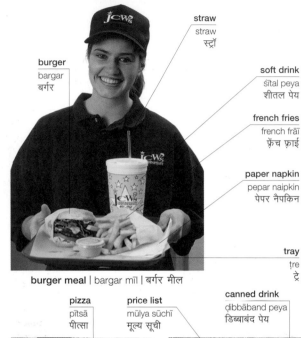

street stall
sṭrīṭ stall | स्ट्रीट स्टॉल

vocabulary • śabdāvalī • शब्दावली

pizza parlour
pītsā pārlar
पीत्सा पार्लर

burger bar
bargar bār
बर्गर बार

menu
vyañjan sūchī
व्यंजन सूची

eat-in
restrāṃ meṃ khānā
रेस्तरां में खाना

take-away
paik karvāke le jānā
पैक करवाके ले जाना

re-heat (v)
dubārā garm karnā
दुबारा गर्म करना

tomato sauce
ṭamāṭar sauce
टमाटर सॉस

Can I have that to go please?
kyā āp ise paik kar sakte haiṃ?
क्या आप इसे पैक कर सकते हैं?

Do you deliver?
kyā āp ḍilīvar karte haiṃ?
क्या आप डिलीवर करते हैं?

hamburger
haim bargar
हैम बर्गर

bun
ban
बन

chicken burger
chikan bargar
चिकन बर्गर

veggie burger
vej bargar
वेज बर्गर

mustard
mastaṛd
मस्टर्ड

sausage
sausage
सॉसेज

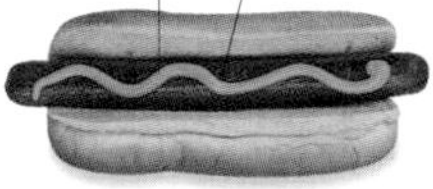

hot dog
hot dog | हॉट डॉग

sandwich
saiṇḍvich
सैंडविच

club sandwich
klab saiṇḍvich
क्लब सैंडविच

open sandwich
khulā saiṇḍvich
खुला सैंडविच

filling
bharāvan
भरावन

wrap
rol | रोल

kebab
kabāb | कबाब

sauce
sauce
सॉस

chicken nuggets | chikan nageṭs | चिकन नगेट्स

savoury
namkīn
नमकीन

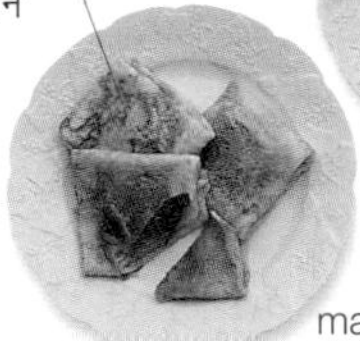

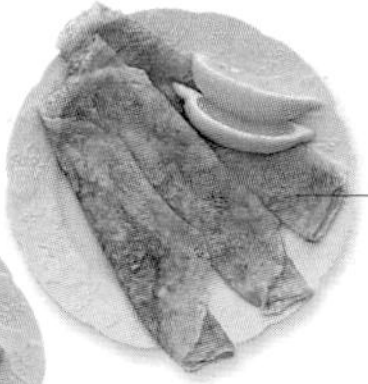

sweet
mīṭhā
मीठा

crêpes
maide kā chīlā
मैदे का चीला

topping
topping
टॉपिंग

fish and chips
talī machhlī aur chips
तली मछली और चिप्स

ribs
chāṃp
चांप

fried chicken
frāiḍ chikan
फ़्राइड चिकन

pizza
pītsā
पीत्सा

breakfast • subah kā nāśtā • सुबह का नाश्ता

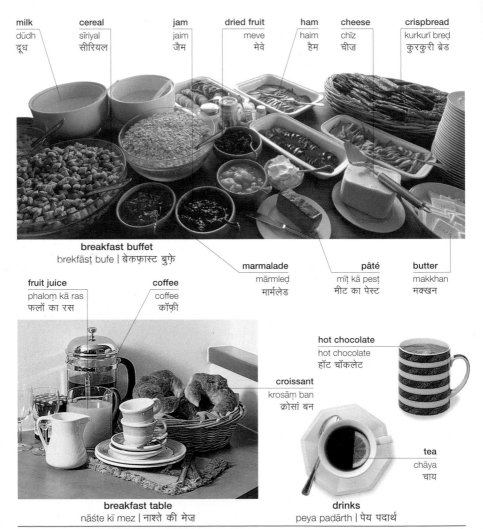

milk
dūdh
दूध
cereal
sīriyal
सीरियल
jam
jaim
जैम
dried fruit
meve
मेवे
ham
haim
हैम
cheese
chīz
चीज़
crispbread
kurkurī breḍ
कुरकुरी ब्रेड
marmalade
mārmleḍ
मार्मलेड
pâté
mīṭ kā pesṭ
मीट का पेस्ट
butter
makkhan
मक्खन

breakfast buffet
brekfāsṭ bufe | ब्रेकफ़ास्ट बुफ़े

fruit juice
phaloṃ kā ras
फलों का रस
coffee
coffee
कॉफ़ी
croissant
krosāṃ ban
क्रोसां बन

breakfast table
nāśte kī mez | नाश्ते की मेज़

hot chocolate
hot chocolate
हॉट चॉकलेट

tea
chāya
चाय

drinks
peya padārth | पेय पदार्थ

brioche
mīṭhe ban | मीठे बन

bread
breḍ | ब्रेड

tomato
ṭamāṭar
टमाटर
black pudding
blaik puḍiṅg
ब्लैक पुडिंग
toast
ṭosṭ
टोस्ट
sausage
sausage
सॉसेज
fried egg
frāiḍ aṇḍā
फ़ाइड अंडा
bacon
bekan
बेकन

English breakfast
aṅgrezī nāśtā | अंग्रेज़ी नाश्ता

kippers
kipars | किपर्स

french toast
french ṭosṭ
फ़्रेंच टोस्ट

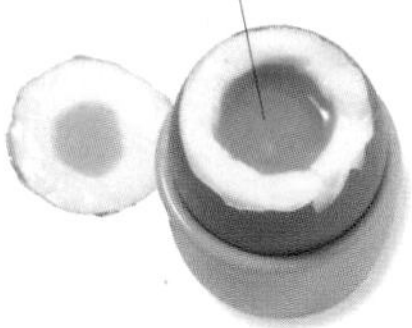

boiled egg
ublā aṇḍā
उबला अंडा

scrambled eggs
aṇḍe kī bhurjī | अंडे की भुर्जी

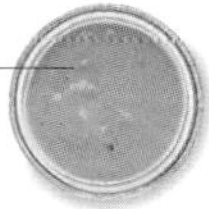
fruit yoghurt
frūṭ dahī
फ़्रूट दही

pancakes
painkek | पैनकेक

cream
krīm
क्रीम

waffles
waffles | वॉफ़ल्स

porridge
daliyā | दलिया

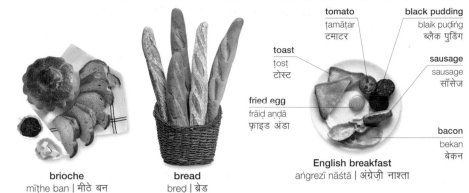

fresh fruit
tāze phal | ताज़े फल

dinner • ḍinar • डिनर

soup
sūp | सूप

broth
śorbā | शोरबा

stew
dampuḳht | दमपुख़्त

curry
rasedār | रसेदार

roast
bhunā | भुना

pie
pāī | पाई

soufflé
sūfle | सूफ़ले

kebab
kabāb | कबाब

meatballs
kofte | कोफ़्ते

omelette
omelette | ऑमलेट

stir fry | kam tel meṃ
bhunā | कम तेल में भुना

pasta
pāstā | पास्ता

rice
chāval | चावल

mixed salad | miśrit
salād | मिश्रित सलाद

green salad
harā salād | हरा सलाद

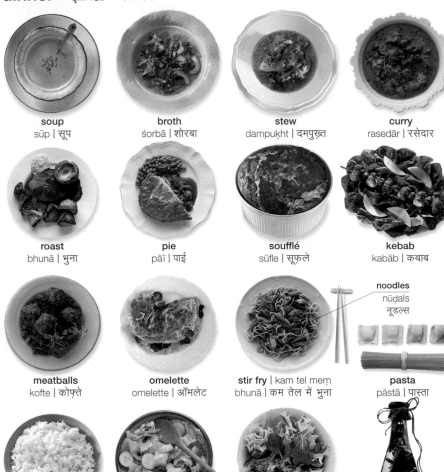

dressing
ḍresiṅg | ड्रेसिंग

techniques • vidhiyāṃ • विधियां

stuffed
bharvāṃ | भरवां

in sauce | sauce meṃ
सॉस में

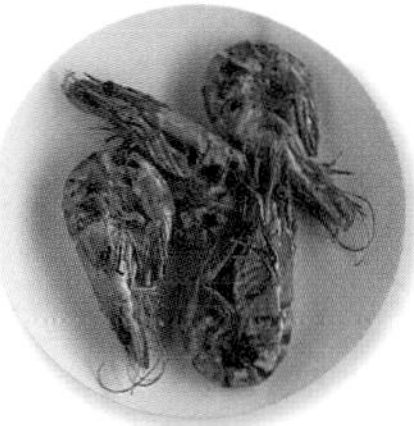

grilled
bhunā huā | भुना हुआ

marinated | masāle meṃ
lipṭā | मसाले में लिपटा

poached
pochaḍ | पोच्ड

mashed
maslā huā | मसला हुआ

baked | bek kiyā
huā | बेक किया हुआ

pan fried | kam tel meṃ
pakā | कम तेल में पका

fried
talā huā | तला हुआ

pickled
achārit | अचारित

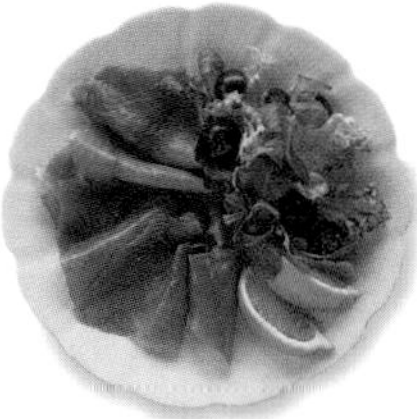

smoked
dhūmrit | धूम्रित

deep fried
talā huā | तला हुआ

syrup | sirap meṃ
banā | सिरप में बना

dressed | ḍresiṅg kiyā
huā | ड्रेसिंग किया हुआ

steamed | bhāp meṃ
pakā | भाप में पका

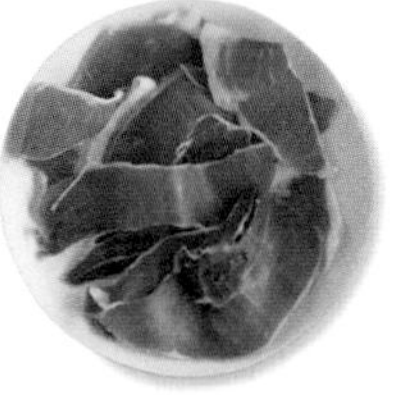

cured
sanrakṣit | संरक्षित

study

adhyayan

अध्ययन

school • vidyālaya • विद्यालय

teacher
adhyāpikā
अध्यापिका

blackboard
śyāmpaṭ
श्यामपट

classroom | kakṣā | कक्षा

pupil
chhātr
छात्र

desk
beñch
बेंच

chalk
chalk
चॉक

schoolboy
skūlī chhātr | स्कूली छात्र

school uniform
skūlī vardī
स्कूली वर्दी

school bag
skūlī bastā
स्कूली बस्ता

schoolgirl
skūlī chhātrā | स्कूली छात्रा

vocabulary • śabdāvalī • शब्दावली

history itihās इतिहास	**science** vijñān विज्ञान	**physics** bhautikī भौतिकी
languages bhāṣāeṃ भाषाएं	**art** kalā कला	**chemistry** rasāyan śāstr रसायन शास्त्र
literature sāhitya साहित्य	**music** saṅgīt संगीत	**biology** jīv vijñān जीव विज्ञान
geography bhūgol भूगोल	**maths** gaṇit गणित	**physical education** śārīrik śikṣā शारीरिक शिक्षा

activities • gatividhiyāṃ • गतिविधियां

read (v) | paṛhnā | पढ़ना

write (v) | likhnā | लिखना

spell (v) | vartanī likhnā
वर्तनी लिखना

draw (v)
chitr banānā | चित्र बनाना

overhead projector
ovarheḍ projekṭar
ओवरहेड प्रोजेक्टर

nib
nib
निब

pen
pen | पेन

colouring pencil
raṅgīn pensil
रंगीन पेंसिल

pencil
pensil | पेंसिल

pencil sharpener
sharpener
शॉपनर

rubber
rabaṛ | रबड़

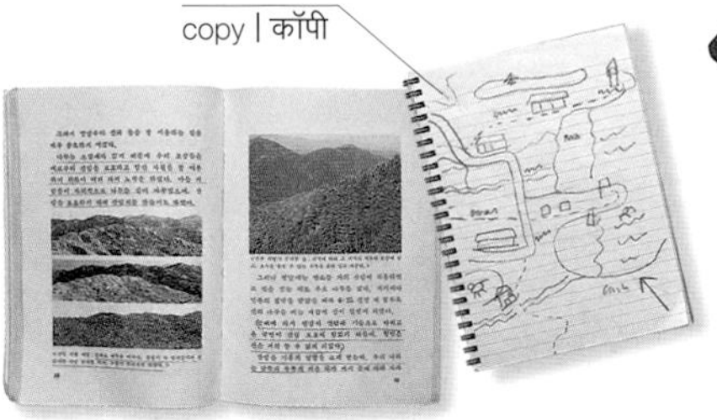

notebook
copy | कॉपी

textbook | pāṭhya pustak | पाठ्य पुस्तक

pencil case
pensil kes | पेंसिल केस

ruler
paimānā | पैमाना

question (v) | praśan
pūchhnā | प्रश्न पूछना

answer (v)
uttar denā | उत्तर देना

discuss (v) | vichār-vimarś
karnā | विचार–विमर्श करना

learn (v)
sīkhnā | सीखना

vocabulary • śabdāvalī • शब्दावली

head teacher mukhyādhyāpikā मुख्याध्यापिका	**answer** uttar उत्तर	**grade** śreṇī श्रेणी
lesson adhyāya अध्याय	**homework** gṛhkārya गृहकार्य	**year** varṣ वर्ष
question praśan प्रश्न	**examination** parīkṣā परीक्षा	**dictionary** śabdkoś शब्दकोश
take notes (v) noṭs lenā नोट्स लेना	**essay** nibandh निबंध	**encyclopaedia** viśvakoś विश्वकोश

maths • gaṇit • गणित

shapes • ākṛtiyāṃ • आकृतियां

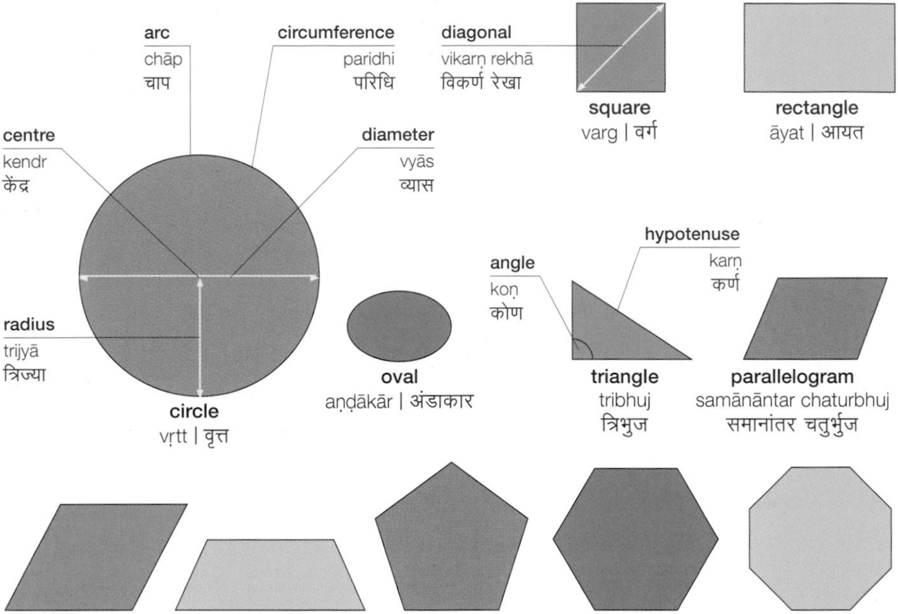
arc
chāp
चाप
circumference
paridhi
परिधि
diagonal
vikarṇ rekhā
विकर्ण रेखा
square
varg | वर्ग
rectangle
āyat | आयत
centre
kendr
केंद्र
diameter
vyās
व्यास
radius
trijyā
त्रिज्या
circle
vṛtt | वृत्त
oval
aṇḍākār | अंडाकार
hypotenuse
karṇ
कर्ण
angle
koṇ
कोण
triangle
tribhuj
त्रिभुज
parallelogram
samānāntar chaturbhuj
समानांतर चतुर्भुज
rhombus
samchaturbhuj
समचतुर्भुज
trapezium
samlamb
समलंब
pentagon
pañchbhuj
पंचभुज
hexagon
ṣaḍbhuj
षड्भुज
octagon
aṣṭbhuj
अष्टभुज

solids • ghanākṛtiyāṃ • घनाकृतियां

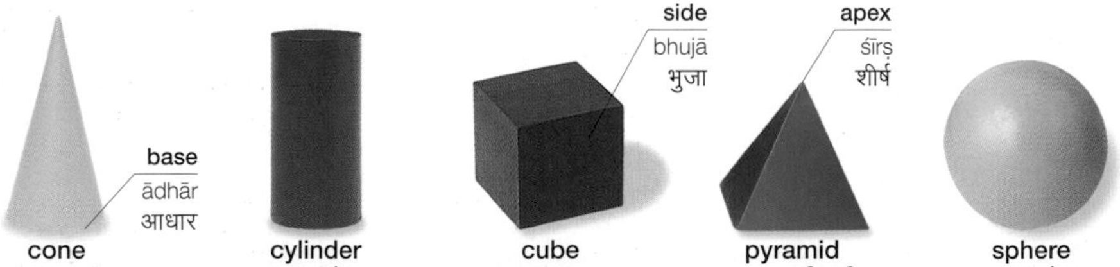
side
bhujā
भुजा
apex
śīrṣ
शीर्ष
base
ādhār
आधार
cone
śaṅku | शंकु
cylinder
belan | बेलन
cube
ghan | घन
pyramid
pirāmiḍ | पिरामिड
sphere
golā | गोला

lines • rekhāeṃ • रेखाएं

straight
sīdhī | सीधी

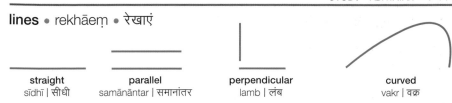

parallel
samānāntar | समानांतर

perpendicular
lamb | लंब

curved
vakr | वक्र

measurements • māpak • मापक

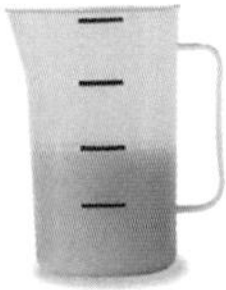

volume
parimāṇ | परिमाण

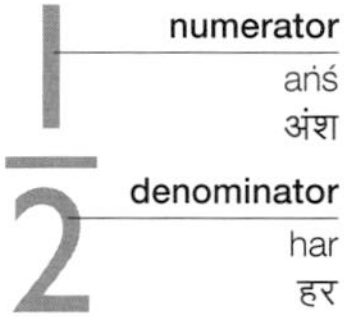
numerator
aṅś
अंश
denominator
har
हर

fraction
bhinn | भिन्न

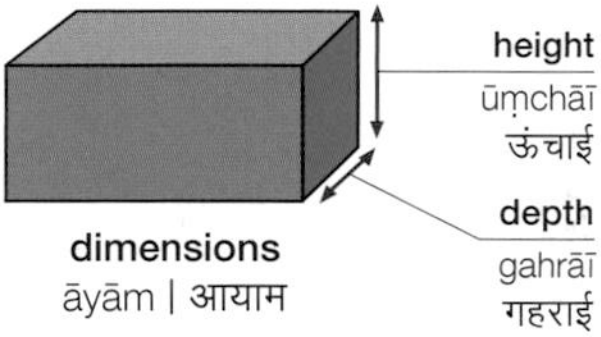
height
ūṃchāī
ऊंचाई
depth
gahrāī
गहराई

dimensions
āyām | आयाम

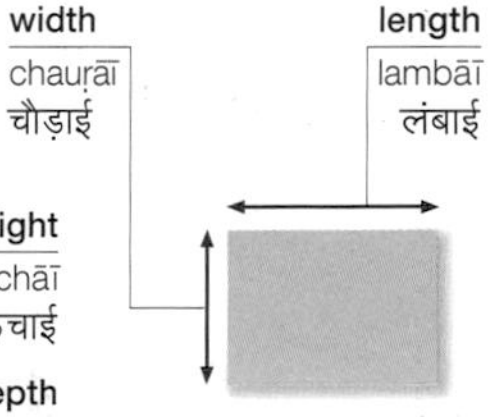
width
chauṛāī
चौड़ाई
length
lambāī
लंबाई

area
kṣetraphal | क्षेत्रफल

equipment • upkaraṇ • उपकरण

set square
samkoṇak
समकोणक

protractor
koṇmāpak/ḍī
कोणमापक/डी

ruler
paimānā
पैमाना

compass
parkār
परकार

calculator
kailkyuleṭar
कैलक्युलेटर

vocabulary • śabdāvalī • शब्दावली

geometry
rekhāgaṇit
रेखागणित

plus
jamā
जमा

times
gunā
गुना

equals
barābar
बराबर

add (v)
joṛnā
जोड़ना

multiply (v)
guṇā karnā
गुणा करना

equation
samīkaraṇ
समीकरण

arithmetic
aṅkgaṇit
अंकगणित

minus
ghaṭā
घटा

divided by
bhājak
भाजक

count (v)
ginnā
गिनना

subtract (v)
ghaṭānā
घटाना

divide (v)
bhāg denā
भाग देना

percentage
pratiśat
प्रतिशत

science • vijñān • विज्ञान

laboratory
prayogśālā | प्रयोगशाला

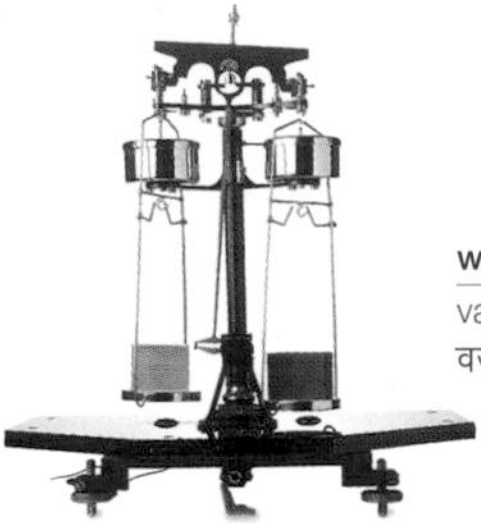

scales
tarāzū | तराज़ू

weight
vazan
वज़न

spring balance
spriṅg tulā | स्प्रिंग तुला

crucible
kuṭhālī
कुठाली

bunsen burner
bansan barnar
बनसन बर्नर

tripod
tipāī | तिपाई

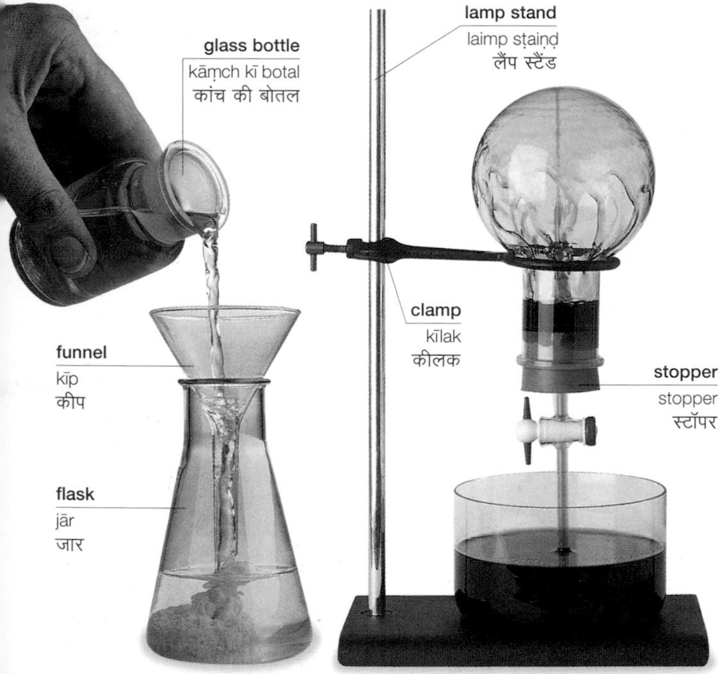

glass bottle
kāṃch kī botal
कांच की बोतल

funnel
kīp
कीप

flask
jār
जार

lamp stand
laimp sṭaiṇḍ
लैंप स्टैंड

clamp
kīlak
कीलक

stopper
stopper
स्टॉपर

experiment | prayog | प्रयोग

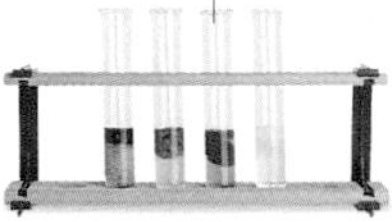

test tube
parakhnalī
परखनली

rack
raik | रैक

timer
ṭāimar | टाइमर

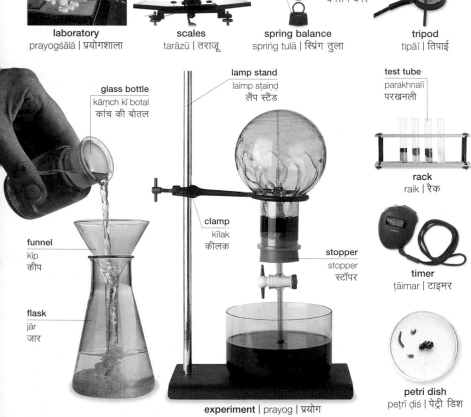

petri dish
peṭrī ḍiś | पेट्री डिश

thermometer
tharmāmīṭar | थर्मामीटर

syringe
siriṅj | सिरिंज

tweezers
chhoṭī chimṭī | छोटी चिमटी

scalpel
chākū | चाकू

dropper
dropper | ड्रॉपर

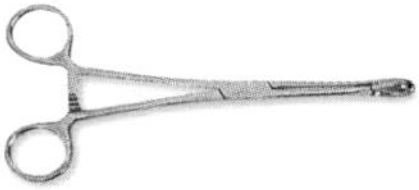

forceps
forceps | फ़ॉरसेप

tongs
baṛī chimṭī | बड़ी चिमटी

spatula
spaiṭyūlā | स्पैट्यूला

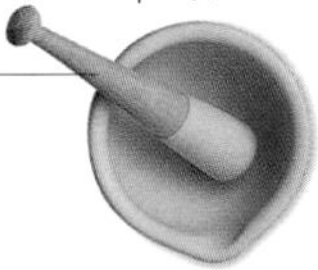
pestle
mūsal
मूसल

mortar
kharal | खरल

filter paper
filṭar pepar | फ़िल्टर पेपर

safety goggles | surakṣā chaśmā | सुरक्षा चश्मा

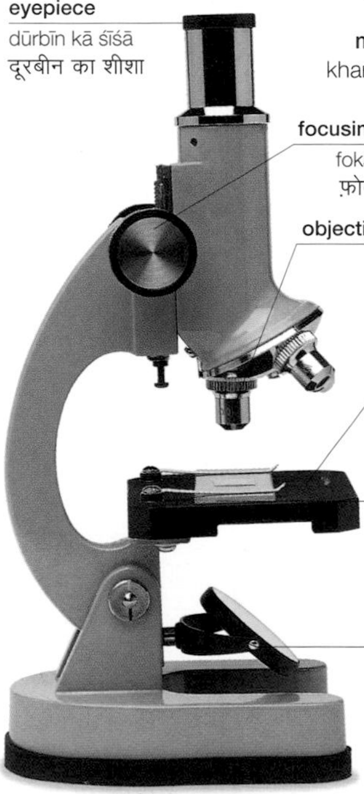
eyepiece
dūrbīn kā śīśā
दूरबीन का शीशा
focusing knob
fokas knob
फ़ोकस नॉब
objective lens
lains
लैंस
stage
tal
तल
slide
slāiḍ
स्लाइड
mirror
śīśā
शीशा

microscope
sūkṣamdarśī | सूक्ष्मदर्शी

pipette
nalikā | नलिका

glass rod
kāṃch kī chhaṛ
कांच की छड़

beaker
bīkar | बीकर

magnet
chumbak
चुंबक

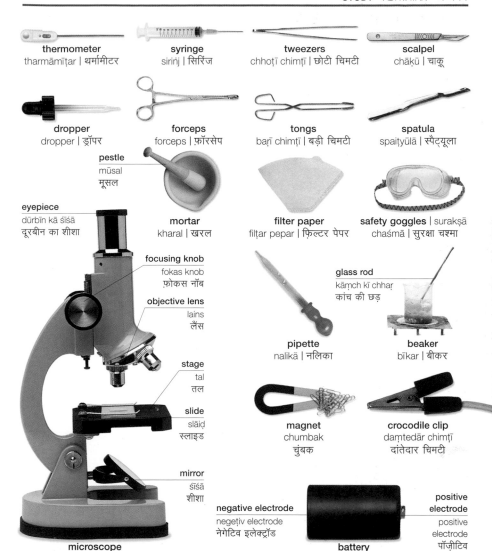

crocodile clip
daṃtedār chimṭī
दांतेदार चिमटी

negative electrode
negeṭiv electrode
नेगेटिव इलेक्ट्रॉड
positive electrode
positive electrode
पॉज़ीटिव इलेक्ट्रॉड

battery
baiṭrī | बैटरी

college • mahāvidyālaya • महाविद्यालय

admissions
praveś
प्रवेश

refectory
bhojan kakṣ
भोजन कक्ष

health centre
svāsthya kendr
स्वास्थ्य केंद्र

sports field
khel kā maidān
खेल का मैदान

hall of residence
chhātrāvās
छात्रावास

campus | parisar | परिसर

catalogue
sūchī
सूची

librarian
pustakālaya adhyakṣ
पुस्तकालय अध्यक्ष

loans desk
pustak prāpti
पुस्तक प्राप्ति

bookshelf
pustakoṃ kī almārī
पुस्तकों की अलमारी

periodical
patrikāeṃ
पत्रिकाएं

journal
patrikāeṃ
पत्रिकाएं

library | pustakālaya | पुस्तकालय

vocabulary • śabdāvalī • शब्दावली

library card pustakālaya kārḍ पुस्तकालय कार्ड	**enquiries** pūchhtāchh पूछताछ	**loan** udhār उधार
reading room adhyayan kakṣ अध्ययन कक्ष	**borrow (v)** udhār lenā उधार लेना	**book** pustak पुस्तक
reading list adhyayan sūchī अध्ययन सूची	**reserve (v)** surakṣit karnā सुरक्षित करना	**title** śīrṣak शीर्षक
return date deya tithi देय तिथि	**renew (v)** navīkṛt karvānā नवीकृत करवाना	**aisle** galiyārā गलियारा

undergraduate
snātak vidyārthī
स्नातक विद्यार्थी

lecturer
prādhyāpak
प्राध्यापक

graduate
snātak
स्नातक

robe
chogā | चोग़ा

lecture theatre
lekchar thiyeṭar | लेक्चर थियेटर

graduation ceremony
snātak samāroh | स्नातक समारोह

schools • vidyālaya • विद्यालय

model
model
मॉडल

art college | kalā
mahāvidyālaya | कला महाविद्यालय

music school
saṅgīt vidyālaya | संगीत विद्यालय

dance academy
nṛtya akādmī | नृत्य अकादमी

vocabulary • śabdāvalī • शब्दावली

scholarship chhātrvṛtti छात्रवृत्ति	**research** anusandhān अनुसंधान	**dissertation** śodh nibandh शोध निबंध	**medicine** āyurvijñān आयुर्विज्ञान	**philosophy** darśan śāstr दर्शन शास्त्र
diploma ḍiplomā डिप्लोमा	**masters** viśārad विशारद	**department** vibhāg विभाग	**zoology** prāṇī vijñān प्राणी विज्ञान	**literature** sāhitya साहित्य
degree upādhi उपाधि	**doctorate** doctorate डॉक्ट्रेट	**law** ḳānūn क़ानून	**physics** bhautikī भौतिकी	**history of art** kalā kā itihās कला का इतिहास
postgraduate snātakottar स्नातकोत्तर	**thesis** śodh prabandh शोध प्रबंध	**engineering** abhiyāntrikī अभियांत्रिकी	**politics** rājnīti राजनीति	**economics** arthśāstr अर्थशास्त्र

work
kārya

कार्य

office • kāryālaya • कार्यालय

office • kāryālaya • कार्यालय

monitor
monitor
मॉनीटर
computer
kampyūṭar
कंप्यूटर
keyboard
kī borḍ
की–बोर्ड
telephone
dūrbhāṣ
दूरभाष
desk
mez
मेज़
wastebasket
raddī kī ṭokrī
रद्दी की टोकरी
swivel chair
ghumāū kursī
घुमाऊ कुर्सी
desktop organizer
desktop organizer
डेस्कटॉप ऑर्गेनाइज़र
file
fāil
फ़ाइल
in-tray
in-ṭre
इन–ट्रे
out-tray
āuṭ-ṭre
आउट–ट्रे
notebook
copy
कॉपी
label
chiṭ
चिट
drawer
darāz
दराज़
filing cabinet
fāil-darāz
फ़ाइल–दराज़

office equipment • kāryālayī upkaraṇ • कार्यालयी उपकरण

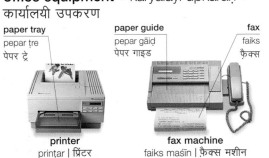

paper tray
pepar ṭre
पेपर ट्रे

printer
prinṭar | प्रिंटर

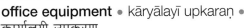

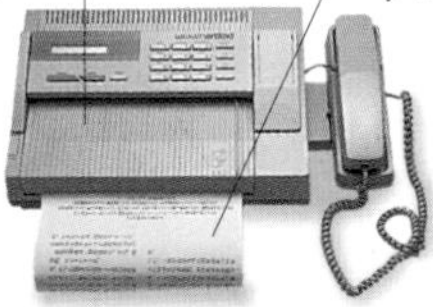
paper guide
pepar gāiḍ
पेपर गाइड
fax
faiks
फ़ैक्स

fax machine
faiks maśīn | फ़ैक्स मशीन

vocabulary • śabdāvalī • शब्दावली

print (v) prinṭ lenā प्रिंट लेना	**enlarge (v)** baṛā karnā बड़ा करना
copy (v) prati banānā प्रति बनाना	**reduce (v)** chhoṭā karnā छोटा करना

I need to make some copies
mujhe kuchh pratiyāṃ banānī haiṃ.
मुझे कुछ प्रतियां बनानी हैं।

office supplies • kāryālayī vastueṃ • कार्यालयी वस्तुएं

compliments slip
preṣak chiṭ
प्रेषक चिट

letterhead
laiṭar haiḍ
लैटर हैड

envelope
lifāfā | लिफ़ाफ़ा

box file
box fāil
बॉक्स फ़ाइल

lever arch file
ārch fāil
आर्च फ़ाइल

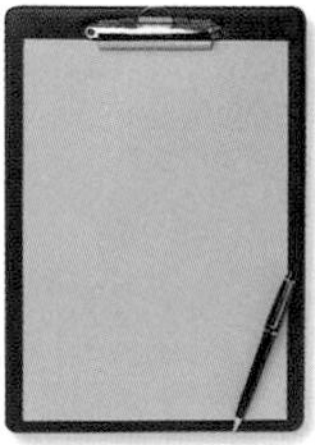

clipboard
klip borḍ
क्लिप बोर्ड

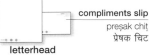

note pad
noṭ paiḍ
नोट पैड

tab
ṭaib
टैब

hanging file
haiṅgiṅg fāil
हैंगिंग फ़ाइल

divider
vibhājak
विभाजक

concertina file
concertina fāil
कॉनसर्टीना फ़ाइल

personal organizer
nijī organizer
निजी ऑर्गेनाइज़र

staples
sṭaipals
स्टैपल्स

stapler
sṭeplar
स्टेप्लर

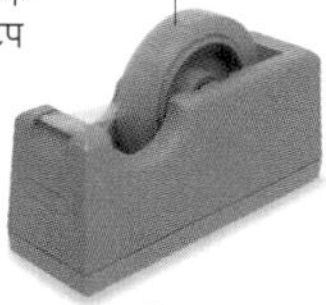

sticky tape
ṭep
टेप

tape dispenser
ṭep ḍispeṅsar
टेप डिस्पेंसर

hole punch
hol pañch
होल पंच

ink pad
syāhī paiḍ
स्याही पैड

rubber stamp
rabaṛ kī mohar
रबड़ की मोहर

rubber band
rabaṛ baiṇḍ
रबड़ बैंड

bulldog clip
baṛī klip
बड़ी क्लिप

paper clip
pepar klip
पेपर क्लिप

drawing pin
drawing pin
ड्रॉइंग पिन

notice board
sūchnāpaṭ | सूचनापट

office • kāryālaya • कार्यालय

flipchart
flip chārṭ
फ़्लिप चार्ट
minutes
kāryavṛtt
कार्यवृत्त
easel
chitrādhār
चित्राधार
report
prativedan
प्रतिवेदन
manager
prabandhak
प्रबंधक
proposal
prastāv
प्रस्ताव
executive
ekzīkyūṭiv
एक्ज़ीक्यूटिव

meeting | sabhā/mīṭiṅg | सभा/मीटिंग

vocabulary • śabdāvalī • शब्दावली

meeting room
sabhā kakṣ
सभा कक्ष

agenda
kāryasūchī
कार्यसूची

attend (v)
upasthit rahnā
उपस्थित रहना

chair (v)
adhyakṣtā karnā
अध्यक्षता करना

What time is the meeting?
mīṭiṅg kis samaya hai?
मीटिंग किस समय है?

What are your office hours?
tumhāre kāryālaya kā kyā samaya hai?
तुम्हारे कार्यालय का क्या समय है?

projector
projekṭar
प्रोजेक्टर
speaker
vaktā
वक्ता

presentation | prastutīkaraṇ | प्रस्तुतीकरण

business • vyavsāya • व्यवसाय

laptop
laptop
लैपटॉप

notes
noṭs
नोट्स

business lunch | biznes lanch | बिज़नेस लंच

businessman
vyavsāyī
व्यवसायी

businesswoman
mahilā vyavsāyī
महिला व्यवसायी

business trip | biznes ṭrip | बिज़नेस ट्रिप

appointment
milne kā samaya
मिलने का समय

palmtop
palmtop
पामटॉप

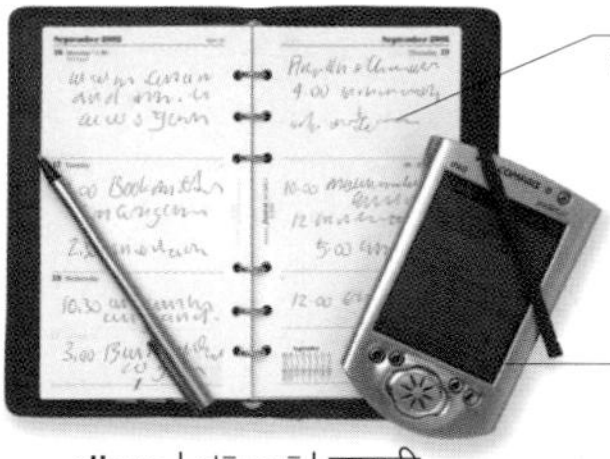

diary | ḍāyarī | डायरी

client
grāhak
ग्राहक

managing director
prabandh nideśak
प्रबंध निदेशक

business deal
vyāvsāyik saudā | व्यावसायिक सौदा

vocabulary • śabdāvalī • शब्दावली

company
kampnī
कंपनी

head office
pradhān kāryālaya
प्रधान कार्यालय

branch
śākhā
शाखा

staff
karmchārī varg
कर्मचारी वर्ग

salary
vetan
वेतन

payroll
vetanbhogī sūchī
वेतनभोगी सूची

accounts department
lekhā vibhāg
लेखा विभाग

marketing department
vipṇan vibhāg
विपणन विभाग

sales department
bikrī vibhāg
बिक्री विभाग

legal department
ḳānūnī vibhāg
क़ानूनी विभाग

customer service department
grāhak sevā vibhāg
ग्राहक सेवा विभाग

personnel department
kārmik vibhāg
कार्मिक विभाग

computer • kampyūṭar • कंप्यूटर

printer
prinṭar
प्रिंटर

monitor
monitor
मॉनीटर

screen
skrīn
स्क्रीन

central processing unit
sentral prosesiñg yūniṭ
सेंट्रल प्रोसेसिंग यूनिट

scanner
skainar
स्कैनर

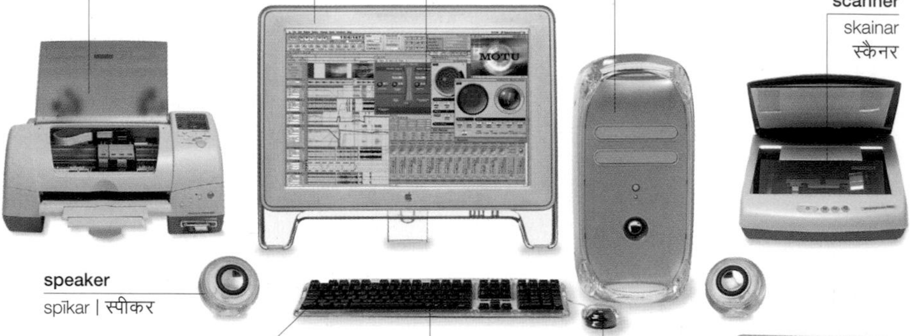

speaker
spīkar | स्पीकर

key
kī | की

KEYBOARD
kī paiḍ | की पैड

mouse
māus | माउस

hardware | hārḍveyar | हार्डवेयर

vocabulary • śabdāvalī • शब्दावली

memory memorī मेमोरी	**software** software सॉफ़्टवेयर	**server** sarvar सर्वर
RAM raim रैम	**application** eplīkeśan एप्लीकेशन	**port** porṭ पोर्ट
bytes bāiṭs बाइट्स	**program** progrām प्रोग्राम	**processor** prosesar प्रोसेसर
system sisṭam सिस्टम	**network** neṭvark नेटवर्क	**power cable** vidyut tār विद्युत तार

disk
ḍisk | डिस्क

laptop
laptop | लैपटॉप

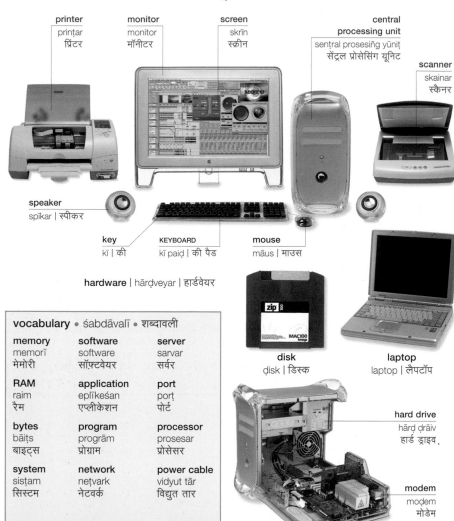

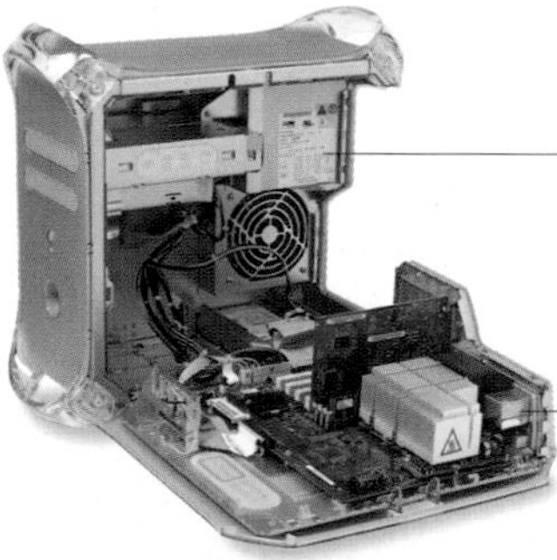

hard drive
hārḍ ḍrāiv
हार्ड ड्राइव

modem
moḍem
मोडेम

desktop • desktop • डेस्कटॉप

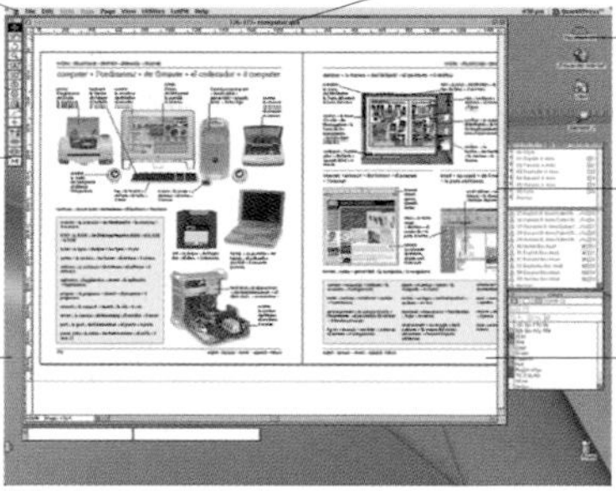

menubar
menyu bār
मेन्यु बार

toolbar
ṭūlbār
टूलबार

wallpaper
wallpaper
वॉलपेपर

font
font
फ़ॉन्ट

icon
āikan
आइकन

scrollbar
scrollbar
स्क्रॉलबार

window
vinḍo
विंडो

file | fāil | फ़ाइल

folder | folḍar | फ़ोल्डर

trash | ṭraiś | ट्रैश

internet • inṭarneṭ • इंटरनेट

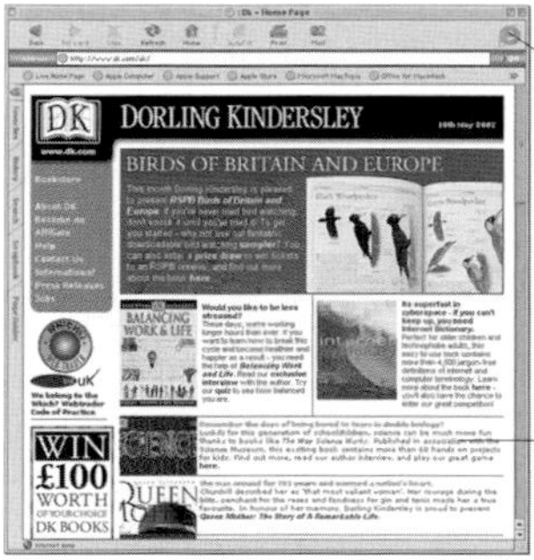

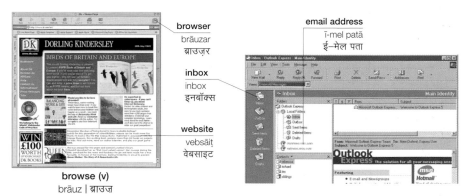

browser
brāuzar
ब्राउज़र

inbox
inbox
इनबॉक्स

website
vebsāiṭ
वेबसाइट

browse (v)
brāuz | ब्राउज़

email • ī-mel • ई–मेल

email address
ī-mel patā
ई–मेल पता

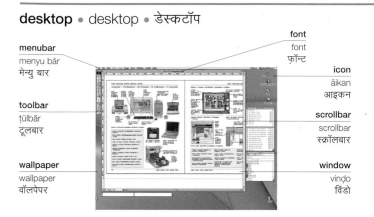

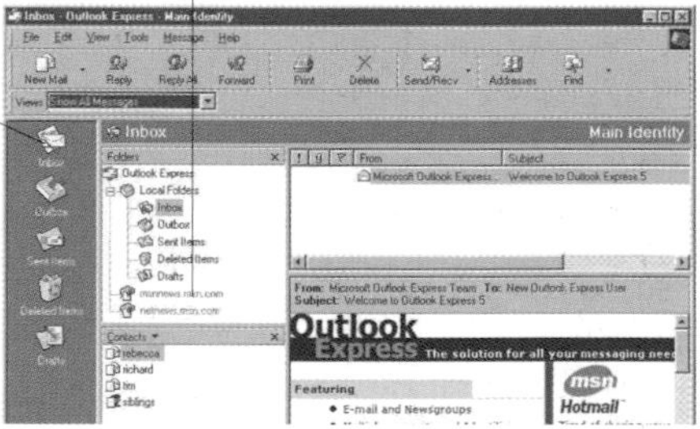

vocabulary • śabdāvalī • शब्दावली

connect (v)
sampark karnā
संपर्क करना

service provider
sevā pradātā
सेवा प्रदाता

log on (v)
log on karnā
लॉग ऑन करना

download (v)
ḍāunloḍ karnā
डाउनलोड करना

send (v)
bhejnā
भेजना

save (v)
surakṣit karnā
सुरक्षित करना

instal (v)
instal karnā
इनस्टॉल करना

email account
ī-mel akāunṭ
ई–मेल अकाउंट

on-line
on lāin
ऑन लाइन

attachment
aṭaichmenṭ
अटैचमेंट

receive (v)
prāpt karnā
प्राप्त करना

search (v)
ḍhūṃṛhnā
ढूंढ़ना

media • mīḍiyā • मीडिया

television studio • ṭelīvizan stūḍiyo • टेलीविज़न स्टूडियो

presenter
prastutkartā
प्रस्तुतकर्ता

light
lāiṭ
लाइट

set
saiṭ
सैट

camera
kaimrā
कैमरा

camera crane
kaimrā kren
कैमरा क्रेन

cameraman
kaimrāmain
कैमरामैन

vocabulary • śabdāvalī • शब्दावली

channel chainal चैनल	**news** samāchār समाचार	**press** prais प्रैस	**soap** nāṭak नाटक	**cartoon** kārṭūn कार्टून	**live** sīdhā prasāraṇ सीधा प्रसारण
programming progrāmiṅg प्रोग्रामिंग	**documentary** vṛttchitr वृत्तचित्र	**television series** ṭelīvizan sṛṅkhlā टेलीविज़न श्रृंखला	**game show** gem śo गेम शो	**prerecorded** pūrv recorded पूर्व रिकॉर्डेड	**broadcast (v)** prasārit karnā प्रसारित करना

interviewer
sākṣātkārkartā
साक्षात्कारकर्ता

reporter
patrakār | पत्रकार

autocue
teli promter | टेली प्रॉम्पटर

newsreader | samāchār vāchak | समाचार वाचक

actors
abhinetā | अभिनेता

sound boom
sāuṇḍ būm | साउंड बूम

clapper board | klaipar borḍ | क्लैपर बोर्ड

film set
film saiṭ | फ़िल्म सैट

radio • reḍiyo • रेडियो

mixing desk
miksiṅg ḍesk
मिक्सिंग डेस्क

microphone
māikrofon
माइक्रोफ़ोन

sound technician
sāuṇḍ taknīśiyan
साउंड तकनीशियन

recording studio | recording sṭūḍiyo | रिकॉर्डिंग स्टूडियो

vocabulary • śabdāvalī • शब्दावली

radio station
reḍiyo sṭeśan
रेडियो स्टेशन

frequency
āvṛtti
आवृत्ति

broadcast
prasāraṇ
प्रसारण

volume
dhvani star
ध्वनि स्तर

wavelength
vevlenth
वेवलैंथ

DJ
ḍīje
डीजे

long wave
long vev
लॉन्ग वेव

short wave
short vev
शॉर्ट वेव

tune (v)
chainal lagānā
चैनल लगाना

medium wave
mīḍiyam vev
मीडियम वेव

law • ḳānūn • क़ानून

court officer
nyāyālaya adhikārī
न्यायालय अधिकारी

witness
gavāh
गवाह

judge
jaj | जज

lawyer
vakīl
वकील

jury
jūrī
जूरी

jury box
jūrī box
जूरी बॉक्स

courtroom
nyāyālaya | न्यायालय

prosecution
abhiyojan
अभियोजन

court official
nyāyālaya karmchārī
न्यायालय कर्मचारी

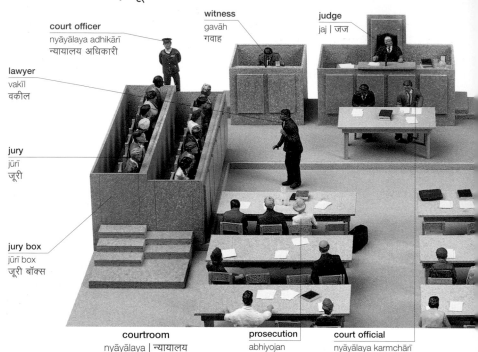

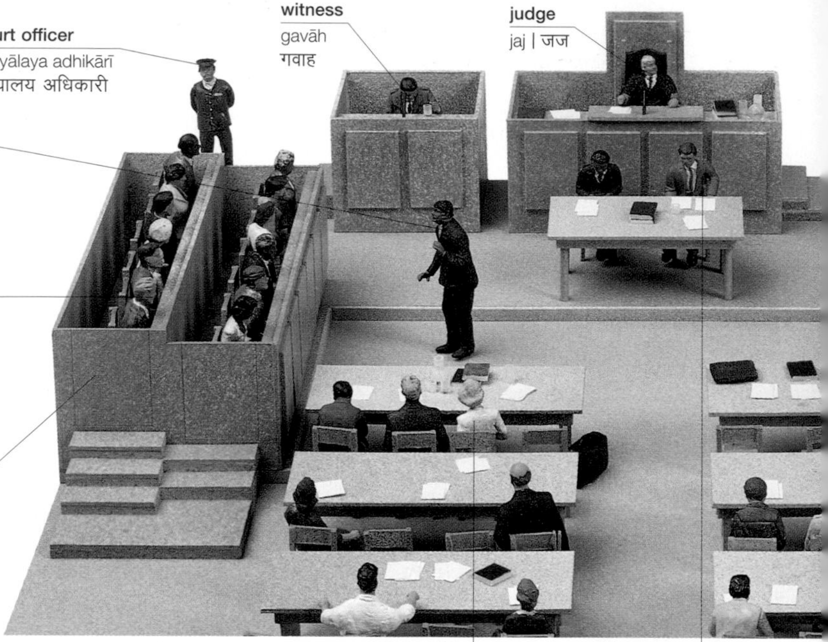

vocabulary • śabdāvalī • शब्दावली

lawyer's office vakīl kā kāryālaya वकील का कार्यालय	**summons** saman समन	**writ** riṭ रिट	**court case** muḳaddmā मुक़द्दमा
legal advice ḳānūnī salāh क़ानूनी सलाह	**statement** bayān बयान	**court date** nyāyālaya kī tārīḳh न्यायालय की तारीख़	**charge** abhiyog अभियोग
client muvakkil मुवक्किल	**warrant** vāraṇṭ वारंट	**plea** pairavī पैरवी	**accused** abhiyukt अभियुक्त

defendant
prativādī
प्रतिवादी

stenographer
āśulipik
आशुलिपिक

defence
bachāv pakṣ
बचाव पक्ष

suspect
sandigdh
संदिग्ध

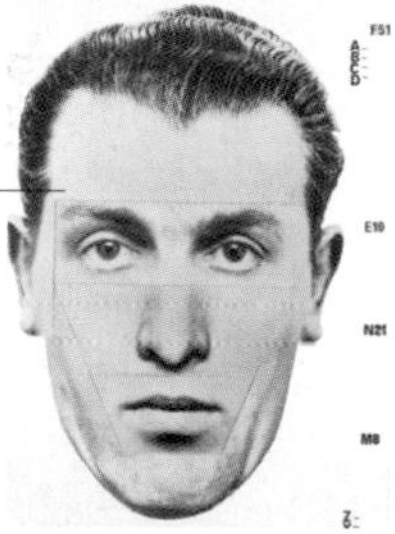

photofit
anumānit tasvīr
अनुमानित तस्वीर

criminal
aprādhī
अपराधी

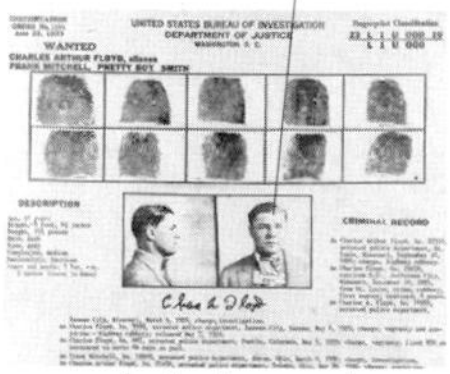

criminal record
āprādhik record
आपराधिक रिकॉर्ड

prison guard | jel kā pahredār | जेल का पहरेदार

cell | jel kī koṭhrī | जेल की कोठरी

prison
jel | जेल

vocabulary • śabdāvalī • शब्दावली

evidence
sabūt
सबूत

verdict
faislā
फ़ैसला

innocent
beḳasūr
बेक़सूर

guilty
doṣī
दोषी

acquitted
abhimukt
अभिमुक्त

sentence
daṇḍādeś
दंडादेश

bail
zamānat
ज़मानत

appeal
apīl
अपील

parole
pairol
पैरोल

I want to see a lawyer.
mujhe ek vakīl chāhie.
मुझे एक वकील चाहिए

Where is the courthouse?
nyāyālaya kahāṃ hai?
न्यायालय कहां है?

Can I post bail?
kyā maiṃ zamānat bhar saktā hūṃ?
क्या मैं ज़मानत भर सकता हूं?

farm • khet • खेत

farmer
kisān
किसान

farmland
kṛṣi bhūmi
कृषि भूमि

farmyard
ahātā
अहाता

outbuilding
āuṭ hāus
आउट हाउस

farmhouse
fārm hāus
फ़ार्म हाउस

field
khet
खेत

barn
khalihān
खलिहान

vegetable plot
śāk khet
शाक खेत

gate
darvāzā
दरवाज़ा

hedge
meṛ
मेड़

fence
bāṛ
बाड़

pasture
charāgāh
चरागाह

livestock
paśudhan
पशुधन

cultivator
phāl
फाल

tractor | ṭrekṭar | ट्रेक्टर

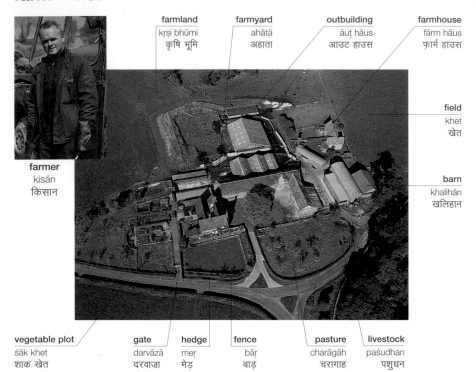

combine harvester | kaṭāī maśīn | कटाई मशीन

types of farm • khetoṃ ke prakār • खेतों के प्रकार

crop
fasal
फ़सल

arable farm
khetī yogya bhūmi
खेती योग्य भूमि

dairy farm
ḍerī fārm
डेरी फ़ार्म

flock
jhuṇḍ
झुंड

sheep farm
bheṛoṃ kā bāṛā
भेड़ों का बाड़ा

poultry farm | murgī pālan kendr | मुर्ग़ी पालन केंद्र

pig farm
śūkar pālan kendr
शूकरपालन केंद्र

fish farm
machhlī pālan kṣetr
मछली पालन क्षेत्र

fruit farm
phaloṃ kā bāg̣
फलों का बाग़

vineyard
aṃgūr kā bāg̣
अंगूर का बाग़

actions • khetoṃ ke kāmkāj • खेतों के कामकाज

furrow
hal rekhā
हल रेखा

plough (v)
jotnā | जोतना

sow (v)
bonā | बोना

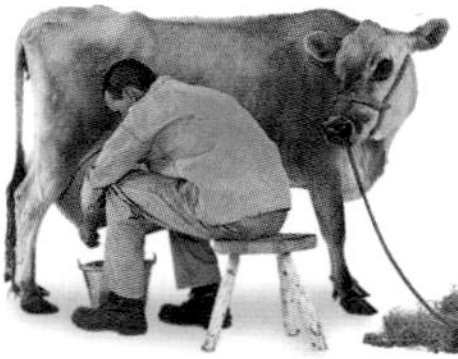

milk (v)
dūdh duhnā | दूध दुहना

feed (v)
charnā | चरना

water (v)
sīṃchnā | सींचना

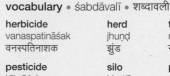

harvest (v)
fasal kāṭnā | फ़सल काटना

vocabulary • śabdāvalī • शब्दावली

herbicide vanaspatināśak वनस्पतिनाशक	**herd** jhuṇḍ झुंड	**trough** nāṃd नांद
pesticide kīṭnāśak कीटनाशक	**silo** khattī खत्ती	**plant (v)** ropnā रोपना

farm • khet • खेत

crops • fasal • फ़सल

wheat
gehūṃ | गेहूं

corn
makaī | मकई

barley
jau | जौ

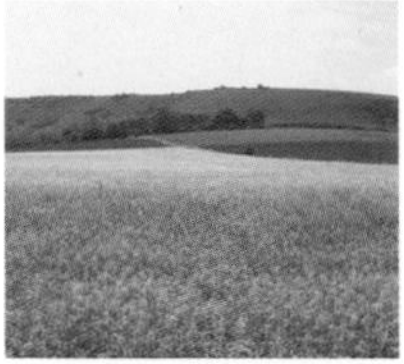

rapeseed | safed sarsoṃ | सफ़ेद सरसों

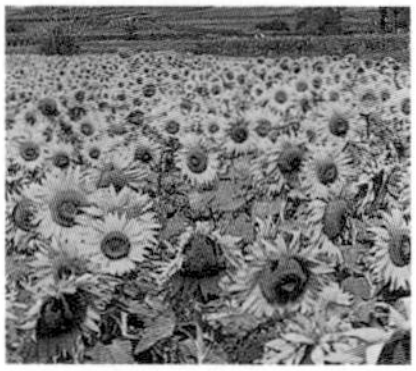

sunflower
sūrajmukhī | सूरजमुखी

hay
sūkhī ghās | सूखी घास

alfalfa
alfālfā | अल्फ़ाल्फ़ा

tobacco
tambāḳū | तंबाक़ू

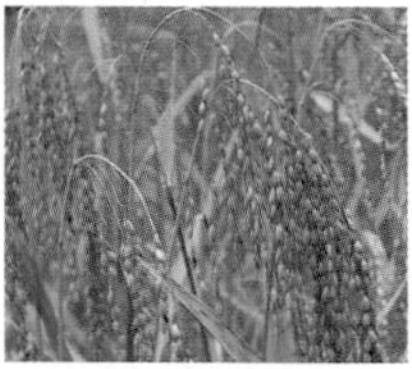

rice
dhān | धान

tea
chāya | चाय

coffee
coffee | कॉफ़ी

flax
alsī
अलसी

sugarcane
gannā
गन्ना

cotton
kapās
कपास

scarecrow
bijūkā
बिजूका

livestock • paśudhan • पशुधन

piglet
śiśu sūar
शिशु सूअर

pig
sūar | सूअर

calf
bachhṛā
बछड़ा

cow
gāya | गाय

bull
bail | बैल

sheep
bheṛ | भेड़

lamb
meṛhā | मेढ़ा

kid
memnā | मेमना

goat
bakrī | बकरी

foal
śiśu aśv
शिशु अश्व

horse
ghoṛā | घोड़ा

donkey
gadhā | गधा

chick
chūzā | चूज़ा

chicken
murgī | मुर्गी

cockerel
murgā | मुर्गा

turkey
ṭarkī | टर्की

duckling
śiśu batakh
शिशु बतख़

duck
batakh | बतख़

stable
astabal | अस्तबल

pen
bāṛā | बाड़ा

chicken coop
daṛbā | दड़बा

pigsty
sūarbāṛā | सूअरबाड़ा

construction • nirmāṇ kārya • निर्माण कार्य

scaffolding
pāṛ | पाड़

pallet
taḳhte
तख़्ते

ladder
sīṛhī
सीढ़ी

window
khiṛkī
खिड़की

rafter
kaṛī/śahtīr
कड़ी/शहतीर

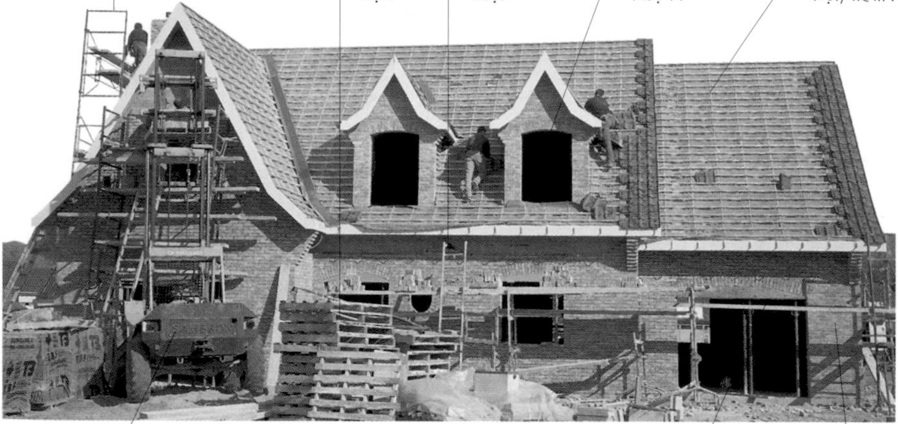

fork-lift truck
kren
क्रेन

building site
nirmāṇ sthal
निर्माण स्थल

lintel
chaukhaṭ
चौखट

wall
dīvār
दीवार

girder
gardar
गर्डर

hard hat
ṭop
टोप

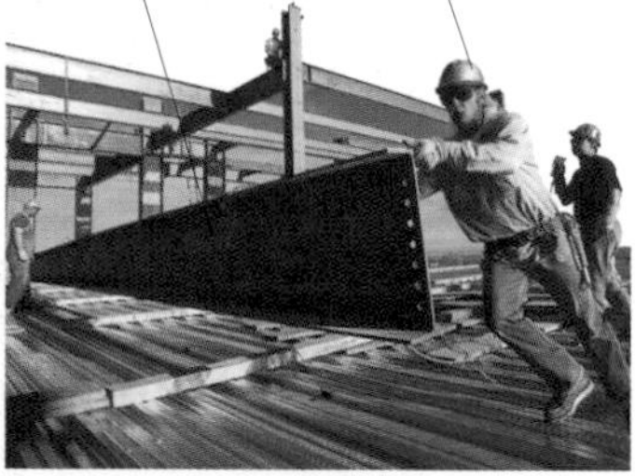

build (v)
nirmāṇ karnā | निर्माण करना

toolbelt
auzār peṭī
औज़ार पेटी

beam
śahtīr
शहतीर

builder
rājgīr | राजगीर

cement
sīmeṇṭ
सीमेंट

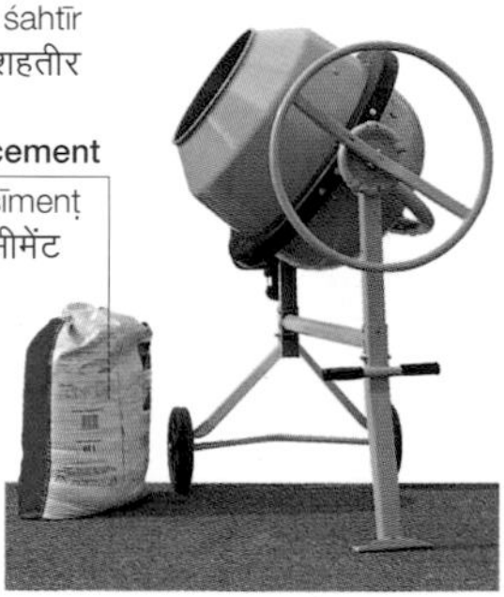

cement mixer | sīmeṇṭ miksar | सीमेंट मिक्सर

materials • sāmān • सामान

brick
īmṭ | ईंट

timber
imāratī lakṛī | इमारती लकड़ी

roof tile
paṭiyā | पटिया

concrete block
concrete block | कॉन्क्रीट ब्लॉक

tools • auzār • औज़ार

mortar
gārā | गारा

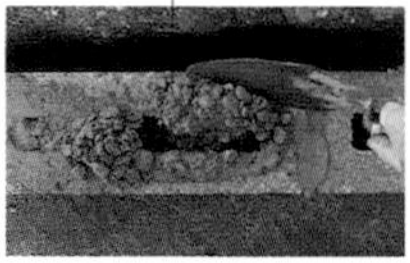

trowel
kannī | कन्नी

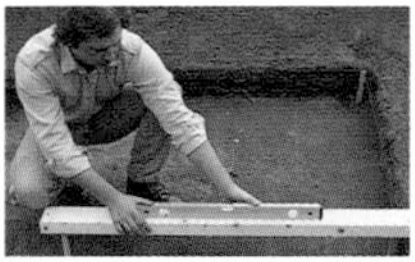

spirit level
talmāpī | तलमापी

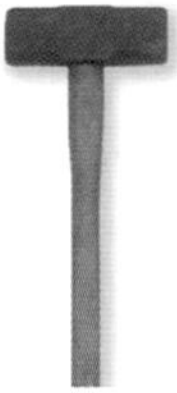

sledgehammer
hathauṛā | हथौड़ा

handle
hatthā
हत्था

pickaxe
kudāl | कुदाल

shovel
belchā | बेलचा

machinery • maśīnarī • मशीनरी

roller
rolar | रोलर

dumper truck
ḍampar | डम्पर

support
ādhār stambh
आधार स्तंभ

hook
huk
हुक

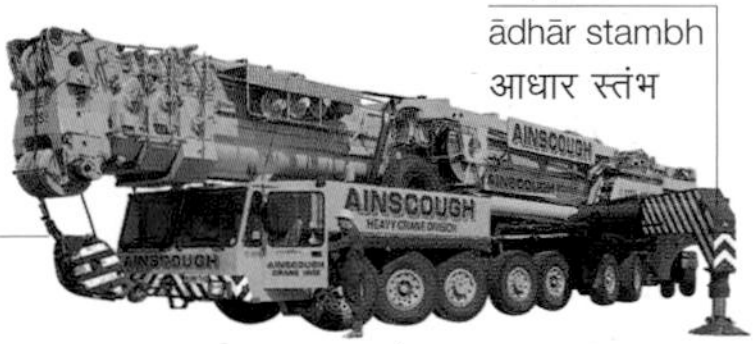

crane | kren | क्रेन

roadworks • saṛak nirmāṇ kārya • सड़क निर्माण कार्य

tarmac
tārkol
तारकोल

cone
kon
कोन

pneumatic drill
nyūmaiṭik ḍril
न्यूमैटिक ड्रिल

resurfacing
punaḥ parat lagānā
पुनः परत लगाना

occupations 1 • vyavasāya 1 • व्यवसाय

carpenter
baṛhaī | बढ़ई

electrician | bijlī mistrī | बिजली मिस्त्री

plumber
nalkār | नलकार

builder
rājgīr | राजगीर

gardener
mālī | माली

vacuum cleaner
vekyūm klīnar
वेक्यूम क्लीनर

cleaner
safaī karmī | सफ़ाई कर्मी

mechanic
mistrī | मिस्त्री

butcher
ḳasāī | क़साई

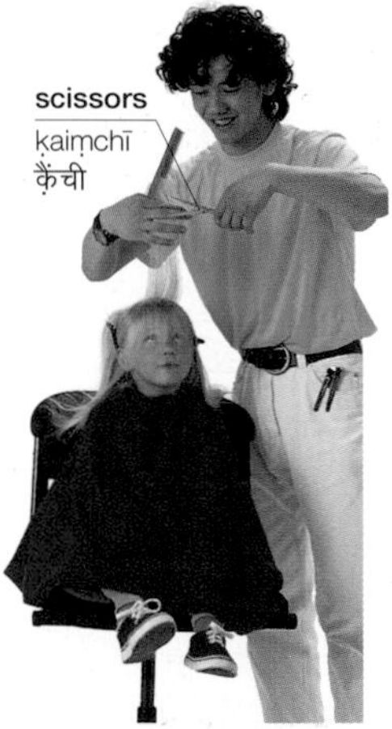
scissors
ḳaiṃchī
कैंची

fishmonger
machhlī vikretā
मछली विक्रेता

greengrocer
sabzī vikretā
सब्ज़ी विक्रेता

florist
phool vikretā
फूल विक्रेता

hairdresser | keś prasādhak | केश प्रसाधक

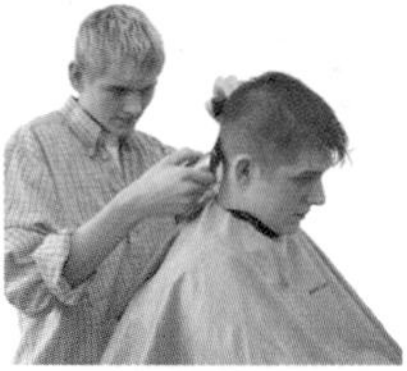

barber
nāī | नाई

jeweller
sunār | सुनार

shop assistant | dukān sahāyak | दुकान सहायक

estate agent | bhūsampatti dalāl | भूसंपत्ति दलाल

optician | dṛṣṭi parīkṣak | दृष्टि परीक्षक

mask
nakạ̄b
नक़ाब

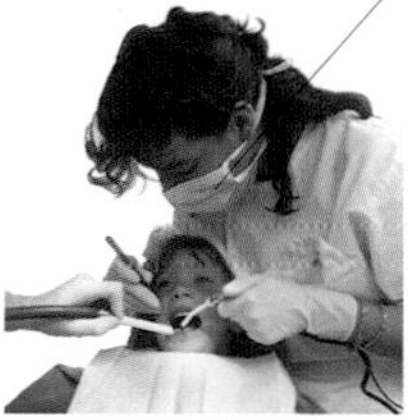

dentist | dant chikitsak | दंत चिकित्सक

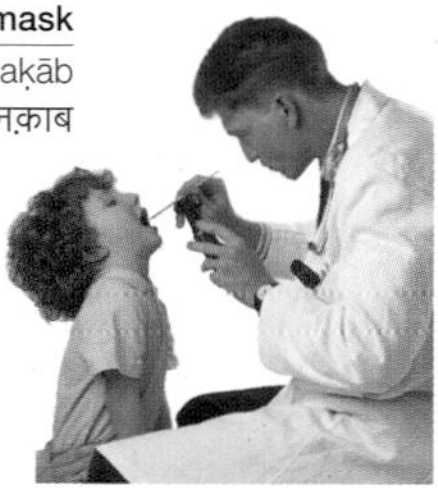

doctor
chikitsak | चिकित्सक

pharmacist
auṣadhkārak | औषधकारक

nurse
nars | नर्स

vet | paśu chikitsak | पशु चिकित्सक

farmer
kisān | किसान

fisherman
machhuārā | मछुआरा

machine-gun
maśīngan
मशीनगन

soldier
sainik | सैनिक

identity badge
pahchān paṭṭikā
पहचान–पट्टिका

uniform
vardī
वर्दी

policeman | pulis karmī | पुलिस कर्मी

security guard | surakṣā karmī | सुरक्षा कर्मी

sailor
nāvik | नाविक

fireman
fāyarmain | फ़ायरमैन

occupations 2 • vyavasāya 2 • व्यवसाय

lawyer
vakīl | वकील

accountant
lekhākār | लेखाकार

model
namūnā
नमूना

architect
vāstukār | वास्तुकार

scientist
vaijñānik | वैज्ञानिक

teacher
adhyāpak | अध्यापक

librarian
pustakālaya adhyakṣ
पुस्तकालय अध्यक्ष

receptionist
svāgatkartā | स्वागतकर्ता

mailbag
ḍāk thailā
डाक–थैला

postman
ḍākiyā | डाकिया

bus driver
bas chālak | बस चालक

lorry driver
ṭrak chālak | ट्रक चालक

taxi driver | ṭaiksī chālak | टैक्सी चालक

pilot | vimān chālak | विमान चालक

air stewardess | vimān parichārikā | विमान परिचारिका

travel agent | ṭreval ejenṭ | ट्रेवल एजेंट

chef's hat
rasoie kī ṭopī
रसोइए की टोपी

chef
rasoiyā | रसोइया

musician
saṅgītkār | संगीतकार

tutu
baile skarṭ
बैले स्कर्ट

dancer
nartakī | नर्तकी

actor
abhinetā | अभिनेता

singer
gāyikā | गायिका

waitress
parichārikā | परिचारिका

barman
bārmain | बारमैन

sportsman
khilāṛī | खिलाड़ी

sculptor
mūrtikār | मूर्तिकार

painter
chitrakār | चित्रकार

photographer
chhāyākār | छायाकार

newsreader | samāchār vāchak | समाचार वाचक

notes
noṭs
नोट्स

journalist
patrakār | पत्रकार

editor
sampādak | संपादक

designer
ḍizāinar | डिज़ाइनर

seamstress
darzin | दर्ज़िन

tailor
darzī | दर्ज़ी

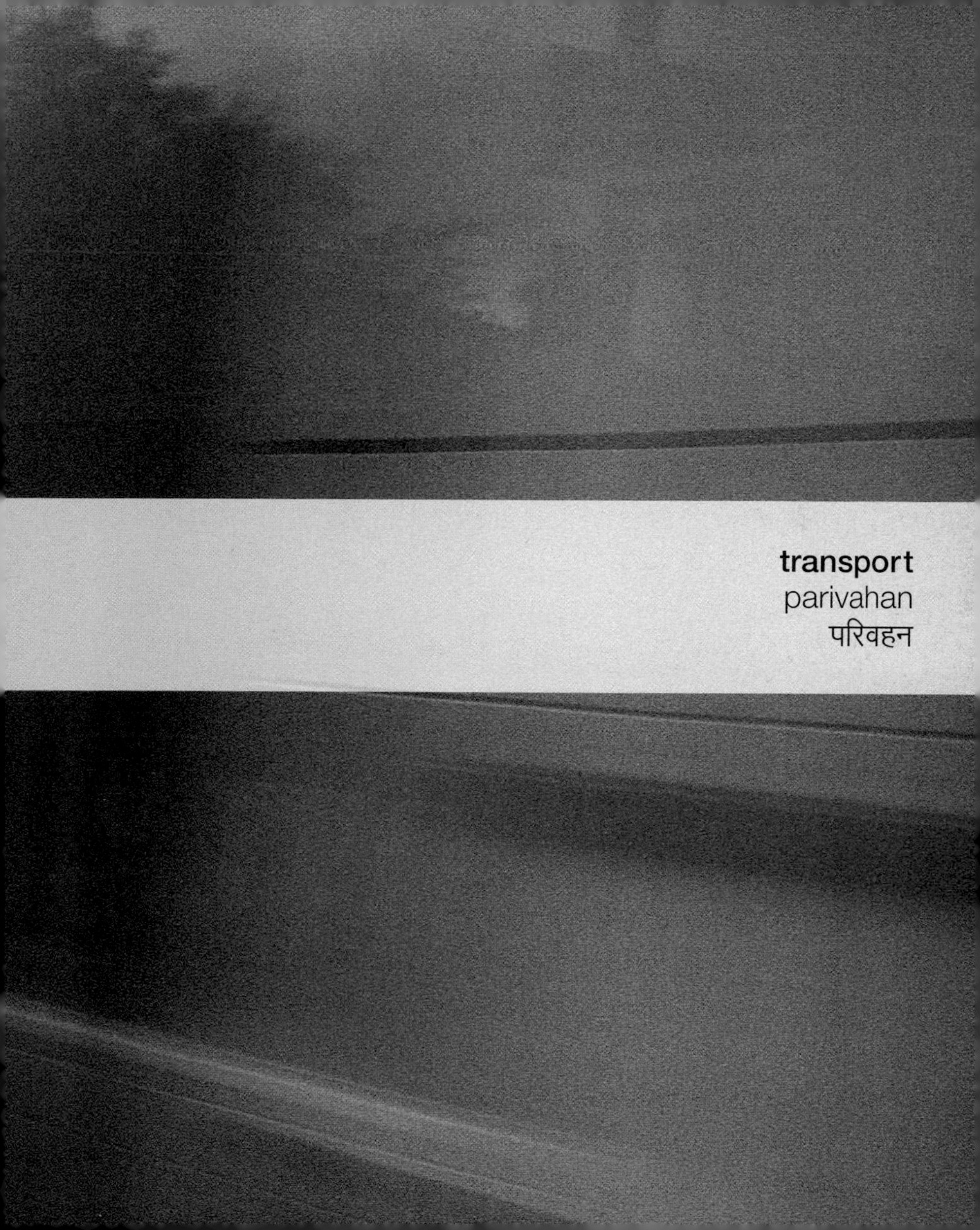

transport
parivahan

परिवहन

roads • saṛkeṃ • सड़कें

motorway
moṭar mārg
मोटर मार्ग

toll booth
ṭol būth
टोल बूथ

road markings
mārg chihn
मार्ग चिह्न

slip road
sāiḍ kī saṛak
साइड की सड़क

one-way
iktarfā rāstā
इकतरफ़ा रास्ता

divider
vibhājak
विभाजक

junction
jaṇkśan
जंक्शन

traffic light
yātāyāt battī
यातायात बत्ती

inside lane
bhītrī len
भीतरी लेन

middle lane
madhya len
मध्य लेन

outside lane
bāhrī len
बाहरी लेन

exit ramp
nikās ḍhalān
निकास ढलान

traffic
yātāyāt
यातायात

flyover
flāī ovar
फ़्लाईओवर

hard shoulder
saṛak kā kinārā
सड़क का किनारा

lorry
ṭrak
ट्रक

central reservation
kendrīya ārakṣaṇ
केंद्रीय आरक्षण

underpass
bhūmigat mārg
भूमिगत मार्ग

pedestrian crossing
paidal pārpath
पैदल पारपथ

emergency phone
āpātkālīn dūrbhāṣ
आपातकालीन दूरभाष

disabled parking
vikläṅg
pārkiṅg sthal
विकलांग
पार्किंग स्थल

traffic jam
yātāyāt jām | यातायात जाम

map
mānchitr
मानचित्र

parking meter
pārkiṅg mīṭar
पार्किंग मीटर

traffic policeman
yātāyāt puliskarmī
यातायात पुलिसकर्मी

vocabulary • śabdāvalī • शब्दावली

roundabout
gol chakkar
गोल चक्कर

tow away (v)
ṭo karnā
टो करना

diversion
parivartit mārg
परिवर्तित मार्ग

crash barrier
ṭakkar avrodh
टक्कर अवरोध

park (v)
pārk karnā
पार्क करना

overtake (v)
āge nikālnā
आगे निकालना

drive (v)
gāṛī chalānā
गाड़ी चलाना

reverse (v)
pīchhe karnā
पीछे करना

roadworks
saṛak nirmāṇ kārya
सड़क निर्माण कार्य

Is this the road to...?
kyā... jāne kā yahī mārg hai?
क्या... जाने का यही मार्ग है?

dual carriageway
dvaya vāhan mārg
द्वय वाहन मार्ग

Where can I park?
maiṃ kahāṃ pārk kar saktā hūṃ?
मैं कहां पार्क कर सकता हूं?

road signs • yātāyāt saṅket • यातायात संकेत

no entry
praveś niṣedh
प्रवेश निषेध

speed limit
gati sīmā
गति सीमा

hazard
sāvdhān
सावधान

no stopping
ruknā manā hai
रुकना मना है

no right turn
dāeṃ muṛnā niṣedh
दाएं मुड़ना निषेध

bus • bas • बस

driver's seat
chālak sīṭ
चालक सीट

handrail
haiṇḍrel
हैंडरेल

automatic door
svachālit darvāzā
स्वचालित दरवाज़ा

front wheel
āge kā pahiyā
आगे का पहिया

luggage hold
sāmān kakṣ
सामान कक्ष

door | darvāzā | दरवाज़ा

coach | bas | बस

types of buses • basoṃ ke prakār • बसों के प्रकार

route number
rūṭ nambar
रूट नंबर

driver
chālak
चालक

double-decker bus
ḍabal-ḍekar bas
डबल–डेकर बस

tram
ṭrām | ट्राम

trolley bus
trolley bas | ट्रॉली बस

school bus | skūl bas | स्कूल बस

rear wheel
pichhlā pahiyā
पिछला पहिया

window
khiṛkī
खिड़की

bus ticket
bas ṭikaṭ | बस टिकट

stop button
stop baṭan
स्टॉप बटन

bell
ghanṭī | घंटी

bus station
bas aḍḍā | बस अड्डा

bus stop
bas stop
बस स्टॉप

vocabulary • śabdāvalī • शब्दावली

timetable
samaya sūchī
समय सूची

fare
kirāyā
किराया

wheelchair access
vhīlcheyar suvidhā
व्हीलचेयर सुविधा

bus shelter
bas khaṛī karne kī jagah
बस खड़ी करने की जगह

Do you stop at...?
kyā āp ... par rokeṅge?
क्या आप ... पर रोकेंगे?

Which bus goes to...?
... ke lie kaun sī bas jātī hai?
... के लिए कौन सी बस जाती है?

minibus
minī bas | मिनी बस

tourist bus | paryaṭak bas | पर्यटक बस

shuttle bus | śaṭal bas | शटल बस

car 1 • kār • कार

exterior • bāhrī svarūp • बाहरी स्वरूप

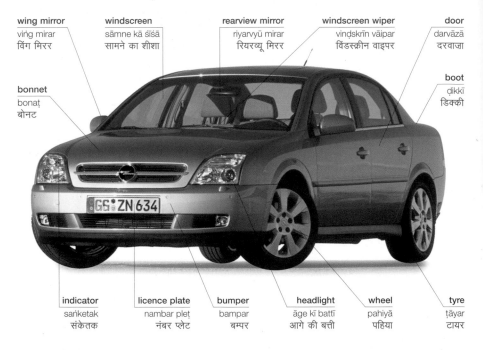

wing mirror
viṅg mirar
विंग मिरर
windscreen
sāmne kā śīśā
सामने का शीशा
rearview mirror
riyarvyū mirar
रियरव्यू मिरर
windscreen wiper
vinḍskrīn vāipar
विंडस्क्रीन वाइपर
door
darvāzā
दरवाज़ा
bonnet
bonaṭ
बोनट
boot
ḍikkī
डिक्की
indicator
saṅketak
संकेतक
licence plate
nambar pleṭ
नंबर प्लेट
bumper
bampar
बम्पर
headlight
āge kī battī
आगे की बत्ती
wheel
pahiyā
पहिया
tyre
ṭāyar
टायर

luggage
sāmān
सामान

roofrack
kairiyar | कैरियर

tailgate | ḍikkī kā darvāzā | डिक्की का दरवाज़ा

seat belt
sīṭ belṭ | सीट बेल्ट

child seat
bālak-sīṭ | बालक–सीट

types • prakār • प्रकार

small car
chhoṭī kār | छोटी कार

hatchback
haichbaik | हैचबैक

saloon
salūn | सलून

estate
vaigan | वैगन

convertible
kanvarṭībal
कन्वर्टीबल

sports car
sporṭs kār
स्पोर्ट्स कार

people carrier
pīpul kairiyar
पीपुल कैरियर

four-wheel drive
for-vhīl ḍrāiv
फ़ोर–व्हील ड्राइव

vintage
vinṭej kār | विंटेज कार

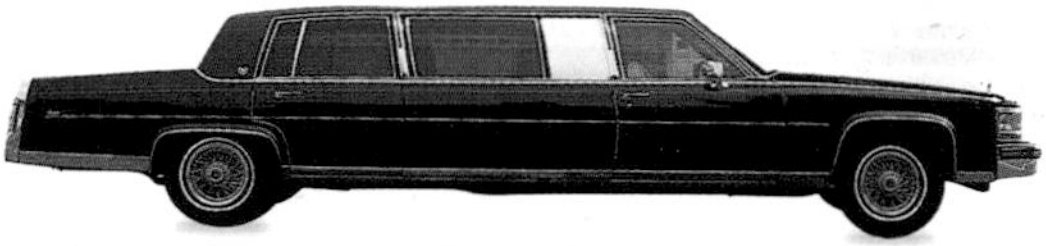

limousine
limozīn | लिमोज़ीन

petrol station • peṭrol sṭeśan • पेट्रोल स्टेशन

petrol pump
peṭrol pamp
पेट्रोल पंप

price
mūlya
मूल्य

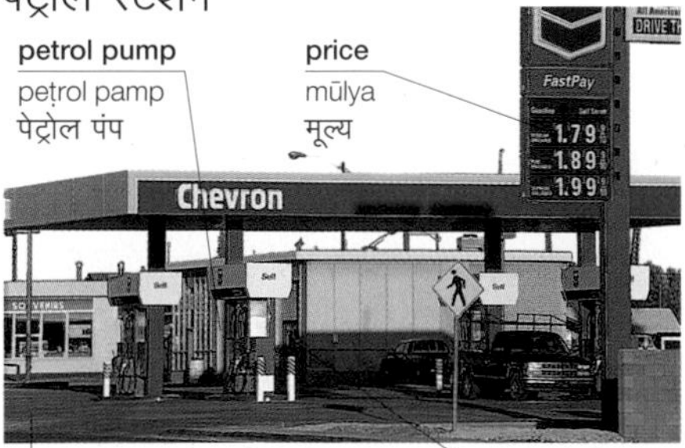

forecourt
dālān
दालान

air supply
havā saplāī
हवा सप्लाई

vocabulary • śabdāvalī • शब्दावली

oil tel तेल	**leaded** sīsā yukt सीसा युक्त	**car wash** kār dhulāī कार धुलाई
petrol peṭrol पेट्रोल	**diesel** ḍīzal डीज़ल	**antifreeze** enṭī frīz एंटी फ़्रीज़
unleaded sīsā rahit सीसा रहित	**garage** gairej गैरेज	**screenwash** screenwash स्क्रीनवॉश

Fill the tank, please.
kṛpyā pūrī ṭaṅkī bhar deṃ
कृपया पूरी टंकी भर दें।

car 2 • kār 2 • कार

interior • inṭīriyar • इंटीरियर

back seat
pichhlī sīṭ | पिछली सीट

headrest
sirhānā | सिरहाना

door lock
darvāze kā lock
दरवाज़े का लॉक

armrest
ārmresṭ
आर्मरेस्ट

handle
haiṇḍil
हैंडिल

vocabulary • śabdāvalī • शब्दावली

two-door
do-darvāzā
दो–दरवाज़ा

four-door
chār-darvāzā
चार–दरवाज़ा

automatic
svachālit
स्वचालित

brake
brek
ब्रेक

accelerator
aiksīlreṭar
ऐक्सीलरेटर

three-door
tīn-darvāzā
तीन–दरवाजा

manual
mānav-chālit
मानव–चालित

ignition
ignīśan
इग्नीशन

clutch
klach
क्लच

air conditioning
vātānukūlan
वातानुकूलन

Can you tell me the way to...?
kyā āp mujhe... jāne kā rāstā batāeṅge?
क्या आप मुझे... जाने का रास्ता बताएंगे?

Where is the car park?
kār pārkiṅg kahāṃ hai?
कार पार्किंग कहां है?

Can I park here?
kyā maiṃ yahāṃ gāṛī khaṛī kar saktā hūṃ?
क्या मैं यहां गाड़ी खड़ी कर सकता हूं?

controls • niyantraṇ • नियंत्रण

steering wheel
sṭīyariṅg
स्टीयरिंग

horn
horn
हॉर्न

dashboard
ḍaiśborḍ
डैशबोर्ड

hazard lights
saṅkaṭ sūchak battī
संकट सूचक बत्ती

satellite navigation
upgrah mārgdarśan
उपग्रह मार्गदर्शन

left-hand drive | bāīṃ or kī ḍrāiv | बाईं ओर की ड्राइव

temperature gauge
tāpmān māpak
तापमान मापक

rev counter
parikramaṇ gaṇak
परिक्रमण गणक

speedometer
spīḍ mīṭar
स्पीड मीटर

fuel gauge
īndhan māpī
ईंधन मापी

car stereo
sṭīriyo
स्टीरियो

heater controls
hīṭar kanṭrol
हीटर कंट्रोल

gearstick
gīyar
गीयर

lights switch
lāiṭ baṭan
लाइट बटन

odometer
pathmāpak yantr
पथमापक यंत्र

air bag
eyar baig
एयर बैग

right-hand drive | dāīṃ or kī ḍrāiv | दाईं ओर की ड्राइव

car 3 • kār 3 • कार

mechanics • yāntrikī • यांत्रिकी

screen wash reservoir
screen wash ḍibbā
स्क्रीन वॉश डिब्बा

dipstick
ḍipasṭik
डिपस्टिक

air filter
vāyu chhalnī
वायु छलनी

brake fluid reservoir
brek dravya ḍibbā
ब्रेक द्रव्य डिब्बा

battery
baiṭrī
बैटरी

bodywork
bodywork
बॉडीवर्क

coolant reservoir
kūlenṭ ḍibbā
कूलेंट डिब्बा

cylinder head
silenḍar
सिलेंडर

pipe
pāip
पाइप

sunroof
kār kī chhat
कार की छत

radiator
reḍieṭar
रेडिएटर

fan
paṅkhā
पंखा

engine
injan
इंजन

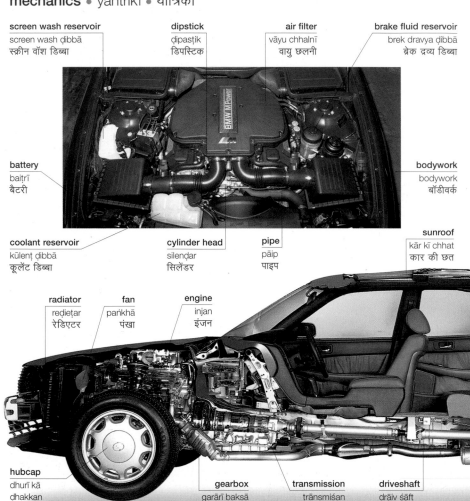

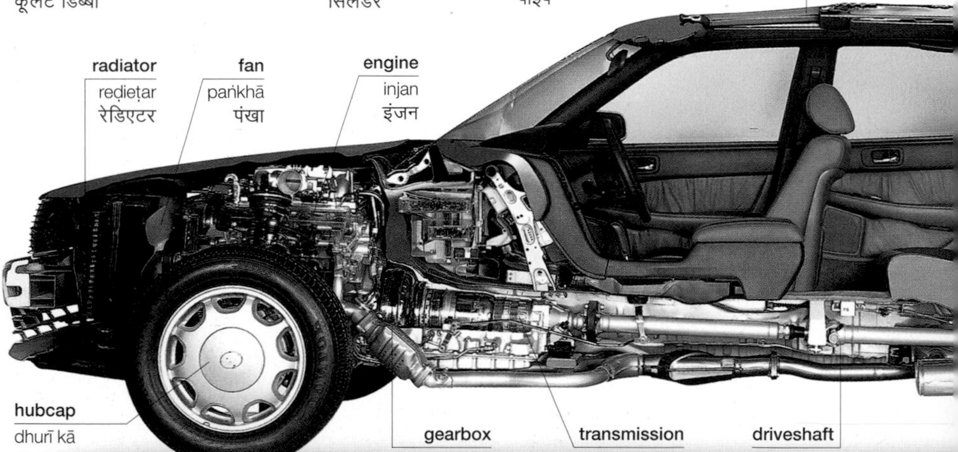

hubcap
dhurī kā ḍhakkan
धुरी का ढक्कन

gearbox
garārī baksā
गरारी बक्सा

transmission
ṭrānsmiśan
ट्रांसमिशन

driveshaft
ḍrāiv śāfṭ
ड्राइव शाफ़्ट

puncture • paṅkchar • पंक्चर

spare tyre
atirikt ṭāyar
अतिरिक्त टायर

wrench
pānā
पाना

wheel nuts
ṭāyar ke pech
टायर के पेच

jack
jaik
जैक

change a wheel (v)
ṭāyar badalnā | टायर बदलना

roof
chhat
छत

suspension
ālamban chhaṛ
आलंबन छड़

silencer
dhvanirodhak
ध्वनिरोधक

exhaust pipe
dhuām̐ nikās nalī
धुआं निकास नली

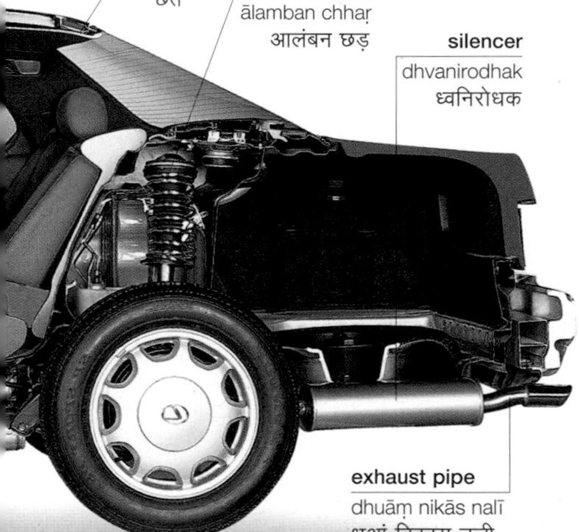

vocabulary • śabdāvalī • शब्दावली

car accident kār durghaṭnā कार दुर्घटना	**turbocharger** ṭarbo chārjar टर्बो चार्जर
breakdown brek ḍāun ब्रेक डाउन	**distributor** vitrak वितरक
insurance bīmā बीमा	**chassis** chesis चेसिस
tow truck ṭo ṭrak टो ट्रक	**handbrake** haiṇḍ brek हैंड ब्रेक
mechanic maikenik मैकेनिक	**alternator** pratyāvartak प्रत्यावर्तक
tyre pressure ṭāyar preśar टायर प्रेशर	**cam belt** kem belṭ केम बेल्ट
fuse box fyūz baksā फ़्यूज़ बक्सा	**timing** ṭāimiṅg टाइमिंग
spark plug spārk plag स्पार्क प्लग	**petrol tank** peṭrol ṭaṅkī पेट्रोल टंकी
fan belt fain belṭ फ़ैन बेल्ट	

My car won't start.
merī kār sṭārṭ nahīṁ
ho rahī.
मेरी कार स्टार्ट नहीं हो रही।

My car has broken down.
merī gāṛī kharāb ho
gaī hai.
मेरी गाड़ी ख़राब हो गई है।

motorbike • moṭarbāik • मोटरबाइक

indicator
saṅketak
संकेतक
speedometer
gatimāpak
गतिमापक
brake
brek
ब्रेक
clutch
klach
क्लच
horn
horn
हॉर्न
throttle
gati niyantrak
गति नियंत्रक

controls
niyantraṇ yantr | नियंत्रण यंत्र

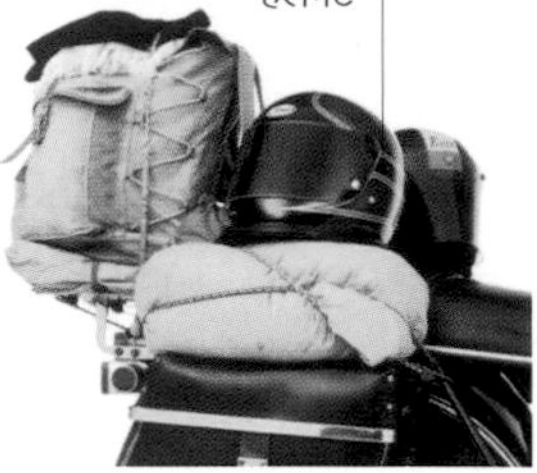
helmet
hailmeṭ
हैलमेट

carrier
samvāhak
संवाहक

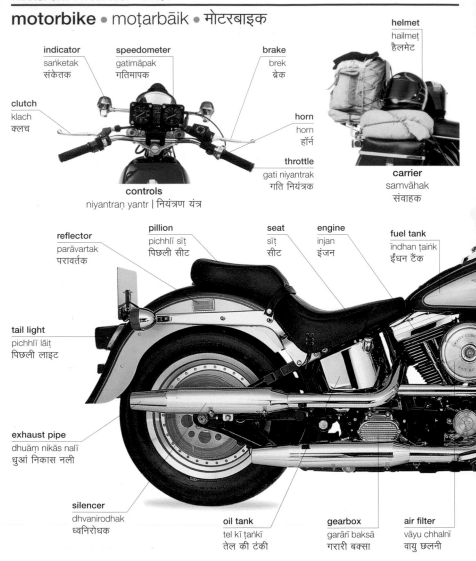

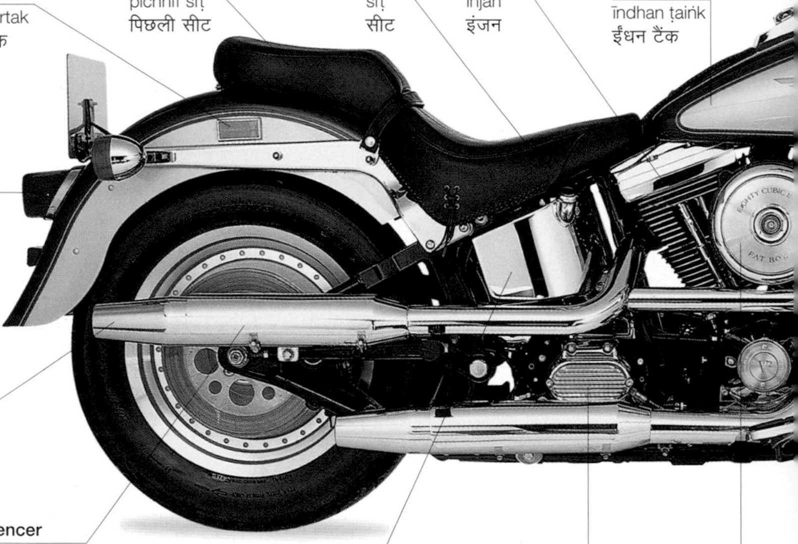
reflector
parāvartak
परावर्तक
pillion
pichhlī sīṭ
पिछली सीट
seat
sīṭ
सीट
engine
injan
इंजन
fuel tank
īndhan ṭaiṅk
ईंधन टैंक
tail light
pichhlī lāiṭ
पिछली लाइट
exhaust pipe
dhuāṃ nikās nalī
धुआं निकास नली
silencer
dhvanirodhak
ध्वनिरोधक
oil tank
tel kī ṭaṅkī
तेल की टंकी
gearbox
garārī baksā
गरारी बक्सा
air filter
vāyu chhalnī
वायु छलनी

visor
hailmeṭ kā śīśā
हैलमेट का शीशा
leathers
laidar vastr
लैदर वस्त्र
reflector strap
parāvartak paṭṭī
परावर्तक पट्टी
knee pad
nī paiḍ
नी पैड

clothing | vastr | वस्त्र

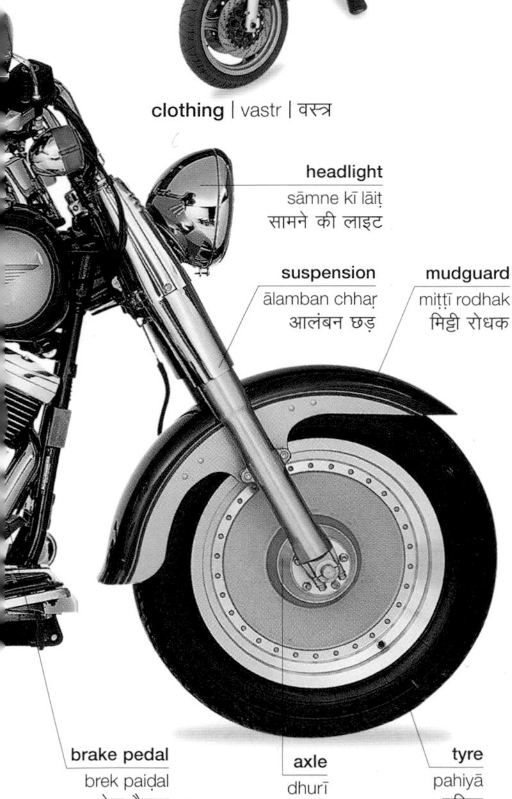
headlight
sāmne kī lāiṭ
सामने की लाइट
suspension
ālamban chhaṛ
आलंबन छड़
mudguard
miṭṭī rodhak
मिट्टी रोधक
brake pedal
brek paiḍal
ब्रेक पैडल
axle
dhurī
धुरी
tyre
pahiyā
पहिया

types • prakār • प्रकार

racing bike | resiṅg bāik | रेसिंग बाइक

windshield
vinḍśīlaḍ
विंडशील्ड

tourer | moṭar sāikil | मोटर साइकिल

dirt bike | ḍarṭ bāik | डर्ट बाइक

stand
sṭainḍ | स्टैंड

scooter | skūṭar | स्कूटर

bicycle • sāikil • साइकिल

tandem | do sīṭoṃ vālī sāikil
दो सीटों वाली साइकिल

racing bike
resiṅg bāik
रेसिंग बाइक

mountain bike
māunṭen bāik
माउंटेन बाइक

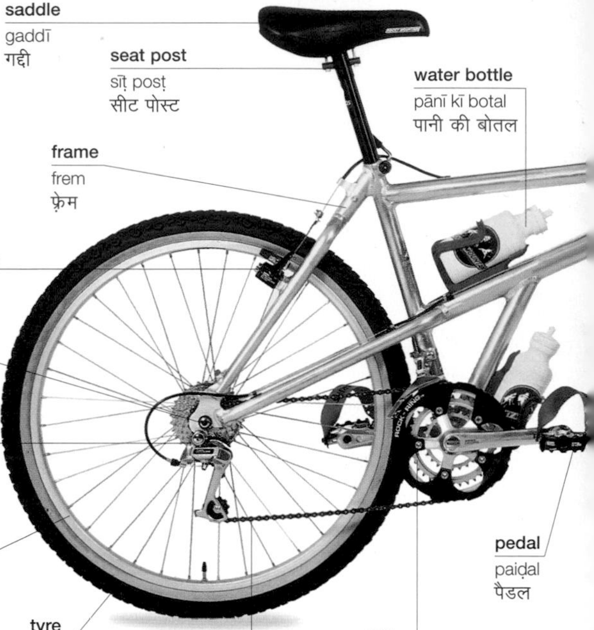

saddle
gaddī
गद्दी

seat post
sīṭ posṭ
सीट पोस्ट

water bottle
pānī kī botal
पानी की बोतल

frame
frem
फ़्रेम

brake
brek
ब्रेक

hub
dhurī
धुरी

gears
gīyar
गीयर

rim
rim
रिम

pedal
paiḍal
पैडल

tyre
ṭāyar
टायर

cog
dāṃtā
दांता

chain
chen
चेन

touring bike
ṭūriṅg bāik | टूरिंग बाइक

helmet
hailmeṭ
हैलमेट

road bike
roḍ bāik | रोड बाइक

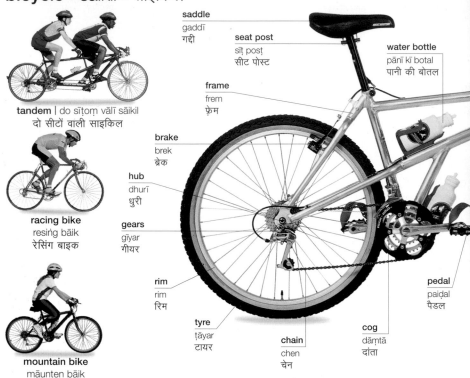

cycle lane | sāikil len | साइकिल लेन

crossbar
crossbar
क्रॉसबार
handlebar
haiṇḍal
हैंडल
gear lever
gīyar līvar
गीयर लीवर
brake lever
brek līvar
ब्रेक लीवर
fork
chimṭā
चिमटा
spoke
tīlī
तीली
wheel
pahiyā
पहिया
valve
vālv
वाल्व
tread
ṭāyar par ḍizāin
टायर पर डिज़ाइन

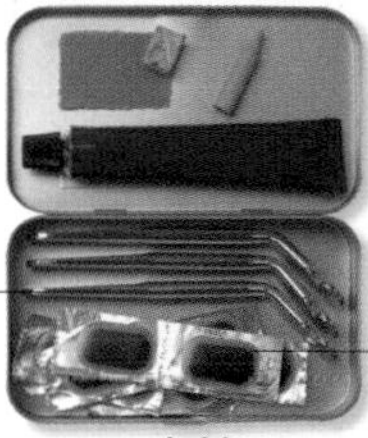
tyre lever
ṭāyar līvar
टायर लीवर
patch
thiglī
थिगली

repair kit
marammat kā sāmān | मरम्मत का सामान

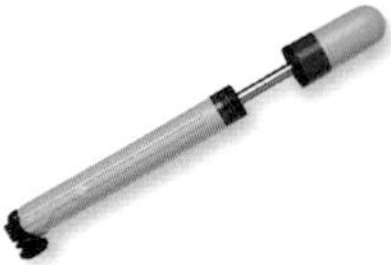

pump
pamp
पंप

key
chābī
चाबी

lock
tālā
ताला

inner tube
bhītrī ṭyūb
भीतरी ट्यूब

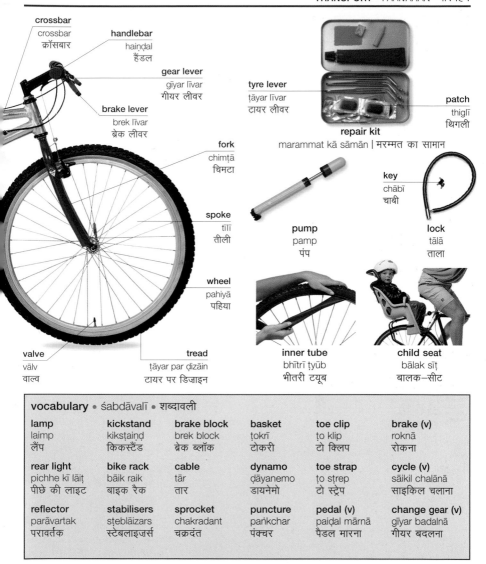

child seat
bālak sīṭ
बालक–सीट

vocabulary • śabdāvalī • शब्दावली

lamp laimp लैंप	**kickstand** kiksṭaiṇḍ किकस्टैंड	**brake block** brek block ब्रेक ब्लॉक	**basket** ṭokrī टोकरी	**toe clip** ṭo klip टो क्लिप	**brake (v)** roknā रोकना
rear light pichhe kī lāiṭ पीछे की लाइट	**bike rack** bāik raik बाइक रैक	**cable** tār तार	**dynamo** ḍāyanemo डायनेमो	**toe strap** ṭo sṭrep टो स्ट्रेप	**cycle (v)** sāikil chalānā साइकिल चलाना
reflector parāvartak परावर्तक	**stabilisers** sṭeblāizars स्टेबलाइज़र्स	**sprocket** chakradant चक्रदंत	**puncture** paṅkchar पंक्चर	**pedal (v)** paiḍal mārnā पैडल मारना	**change gear (v)** gīyar badalnā गीयर बदलना

train • relgāṛī • रेलगाड़ी

carriage
relgāṛī
ḍibbā
रेलगाड़ी
डिब्बा

platform number
platform saṃkhyā
प्लेटफ़ॉर्म संख्या

commuter
yātrī
यात्री

trolley
trolley
ट्रॉली

platform
platform
प्लेटफ़ॉर्म

train station | relve sṭeśan | रेलवे स्टेशन

types of train • relgaṛī ke prakār • रेलगाड़ी के प्रकार

engine
injan
इंजन

steam train
bhāp chālit rel | भाप चालित रेल

driver's cab
chālak kakṣ
चालक कक्ष

rail
paṭrī
पटरी

diesel train | ḍīzal rel | डीज़ल रेल

electric train
vidyut rel | विद्युत रेल

high-speed train
tez gati rel | तेज़ गति रेल

monorail
ekpaṭrī rel | एकपटरी रेल

underground train
bhūmigat rel | भूमिगत रेल

tram
ṭrām gāṛī | ट्राम गाड़ी

freight train
mālgāṛī | मालगाड़ी

luggage rack
sāmān kī jagah
सामान की जगह

window
khiṛkī
खिड़की

track
paṭrī
पटरी

door
darvāzā
दरवाज़ा

seat
sīṭ
सीट

compartment | ḍibbā | डिब्बा

ticket barrier
ṭikaṭ bairiyar | टिकट बैरियर

ticket
ṭikaṭ | टिकट

dining car | bhojanyān | भोजनयान

public address system
jan sūchnā praṇālī
जन सूचना प्रणाली

timetable
samaya sāriṇī
समय–सारिणी

concourse | relve parisar | रेलवे परिसर

sleeping compartment
śayan yān | शयन यान

vocabulary • śabdāvalī • शब्दावली

rail network
relgāṛī tantr
रेलगाड़ी तंत्र

inter-city train
antar nagarīya relgāṛī
अंतर नगरीय रेलगाड़ी

rush hour
vyast samaya
व्यस्त समय

underground map
bhūmigat nakśā
भूमिगत नक़्शा

delay
vilamb
विलंब

fare
kirāyā
किराया

ticket office
ṭikaṭ ghar
टिकट घर

ticket inspector
ṭikaṭ nirīkṣak
टिकट निरीक्षक

change (v)
badalnā
बदलना

live rail
chālū paṭrī
चालू पटरी

signal
signal
सिग्नल

emergency lever
āpātkālīn līvar
आपातकालीन लीवर

aircraft • vāyuyān • वायुयान

airliner • yātrī vimān • यात्री विमान

cockpit
chālak kakṣ
चालक कक्ष

exit
nikās dvār
निकास द्वार

engine
injan
इंजन

fuselage
fyūzilej
फ़्यूज़िलेज

wing
paṅkh
पंख

tail
pūṃchh
पूंछ

rudder
raḍar | रडर

nose
agra bhāg
अग्र भाग

nosewheel
āge kā pahiyā
आगे का पहिया

landing gear
lenḍiṅg gīyar
लेंडिंग गीयर

aileron
pichhlī patvār
पिछली पतवार

fin
paṅkh
पंख

tailplane
pichhlā samtal paṅkh
पिछला समतल पंख

cabin • kebin • केबिन

emergency exit
āpātkālīn nikās
आपातकालीन निकास

flight attendant
vimān parichārikā
विमान परिचारिका

overhead locker
ūprī locker
ऊपरी लॉकर

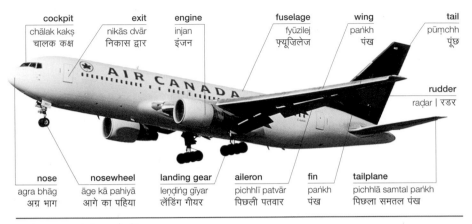

window
khiṛkī
खिड़की

air vent
vāyu chhidr
वायु छिद्र

reading light
battī
बत्ती

seat
sīṭ
सीट

row
ḳatār
क़तार

armrest
hatthā
हत्था

aisle
galiyārā
गलियारा

tray-table
ṭre-ṭebal
ट्रे–टेबल

seat back
sīṭ kī pīṭh
सीट की पीठ

hot-air balloon
garm havā kā gubbārā
गर्म हवा का ग़ुब्बारा

microlight
māikrolāiṭ
माइक्रोलाइट

glider
glāiḍar
ग्लाइडर

biplane
bāiplen
बाइप्लेन

propeller
chālak yantr
चालक यंत्र

light aircraft
halkā vayuyān
हल्का वायुयान

sea plane
naukā vimān
नौका विमान

private jet
nijī vimān | निजी विमान

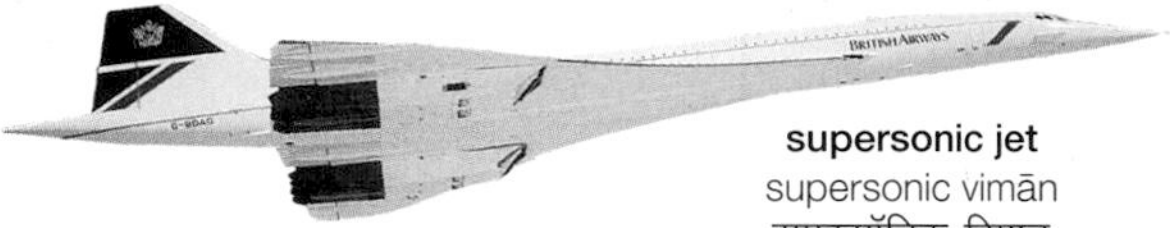

supersonic jet
supersonic vimān
सुपरसॉनिक विमान

rotor blade
roṭar bleḍ
रोटर ब्लेड

helicopter
helicopter | हैलीकॉप्टर

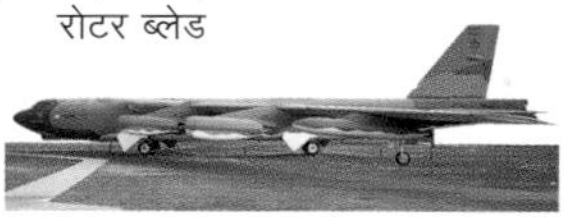

bomber
bamvarṣak | बमवर्षक

missile
misāil | मिसाइल

fighter plane
laṛākū vimān | लड़ाकू विमान

vocabulary • śabdāvalī • शब्दावली

pilot vimān chālak विमान चालक	**take off (v)** uṛān bharnā उड़ान भरना	**land (v)** utarnā उतरना	**economy class** sāmānya śreṇī सामान्य श्रेणी	**hand luggage** halkā sāmān हल्का सामान
co-pilot sah-vimān chālak सह–विमान चालक	**fly (v)** uṛnā उड़ना	**altitude** ūṃchāī ऊंचाई	**business class** vyāvasāyik śreṇī व्यावसायिक श्रेणी	**seat belt** sīṭ belṭ सीट बेल्ट

airport • havāī aḍḍā • हवाई अड्डा

apron
epran
एप्रन

baggage trailer
sāmān gāṛī
सामान गाड़ी

terminal
ṭarminal
टर्मिनल

service vehicle
sevā vāhan
सेवा वाहन

walkway
mārg
मार्ग

airliner | vāyuyān | वायुयान

---

vocabulary • śabdāvalī • शब्दावली

runway
havāī paṭṭī
हवाई पट्टी

international flight
antarrāṣṭrīya uṛān
अंतरराष्ट्रीय उड़ान

domestic flight
gharelū uṛān
घरेलू उड़ान

connection
saṃyojī
संयोजी

flight number
uṛān nambar
उड़ान नंबर

immigration
āpravās
आप्रवास

customs
sīmā śulk
सीमा शुल्क

excess baggage
atirikt sāmān
अतिरिक्त सामान

carousel
sāmān kī chal paṭṭī
सामान की चल पट्टी

security
surakṣā
सुरक्षा

x-ray machine
eksare maśīn
एक्सरे मशीन

holiday brochure
paryaṭan sūchnā pustikā
पर्यटन सूचना पुस्तिका

holiday
chhuṭṭiyāṃ
छुट्टियां

check in (v)
chek in
चेक इन

control tower
niyantraṇ tower
नियंत्रण टॉवर

book a flight (v)
uṛān buk karnā
उड़ान बुक करना

---

hand luggage
halkā sāmān
हल्का सामान

luggage
sāmān
सामान

trolley
trolley
ट्रॉली

check-in desk
chek in ḍesk
चेक इन डेस्क

visa
vīzā
वीज़ा

passport | pāsporṭ | पासपोर्ट

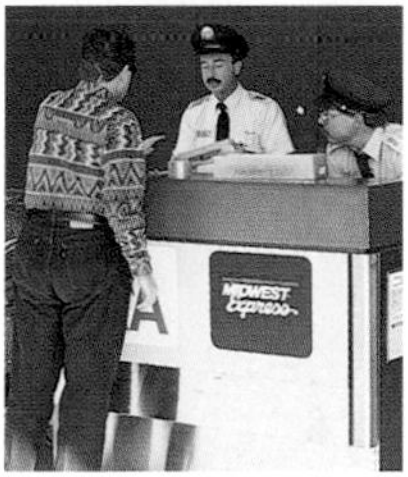

passport control
pāsporṭ kanṭrol
पासपोर्ट कंट्रोल

boarding pass
borḍiṅg pās
बोर्डिंग पास

ticket
ṭikaṭ
टिकट

gate number
dvār saṃkhyā
द्वार संख्या

departure lounge
prasthān kakṣ | प्रस्थान कक्ष

destination
gantavya
sthān
गंतव्य स्थान

departures
prasthān
प्रस्थान

arrivals
āgman
आगमन

information screen
sūchnā skrīn | सूचना स्क्रीन

duty-free shop
śulk mukt dukān
शुल्क मुक्त दुकान

baggage reclaim
sāmān vāpsī
सामान वापसी

taxi rank
ṭaiksī ḳatār
टैक्सी–क़तार

car hire
kirāe kī kār
किराए की कार

ship • jahāz • जहाज़

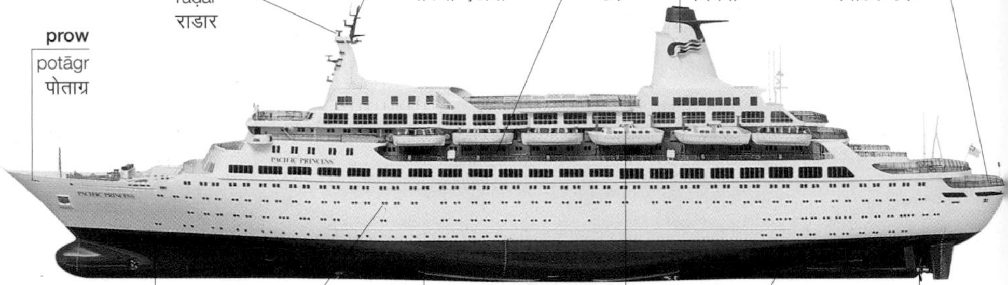
radio antenna
reḍiyo enṭīnā
रेडियो एंटीना
deck
ḍaik
डैक
funnel
chimnī
चिमनी
quarterdeck
kvārṭar ḍaik
क्वार्टर डैक
radar
rāḍār
राडार
prow
potāgr
पोताग्र
plimsoll line
tal rekhā
तल रेखा
porthole
gavākṣ
गवाक्ष
hull
peṭā
पेटा
lifeboat
rakṣā naukā
रक्षा नौका
keel
nautal
नौतल
propeller
chālak yantr
चालक यंत्र

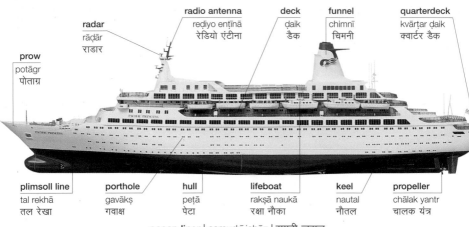

ocean liner | samudrī jahāz | समुद्री जहाज़

bridge
potādhikārī kakṣ
पोताधिकारी कक्ष

engine room
injan kakṣ
इंजन कक्ष

cabin
kaibin | कैबिन

galley
pot | पोत

vocabulary • śabdāvalī • शब्दावली

dock
dock
डॉक

port
bandargāh
बंदरगाह

gangway
mārgikā
मार्गिका

anchor
laṅgar
लंगर

bollard
rakṣā stambh
रक्षा–स्तंभ

windlass
charkhī
चरखी

captain
kaptān
कप्तान

speedboat
moṭar naukā
मोटर नौका

rowing boat
chappū vālī nāv
चप्पू वाली नाव

canoe
ḍoṅgī
डोंगी

other ships • anya jahāz • अन्य जहाज़

ferry | yātrī vāhak jahāz | यात्री वाहक जहाज़

outboard motor
āuṭborḍ moṭar
आउटबोर्ड मोटर

inflatable dinghy | havā bharī ḍoṅgī | हवा भरी डोंगी

hydrofoil | jal patrak
जल पत्रक

yacht
krīṛā naukā | क्रीड़ा नौका

catamaran
donāvā | दोनावा

tug boat
karṣ naukā | कर्ष नौका

hovercraft
hover krāfṭ | हॉवर क्राफ़्ट

container ship
māl pot | माल पोत

rigging
sāj sāmān
साज सामान

sailboat
pāl naukā | पाल नौका

hold
māl kakṣ
माल कक्ष

freighter | mālvāhak
मालवाहक

oil tanker
tel pot | तेल पोत

aircraft carrier | vāyuyān vāhak | वायुयान वाहक

battleship
jaṅgī jahāz | जंगी जहाज़

conning tower
chālak kakṣ
चालक कक्ष

submarine
panḍubbī | पनडुब्बी

port • bandargāh • बंदरगाह

warehouse
mālgodām
मालगोदाम

crane
kren
क्रेन

fork-lift truck
kren
क्रेन

access road
praveś mārg
प्रवेश मार्ग

customs house
sīmā śulk chaukī
सीमा शुल्क चौकी

dock
godī
गोदी

container
māl ḍibbā
माल डिब्बा

quay
jahāz ghāṭ
जहाज़ घाट

cargo
kārgo
कार्गो

container port | māl vāhak bandargāh
माल वाहक बंदरगाह

ferry terminal
yātrī jahāz ṭarminal
यात्री जहाज़ टर्मिनल

ferry
yātrī jahāz
यात्री जहाज़

ticket office
ṭikaṭ ghar
टिकट घर

passenger
yātrī
यात्री

passenger port
yātrī bandargāh | यात्री बंदरगाह

net
jāl
जाल
fishing boat
machhuārī nāv
मछुआरी नाव

fishing port | matsya bandargāh | मत्स्य बंदरगाह

mooring
laṅgargāh
लंगरगाह

marina | taṭvartī ḳasbā | तटवर्ती क़स्बा

harbour | bandargāh | बंदरगाह

pier | potghāṭ | पोतघाट

jetty | jeṭī | जेटी

shipyard | pot nirmāṇ ghāṭ | पोत निर्माण घाट

lamp
laimp
लैंप

lighthouse | prakāś stambh | प्रकाश स्तंभ

buoy
boyā | बोया

vocabulary • śabdāvalī • शब्दावली

coastguard taṭrakṣak तटरक्षक	**dry dock** sūkhā bandargāh सूखा बंदरगाह	**board (v)** chaṛhnā चढ़ना
harbour master bandargāh pramukh बंदरगाह प्रमुख	**moor (v)** nāv bāndhnā नाव बांधना	**disembark (v)** jahāz se utarnā जहाज़ से उतरना
drop anchor (v) laṅgar ḍālnā लंगर डालना	**dock (v)** bandargāh meṃ lānā बंदरगाह में लाना	**set sail (v)** yātrā ārambh karnā यात्रा आरंभ करना

ULTRA
3
DUNLOP
DDH III
4
DUNLOP
MOLITOR
TOUR
EDITION
1
ProStaff
4
SPRINGS
GOLF CLUB
TOP-FLITE
HOT XL
4
ProStaff
4
RAM TOUR
1
MAXFLI
TOP-FLITE
STRATA
3
DISTANCE

sports
khelkūd
खेलकूद

American football • amerikan football • अमेरिकन फ़ुटबॉल

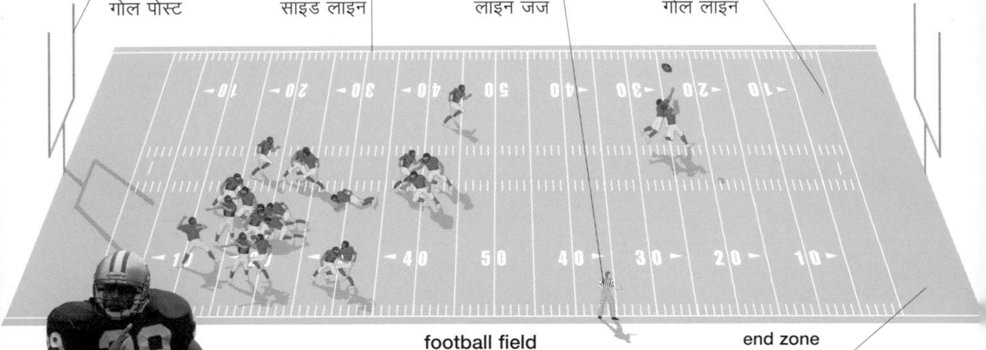
goalpost
gol posṭ
गोल पोस्ट
sideline
sāiḍ lāin
साइड लाइन
line judge
lāin jaj
लाइन जज
goal line
gol lāin
गोल लाइन
football field
football kā maidān | फ़ुटबॉल का मैदान
end zone
samāpti kṣetr
समाप्ति क्षेत्र

football
football | फ़ुटबॉल
pads
paid | पैड
helmet
hailmeṭ | हैलमेट
boot
jūtā
जूता

football player
football khilāṛī
फ़ुटबॉल खिलाड़ी

tackle (v)
pratirodh karnā | प्रतिरोध करना

pass (v)
pās denā | पास देना

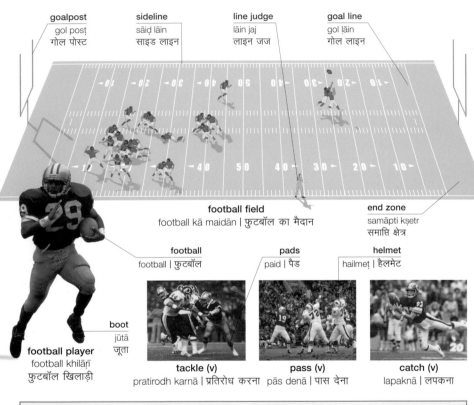

catch (v)
lapaknā | लपकना

vocabulary • śabdāvalī • शब्दावली

time out
samaya samāpt
समय समाप्त

team
ṭīm
टीम

defence
bachāv
बचाव

cheerleader
protsāhak ṭīm netā
प्रोत्साहक टीम नेता

fumble
binā soche kik mārnā
बिना सोचे किक मारना

attack
hamlā
हमला

score
skor
स्कोर

touchdown
gend se zamīn chhūnā
गेंद से ज़मीन छूना

What is the score?
kyā skor huā hai?
क्या स्कोर हुआ है?

Who is winning?
kaun jīt rahā hai?
कौन जीत रहा है?

rugby • ragbī • रग्बी

dead ball line
ḍed ball lāin
डेड बॉल लाइन
in-goal area
gol kā kṣetr
गोल का क्षेत्र
touch line
pārśv rekhā
पार्श्व रेखा
flag
jhaṇḍā
झंडा
goal
gol
गोल

rugby pitch | ragbī kā maidān | रग्बी का मैदान

throw (v)
ball pheṃknā
बॉल फेंकना

ball
ball
बॉल

kick (v)
kik mārnā
किक मारना

rugby strip
ragbī sṭrip
रग्बी स्ट्रिप

pass (v)
ball ek-dūsre ko denā
बॉल एक – दूसरे को देना

tackle (v)
pratirodh karnā
प्रतिरोध करना

try
ṭraī | ट्राई

player
khilāṛī
खिलाड़ी

ruck | khilāṛiyoṃ kā dal | खिलाड़ियों का दल

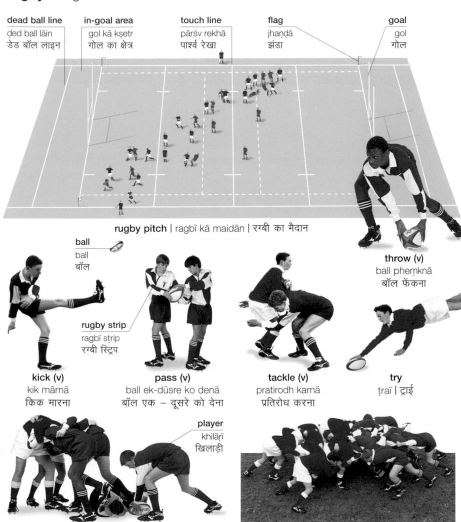

scrum | ball ko ghernā | बॉल को घेरना

soccer • soccer • सॉकर

football
football
फ़ुटबॉल

football strip
football sṭrip
फ़ुटबॉल स्ट्रिप

footballer
footballer
फ़ुटबॉलर

forward
agrim paṅkti kā khilāṛī
अग्रिम पंक्ति का खिलाड़ी

referee
refrī
रेफ़री

centre circle
kendrīya gherā
केंद्रीय घेरा

goalkeeper
golkīpar
गोलकीपर

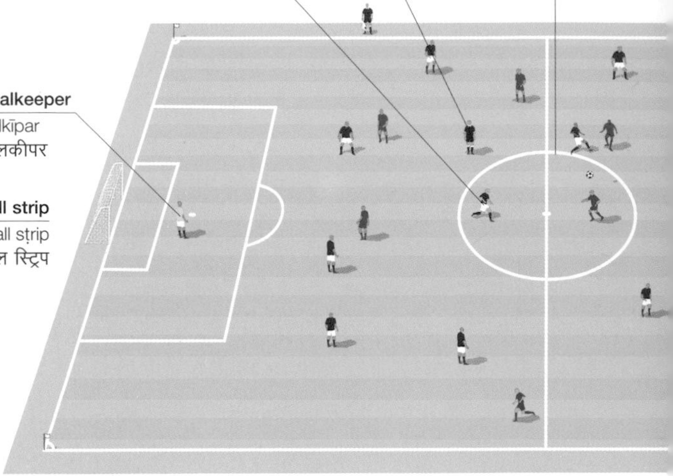

football pitch
football maidān | फ़ुटबॉल मैदान

goalpost
gol posṭ
गोल पोस्ट

net
jāl
जाल

crossbar
crossbar
क्रॉसबार

goal | gol | गोल

dribble (v) | gend dhakelnā
गेंद धकेलना

head (v)
sir se mārnā | सिर से मारना

wall
pratirakṣak
paṅkti
प्रतिरक्षक पंक्ति

free kick | frī kik | फ़्री किक

penalty area
penalṭī kṣetr
पेनल्टी क्षेत्र

goal line
gol sīmā
गोल – सीमा

goal area
gol kṣetr
गोल–क्षेत्र

goal
gol
गोल

defender
pratirakṣak
प्रतिरक्षक

linesman
lāins main
लाइन्स मैन

corner flag
corner jhaṇḍā
कॉर्नर–झंडा

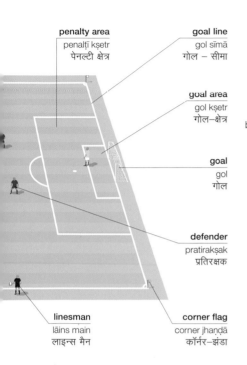

throw-in
ball pheṃknā | बॉल फेंकना

kick (v) | kik mārnā |
किक मारना

boot
jūtā
जूता

pass (v) | pāss denā |
पास देना

shoot (v) | zor se
mārnā | ज़ोर से मारना

save (v)
gol roknā | गोल रोकना

tackle (v)
pratirodh karnā
प्रतिरोध करना

vocabulary • śabdāvalī • शब्दावली

stadium steḍiyam स्टेडियम	**foul** niyam ullaṅghan नियम उल्लंघन	**yellow card** pīlā kārḍ पीला कार्ड	**league** līg लीग	**extra time** atirikt samaya अतिरिक्त समय
score a goal (v) gol dāgnā गोल दाग़ना	**corner** corner कॉर्नर	**off-side** off - sāiḍ ऑफ़–साइड	**draw** anirṇit maich अनिर्णित मैच	**substitute** vaikalpik khilāṛī वैकल्पिक खिलाड़ी
penalty penalṭī पेनल्टी	**red card** lāl kārḍ लाल कार्ड	**send off** saiṇḍ off सैंड ऑफ़	**half time** ādhā vakt आधा वक़्त	**substitution** vikalp bulānā विकल्प बुलाना

hockey • hockey • हॉकी

ice hockey • āis hockey • आइस हॉकी

defending zone
rakṣā kṣetr
रक्षा क्षेत्र
goal line
gol lāin
गोल लाइन
attack zone
ākramaṇ kṣetr
आक्रमण क्षेत्र
neutral zone
taṭasth kṣetr
तटस्थ क्षेत्र
goalkeeper
golkīpar
गोलकीपर
goal
gol
गोल
face-off circle
fes off sarkal
फ़ेस ऑफ़ सर्कल
centre circle
kendrīya gherā
केंद्रीय घेरा

ice hockey rink
āis hockey kā maidān
आइस हॉकी का मैदान

pad
paiḍ
पैड
glove
dastānā
दस्ताना
ice-skate
āis sket
आइस स्केट
stick
sṭik | स्टिक
puck
ḍisk | डिस्क

ice hockey player | āis hockey khilāṛī
आइस हॉकी खिलाड़ी

field hockey • fīlḍ hockey • फ़ील्ड हॉकी

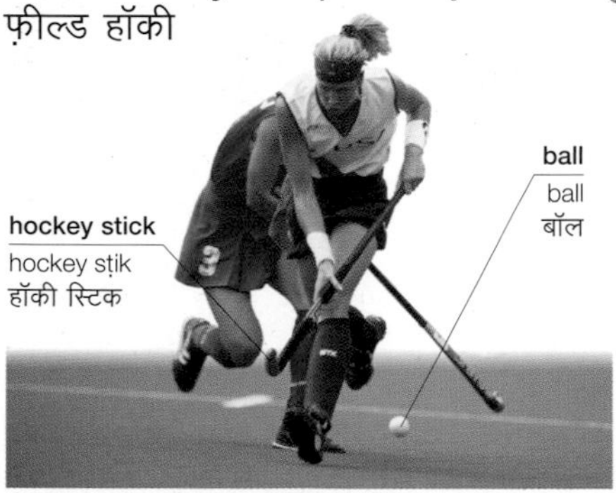
ball
ball
बॉल
hockey stick
hockey sṭik
हॉकी स्टिक

skate (v) | skeṭiṅg karnā | स्केटिंग करना

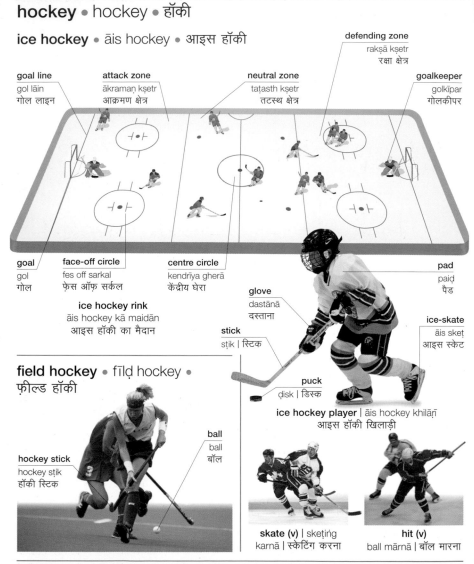

hit (v)
ball mārnā | बॉल मारना

cricket • kriket̤ • क्रिकेट

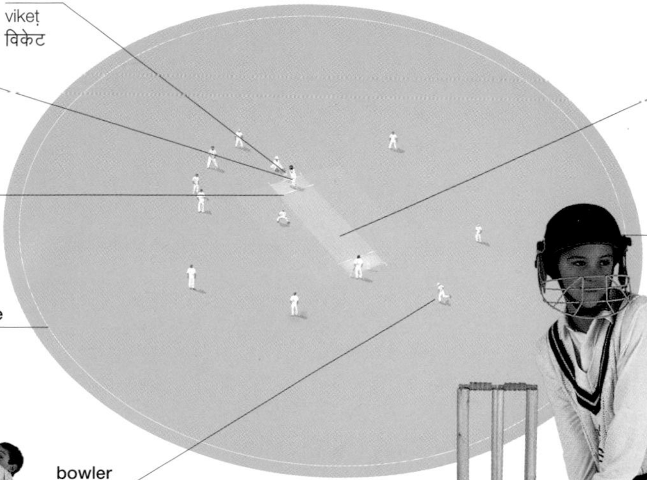
wicket
viket̤
विकेट
batsman
ballebāz
बल्लेबाज़
crease
krīz
क्रीज़
boundary line
sīmā rekhā
सीमा रेखा
pitch
pich
पिच
bowler
gendbāz
गेंदबाज़

bowl (v)
gendbāzī karnā
गेंदबाज़ी करना

bat (v)
ballebāzī karnā | बल्लेबाज़ी करना

face mask
hailmet̤
हैलमेट
stump
st̤amp
स्टंप
leg pad
paid̤
पैड
bat
ballā
बल्ला

cricketer
kriket̤ khilāṛī | क्रिकेट खिलाड़ी

cricket ball
kriket̤ gend
क्रिकेट गेंद

field (v) | fīld̤iṅg karnā | फ़ील्डिंग करना

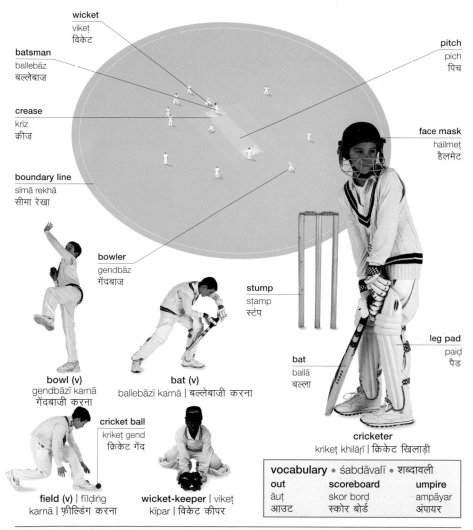

wicket-keeper | viket̤ kīpar | विकेट कीपर

vocabulary • śabdāvalī • शब्दावली

out āut̤ आउट	**scoreboard** skor bord̤ स्कोर बोर्ड	**umpire** ampāyar अंपायर

basketball • bāskeṭ ball • बास्केट बॉल

sideline
sāiḍ lāin
साइड लाइन
referee
refrī
रेफ़री
centre circle
kendrīya gherā
केंद्रीय घेरा
free-throw line
frī thro lāin
फ़्री थ्रो लाइन
endline
samāpti rekhā
समाप्ति रेखा
centreline
madhya rekhā
मध्य रेखा
three-point line
thrī point lāin
थ्री पॉइन्ट लाइन

court | maidān | मैदान

number
saṃkhyā
संख्या
ball
ball
बॉल

basketball player | bāskeṭ ball khilāṛī
बास्केट बॉल खिलाड़ी

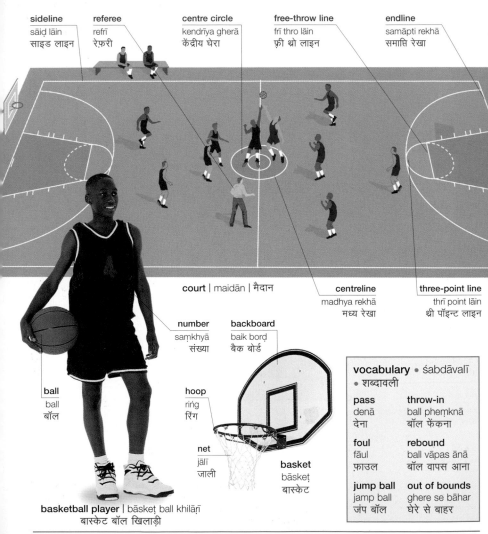

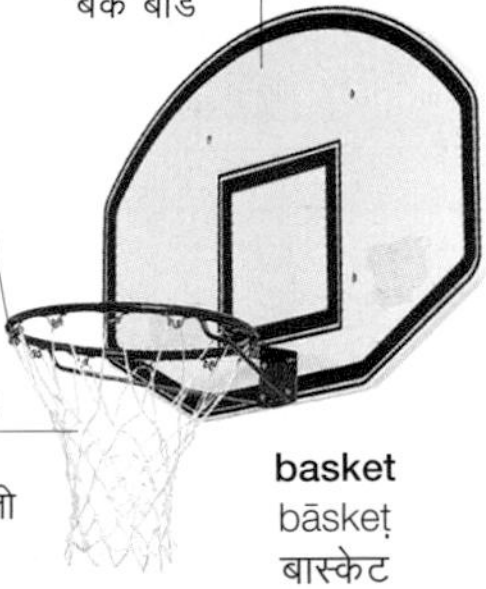
backboard
baik borḍ
बैक बोर्ड
hoop
riṅg
रिंग
net
jālī
जाली
basket
bāskeṭ
बास्केट

vocabulary • śabdāvalī • शब्दावली

pass denā देना	**throw-in** ball pheṃknā बॉल फेंकना
foul fāul फ़ाउल	**rebound** ball vāpas ānā बॉल वापस आना
jump ball jamp ball जंप बॉल	**out of bounds** ghere se bāhar घेरे से बाहर

actions • gatividhiyāṃ • गतिविधियां

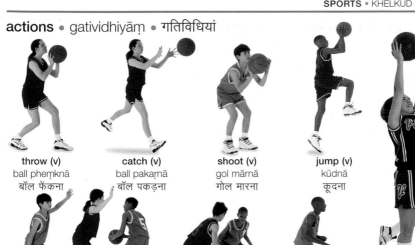

throw (v)
ball pheṃknā
बॉल फेंकना

catch (v)
ball pakaṛnā
बॉल पकड़ना

shoot (v)
gol mārnā
गोल मारना

jump (v)
kūdnā
कूदना

mark (v) | ball niśāne par mārnā | बॉल निशाने पर मारना

block (v) | ball roknā | बॉल रोकना

bounce (v) | ṭappā mārnā | टप्पा मारना

dunk (v) | ball bāskeṭ meṃ ḍālnā | बॉल बास्केट में डालना

volleyball • volleyball • वॉलीबॉल

block (v)
ball roknā
बॉल रोकना

net
jāl
जाल

dig (v)
ball lapakne ko taiyār rahnā
बॉल लपकने को तैयार रहना

referee
refrī
रेफ़री

knee support
nī saporṭ
नी सपोर्ट

court | maidān | मैदान

baseball • baseball • बेसबॉल

field • maidān • मैदान

left field
left fīld
लेफ्ट फ़ील्ड

infield
in fīld
इन फ़ील्ड

centre field
senṭar fīld
सेंटर फ़ील्ड

bat
ballā
बल्ला

helmet
hailmeṭ
हैलमेट

baseman
besmain
बेसमैन

pitcher's mound
pichar kā sthān
पिचर का स्थान

home plate
vāpas apne sthān par
pahuṃchnā
वापस अपने स्थान पर पहुंचना

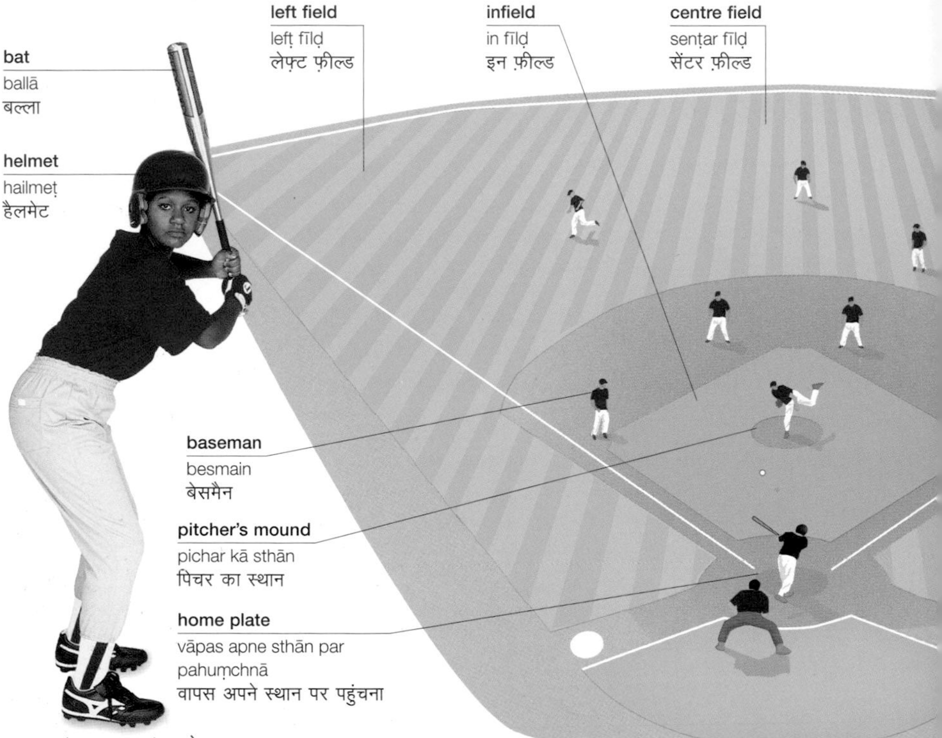

batter | ballebāz | बल्लेबाज़

vocabulary • śabdāvalī • शब्दावली

inning	safe	foul ball
pārī	surakṣit	fāul gend
पारी	सुरक्षित	फ़ाउल गेंद
run	**out**	**strike**
ran	āuṭ	sṭrāik
रन	आउट	स्ट्राइक

ball
gend
गेंद

mitt | dastānā |
दस्ताना

mask | mukhauṭā
मुखौटा

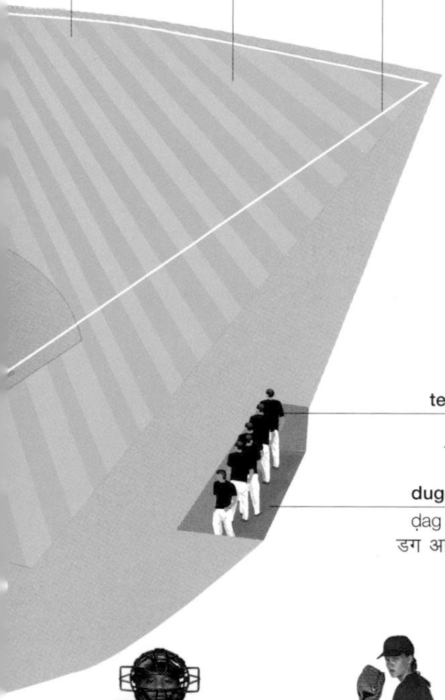
outfield
āuṭ fīlḍ
आउट फ़ील्ड
right field
rāiṭ fīlḍ
राइट फ़ील्ड
foul line
fāul lāin
फ़ाउल लाइन
team
ṭīm
टीम
dugout
ḍag āuṭ
डग आउट

catcher
kaichar | कैचर

pitcher
pichar | पिचर

actions • kriyāeṃ • क्रियाएं

throw (v) | ball pheṃknā
बॉल फेंकना

catch (v) | gend
pakaṛnā | गेंद पकड़ना

run (v)
dauṛnā | दौड़ना

field (v) | fīlḍiṅg karnā
फ़ील्डिंग करना

slide (v)
phisalnā
फिसलना
tag (v)
pīchhe dauṛnā | पीछे दौड़ना

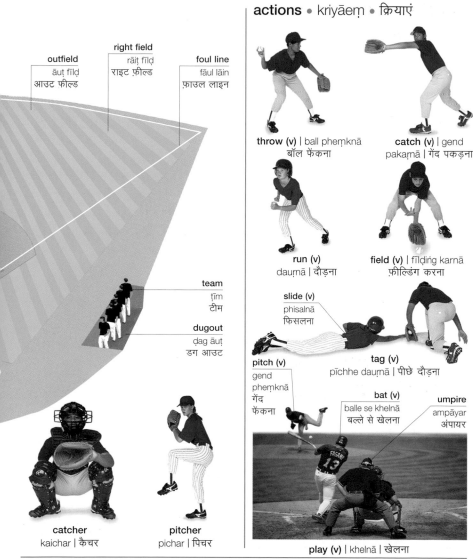

pitch (v)
gend
pheṃknā
गेंद
फेंकना
bat (v)
balle se khelnā
बल्ले से खेलना
umpire
ampāyar
अंपायर
FASANO
13
play (v) | khelnā | खेलना

tennis • ṭenis • टेनिस

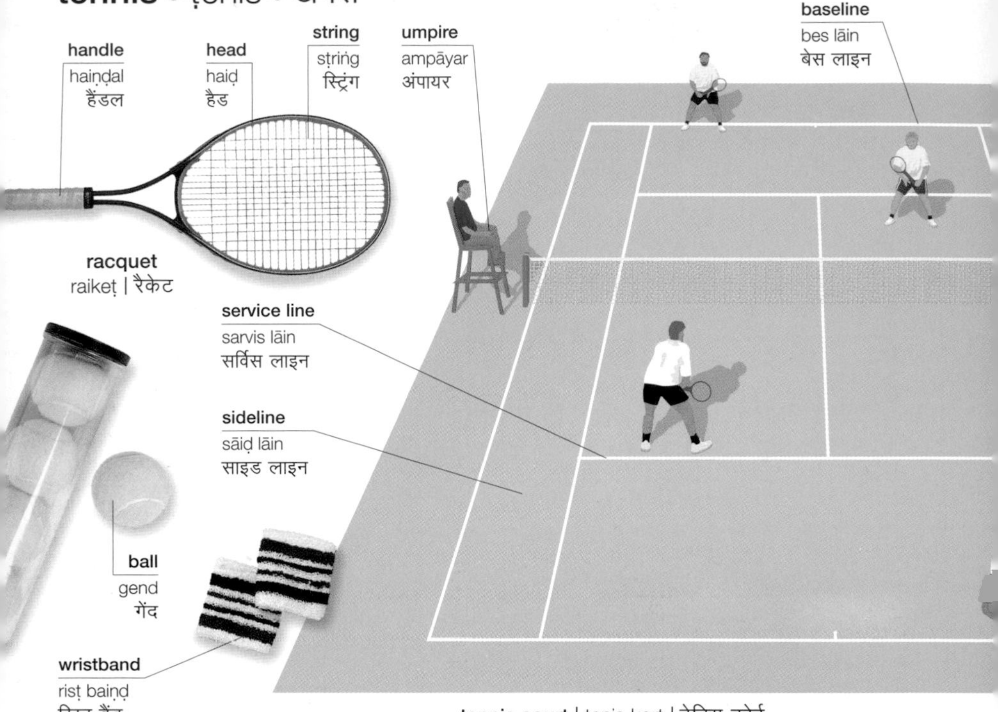
handle
haiṇḍal
हैंडल
head
haiḍ
हैड
string
striṅg
स्ट्रिंग
umpire
ampāyar
अंपायर
baseline
bes lāin
बेस लाइन
racquet
raikeṭ | रैकेट
service line
sarvis lāin
सर्विस लाइन
sideline
sāiḍ lāin
साइड लाइन
ball
gend
गेंद
wristband
risṭ baiṇḍ
रिस्ट बैंड

tennis court | ṭenis korṭ | टेनिस कोर्ट

vocabulary • śabdāvalī • शब्दावली

singles ekal एकल	**set** saiṭ सैट	**deuce** barābarī बराबरी	**fault** galat shot ग़लत शॉट	**slice** galat prahār ग़लत प्रहार	**let!** khilāṛī ko roknā खिलाड़ी को रोकना
doubles yugal युगल	**match** maich मैच	**love** śūnya शून्य	**dropshot** dropshot ड्रॉप शॉट	**rally** kaṛā pariśram कड़ा परिश्रम	**championship** chaimpiyanśip चैम्पियनशिप
game khel खेल	**spin** spin स्पिन	**tiebreak** nirṇāyak aṃk निर्णायक अंक	**advantage** anukūl sthiti अनुकूल स्थिति	**linesman** lāins main लाइन्स मैन	**ace** pahlī sarvis se banā aṃk पहली सर्विस से बना अंक

net
neṭ
नेट
smash
zor se mārnā
ज़ोर से मारना
ballboy
ball boy
बॉल बॉय
serve (v)
sarvis karnā
सर्विस करना
tennis shoes
ṭenis jūte
टेनिस जूते

player
khilāṛī | खिलाड़ी

strokes • sṭroks • स्ट्रोक्स

serve
sarv | सर्व

volley
volley | वॉली

return
riṭarn | रिटर्न

lob | lob
लोब

forehand
forhaiṇḍ | फ़ोरहैंड

backhand
baikhaiṇḍ | बैकहैंड

racquet games • raikeṭ ke khel • रैकेट के खेल

shuttlecock
chiṛiyā
चिड़िया

bat
baiṭ
बैट

badminton
baiḍminṭan | बैडमिंटन

table tennis
ṭebal ṭenis | टेबल टेनिस

squash
skvaiś | स्क्वैश

racquetball
raikeṭ ball | रैकेट बॉल

golf • golf • गोल्फ़

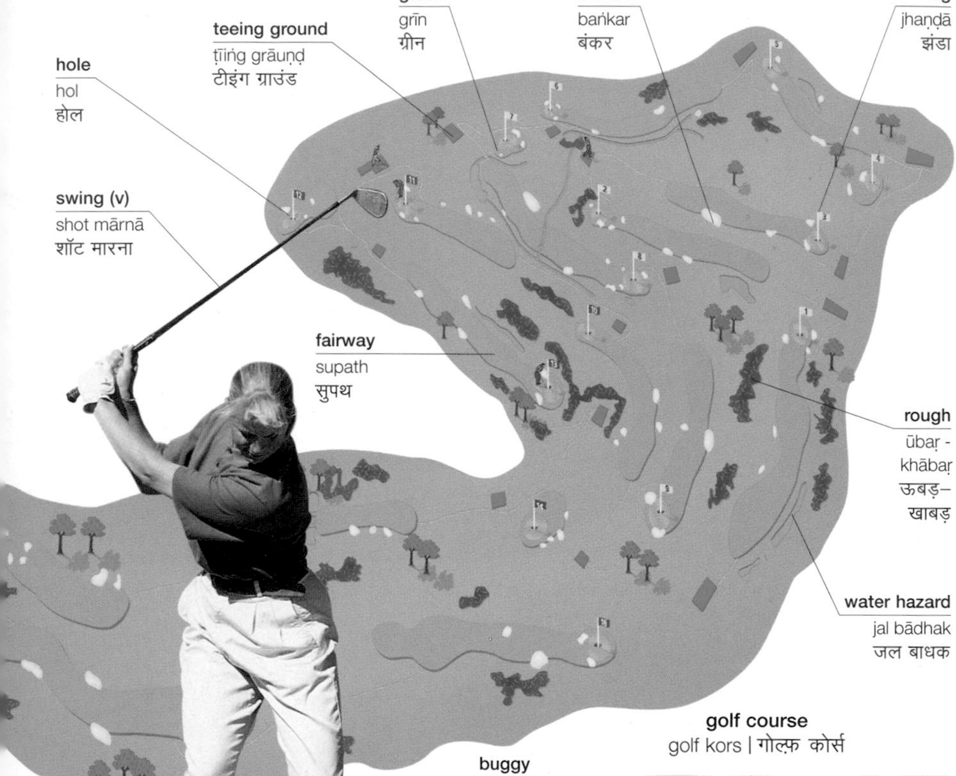
hole
hol
होल
teeing ground
ṭīiṅg grāuṇḍ
टीइंग ग्राउंड
green
grīn
ग्रीन
bunker
baṅkar
बंकर
flag
jhaṇḍā
झंडा
swing (v)
shot mārnā
शॉट मारना
fairway
supath
सुपथ
rough
ūbaṛ - khābaṛ
ऊबड़–खाबड़
water hazard
jal bādhak
जल बाधक
buggy
baggī
बग्गी
stance
shot mārne kā tarīḳā
शॉट मारने का तरीक़ा

golf course
golf kors | गोल्फ़ कोर्स

golfer | golf khilāṛī | गोल्फ़ खिलाड़ी

clubhouse | klab sadan | क्लब सदन

equipment • upkaraṇ • उपकरण

golf ball
golf ball
गोल्फ़ बॉल

tee | ṭī | टी

umbrella
chhātā
छाता

golf bag
golf baig
गोल्फ़ बैग

golf trolley
golf trolley | गोल्फ़ ट्रॉली

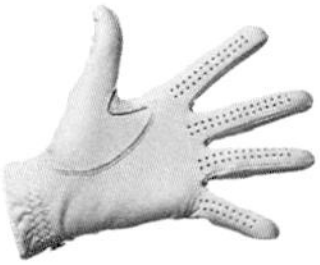

glove
dastānā | दस्ताना

spikes
kīloṃ vāle jūte
कीलों वाले जूते

golf shoe
golf ke jūte | गोल्फ़ के जूते

actions • gatividhiyāṃ • गतिविधियां

tee-off (v) | khel ārambh karnā
खेल आरंभ करना

drive (v)
ḍrāiv mārnā
ड्राइव मारना

putt (v) | gend par prahār karnā
गेंद पर प्रहार करना

chip (v)
chip shot lenā
चिप शॉट लेना

golf clubs • golf klab • गोल्फ़ क्लब

wood
vuḍ | वुड

putter
paṭar | पटर

iron
āyaran | आयरन

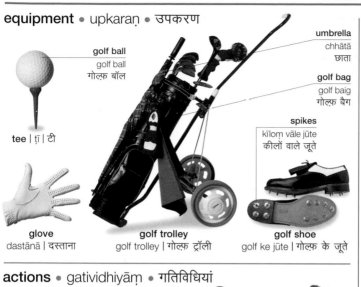

wedge
vej | वेज

vocabulary • śabdāvalī • शब्दावली

par ausat khel औसत खेल	**over par** utkṛṣṭ khel उत्कृष्ट खेल	**handicap** haiṇḍīkaip हैंडीकैप	**caddy** golf sahāyak गोल्फ़ सहायक	**backswing** baiksviṅg बैकस्विंग	**stroke** sṭrok स्ट्रोक
under par nimn khel निम्न खेल	**hole in one** hol in van होल इन वन	**tournament** muḳāblā मुक़ाबला	**spectators** darśak दर्शक	**practice swing** praikṭis shot प्रैक्टिस शॉट	**line of play** khel rekhā खेल रेखा

athletics • ethleṭiks • एथलेटिक्स

lane
len
लेन

track
paṅkti
पंक्ति

finishing line
samāpti rekhā
समाप्ति रेखा

starting line
prārambhik rekhā
प्रारंभिक रेखा

field
maidān | मैदान

starting blocks
ārambhik avrodh | आरंभिक अवरोध

sprinter
tez dhāvak
तेज़ धावक

discus
chakkā pheṃk
चक्का फेंक

athlete
ethlīṭ
एथलीट

shotput
golā pheṃk
गोला फेंक

javelin
bhālā pheṃk
भाला फेंक

vocabulary • śabdāvalī • शब्दावली

race dauṛ दौड़	**record** record रिकॉर्ड	**photo finish** barābarī kī dauṛ बराबरी की दौड़	**personal best** apnā viśeṣ pradarśan अपना विशेष प्रदर्शन
time samaya समय	**pole vault** bāṃs kūd बांस–कूद	**marathon** mairāthan मैराथन	**break a record (v)** record toṛnā रिकॉर्ड तोड़ना

stopwatch
virām ghaṛī | विराम घड़ी

baton
ḍanḍī
डंडी

relay race
rile dauṛ | रिले दौड़

crossbar
chhaṛ
छड़

high jump
ūṃchī kūd | ऊंची कूद

long jump
lambī kūd | लंबी कूद

hurdles | bādhā dauṛ | बाधा दौड़

gymnastics • jimnāsṭik • जिमनास्टिक

horse
horse
हॉर्स

vault
chhalāṅg mārnā
छलांग मारना

springboard
spriṅgborḍ
स्प्रिंगबोर्ड

somersault
kalābāzī | कलाबाज़ी

gymnast
jimnāsṭ
जिमनास्ट

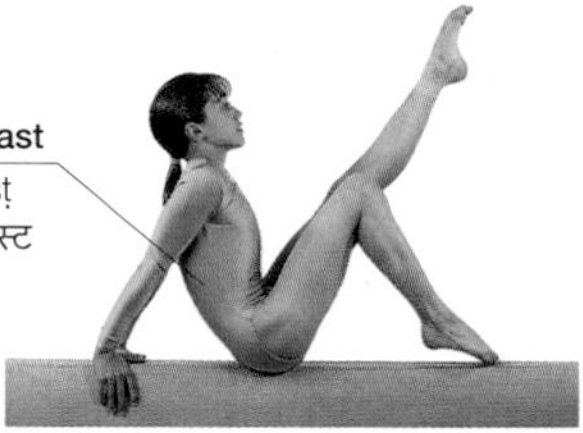

beam | bīm | बीम

mat
chaṭāī | चटाई

floor exercises
zamīnī vyāyām
ज़मीनी व्यायाम

tumble
kalābāzī
कलाबाज़ी

ribbon
fītā
फ़ीता

rhythmic gymnastics
saṅgītmaya jimnāsṭik
संगीतमय जिमनास्टिक

vocabulary • śabdāvalī • शब्दावली

horizontal bar
āṛī chhaṛ
आड़ी छड़

parallel bars
samānāntar chhaṛeṃ
समानांतर छड़ें

pommel horse
pommel horse
पॉमेल हॉर्स

asymmetric bars
asamān chhaṛeṃ
असमान छड़ें

rings
riṅg
रिंग

podium
poḍiyam
पोडियम

medals
padak
पदक

gold
svarṇ
स्वर्ण

silver
rajat
रजत

bronze
kāṃsya
कांस्य

combat sports • mall krīṛā • मल्ल क्रीड़ा

opponent
pratidvandī
प्रतिद्वंद्वी

guard
hailmeṭ
हैलमेट

glove
dastānā
दस्ताना

belt
peṭī
पेटी

tae-kwon-do | tāikvāṅḍo | ताइक्वांडो

karate | karāṭe | कराटे

judo | jūḍo | जूडो

aikido
ekāiḍo | एकाइडो

mask
mukhauṭā
मुखौटा

sword
talvār
तलवार

kendo
kenḍo | केनडो

kung fu
kuṅgfū | कुंगफ़ू

kickboxing
kik boxing | किक बॉक्सिंग

wrestling
kuśtī | कुश्ती

boxing
mukkebāzī | मुक्केबाज़ी

actions • dāṅvpeṅch • दांवपेंच

fall
girnā | गिरना

hold
pakaṛnā | पकड़ना

throw
girānā | गिराना

pin | paṭkanī
denā | पटकनी देना

kick
kik | किक

punch
mukkā | मुक्का

strike
mukkā mārnā | मुक्का मारना

jump
kūdnā | कूदना

block
prahār roknā | प्रहार रोकना

chop | nīche vār
karnā | नीचे वार करना

vocabulary • śabdāvalī • शब्दावली

boxing ring
boxing riṅg
बॉक्सिंग रिंग

boxing gloves
boxing dastāne
बॉक्सिंग–दस्ताने

mouth guard
māuth gārḍ
माउथ गार्ड

round
charaṇ
चरण

bout
śakti parīkṣā
शक्ति परीक्षा

sparring
paiṅtrebāzī
पैंतरेबाज़ी

fist
muṭṭhī
मुट्ठी

knock out
paṭkanī
पटकनी

punch bag
pañch baig
पंच बैग

black belt
blaik belṭ
ब्लैक बेल्ट

self defence
ātmrakṣā
आत्मरक्षा

martial arts
mārśal ārṭs
मार्शल आर्ट्स

capoeira
kepoirā
केपोइरा

sumo wrestling
sūmo kuśtī
सूमो कुश्ती

tai-chi
tāī chī
ताई–ची

swimming • tairākī • तैराकी

equipment • upkaraṇ • उपकरण

armband
bāzū paṭṭī | बाजू पट्टी

nose clip
noz klip
नोज़ क्लिप

goggles
chaśmā | चश्मा

float
floṭ | फ़्लोट

swimsuit
svimsūṭ | स्विमसूट

lane
len
लेन

water
pānī
पानी

starting block
ārambh sthal
आरंभ स्थल

swimming pool | taranṭāl | तरणताल

cap
ṭopī
टोपी

trunks
jāṅghiyā
जांघिया

swimmer | tairāk | तैराक

springboard
spriṅgborḍ
स्प्रिंगबोर्ड

diver
gotāḳhor
गोताख़ोर

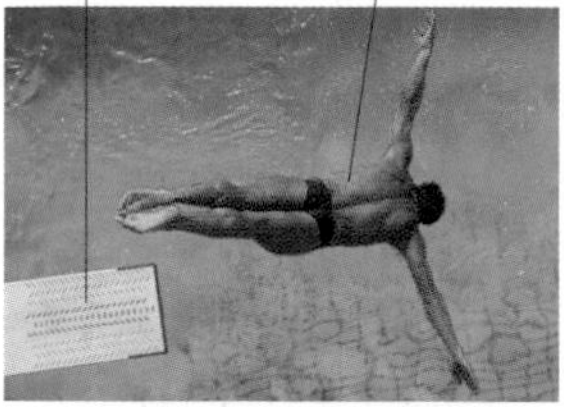
dive (v) | ḍāiv mārnā | डाइव मारना

swim (v) | tairnā | तैरना

turn | palaṭnā | पलटना

styles • śailiyāṃ • शैलियां

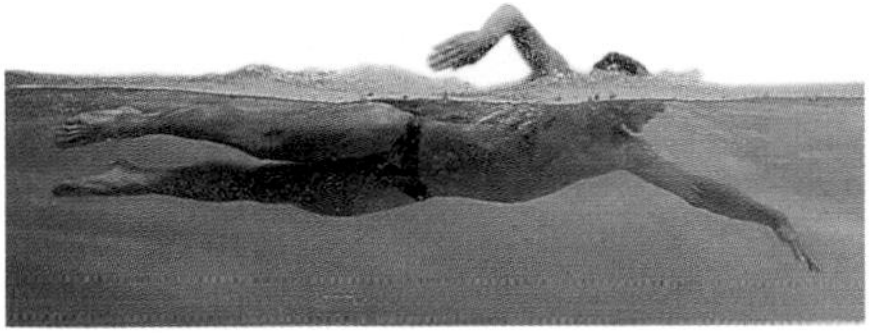

front crawl | franṭ crawl | फ़्रंट क्रॉल

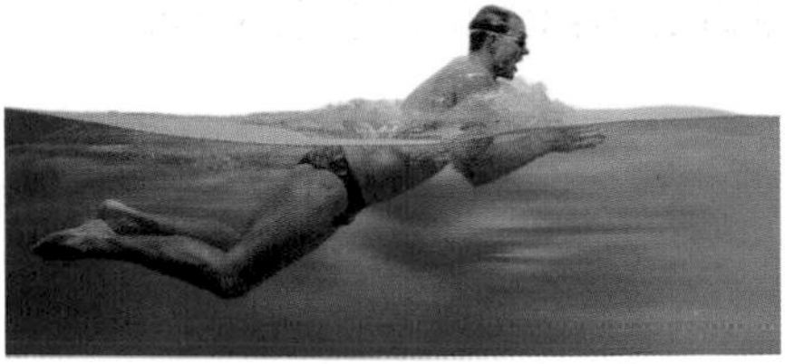

breaststroke | bresṭsṭrok | ब्रेस्टस्ट्रोक

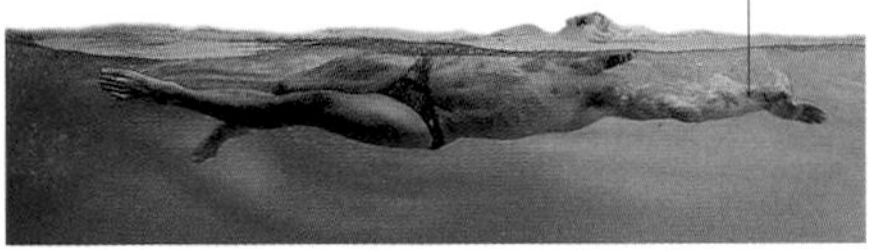
stroke
sṭrok | स्ट्रोक

backstroke | baiksṭrok | बैकस्ट्रोक

kick
kik | किक

butterfly | baṭarflāī | बटरफ़्लाई

scuba diving • skūbā ḍāiviṅg • स्कूबा डाइविंग

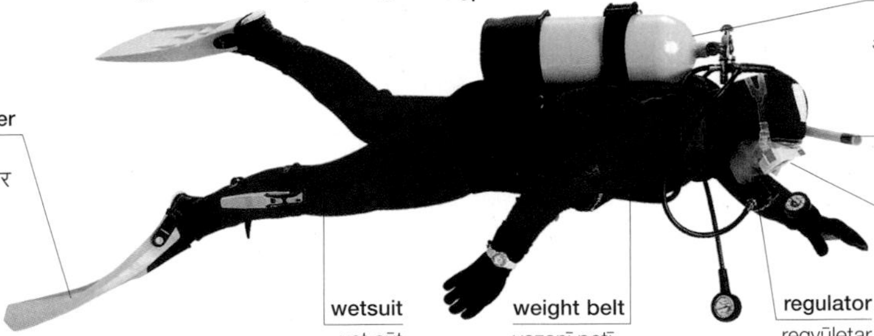
air cylinder
oxygen slienḍar
ऑक्सीज़न सिलेंडर
flipper
flipar
फ़्लिपर
snorkel
śvās nalī
श्वास नली
mask
naḳāb
नक़ाब
wetsuit
veṭ sūṭ
वेट सूट
weight belt
vazanī peṭī
वज़नी पेटी
regulator
regyūleṭar
रेग्यूलेटर

vocabulary • śabdāvalī • शब्दावली

dive ḍāiv डाइव	**racing dive** resiṅg ḍāiv रेसिंग डाइव	**lockers** lockers लॉकर्स	**water polo** water polo वॉटर पोलो	**shallow end** uthlā chhor उथला छोर	**cramp** nas charhnā नस चढ़ना
high dive ūṃchī ḍāiv ऊंची डाइव	**tread water (v)** pānī meṃ pair mārnā पानी में पैर मारना	**lifeguard** jīvan rakṣak जीवन रक्षक	**deep end** gahrā chhor गहरा छोर	**synchronized swimming** siṅkronāizḍ tairākī सिंक्रोनाइज़्ड तैराकी	**drown (v)** ḍūbnā डूबना

sailing • pāl naukāyan • पाल नौकायन

compass
kampās | कंपास

anchor
laṅgar | लंगर

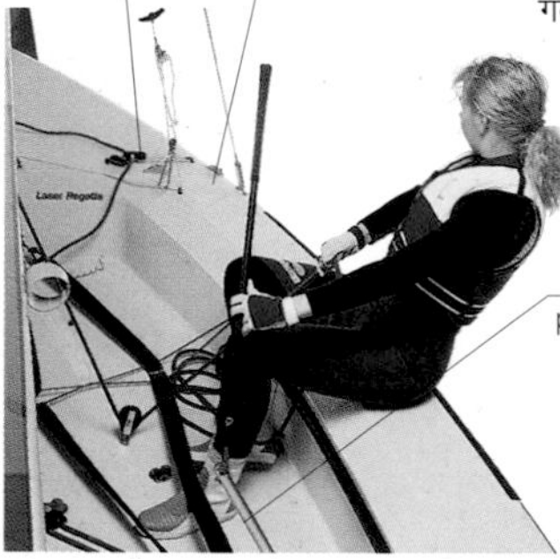
cleat
phannī
फन्नी
sidedeck
sāiḍ ḍek
साइड डेक
tiller
patvār hatthā
पतवार हत्था

navigate (v) | mārg nirdeśan karnā | मार्ग निर्देशन करना

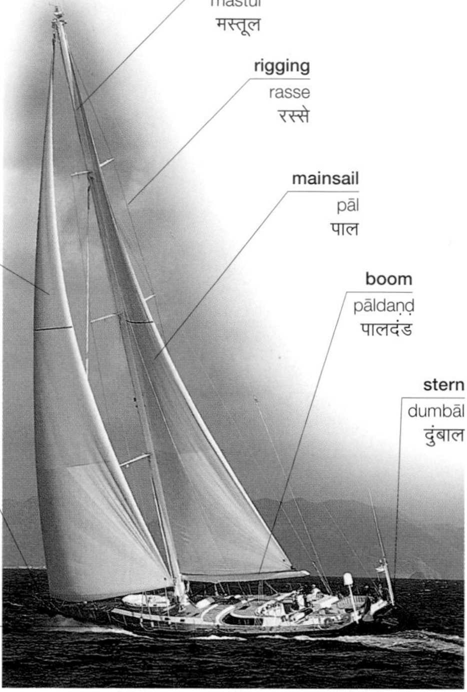
mast
mastūl
मस्तूल
rigging
rasse
रस्से
headsail
aglā pāl
अगला पाल
mainsail
pāl
पाल
boom
pāldaṇḍ
पालदंड
bow
galhī
गलही
stern
dumbāl
दुंबाल
hull
peṭā
पेटा

yacht | krīṛā naukā | क्रीड़ा–नौका

safety • surakṣā • सुरक्षा

flare
tīvr prakaś saṅketak
तीव्र प्रकाश संकेतक

lifebuoy
jīvan rakṣā ṭyūb
जीवन रक्षा ट्यूब

life jacket
rakṣā jaikeṭ
रक्षा जैकेट

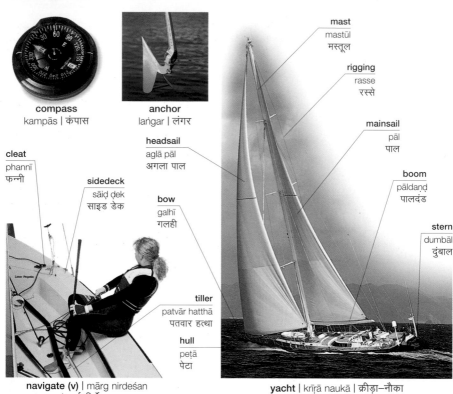

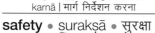

life raft
jīvan rakṣā naukā
जीवन रक्षा नौका

watersports • jalkrīṛā • जलक्रीड़ा

rower
nāvik
नाविक

oar
chappū
चप्पू

kayak
pansuiyā
पनसुइया

paddle
chhoṭā chappū
छोटा चप्पू

row (v) | nāv khenā | नाव खेना

canoeing | naukā vihār | नौका विहार

sail
pāl
पाल

windsurfer
viṇḍ sarfar
विंड सर्फ़र

board
borḍ
बोर्ड

footstrap
fuṭ strep
फुट स्ट्रेप

surfboard
sarf borḍ
सर्फ़ बोर्ड

ski
skī | स्की

surfing
sarfing | सर्फ़िंग

waterskiing | water
skīing | वॉटर स्कीइंग

speed boating | spīḍ
boṭing | स्पीड बोटिंग

windsurfing | viṇḍ sarfing | विंड सर्फ़िंग

rafting
naukāyan | नौकायन

jet skiing
jeṭ skīing | जेट स्कीइंग

---

vocabulary • śabdāvalī • शब्दावली

waterskier	**crew**	**wind**	**surf**	**sheet**	**centreboard**
water skīar	karmīdal	havā	samudrī lahreṅ	naukā pāl	senṭar borḍ
वॉटर स्कीअर	कर्मीदल	हवा	समुद्री लहरें	नौका पाल	सेंटर बोर्ड
surfer	**tack (v)**	**wave**	**rapids**	**rudder**	**capsize (v)**
sarfar	diśā badalnā	lahar	tīvr nadī	patvār	nāv ulaṭnā
सर्फ़र	दिशा बदलना	लहर	तीव्र नदी	पतवार	नाव उलटना

horse riding • ghuṛsavārī • घुड़सवारी

riding hat
haiṭ
हैट
mane
ayāl
अयाल
rider
ghuṛsavār
घुड़सवार
saddle
zīn
ज़ीन
reins
lagām
लगाम
horse
ghoṛā
घोड़ा
jodhpurs
taṅg pajāmī
तंग पजामी
tail
pūṃchh
पूंछ
girth
ghoṛe kī taṅg
घोड़े की तंग
riding boot
ghuṛsavārī ke jūte
घुड़सवारी के जूते
stirrup
rakāb
रकाब
hoof
khur
खुर

horseshoe
ghuṛnāl | घुड़नाल

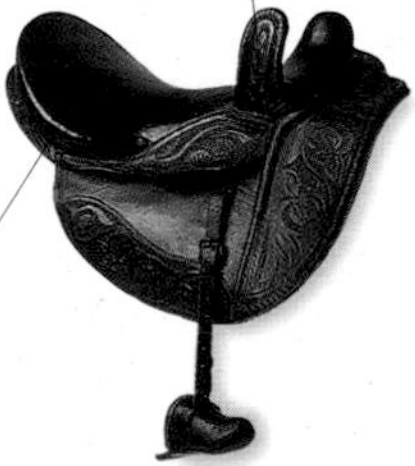
pommel
haiṇḍal
हैंडल
seat
sīṭ
सीट

side-saddle
sāiḍ zīn | साइड ज़ीन

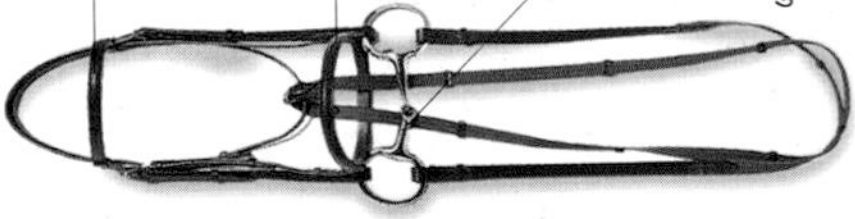
browband
sir paṭṭā
सिर–पट्टा
noseband
nakel
नकेल
bit
lagām kī
mukhrī
लगाम की
मुखरी

bridle | lagām | लगाम

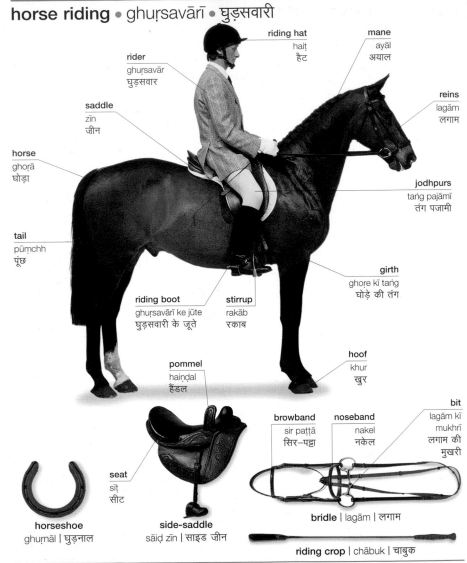

riding crop | chābuk | चाबुक

events • pratispardhā • प्रतिस्पर्धा

racehorse
dauṛ kā ghoṛā | दौड़ का घोड़ा

fence
bāṛ | बाड़

horse race
ghuṛdauṛ | घुड़दौड़

steeplechase
bādhā dauṛ | बाधा दौड़

harness race | ghoṛā gāṛī
dauṛ | घोड़ा गाड़ी दौड़

rodeo
ghuṛsavārī khel | घुड़सवारी खेल

showjumping
śo jamping | शो जंपिंग

carriage race
baggī dauṛ | बग्गी दौड़

trekking
ṭraiking | ट्रैकिंग

dressage
ghoṛā sadhānā | घोड़ा सधाना

polo
polo | पोलो

vocabulary • śabdāvalī • शब्दावली

walk	canter	jump	halter	paddock	flat race
chāl	ghoṛe kī mand chāl	kūd	rassī	ghoroṃ kā bāṛā	sīdhī dauṛ
चाल	घोड़े की मंद चाल	कूद	रस्सी	घोड़ों का बाड़ा	सीधी दौड़
trot	gallop	groom	stable	arena	racecourse
dulkī	sarpaṭ chāl	sāīs	astabal	khel kā maidān	dauṛ kā maidān
दुलकी	सरपट चाल	साईस	अस्तबल	खेल का मैदान	दौड़ का मैदान

fishing • machhlī pakaṛnā • मछली पकड़ना

weight | bhār | भार

barb
kāṃṭā
कांटा

eye
āṃkh
आंख

fishhook | machhlī huk | मछली हुक

bait | machhlī chārā | मछली–चारा

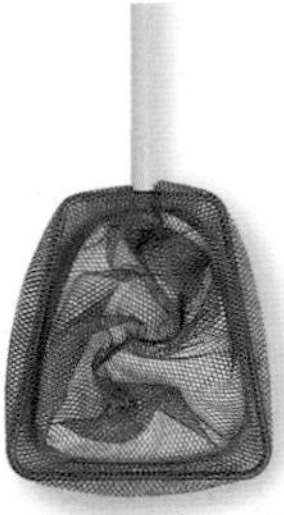

float
floṭ | फ़्लोट

fly | kṛtrim makkhī | कृत्रिम मक्खी

landing net | machhlī pakaṛne kā jāl | मछली पकड़ने का जाल

lure
chārā | चारा

tackle box
upkaraṇ baksā
उपकरण बक्सा

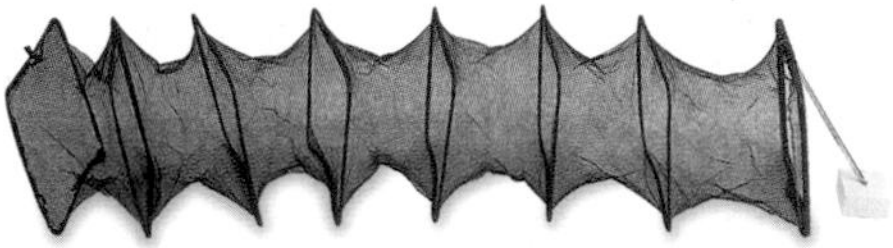

keep net | machhlī rakhne kā jāl | मछली रखने का जाल

fishing rod
machhlī pakaṛne ka kāṃṭā
मछली पकड़ने का कांटा

line
ḍorī | डोरी

reel
rīl
रील

waders
jalsah jūte
जलसह जूते

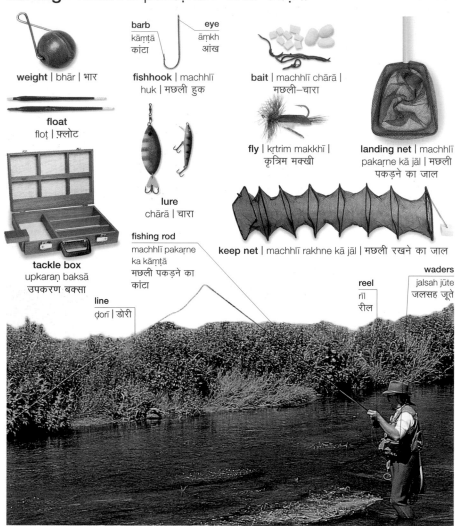

angler | machhlı pakaṛne vālā | मछली पकड़ने वाला

types of fishing • machhlī pakaṛne ke prakār • मछली पकड़ने के प्रकार

freshwater fishing | nadī meṃ machhlī pakaṛnā | नदी में मछली पकड़ना

fly fishing | makkhī se machhlī pakaṛnā | मक्खी से मछली पकड़ना

sport fishing
śaukiyā machhlī pakaṛnā
शौक़िया मछली पकड़ना

deep sea fishing
gahre samudr meṃ machhlī pakaṛnā
गहरे समुद्र में मछली पकड़ना

surfcasting | samudr kināre machhlī pakaṛnā
समुद्र किनारे मछली पकड़ना

activities • gatividhiyāṃ • गतिविधियां

cast (v)
jāl ḍālnā
जाल डालना

catch (v)
pakaṛnā
पकड़ना

reel in (v)
ḍorī khīṃchnā
डोरी खींचना

net (v)
jāl se pakaṛnā
जाल से पकड़ना

release (v)
pānī meṃ chhoṛnā
पानी में छोड़ना

vocabulary • śabdāvalī • शब्दावली

bait (v) chārā lagānā चारा लगाना	**tackle** upkaraṇ उपकरण	**waterproofs** jalvārak जलवारक	**fishing permit** fiśiṅg parmiṭ फ़िशिंग परमिट	**creel** machhlī kī ṭokrī मछली की टोकरी
bite (v) chārā khānā चारा खाना	**spool** charkhī चरखी	**pole** bāṃs बांस	**marine fishing** samudr meṃ machhlī pakaṛnā समुद्र में मछली पकड़ना	**spearfishing** bhāle se machhlī pakaṛnā भाले से मछली पकड़ना

skiing • skīiṅg • स्कीइंग

ski slope
skī slop
स्की स्लोप
chairlift
cheyarlifṭ
चेयरलिफ़्ट
cable car
kebal kār
केबल कार
ski suit
skī sūṭ
स्की सूट
ski pole
skī pol
स्की पोल
glove
dastānā
दस्ताना
ski run
skī mārg
स्की मार्ग
ski boot
skī būṭ
स्की बूट
safety barrier
surakṣā bairiyar
सुरक्षा बैरियर
ski
skī
स्की
edge
kinārā
किनारा
tip
nok
नोक
skier
skīyar | स्कीयर
les 3 vallées

events • pratispardhāeṃ • प्रतिस्पर्धाएं

downhill skiing | ḍāun hil skīiṅg | डाउन हिल स्कीइंग

gate
prārambh sthān
प्रारंभ स्थान

slalom | barfānī dauṛ | बर्फ़ानी दौड़

ski jump
skī kūd | स्की कूद

cross-country skiing
cross kanṭrī skīiṅg
क्रॉस कंट्री स्कीइंग

winter sports • śaradiya krīṛāeṃ • शरदीय क्रीड़ाएं

ice climbing
āis klāimbiṅg
आइस क्लाइम्बिंग

ice-skating
āis skeṭiṅg
आइस स्केटिंग

skate
skeṭ
स्केट

figure skating
figar skeṭiṅg
फ़िगर स्केटिंग

goggles
chaśmā
चश्मा

snowboarding
sno borḍiṅg | स्नो बोर्डिंग

bobsleigh
slej gāṛī | स्लेज गाड़ी

luge
him vāhan | हिम वाहन

snowmobile
slej | स्लेज

sledding | slej par phisalnā | स्लेज पर फिसलना

vocabulary • śabdāvalī • शब्दावली

giant slalom
baṛī barfānī dauṛ
बड़ी बर्फ़ानी दौड़

curling
karliṅg khel
कर्लिंग खेल

off-piste
ṭhos baraf par skīiṅg
ठोस बर्फ़ पर स्कीइंग

alpine skiing
ucch parvatīya skīiṅg
उच्च पर्वतीय स्कीइंग

dog sledding
dog slejiṅg
डॉग स्लेजिंग

speed skating
spīḍ skeṭiṅg
स्पीड स्केटिंग

biathlon
skīiṅg pratiyogitā
स्कीइंग प्रतियोगिता

avalanche
him skhalan
हिम स्खलन

other sports • anya khelkūd • अन्य खेलकूद

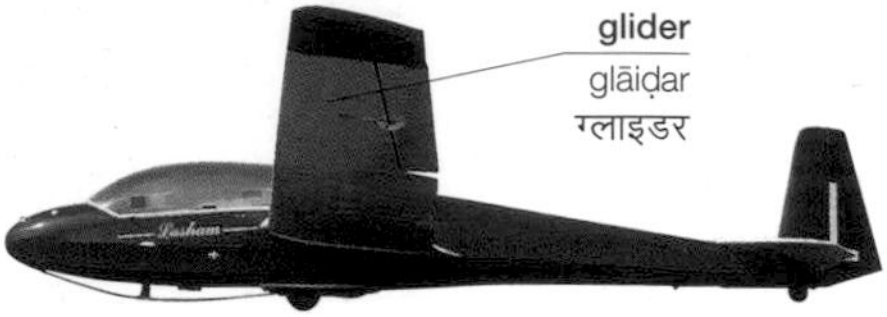

glider
glāiḍar
ग्लाइडर

hang-glider
haiṅg glāiḍar
हैंग–ग्लाइडर

gliding
glāiḍiṅg
ग्लाइडिंग

parachute
pairāśūṭ
पैराशूट

hang-gliding
haiṅg glāiḍiṅg
हैंग–ग्लाइडिंग

rope
rassī
रस्सी

rock climbing
parvatārohaṇ | पर्वतारोहण

parachuting
pairāśūṭ se utarnā | पैराशूट से उतरना

paragliding
pairāglāiḍiṅg | पैराग्लाइडिंग

skydiving
ākāśīya gotākhorī | आकाशीय ग़ोताख़ोरी

abseiling
parvat avrohaṇ | पर्वत अवरोहण

bungee jumping
bañjī kūd | बंजी कूद

rally driving
railī ḍrāiviṅg
रैली ड्राइविंग

racing driver
resiṅg ḍrāivar
रेसिंग ड्राइवर

motor racing
moṭar res
मोटर रेस

motorcross
moṭar cross
मोटर क्रॉस

motorbike racing
moṭarbāik res
मोटरबाइक रेस

skateboard
skeṭ borḍ
स्केट बोर्ड

skateboarding
skeṭborḍiṅg
स्केटबोर्डिंग

rollerskate
rolar skeṭ
रोलर स्केट

roller skating
rolar skeṭiṅg
रोलर स्केटिंग

stick
sṭik
स्टिक

lacrosse
cross balle kā khel
क्रॉस बल्ले का खेल

mask
naḳāb
नक़ाब

foil
talvār
तलवार

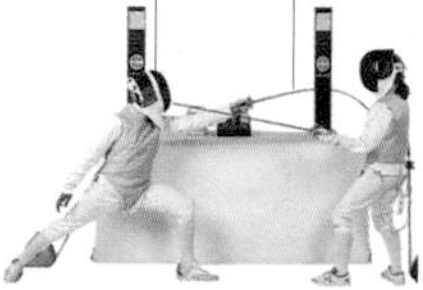

fencing
talvārbāzī
तलवारबाज़ी

pin
pin | पिन

bowling ball
boliṅg ball
बोलिंग बॉल

bowling
boliṅg | बोलिंग

bow
dhanuṣ | धनुष

arrow
tīr
तीर

quiver
tarkaś
तरकश

archery
dhanurvidyā
धनुर्विद्या

target
niśānā | निशाना

target shooting
niśānebāzī
निशानेबाज़ी

pool
pūl biliyarḍ | पूल बिलियर्ड

snooker
snūkar | स्नूकर

fitness • svasthtā • स्वस्थता

exercise bike
vyāyām
sāikil
व्यायाम
साइकिल

free weights
vazan
वज़न

bar
chhaṛ
छड़

gym machine
jim maśīn
जिम मशीन

bench
bench
बेंच

gym
jim
जिम

rowing machine
roiṅg maśīn
रोइंग मशीन

treadmill
ṭreḍmil
ट्रेडमिल

cross trainer
cross ṭrenar
क्रॉस ट्रेनर

personal trainer
nijī praśikṣak
निजी प्रशिक्षक

step machine
sṭep maśīn
स्टेप मशीन

swimming pool
taraṇtāl
तरणताल

sauna
vāṣp snān
वाष्प स्नान

exercises • vyāyām • व्यायाम

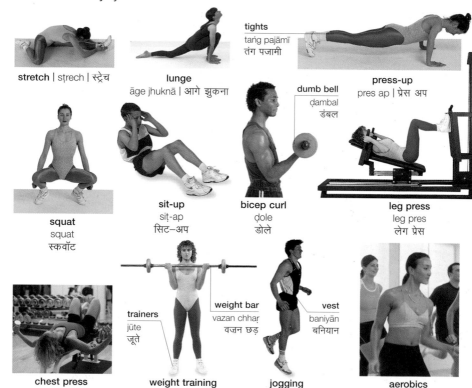

stretch | sṭrech | स्ट्रेच

lunge
āge jhuknā | आगे झुकना

tights
taṅg pajāmī
तंग पजामी

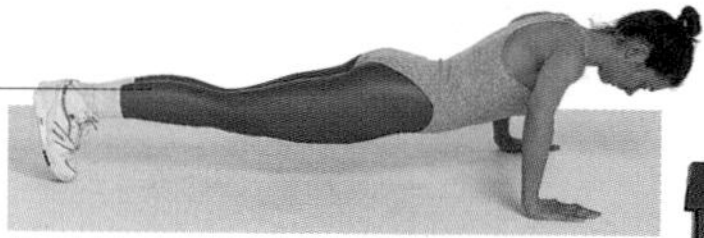

press-up
pres ap | प्रेस अप

squat
squat
स्कवॉट

sit-up
siṭ-ap
सिट–अप

dumb bell
ḍambal
डंबल

bicep curl
ḍole
डोले

leg press
leg pres
लेग प्रेस

chest press
chesṭ pres
चेस्ट प्रेस

trainers
jūte
जूते

weight bar
vazan chhaṛ
वज़न छड़

weight training
bhārottolan
भारोत्तोलन

vest
baniyān
बनियान

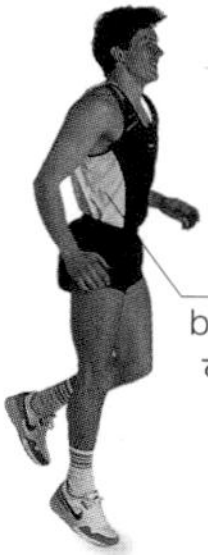

jogging
jogging
जॉगिंग

aerobics
airobiks
ऐरोबिक्स

vocabulary • śabdāvalī • शब्दावली

train (v)
abhyās karnā
अभ्यास करना

warm up (v)
māṃspeśiyāṃ garmānā
मांसपेशियां गरमाना

circuit training
sarkiṭ ṭreniṅg
सर्किट ट्रेनिंग

flex (v)
jhukānā
झुकाना

extend (v)
baṛhnā
बढ़ना

pull up (v)
pul-ap karnā
पुल–अप करना

Pilates
pilātīz
पिलातीज़

boxercise
boxing vyāyām
बॉक्सिंग व्यायाम

skipping
rassī kūd
रस्सी कूद

jog on the spot (v)
ek jagah jog karnā
एक जगह जॉग करना

leisure
manorañjan
मनोरंजन

theatre • thieṭar • थिएटर

curtain
pardā
पर्दा

wings
pārśv
पार्श्व

set
saiṭ
सैट

audience
darśak
दर्शक

orchestra
orchestra
ऑर्केस्ट्रा

stage | manch | मंच

seat
sīṭ
सीट

upper circle
ūprī dīrghā
ऊपरी दीर्घा

row
kaṭār
क़तार

box
box
बॉक्स

circle
dīrghā
दीर्घा

balcony
bālkanī
बालकनी

aisle
vīthikā
वीथिका

stalls
stalls
स्टॉल

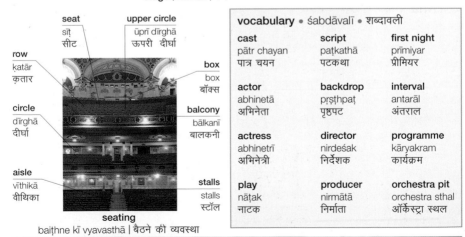

seating
baiṭhne kī vyavasthā | बैठने की व्यवस्था

cast	**script**	**first night**
pātr chayan	paṭkathā	prīmiyar
पात्र चयन	पटकथा	प्रीमियर
actor	**backdrop**	**interval**
abhinetā	pṛṣṭhpaṭ	antarāl
अभिनेता	पृष्ठपट	अंतराल
actress	**director**	**programme**
abhinetrī	nirdeśak	kāryakram
अभिनेत्री	निर्देशक	कार्यक्रम
play	**producer**	**orchestra pit**
nāṭak	nirmātā	orchestra sthal
नाटक	निर्माता	ऑर्केस्ट्रा स्थल

concert
concert | कॉन्सर्ट

musical
myūzikal | म्यूज़िकल

ballet
baile | बैले

vocabulary • śabdāvalī • शब्दावली

usher
praveśak
प्रवेशक

classical music
śāstrīya saṅgīt
शास्त्रीय संगीत

musical score
svarlipi
स्वरलिपि

soundtrack
dhvani paṭṭī
ध्वनि पट्टी

applaud (v)
talī bajānā
ताली बजाना

encore
punaḥ prastuti
पुनः प्रस्तुति

What time does it start?
yah kis samaya śurū hogā?
यह किस समय शुरू होगा?

I'd like two tickets for tonight's performance.
mujhe āj rāt ke kāryakram kī do ṭikṭeṃ chāhie
मुझे आज रात के कार्यक्रम की दो टिकटें चाहिए।

opera
opera | ऑपेरा

cinema • sinemā • सिनेमा

popcorn
popcorn
पॉपकॉर्न

box office
box office
बॉक्स ऑफ़िस

lobby
lobby
लॉबी

poster
posṭar
पोस्टर

cinema hall
sinemā hall | सिनेमा हॉल

screen
pardā | पर्दा

vocabulary • śabdāvalī • शब्दावली

comedy
comedy
कॉमेडी

thriller
thrilar
थ्रिलर

horror film
ḍarāvanī film
डरावनी फ़िल्म

western
paśchimī
पश्चिमी

romance
romāns
रोमांस

science fiction film
vijñān kathā film
विज्ञान कथा फ़िल्म

adventure
romānch kathā
रोमांच कथा

animated film
ainimeṭeḍ film
ऐनिमेटेड फ़िल्म

orchestra • vādyavṛṅd • वाद्यवृंद

strings • tantrī vādya • तंत्री वाद्य

harp
hārp
हार्प

conductor
sanchālak
संचालक

double bass
ḍabal bās
डबल बास

violin
vāyalin
वायलिन

podium
poḍiyam
पोडियम

viola
vāyolā
वायोला

cello
chelo
चेलो

score
svar lipi
स्वर लिपि

piano | piyāno | पियानो

treble clef
ṭrebal klaif
ट्रेबल क्लैफ़

note
svar
स्वर

staff
sṭāf
स्टाफ़

bass clef
bās klaif
बास क्लैफ़

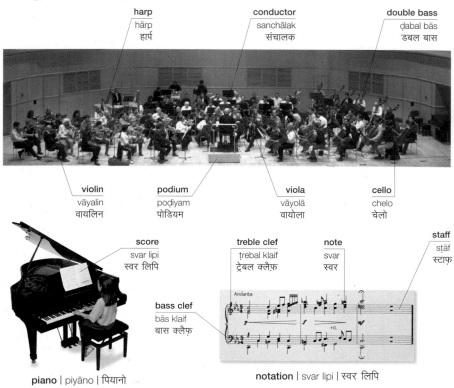

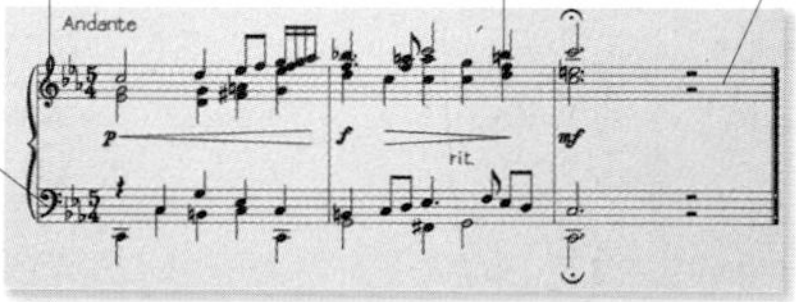

notation | svar lipi | स्वर लिपि

vocabulary • śabdāvalī • शब्दावली

overture pūrvraṅg पूर्वरंग	**sonata** sonāṭā सोनाटा	**rest** virām विराम	**sharp** ucch svar उच्च स्वर	**natural** piyāno kā śvet pardā पियानो का श्वेत पर्दा	**scale** saptak सप्तक
symphony svar saṅgati स्वर संगति	**instruments** vādya yantr वाद्य यंत्र	**pitch** svarmān स्वरमान	**flat** komal sur कोमल सुर	**bar** tālkhaṇḍ तालखंड	**baton** chhaṛī छड़ी

woodwind • kāṣṭh vādya yantr • काष्ठ वाद्य यंत्र

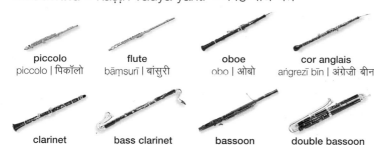

piccolo
piccolo | पिकॉलो

flute
bāṃsurī | बांसुरी

oboe
obo | ओबो

cor anglais
aṅgrezī bīn | अंग्रेज़ी बीन

clarinet
klairineṭ
क्लैरिनेट

bass clarinet
mandr klairineṭ
मंद्र क्लैरिनेट

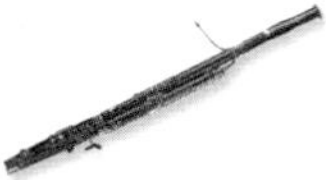
bassoon
basūn
बसून

double bassoon
ḍabal basūn
डबल बसून

saxophone
seksofon
सेक्सोफ़ोन

percussion • tāl vādya • ताल वाद्य

kettledrum
nagāṛā | नगाड़ा

gong
ghaṇṭā | घंटा

bongos
baumgo
बौंगो

snare drum
chhoṭā ḍram
छोटा ड्रम

cymbals
manjīrā | मंजीरा

tambourine
ḍaphlī | डफली

vibraphone
vāibrāfon | वाइब्राफ़ोन

triangle
ṭrāieṅgal
ट्राइएंगल

maracas
marākas
मराकस

brass • pītal ke vādya • पीतल के वाद्य

trumpet
ṭrampeṭ | ट्रम्पेट

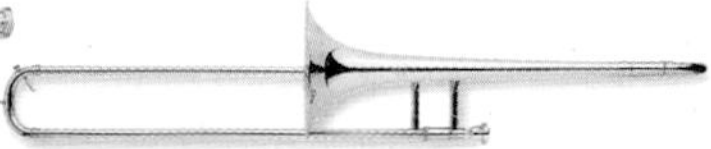
trombone
trombone | ट्रॉमबोन

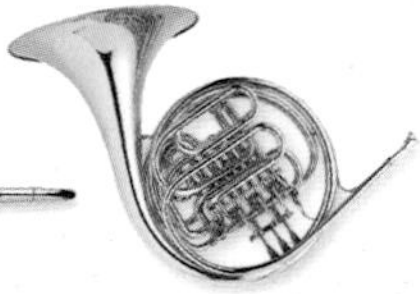
French horn
french horn | फ़्रेंच हॉर्न

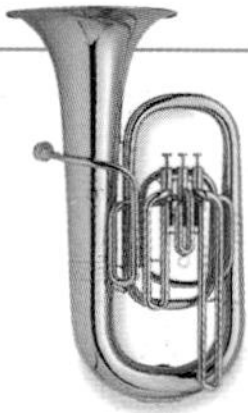
tuba
ṭyūbā | ट्यूबा

concert • concert • कॉन्सर्ट

lead singer
pramukh gāyak
प्रमुख गायक
microphone
māikrofon
माइक्रोफ़ोन
drummer
ḍramar
ड्रमर
guitarist
giṭār vādak
गिटार वादक
fans
praśansak
प्रशंसक
bass guitarist
bais giṭār vādak
बैस गिटार वादक
speaker
spīkar | स्पीकर

rock concert | rock concert | रॉक कॉन्सर्ट

instruments • vādya yantr • वाद्य यंत्र

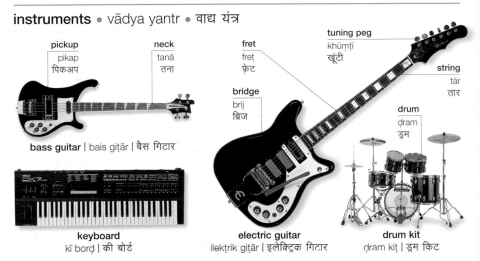

pickup
pikap
पिकअप
neck
tanā
तना

bass guitar | bais giṭār | बैस गिटार

keyboard
kī borḍ | की बोर्ड

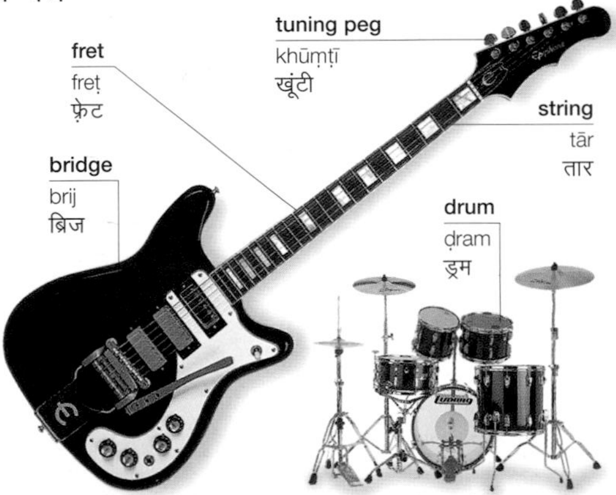
fret
freṭ
फ़्रेट
tuning peg
khūṃṭī
खूंटी
string
tār
तार
bridge
brij
ब्रिज
drum
ḍram
ड्रम

electric guitar
ilekṭrik giṭār | इलेक्ट्रिक गिटार

drum kit
ḍram kiṭ | ड्रम किट

musical styles • saṅgīt śailiyāṃ • संगीत शैलियां

jazz | jaiz | जैज़

blues | blūz | ब्लूज़

punk | paṅk | पंक

folk music
lok saṅgīt | लोक संगीत

pop | pop | पॉप

dance | dāns | डांस

rap
raip | रैप

heavy metal
rock | रॉक

classical music
śāstrīya saṅgīt | शास्त्रीय संगीत

vocabulary • śabdāvalī • शब्दावली

song	**lyrics**	**melody**	**beat**	**reggae**	**country**	**spotlight**
gānā	gīt	madhur saṅgīt	thāp	raige	kanṭrī myūzik	spot lāiṭ
गाना	गीत	मधुर संगीत	थाप	रैगे	कंट्री म्यूजिक	स्पॉट लाइट

sightseeing • sair-sapāṭā • सैर–सपाटा

tourist
paryaṭak
पर्यटक

tourist attraction
paryaṭan sthal | पर्यटन स्थल

itinerary
mārg nirdeśikā
मार्ग निर्देशिका

open-top
khulī chhat
खुली छत

tour bus | paryaṭan bas | पर्यटन बस

tour guide
paryaṭan gāiḍ
पर्यटन–गाइड

guided tour
mārgdarśit paryaṭan
मार्गदर्शित पर्यटन

statuette
laghu pratimā
लघु प्रतिमा

souvenirs
smṛti chihn
स्मृति चिह्न

vocabulary • śabdāvalī • शब्दावली

open khulā खुला	**guide book** nirdeśikā निर्देशिका	**camcorder** haiṇḍīkaim हैंडीकैम	**left** bāyāṃ बायां	**Where is...?** ... kahāṃ hai? ... कहां है?
straight on sīdh meṃ सीध में	**film closed** band बंद	**camera** kaimrā कैमरा	**right** dāyāṃ दायां	**I'm lost.** maiṃ kho gayā hūṃ मैं खो गया हूं।
film entrance fee praveś śulk प्रवेश शुल्क	**batteries** baiṭriyāṃ बैटरियां	**directions** nirdeśan निर्देशन	**film** film फ़िल्म	**Can you tell me the way to...?** kyā āp mujhe ... jāne kā rāstā batā sakte haiṃ? क्या आप मुझे ... जाने का रास्ता बता सकते हैं?

attractions • ramaṇīya sthal • रमणीय स्थल

painting
peṇṭiṅg
पेंटिंग

exhibit
pradarśit vastu
प्रदर्शित वस्तु

art gallery
kalā dīrghā | कला दीर्घा

monument
smārak | स्मारक

exhibition
pradarśanī | प्रदर्शनी

museum
saṅgrahālya | संग्रहालय

famous ruin
prasiddh khaṅḍahar
प्रसिद्ध खंडहर

historic building
aitihāsik imārat
ऐतिहासिक इमारत

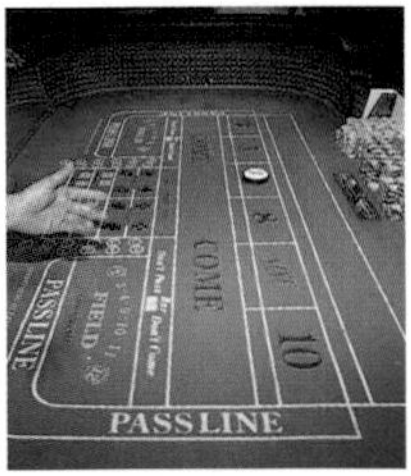

casino
juāghar | जुआघर

gardens
bāg̣ | बाग़

national park
rāṣṭrīya udyān | राष्ट्रीय उद्यान

information • jānkarī • जानकारी

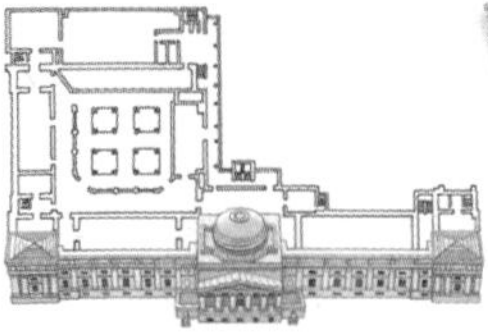

floor plan
bhavan nak̠śā | भवन नक़्शा

map
nak̠śā | नक़्शा

times
samaya
समय

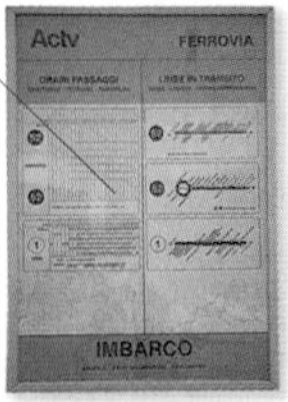

timetable
samaya sāriṇī
समय सारिणी

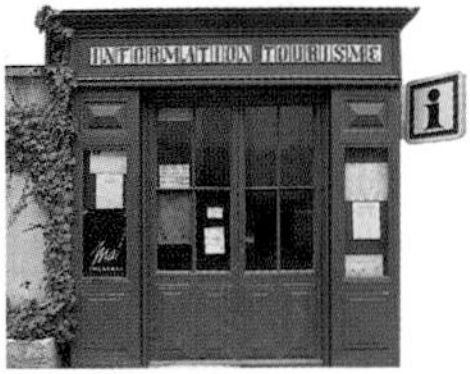

tourist information
paryaṭak sūchnā kendr
पर्यटक सूचना केंद्र

outdoor activities • bāhrī gatividhiyāṃ • बाहरी गतिविधियां

footpath
paidal rāstā
पैदल रास्ता

sundial
dhūp gharī
धूप घड़ी

café
kaife
कैफ़े

park | udyān | उद्यान

grass
ghās
घास

bench
bench
बेंच

formal gardens
bagīchā
बग़ीचा

roller coaster
rolar kosṭar
रोलर कोस्टर

fairground
melā sthal | मेला स्थल

theme park
thīm pārk | थीम पार्क

safari park
safārī pārk | सफ़ारी पार्क

zoo
chiṛiyāghar | चिड़ियाघर

activities • gatividhiyāṃ • गतिविधियां

cycling | sāikil chalānā | साइकिल चलाना

jogging jogging | जॉगिंग

skateboarding | skeṭ borḍiṅg | स्केट बोर्डिंग

rollerblading | rolar bleḍiṅg | रोलर ब्लेडिंग

bird watching | pakṣī nihārnā | पक्षी निहारना

bridle path
aśv mārg
अश्व मार्ग

horse riding ghuṛsavārī | घुड़सवारी

hiking padyātrā | पदयात्रा

hamper
ṭokrī
टोकरी

picnic piknik | पिकनिक

playground • khel kā maidān • खेल का मैदान

sandpit ret kā akhāṛā रेत का अखाड़ा

paddling pool kṛtrim tālāb कृत्रिम तालाब

swings jhūlā | झूला

climbing frame sīṛhīnumā jhūlā | सीढ़ीनुमा झूला

seesaw | seesaw | सीसॉ

slide | phisal paṭṭī | फिसल पट्टी

beach • taṭ • तट

hotel
hoṭal
होटल
beach umbrella
taṭīya chhātā
तटीय छाता
beach hut
taṭīya jhopṛī
तटीय झोपड़ी
sand
ret
रेत
wave
lahar
लहर
sea
samudr
समुद्र

beach bag
bīch thailā
बीच थैला
bikini
biknī
बिकनी

sunbathe (v) | sūrya snān karnā | सूर्य स्नान करना

lifeguard
jīvan rakṣak
जीवन रक्षक

lifeguard tower
jīvan rakṣak ṭāvar
जीवन रक्षक टावर

windbreak | havā rodhak | हवा रोधक

promenade | vihār sthal | विहार स्थल

deck chair | ḍaik kursī | डैक कुर्सी

sunglasses | dhūp kā chaśmā | धूप का चश्मा

sunhat
haiṭ | हैट

suntan lotion | sanṭain lośan | सनटैन लोशन

sunblock | san block | सन ब्लॉक

beach ball
bīch ball | बीच बॉल

rubber ring | rabaṛ kī ṭyūb | रबड़ की ट्यूब

beach towel
bīch tauliyā | बीच तौलिया

swimsuit
tairākī sūṭ
तैराकी सूट
spade
khurpī
खुरपी
bucket
ṭokrī
टोकरी
sandcastle
ret kā mahal
रेत का महल
shell
sīp
सीप

camping • śivir lagānā • शिविर लगाना

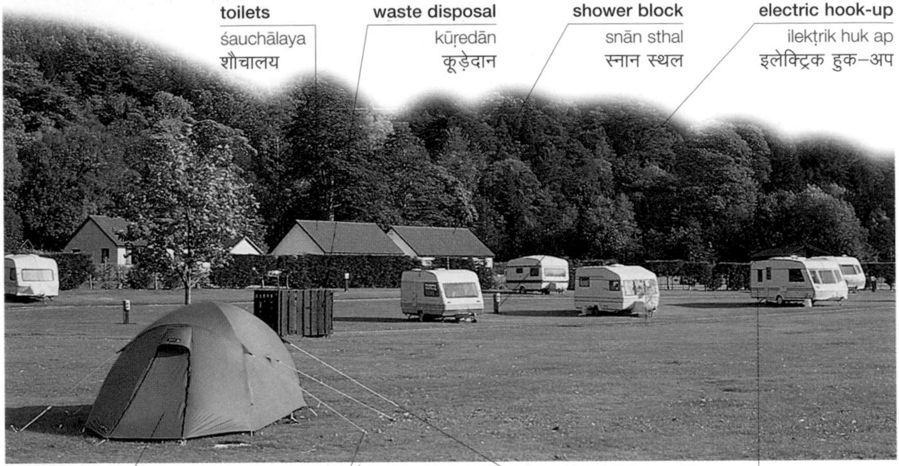
toilets
śauchālaya
शौचालय
waste disposal
kūṛedān
कूड़ेदान
shower block
snān sthal
स्नान स्थल
electric hook-up
ilekṭrik huk ap
इलेक्ट्रिक हुक–अप
flysheet
dvār pardā
द्वार पर्दा
tent peg
khūṃṭā
खूंटा
guy rope
rassī
रस्सी
caravan
gāṛī
गाड़ी

campsite
śivir sthal | शिविर स्थल

vocabulary • śabdāvalī • शब्दावली

camp (v)
śivir lagānā
शिविर लगाना

site manager's office
sāiṭ prabandhak kāryālaya
साइट प्रबंधक कार्यालय

pitches available
sthān uplabdh
स्थान उपलब्ध

full
pūrā
पूरा

pitch
sthān
स्थान

pitch a tent (v)
tambū gāṛnā
तंबू गाड़ना

tent pole
tambū kā khambhā
तंबू का खंभा

camp bed
safrī palaṅg
सफ़री पलंग

picnic bench
piknik bench
पिकनिक बेंच

hammock
jhūlā
झूला

camper van
śivir vāhan
शिविर वाहन

trailer
ṭrelar
ट्रेलर

charcoal
kacchā koyalā
कच्चा कोयला

firelighter
āg jalāne kā upkaraṇ
आग जलाने का उपकरण

light a fire (v)
āg jalānā
आग जलाना

campfire
alāv
अलाव

frame
frem
फ़्रेम

ground sheet
darī
दरी

backpack
piṭṭhū
पिट्ठू

vacuum flask
vaikyūm flāsk
वैक्यूम फ़्लास्क

water bottle
pānī kī botal
पानी की बोतल

tent
śivir | शिविर

insect repellent
macchhar avrodhak
मच्छर अवरोधक

torch
torch | टॉर्च

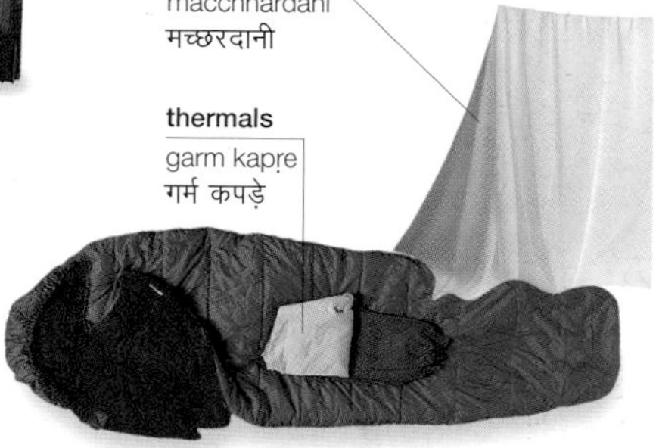

mosquito net
macchhardānī
मच्छरदानी

thermals
garm kapṛe
गर्म कपड़े

sleeping bag
slīpiṅg baig | स्लीपिंग बैग

walking boots
jūte | जूते

waterproofs
waterproofs | वॉटरप्रूफ़

camping stove
safrī sṭov | सफ़री स्टोव

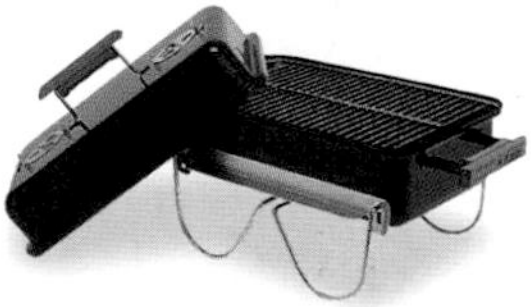

barbecue
gril | ग्रिल

sleeping mat
gaddā
गद्दा

air mattress | havā bharā gaddā | हवा भरा गद्दा

home entertainment • gharelū manorañjan • घरेलू मनोरंजन

personal CD player
parsnal CD pleyar
पर्सनल सीडी प्लेयर

mini disk recorder
minī ḍisk recorder
मिनी डिस्क रिकॉर्डर

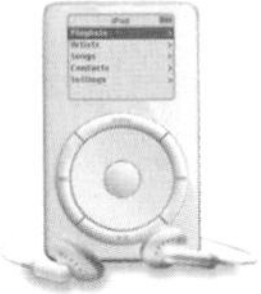

MP3 player
MP3 pleyar
एम पी थ्री प्लेयर

DVD disk
DVD ḍisk
डीवीडी डिस्क

DVD player
DVD pleyar
डीवीडी प्लेयर

record player
record pleyar
रिकॉर्ड प्लेयर

CD player
CD pleyar
सीडी प्लेयर

radio
reḍiyo
रेडियो

amplifier
emplīfāyar
एंप्लीफ़ायर

headphones
haiḍfon
हैडफ़ोन

stand
sṭainḍ
स्टैंड

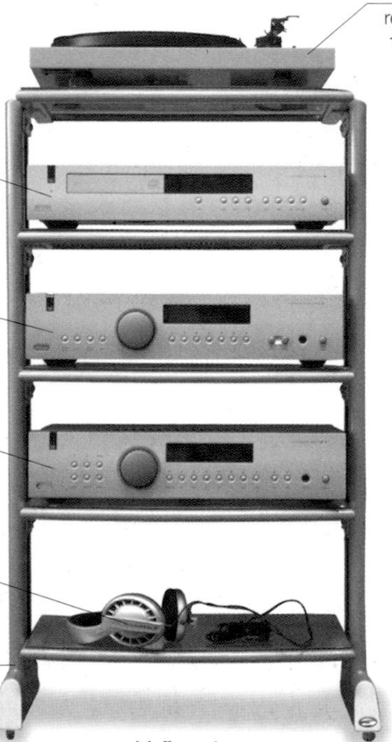

hi-fi system
haɪ faɪ sisṭam | हाई–फ़ाई सिस्टम

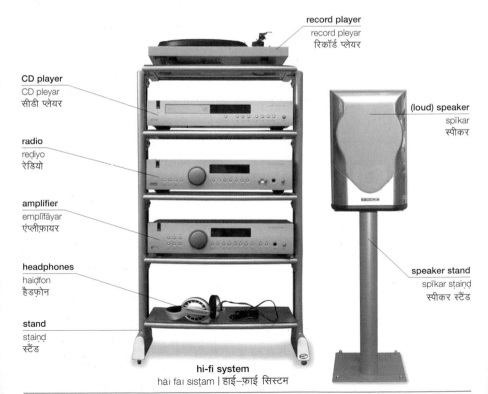

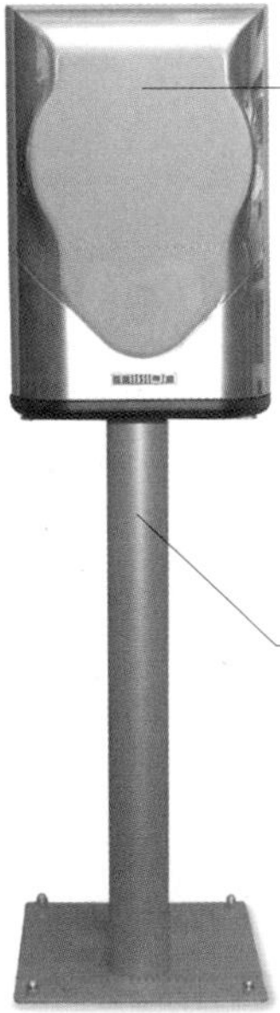

(loud) speaker
spīkar
स्पीकर

speaker stand
spīkar sṭainḍ
स्पीकर स्टैंड

video tape
vīḍiyo ṭep
वीडियो टेप

video recorder
vīḍiyo recorder | वीडियो रिकॉर्डर

screen
skrīn
स्क्रीन
eyecup
aī kap
आई कप

camcorder
haiṇḍīkaim | हैंडीकैम

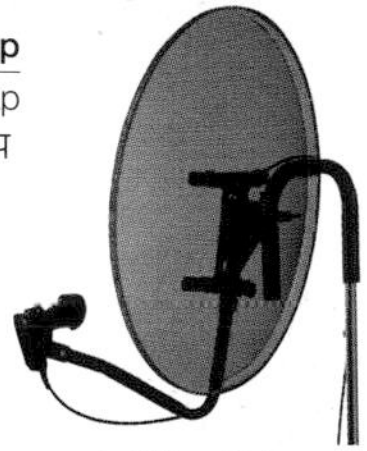

satellite dish
upgrah ḍiś | उपग्रह डिश

widescreen television
baṛe skrīn vālā ṭīvī
बड़े स्क्रीन वाला टीवी
console
console
कॉन्सोल
controller
kanṭrolar
कंट्रोलर

video game | vīḍiyo gem | वीडियो गेम

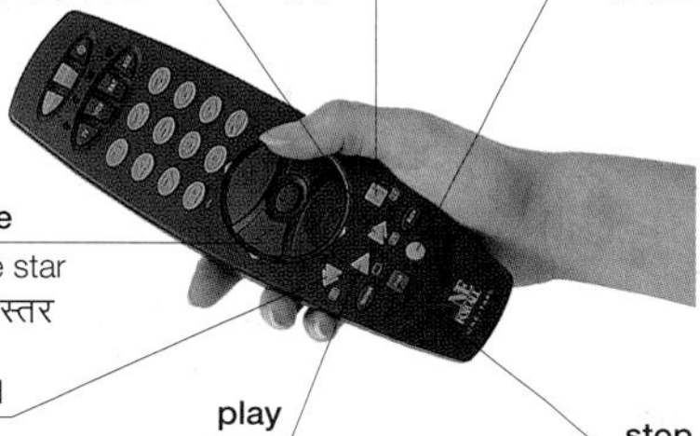
fast forward
fāsṭ forward
फ़ास्ट फ़ॉरवर्ड
pause
pause
पॉज़
record
record
रिकॉर्ड
volume
volume star
वॉल्यूम स्तर
rewind
rivāiṇḍ
रिवाइंड
play
ple
प्ले
stop
stop
स्टॉप

remote control
rimoṭ kanṭrol | रिमोट कंट्रोल

vocabulary • śābdāvalī • शब्दावली

compact disc
compact ḍisk
कॉम्पेक्ट डिस्क

cassette tape
kaiseṭ ṭep
कैसेट टेप

cassette player
kaiseṭ pleyar
कैसेट प्लेयर

feature film
fīchar film
फ़ीचर फ़िल्म

advertisement
vijñāpan
विज्ञापन

digital
ḍijīṭal
डिजीटल

programme
kāryakram
कार्यक्रम

stereo
sṭīriyo
स्टीरियो

cable television
kebal ṭelīvizan
केबल टेलीविज़न

change channel (v)
chainal badalnā
चैनल बदलना

tune the radio (v)
reḍiyo saiṭ karnā
रेडियो सैट करना

watch television (v)
ṭīvī dekhnā
टीवी देखना

turn the television on (v)
ṭelīvizan chalānā
टेलीविज़न चलाना

turn the television off (v)
ṭelīvizan band karnā
टेलीविज़न बंद करना

pay per view channel
prati chainal bhugtān
प्रति चैनल भुगतान

photography • foṭogrāfī • फ़ोटोग्राफ़ी

frame counter
frem kāunṭar
फ़्रेम काउंटर
flash
flaiś
फ़्लैश
aperture dial
aparchar niyantrak
अपर्चर नियंत्रक
shutter release
śaṭar rilīz
शटर रिलीज़
shutter-speed dial
śaṭar-spīḍ ḍāyal
शटर–स्पीड डायल
lens
lains
लैंस

SLR camera | SLR kaimrā | एस एल आर कैमरा

filter
filṭar | फ़िल्टर

lens caps
lains kaip | लैंस कैप

flash gun
flaiś gan | फ़्लैश गन

lightmeter
lāiṭmīṭar | लाइटमीटर

zoom lens
zūm lains | ज़ूम लैंस

tripod
tipāyā sṭaiṇḍ | तिपाया स्टैंड

types of camera • kaimre ke prakār • कैमरे के प्रकार

digital camera
ḍijīṭal kaimrā
डिजीटल कैमरा

APS camera
APS kaimrā
ए पी एस कैमरा

instant camera
insṭenṭ kaimrā
इंस्टेंट कैमरा

disposable camera
ḍispozebal kaimrā
डिस्पोजेबल कैमरा

photograph (v) • foṭo khīṃchnā • फ़ोटो खींचना

film spool
film rīl
फ़िल्म रील

film
film | फ़िल्म

focus (v) | kendrit karnā | केंद्रित करना

develop (v)
film dhonā | फ़िल्म धोना

negative
negeṭiv | नेगेटिव

landscape
prakṛtik dṛśya
प्राकृतिक दृश्य

portrait
vyakti chitr
व्यक्ति चित्र

photograph | tasvīr | तस्वीर

photo album
foṭo elbam | फ़ोटो एल्बम

photo frame | foṭo frem | फ़ोटो फ़्रेम

problems • samasyāeṃ • समस्याएं

underexposed
kam udbhāsit
कम उद्भासित

overexposed
atyadhik udbhāsit
अत्यधिक उद्भासित

out of focus | fokas se bāhar | फ़ोकस से बाहर

red eye
raid āī | रैड आई

vocabulary • śabdāvalī • शब्दावली

viewfinder
dṛśyadarśī
दृश्यदर्शी

camera case
kaimrā kes
कैमरा केस

exposure
udbhāsan
उद्भासन

darkroom
ḍārk rūm
डार्क रूम

print
foṭo prati
फ़ोटो प्रति

mat
khurdurā
खुरदुरा

gloss
chiknā
चिकना

enlargement
foṭo baṛī karānā
फ़ोटो बड़ी कराना

I'd like this film processed
maiṃ ye rīl dhulvānā chāhtī hūṃ
मैं ये रील धुलवाना चाहती हूं।

games • khel • खेल

chessboard
bisāt
बिसात

black
kālā
काला

white
safed
सफ़ेद

queen
vazīr
वज़ीर

king
rājā
राजा

bishop
ūṃṭ
ऊंट

pawn
pyādā
प्यादा

knight
ghoṛā
घोड़ा

rook
hāthī
हाथी

chess
śatranj | शतरंज

square
ḳhānā
ख़ाना

piece
goṭī
गोटी

draughts | draughts | ड्रॉट्स

tile
ṭāil
टाइल

scrabble | skraibal | स्क्रैबल

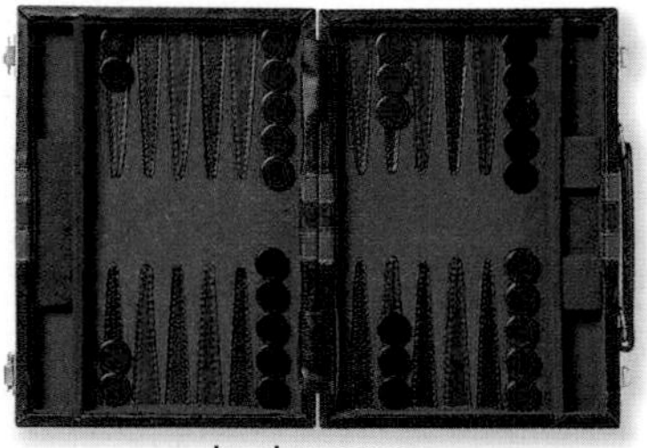

backgammon
balk galman | बैक गैमन

dice
pāsā
पासा

counter
mohrā | मोहरा

monopoly
monopolī
मोनोपोली

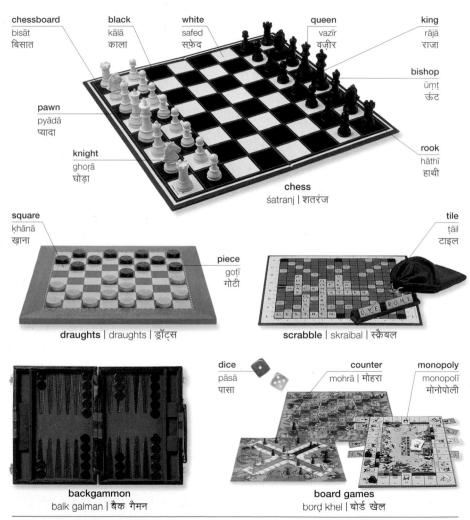

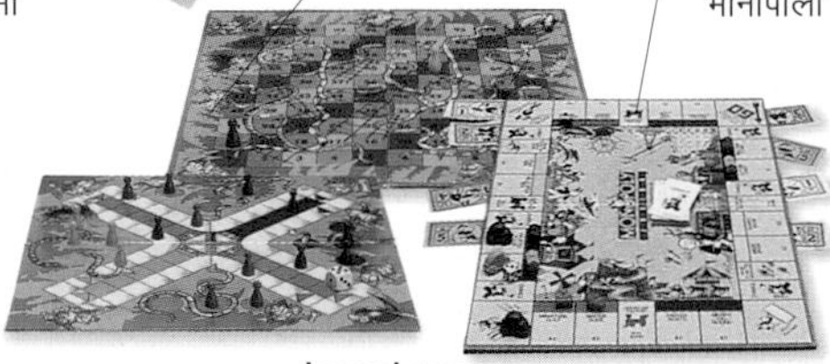

board games
borḍ khel | बोर्ड खेल

stamp collecting
ḍāk ṭikaṭ saṅgrah
डाक टिकट संग्रह

jigsaw puzzle | chitrakhaṇḍ pahelī | चित्रखंड पहेली

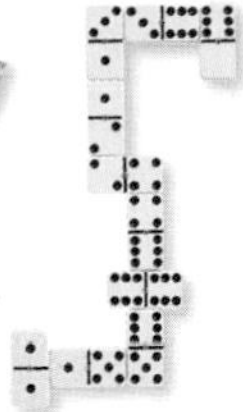

dominoes
ḍominos | डोमिनोस

dartboard
ḍārṭ borḍ
डार्टबोर्ड

bullseye
lakṣya
लक्ष्य

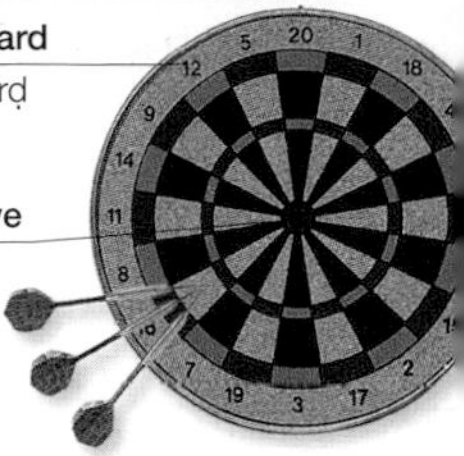

darts
ḍārṭs | डार्ट्स

joker
jokar
जोकर

jack
gulām
ग़ुलाम

queen
begam
बेगम

king
bādśāh
बादशाह

ace
ikkā
इक्का

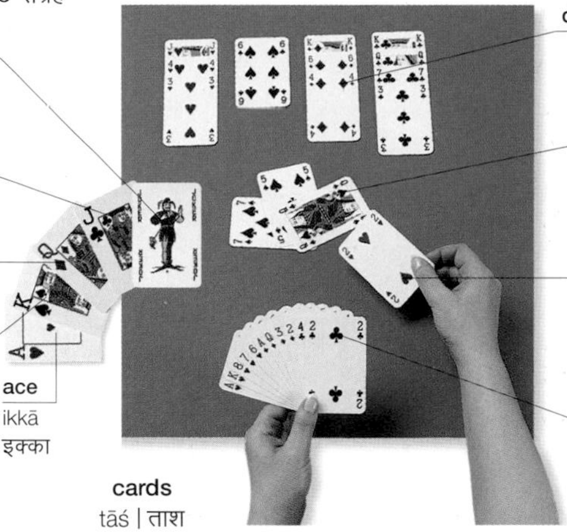

diamond
īnṭ
ईंट

spade
hukum
हुकुम

heart
pān
पान

club
chiṛī
चिड़ी

cards
tāś | ताश

shuffle (v)
tāś pheṃṭnā | ताश फेंटना

deal (v)
patte bāṃṭnā | पत्ते बांटना

vocabulary • śabdāvalī • शब्दावली

move chāl चाल	**win (v)** jītnā जीतना	**loser** parājit पराजित	**point** nambar नंबर	**bridge** brij ब्रिज	**Roll the dice.** pāsā pheṃko पासा फेंको
play (v) khelnā खेलना	**winner** vijetā विजेता	**game** khel खेल	**score** arjit aṃk अर्जित अंक	**pack of cards** tāś kī gaḍḍī ताश की गड्डी	**Whose turn is it?** kiskī bārī hai? किसकी बारी है?
player khilāṛī खिलाड़ी	**lose (v)** hārnā हारना	**bet** śart शर्त	**poker** pokar पोकर	**suit** tāś raṅg ताश रंग	**It's your move.** ab tumhārī chāl hai अब तुम्हारी चाल है।

arts and crafts 1 • kalā aur śilp 1 • कला और शिल्प 1

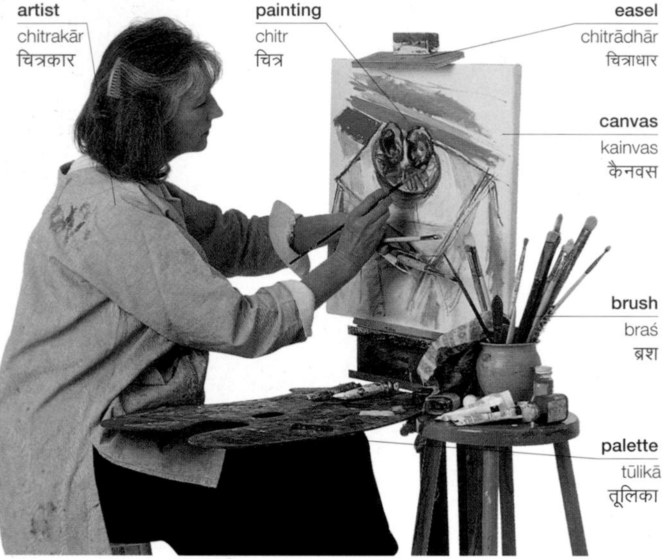

painting | chitrakārī | चित्रकारी

colours • raṅg • रंग

red lāl | लाल	**blue** nīlā | नीला	**yellow** pīlā | पीला	**green** harā | हरा
orange nāraṅgī | नारंगी	**purple** baiṅganī | बैंगनी	**white** safed | सफ़ेद	**black** kālā | काला
grey slēṭī | स्लेटी	**pink** gulābī | गुलाबी	**brown** bhūrā | भूरा	**indigo** nīl | नील

paints • raṅg • रंग

oil paints
tail raṅg | तैल रंग

watercolour paint
pānī ke raṅg | पानी के रंग

pastels
raṅgīn khaṛiyā | रंगीन खड़िया

acrylic paint
aikrilīk raṅg | ऐक्रिलीक रंग

poster paint
pōsṭar raṅg | पोस्टर रंग

other crafts • anya kalāeṃ • अन्य कलाएं

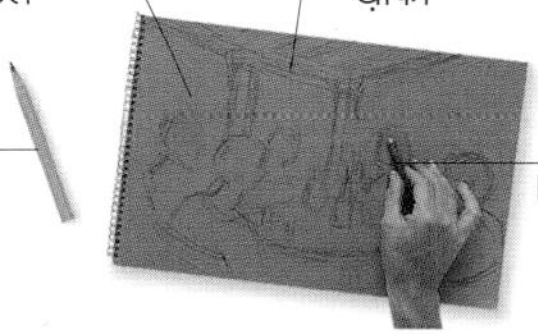
sketch pad
rekhāṅkan paṭal
रेखांकन पटल
sketch
ḳhākā
ख़ाका
pencil
pensil
पेंसिल
charcoal
koyalā battī
कोयला बत्ती

drawing | rekhāṅkan | रेखांकन

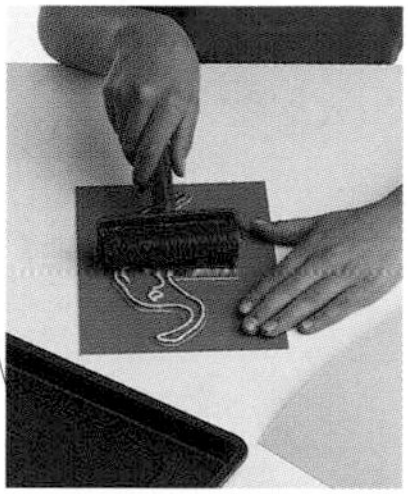
ink
syāhī
स्याही

printing
chhapāī | छपाई

engraving
utkīrṇan | उत्कीर्णन

stone
patthar
पत्थर
mallet
muṅgrā
मुंगरा

sculpting
mūrti śilp | मूर्ति शिल्प

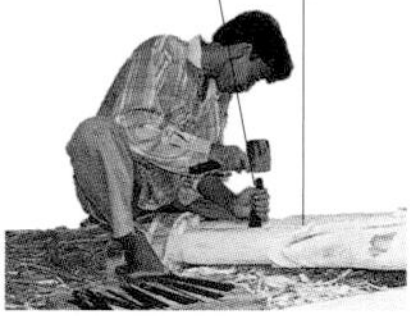
chisel
chhainī
छैनी
wood
lakṛī
लकड़ी

woodworking
kāṣṭh-kalā | काष्ठ–कला

modelling tool
hastkalā upkaraṇ
हस्तकला उपकरण
potter's wheel
chāk
चाक
clay
chiknī miṭṭī
चिकनी
मिट्टी

pottery
kumhār karm | कुम्हार कर्म

glue
gond
गोंद
cardboard
gattā
गत्ता

collage | kolāj | कोलाज

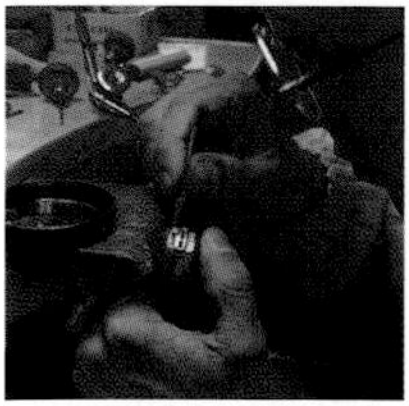

jewellery making | ābhūṣaṇ-nirmāṇ | आभूषण निर्माण

papier-mâché | paipya māśe | पैप्य माशे

origami
aurigāmī | औरिगामी

model making | model banānā | मॉडल बनाना

arts and crafts 2 • kalā aur śilp 2 • कला और शिल्प 2

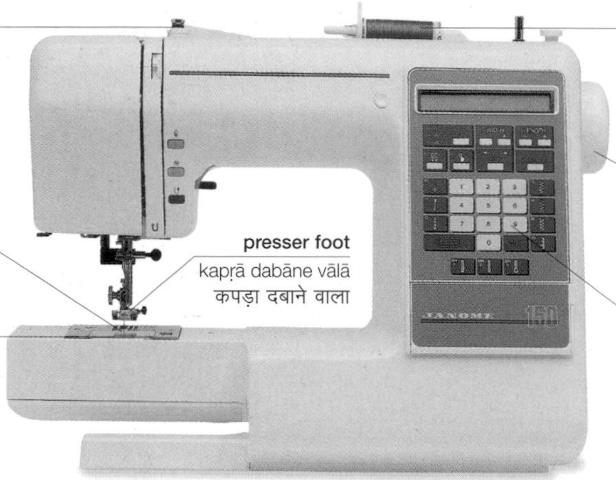

thread guide
dhāgā
धागा

needle
sūī
सूई

presser foot
kapṛā dabāne vālā
कपड़ा दबाने वाला

needle plate
sūī ke nīche
kī pattī
सूई के नीचे
की पत्ती

thread reel
dhāge kī rīl
धागे की रील

balance wheel
pahiyā
पहिया

stitch selector
silāī chayan baṭan
सिलाई चयन बटन

sewing machine
silāī maśīn | सिलाई मशीन

scissors
ḳaiṃchī
क़ैंची

pattern
ḳhākā
ख़ाका

tape measure
inchṭep
इंचटेप

material
kapṛā | कपड़ा

pincushion
pinkuśan
पिनकुशन

pin
pin
पिन

sewing basket
silāī kī ṭokrī | सिलाई की टोकरी

thread
dhāgā
धागा

bobbin
phirkī
फिरकी

eye
āī | आई

hook
huk
हुक

thimble
aṃguśtānā
अंगुश्ताना

tailor's chalk
darzī kā chalk
दर्ज़ी का चॉक

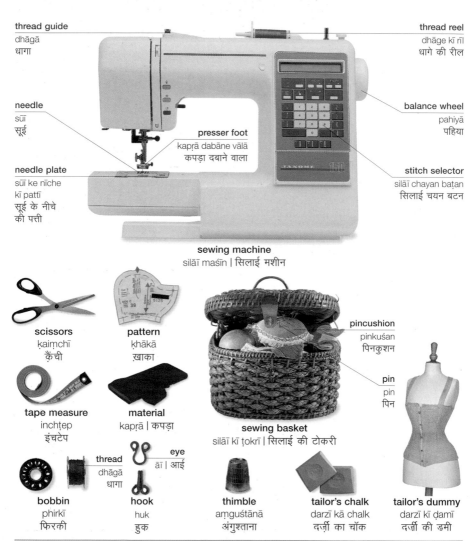

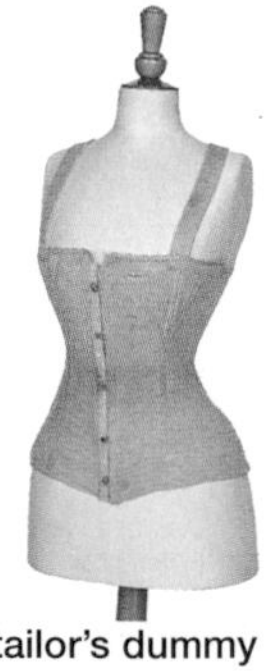

tailor's dummy
darzī kī ḍamī
दर्ज़ी की डमी

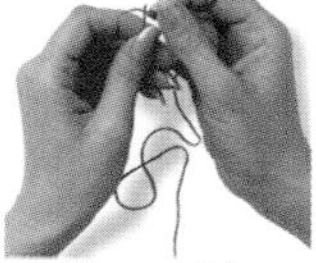

thread (v)
dhāgā ḍālnā
धागा डालना

stitch
bakhiyā
बखिया

sew (v)
silnā
सिलना

darn (v)
rafū karnā
रफ़ू करना

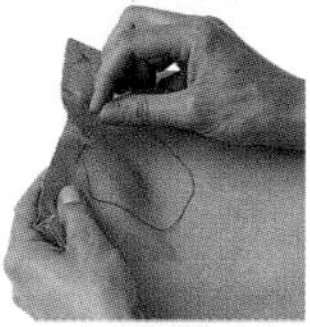

tack (v)
ṭāṃknā
टांकना

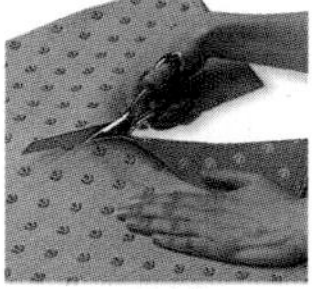

cut (v)
kāṭnā
काटना

needlepoint
sūī kī nok
सूई की नोक

embroidery
kaṛhāī
कढ़ाई

crochet hook
krośiyā huk
क्रोशिया हुक

crochet
krośiyā
क्रोशिया

macramé
jhālar
झालर

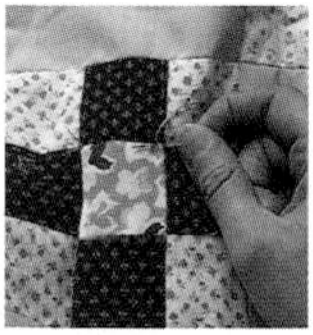

patchwork
paiband
पैबंद

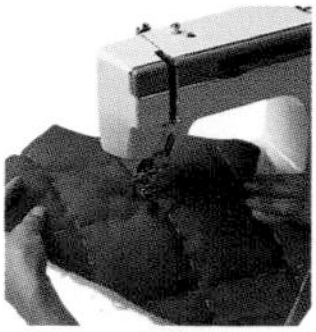

quilting
parat lagānā
परत लगाना

lace bobbin
les bobbin
लेस बॉबिन

lace-making
les banānā
लेस बनाना

loom
karghā
करघा

weaving
bunnā
बुनना

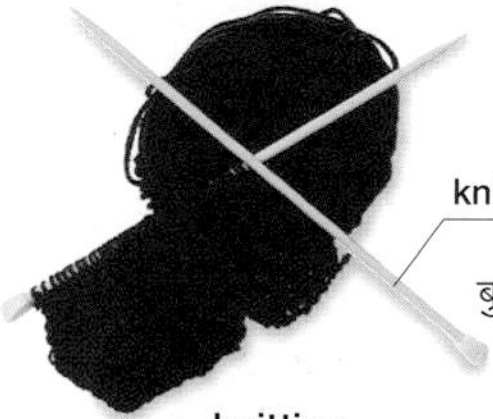

knitting needle
bunne kī slāī
बुनने की सलाई

knitting
bunāī | बुनाई

wool
ūn
ऊन

skein
lacchhī | लच्छी

vocabulary • śabdāvalī • शब्दावली

unpick (v)
udheṛnā
उधेड़ना

fabric
kapṛā
कपड़ा

cotton
sūtī kapṛā
सूती कपड़ा

linen
linen
लिनेन

polyester
polyester
पॉलीएस्टर

nylon
nāyalon
नायलोन

silk
reśam
रेशम

designer
ḍizāinar
डिज़ाइनर

fashion
faiśan
फ़ैशन

zip
zip
ज़िप

environment

paryāvaraṇ

पर्यावरण

space • antarikṣ • अंतरिक्ष

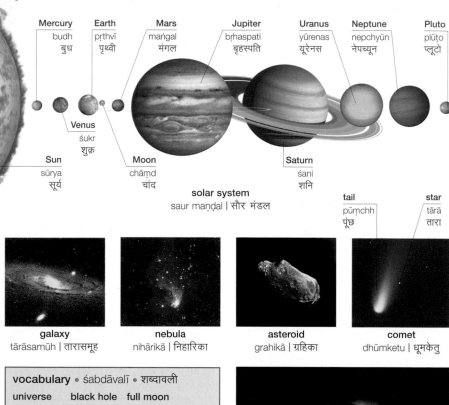

Mercury
budh
बुध
Earth
pṛthvī
पृथ्वी
Mars
maṅgal
मंगल
Jupiter
bṛhaspati
बृहस्पति
Uranus
yūrenas
यूरेनस
Neptune
nepchyūn
नेपच्यून
Pluto
plūṭo
प्लूटो
Venus
śukr
शुक्र
Sun
sūrya
सूर्य
Moon
chāṃd
चांद
Saturn
śani
शनि

solar system
saur maṇḍal | सौर मंडल

galaxy
tārāsamūh | तारासमूह

nebula
nihārikā | निहारिका

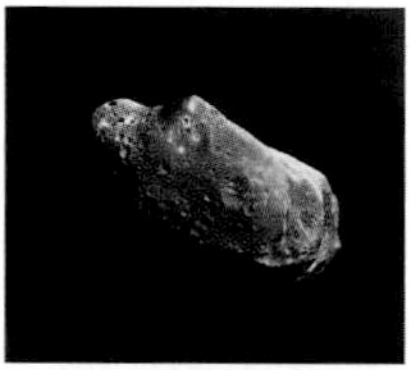

asteroid
grahikā | ग्रहिका

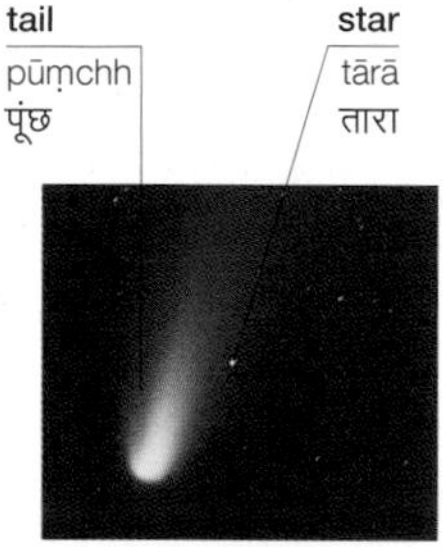
tail
pūṃchh
पूंछ
star
tārā
तारा

comet
dhūmketu | धूमकेतु

vocabulary • śabdāvalī • शब्दावली

universe
brahamāṇḍ
ब्रह्मांड

black hole
blaik hol
ब्लैक होल

full moon
pūrā chāṃd
पूरा चांद

orbit
kakṣā
कक्षा

planet
grah
ग्रह

crescent moon
ardhchandr
अर्धचंद्र

gravity
gurutv
गुरुत्व

meteor
ulkā
उल्का

new moon
pratipadā kā chāṃd
प्रतिपदा का चांद

eclipse | grahan | ग्रहण

space exploration • antarikṣ anveṣaṇ • अंतरिक्ष अन्वेषण

space shuttle
antarikṣ yān
अंतरिक्ष यान

booster
būsṭar
बूस्टर

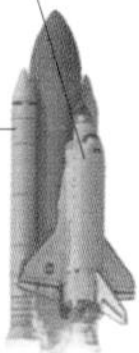

space suit
antarikṣ sūṭ
अंतरिक्ष सूट

astronaut | antarikṣ yātrī | अंतरिक्ष यात्री

thruster
thrasṭar
थ्रस्टर

radar
rāḍār
राडार

crew hatch
updvār
उपद्वार

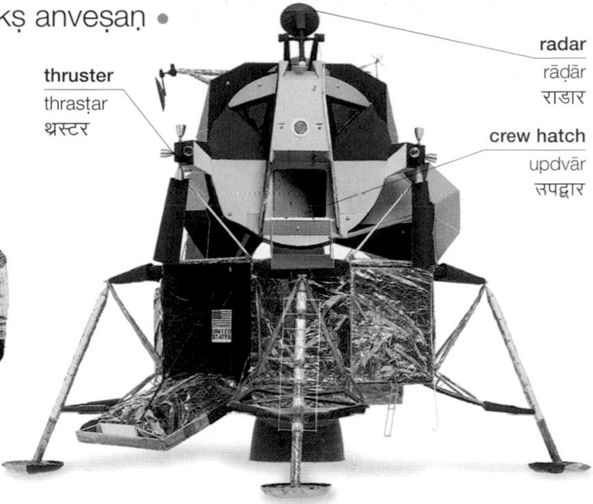

lunar module | chandryān | चंद्रयान

launch pad
prakṣepaṇ sthal
प्रक्षेपण स्थल

launch
prakṣepaṇ | प्रक्षेपण

satellite
upgrah | उपग्रह

space station | antarikṣ kendr
अंतरिक्ष केंद्र

astronomy • khagol vijñān • खगोल विज्ञान

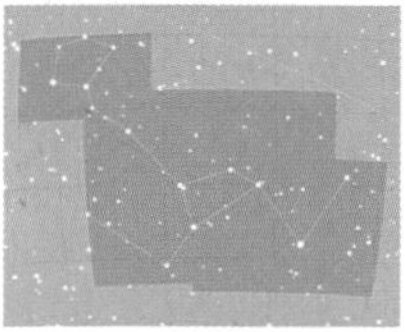

constellation
tārāmaṇḍal | तारामंडल

binoculars
dūrbīn | दूरबीन

telescope
dūrbīn
दूरबीन

tripod
tipāyā sṭaiṇḍ
तिपाया स्टैंड

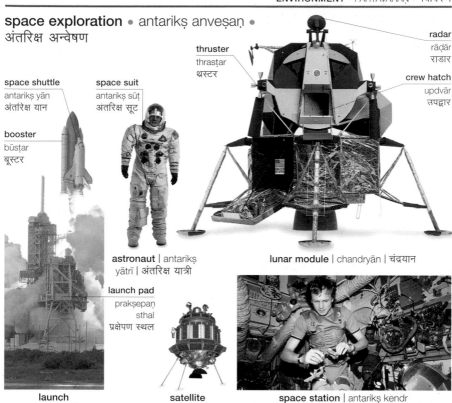

Earth • pṛthvī • पृथ्वी

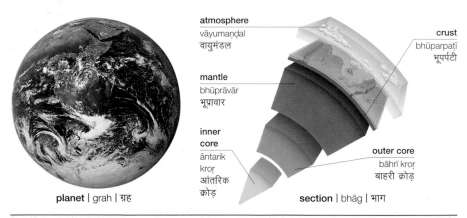

pole
dhruv
ध्रुव
land
bhūmi
भूमि
ocean
mahāsāgar
महासागर
mountain range
parvat śreṇī
पर्वत श्रेणी
sea
sāgar
सागर
peninsula
prāyadvīp
प्रायद्वीप
continent
mahādvīp
महाद्वीप
island
dvīp
द्वीप

planet | grah | ग्रह

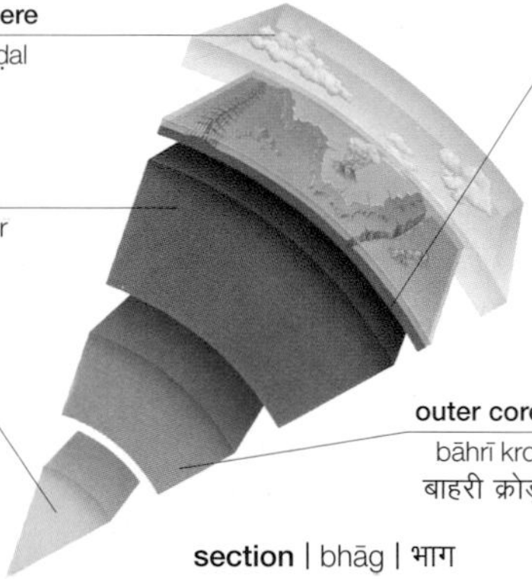
atmosphere
vāyumaṇḍal
वायुमंडल
crust
bhūparpaṭī
भूपर्पटी
mantle
bhūprāvār
भूप्रावार
inner
core
āntarik
kroṛ
आंतरिक
क्रोड़
outer core
bāhrī kroṛ
बाहरी क्रोड़

section | bhāg | भाग

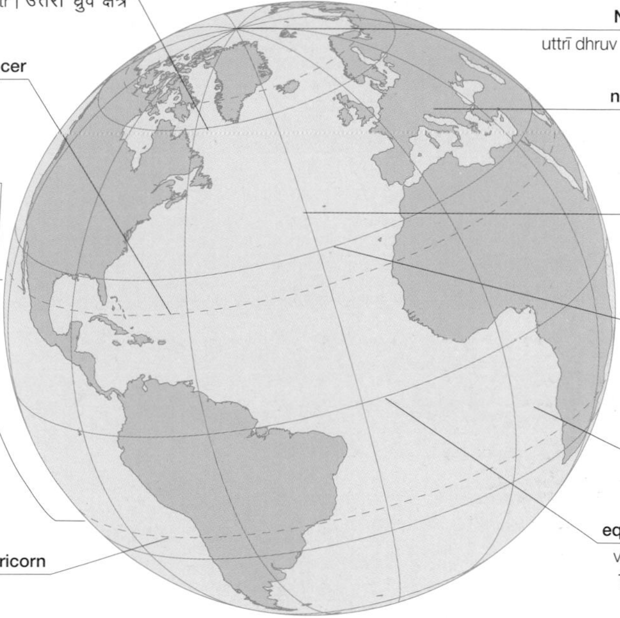
Arctic Circle
uttrī dhruv kṣetr | उत्तरी ध्रुव क्षेत्र
North Pole
uttrī dhruv | उत्तरी ध्रुव
Tropic of Cancer
kark rekhā
कर्क रेखा
northern hemisphere
uttrī golārdh
उत्तरी गोलार्ध
tropics
uṣṇ kaṭibandh
उष्ण कटिबंध
longitude
deśāntar rekhāṅś
देशांतर रेखांश
latitude
akṣāṅś
अक्षांश
southern hemisphere
dakṣiṇī golārdh
दक्षिणी गोलार्ध
equator
viṣuvat
विषुवत
Tropic of Capricorn
makar rekhā
मकर रेखा

zones | kaṭibandh | कटिबंध

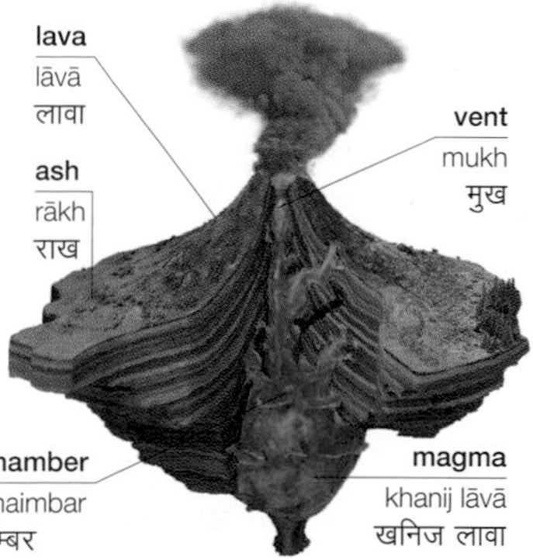
lava
lāvā
लावा
ash
rākh
राख
vent
mukh
मुख
chamber
chaimbar
चैम्बर
magma
khanij lāvā
खनिज लावा

volcano | jvālāmukhī | ज्वालामुखी

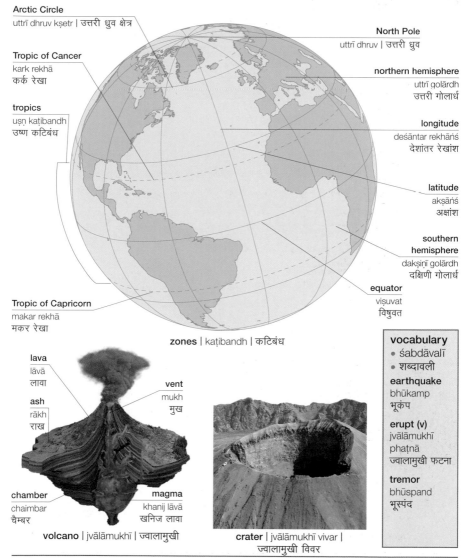

crater | jvālāmukhī vivar | ज्वालामुखी विवर

vocabulary • śabdāvalī • शब्दावली

earthquake
bhūkamp
भूकंप

erupt (v)
jvālāmukhī phaṭnā
ज्वालामुखी फटना

tremor
bhūspand
भूस्पंद

landscape • bhūdṛśaya • भूदृश्य

mountain
parvat | पर्वत
slope
ḍhalān
ढलान
bank
kinārā
किनारा
river
nadī
नदी
rapids
tīvr dhārā
तीव्र धारा
rocks
chaṭṭān
चट्टान

glacier
himnad | हिमनद

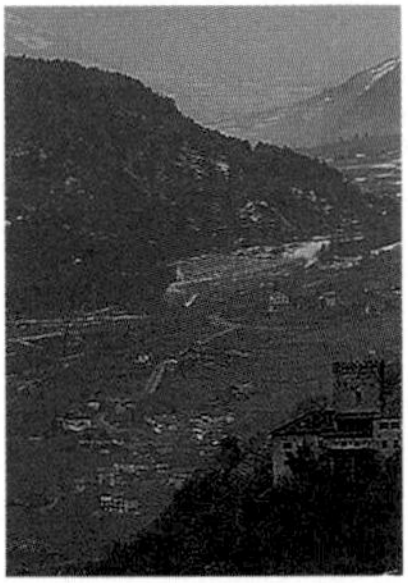
valley | ghāṭī | घाटी

hill
pahāṛī | पहाड़ी

plateau
paṭhār | पठार

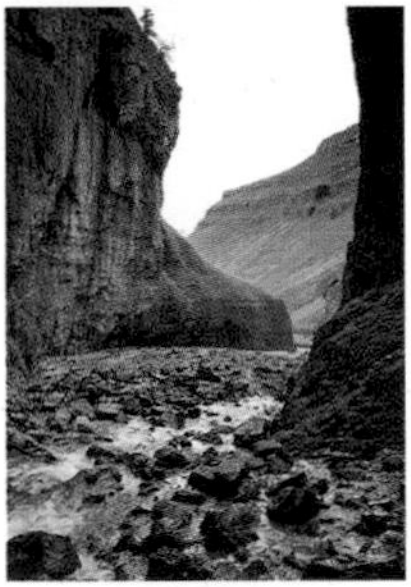
gorge
darrā | दर्रा

cave
guphā | गुफा

plain | maidān | मैदान

desert | registān
रेगिस्तान

forest | jaṅgal | जंगल

wood | van | वन

rainforest
varṣā van | वर्षा वन

swamp
daldal | दलदल

meadow
charāgāh | चरागाह

grassland | ghās kā
maidān | घास का मैदान

waterfall
jalprapāt | जलप्रपात

stream
dhārā | धारा

lake
jhīl | झील

geyser
garm jalsarot | गर्म जलस्रोत

coast
samudr taṭ | समुद्र तट

cliff | khaṛī chaṭṭān
खड़ी चट्टान

coral reef
pravāl dvīp | प्रवाल द्वीप

estuary | sāgar vilyan
सागर विलयन

weather • mausam • मौसम

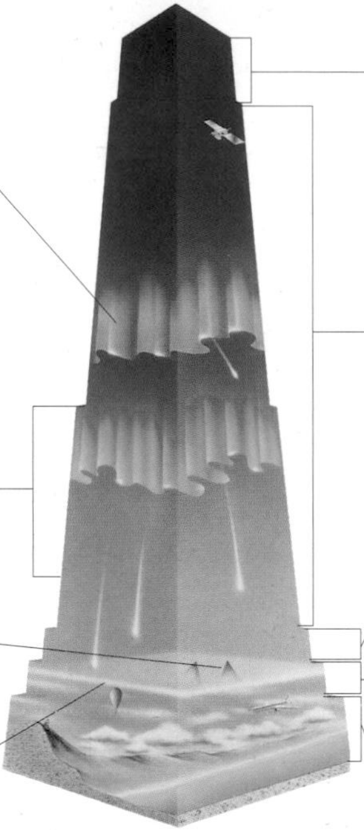
exosphere
parāmaṇḍal
परामंडल
aurora
dhruvjyoti
ध्रुवज्योति
thermosphere
tāpmaṇḍal
तापमंडल
ionosphere
āyan maṇḍal
आयन मंडल
mesosphere
madhya
maṇḍal
मध्य मंडल
ultraviolet
rays
parābaiṅganī
kirṇeṃ
पराबैंगनी किरणें
stratosphere
samtāp maṇḍal
समताप मंडल
ozone layer
ozon parat
ओज़ोन परत
troposphere
nimntāp maṇḍal
निम्नताप मंडल

atmosphere | vayumaṇḍal | वायुमंडल

sunshine | dhūp | धूप

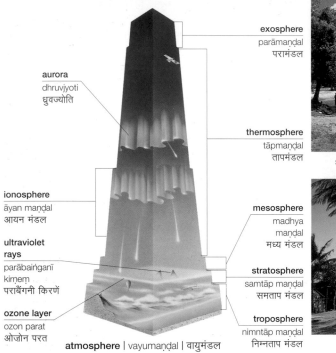

wind | pavan | पवन

vocabulary • śabdāvalī • शब्दावली

sleet himvarṣā हिमवर्षा	**shower** bauchhār बौछार	**hot** garm गर्म	**dry** sūkhā सूखा	**windy** tūfānī तूफ़ानी
hail ole ओले	**sunny** dhūpdār धूपदार	**cold** ṭhaṇḍā ठंडा	**wet** gīlā गीला	**gale** āṅdhī आंधी
thunder garaj गरज	**cloudy** meghācchhann मेघाच्छन्न	**warm** gunguṇā गुनगुना	**humid** nam नम	**temperature** tāpmān तापमान

I'm hot/cold.
mujhe garmī / ṭhaṇḍ lag rahī hai
मुझे गर्मी/ठंड लग रही है।

It's raining.
bāriś ho rahī hai
बारिश हो रही है।

It's ... degrees.
tāpmān ... ḍigrī hai
तापमान... डिग्री है।

cloud | bādal | बादल

rain | bāriś | बारिश

lightning
bijlī | बिजली

storm | tūfān | तूफ़ान

mist | kohrā | कोहरा

fog | dhundh | धुंध

rainbow | indrdhanuṣ | इंद्रधनुष

snow | him | हिम

frost | tuṣār | तुषार

ice | baraf | बर्फ़

icicle
āisikal | आइसिकल

freeze | ṭhaṇḍ | ठंड

hurricane
chakrvāt | चक्रवात

tornado
bavaṇḍar | बवंडर

monsoon
varṣā | वर्षा

flood
bāṛh | बाढ़

rocks • pāṣāṇ • पाषाण

igneous • jvalāmukhīya śail • ज्वालामुखीय शैल

granite
grenāiṭ
ग्रेनाइट

obsidian
obsiḍiyan
ओबसिडियन

basalt
kālā patthar
काला पत्थर

pumice
jhāmak
झामक

sedimentary • avsādī śail • अवसादी शैल

sandstone
baluā patthar
बलुआ पत्थर

limestone
chūnā patthar
चूना पत्थर

chalk
khaṛiyā
खड़िया

flint
chakmak
चकमक

conglomerate
pāṣāṇit kaṅkaṛ
पाषाणित कंकड़

coal
koyalā
कोयला

metamorphic • rūpāntarit śail • रूपांतरित शैल

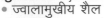

slate
sleṭ
स्लेट

schist
starit chaṭṭān
स्तरित चट्टान

gneiss
śail
शैल

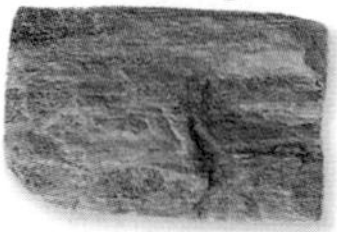

marble
saṅgmarmar
संगमरमर

gems • ratan • रत्न

ruby
māṇik | माणिक

aquamarine
haritnīl
हरितनील

amethyst
jambumaṇi
जंबुमणि

jade
jeḍ
जेड

diamond
hīrā
हीरा

jet
lāvā maṇi
लावा मणि

emerald
pannā
पन्ना

opal
upal
उपल

sapphire
nīlam
नीलम

moonstone
chandrakānt maṇi
चंद्रकांत मणि

garnet
raktmaṇi
रक्तमणि

topaz
pukhrāj
पुखराज

tourmaline
turmalī
तुरमली

minerals • khanij • खनिज

quartz
sphaṭik
स्फटिक

mica
abhrak
अभ्रक

sulphur
gandhak
गंधक

hematite
hemeṭāiṭ
हेमेटाइट

calcite
kailsāiṭ
कैल्साइट

malachite
melākāiṭ
मेलाकाइट

turquoise
fīrojā
फ़ीरोजा

onyx
sarpmaṇi
सर्पमणि

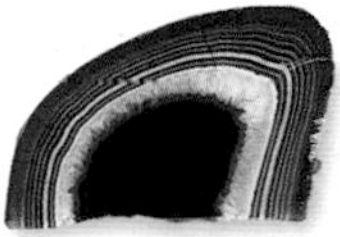

agate
akīk
अकीक

graphite
grefāiṭ
ग्रेफ़ाइट

metals • dhātu • धातु

gold
sonā | सोना

silver
chāndī
चांदी

platinum
pleṭinam
प्लेटिनम

nickel
nikal | निकल

iron
lohā | लोहा

copper
tāmbā | तांबा

tin
ṭin | टिन

aluminium
alyūminiyam
अल्यूमिनियम

mercury
pārā | पारा

zinc
jastā | जस्ता

animals 1 • paśu 1 • पशु

mammals • standhārī jīv • स्तनधारी जीव

rabbit
ḳhargoś
ख़रगोश

hamster
haimsṭar | हैमस्टर

whiskers
mūṃchheṃ
मूंछें

mouse
mūṣak | मूषक

tail
pūṃchh
पूंछ

rat
chūhā | चूहा

hedgehog
sāhī | साही

squirrel
gilahrī
गिलहरी

bat
chamgādaṛ
चमगादड़

raccoon
raikūn
रैकून

fox
lomṛī
लोमड़ी

wolf
bheṛiyā
भेड़िया

puppy
pillā
पिल्ला

dog
kuttā | कुत्ता

kitten
billī kā bacchā
बिल्ली का बच्चा

cat
billī | बिल्ली

otter
ūdbilāv | ऊदबिलाव

pup
śiśu sīl
शिशु सील

seal
sīl | सील

sea lion
samudr siṅh
समुद्र सिंह

flipper
mīn paṅkh
मीन पंख

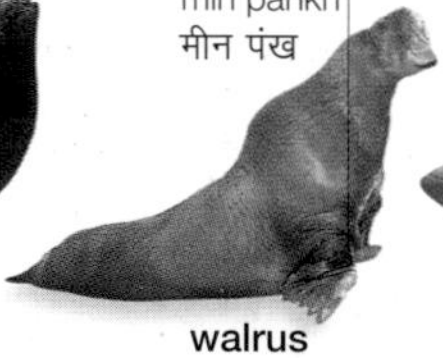

walrus
hāthī sīl
हाथी सील

blowhole
śvās chhidr
श्वास छिद्र

whale
vhel | व्हेल

dolphin
dolphin
डॉल्फ़िन

antler
sīng
सींग

deer
hiran | हिरन

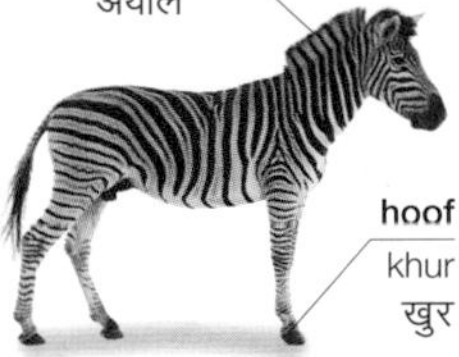

mane
ayāl
अयाल

hoof
khur
खुर

zebra
zebrā | ज़ेबरा

giraffe
jirāf | जिराफ़

hump
kūbaṛ
कूबड़

camel
ūṃṭ | ऊंट

hippopotamus
dariyāī ghoṛā | दरियाई घोड़ा

trunk
sūṃṛ | सूंड़

tusk
hāthī dāṃt
हाथी दांत

elephant
hāthī | हाथी

horn
sīng | सींग

rhinoceros
gaiṇḍā | गैंडा

tiger
bāgh | बाघ

mane
ayāl | अयाल

lion
babbar śer | बब्बर शेर

monkey
bandar | बंदर

gorilla
gorillā | गोरिल्ला

koala
koālā | कोआला

pouch
thailī
थैली

kangaroo
kaṅgārū | कंगारू

claw
panjā
पंजा

bear
bhālū | भालू

polar bear
dhruviya bhālū | ध्रुवीय भालू

panda
pāṃḍā
पांडा

animals 2 • paśu • पशु

birds • pakṣī • पक्षी

canary
chhoṭī pīlī chiṛiyā
छोटी पीली चिड़िया

sparrow
goraiyā | गोरैया

hummingbird | marmar pakṣī | मर्मर पक्षी

swallow
abābīl | अबाबील

crow
kauā | कौआ

pigeon
kabūtar | कबूतर

woodpecker
kaṭhphoṛvā
कठफोड़वा

falcon
bāz | बाज़

owl
ullū | उल्लू

gull
ghomrā | घोमरा

eagle
ukāb | उक़ाब

pelican
pelikan | पेलिकन

flamingo
rājhaṃs | राजहंस

stork
bagulā | बग़ुला

crane
sāras | सारस

penguin
penguin | पेंगुइन

ostrich
śuturmurg | शुतुर्मुर्ग़

goose
bataḳh | बतख़

swan
haṃs | हंस

peacock
mor | मोर

pheasant
tītar | तीतर

turkey
ṭarkī | टर्की

cockatoo
kākātū totā
काकातू तोता

bill
choṃch
चोंच
feather
far
फ़र
wing
paṅkh
पंख
claw
panjā
पंजा

parrot
totā | तोता

reptiles • sarīsṛp • सरीसृप

scales
sūkhī chamṛī
सूखी चमड़ी

alligator
ghaṛiyāl | घड़ियाल

lizard
chhipkalī | छिपकली

iguana
goh | गोह

shell
kavach
कवच

turtle | samudrī
kachhuā | समुद्री कछुआ

tortoise
kachhuā | कछुआ

snake
sāṃp | सांप

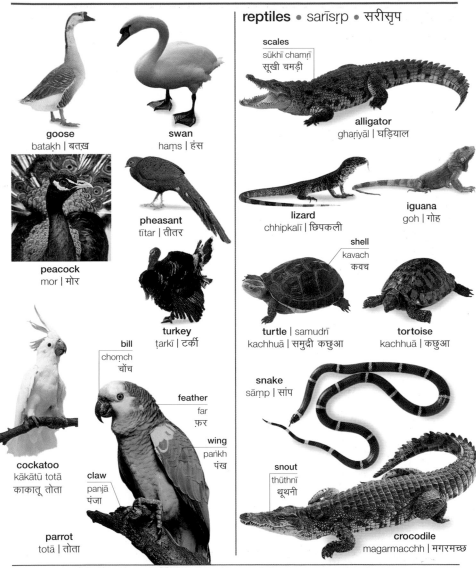

snout
thūthnī
थूथनी

crocodile
magarmacchh | मगरमच्छ

animals 3 • paśu 3 • पशु

amphibians • ubhayachar jīv • उभयचर जीव

frog
meṃḍhak | मेंढक

toad
thal meṃḍhak | थल मेंढक

tadpole
śiśu meṃḍhak | शिशु मेंढक

salamander
sarṭak | सरटक

fish • machhlī • मछली

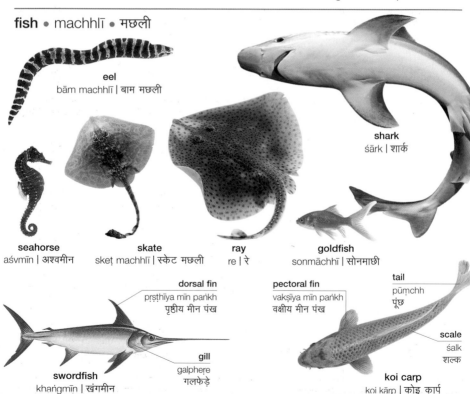

eel
bām machhlī | बाम मछली

shark
śārk | शार्क

seahorse
aśvmīn | अश्वमीन

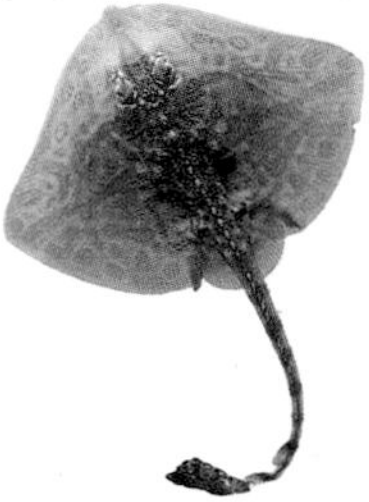

skate
skeṭ machhlī | स्केट मछली

ray
re | रे

goldfish
sonmāchhī | सोनमाछी

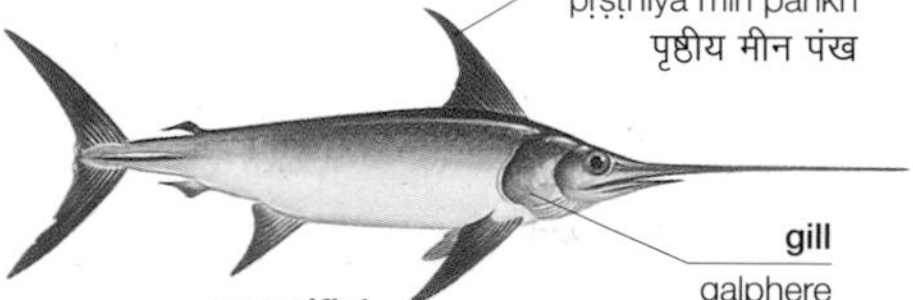

dorsal fin
pṛṣṭhīya mīn paṅkh
पृष्ठीय मीन पंख

gill
galphere
गलफेड़े

swordfish
khaṅgmīn | खंगमीन

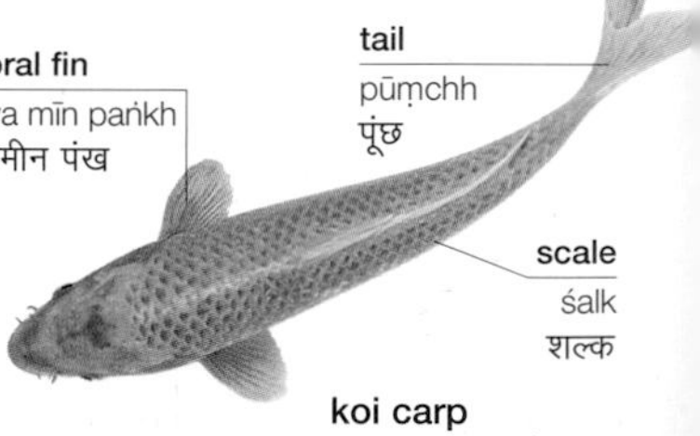

pectoral fin
vakṣīya mīn paṅkh
वक्षीय मीन पंख

tail
pūṃchh
पूंछ

scale
śalk
शल्क

koi carp
koi kārp | कोइ कार्प

invertebrates • akaśerukī jīv • अकशेरुकी जीव

ant
chīṃṭī | चींटी

termite
dīmak | दीमक

bee
madhumakkhī | मधुमक्खी

wasp
barr | बर्र

beetle
phūṅgā | फूंगा

cockroach
tilchaṭṭā | तिलचट्टा

moth
pataṅgā | पतंगा

butterfly
titlī | तितली

cocoon
koyā | कोया

caterpillar
illī | इल्ली

cricket
jhīṅgur | झींगुर

grasshopper
ṭiḍḍā | टिड्डा

praying mantis
mantris
मंत्रिस

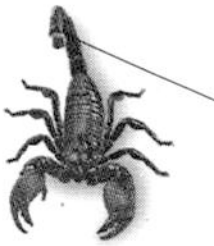

scorpion
bicchhū | बिच्छू

centipede
kankhajūrā | कनखजूरा

dragonfly
ḍraigan flāī
ड्रैगन फ़्लाई

fly
makkhī | मक्खी

mosquito
macchhar | मच्छर

ladybird
leḍībarḍ | लेडीबर्ड

spider
makṛī | मकड़ी

slug
kambu | कंबु

snail
ghoṃghā | घोंघा

worm
kṛmi | कृमि

starfish
sṭār fiś | स्टार फ़िश

mussel
śambuk | शंबुक

crab
kekṛā | केकड़ा

lobster
lobster | लॉबस्टर

octopus
aṣṭbhuj | अष्टभुज

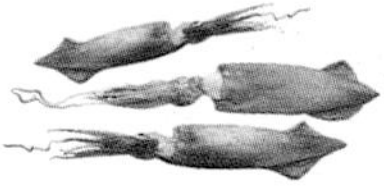
squid
skviḍ | स्क्विड

jellyfish
jailī fiś | जैली फ़िश

plants • vanaspati • वनस्पति

tree • peṛ • पेड़

leaf
pattī
पत्ती

twig
ṭahnī
टहनी

willow
śarpat | शरपत

branch
śākhā
शाखा

bark
chhāl
छाल

trunk
tanā
तना

root
jaṛ
जड़

oak | bāṃj | बांज

poplar | vilāyatī pīpal | विलायती पीपल

eucalyptus
nīlgiri | नीलगिरि

larch
śrīdāru | श्रीदारु

beech
bīch | बीच

birch
bhojvṛkṣ | भोजवृक्ष

pine
chīṛ | चीड़

cedar
devdār | देवदार

maple
mepal | मेपल

elm
chirābel | चिराबेल

lime | nībū kā vṛkṣ | नीबू का वृक्ष

berry
saras phal
सरस फल

holly
śūlparṇī | शूलपर्णी

palm
tāṛ | ताड़

flowering plant • puṣpī paudhe • पुष्पी पौधे

flower
phūl
फूल

stamen
puṅkesar
पुंकेसर

petal
paṅkhuṛī
पंखुड़ी

calyx
karṇikā
कर्णिका

stalk
ḍaṇṭhal
डंठल

bud
kalī
कली

stem
ḳalam
क़लम

buttercup
baṭarkap | बटरकप

daisy
ḍezī | डेज़ी

thistle
ikṣugandhā
इक्षुगंधा

dandelion
kukrauṃdhā
कुकरौंधा

heather
haidar
हैदर

poppy
ahipuṣp
अहिपुष्प

foxglove
apsaroṅguli
अप्सरोंगुलि

honeysuckle
hanīsakal
हनीसकल

sunflower
sūryamukhī
सूर्यमुखी

clover
tinpatiyā
तिनपतिया

bluebells
jaṅglī gomed
जंगली गोमेद

primrose
primroz
प्रिमरोज़

lupins
lyūpin
ल्यूपिन

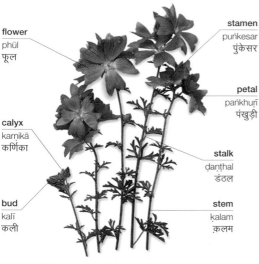

nettle
bicchhū-būṭī
बिच्छू–बूटी

town • śahar • शहर

street
saṛak
सड़क

kerb
paṭrī
पटरी

street corner
galī kā nukkaṛ
गली का नुक्कड़

shop
dukān
दुकान

intersection
chaurāhā
चौराहा

one-way system
iktarfā rāstā
इकतरफ़ा रास्ता

pavement
fuṭpāth
फ़ुटपाथ

office block
karyālaya khaṇḍ
कार्यालय खंड

apartment block
apārṭmenṭ khaṇḍ
अपार्टमेंट खंड

alley
galī
गली

car park
kār pārk
कार पार्क

street sign
mārg saṅketak
मार्ग संकेतक

bollard
khambhā
खंभा

street light
sṭrīṭ lāiṭ
स्ट्रीट लाइट

buildings • imārat • इमारत

town hall
ṭāun hall | टाउन हॉल

library
pustakālaya | पुस्तकालय

cinema
sinemā | सिनेमा

theatre
thieṭar | थिएटर

university
viśvvidyālaya | विश्वविद्यालय

school
vidyālaya | विद्यालय

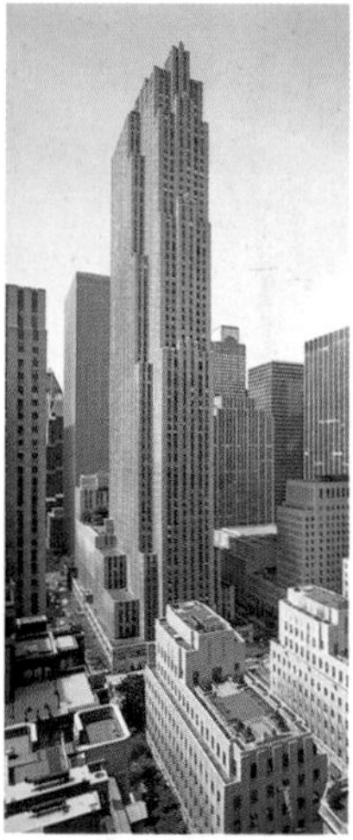

skyscraper
gaganchumbī imārat
गगनचुंबी इमारत

areas • kṣetr • क्षेत्र

industrial estate
audyogik kṣetr
औद्योगिक क्षेत्र

city
śahar | शहर

suburb
upnagar | उपनगर

village
gāṃv | गांव

vocabulary • śabdāvalī • शब्दावली

pedestrian zone
paidal rāstā
पैदल रास्ता

avenue
rāstā
रास्ता

side street
galī
गली

square
chauk
चौक

manhole
mainhol
मैनहोल

bus stop
bas stop
बस स्टॉप

gutter
nālā
नाला

factory
kārḳhānā
कारख़ाना

church
charch
चर्च

drain
nālī
नाली

architecture • vāstuśilp • वास्तुशिल्प

buildings and structures • bhavan evam imāratem̩ • भवन एवं इमारतें

skyscraper | gaganchumbī imārat | गगनचुंबी इमारत

turret
burj
बुर्ज

moat
khāī
खाई

castle
ķilā | क़िला

church
girjāghar | गिरजाघर

dome
gumbad
गुम्बद

mosque
masjid | मस्जिद

temple
mandir | मंदिर

vault
mehrābdār chhat
मेहराबदार छत

synagogue | yahūdī pūjāsthal
यहूदी पूजास्थल

dam
bāndh | बांध

bridge
pul | पुल

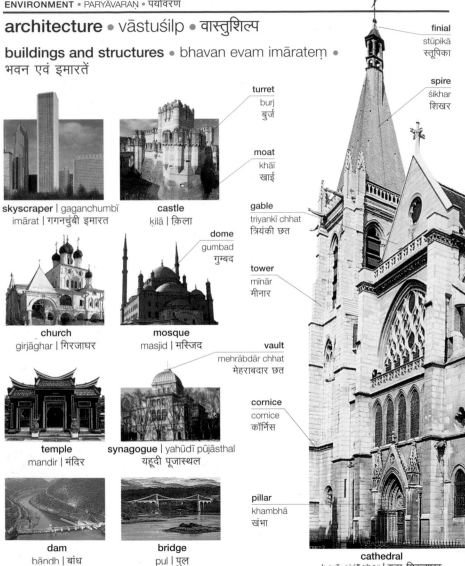

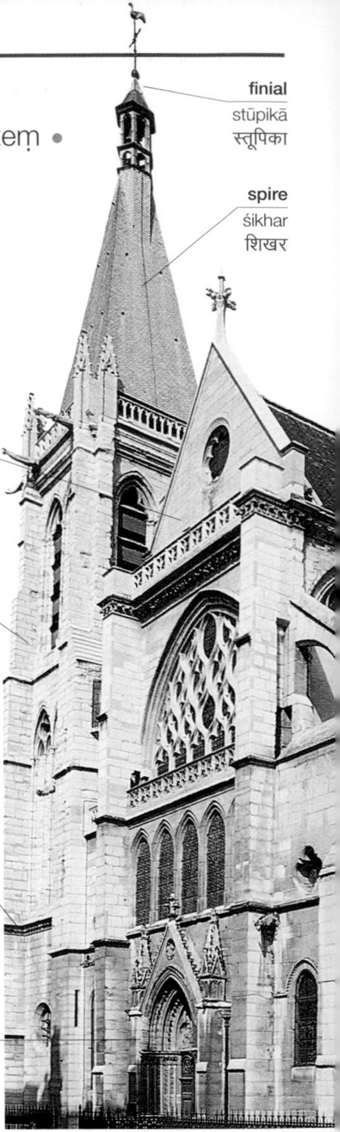

finial
stūpikā
स्तूपिका

spire
śikhar
शिखर

gable
triyankī chhat
त्रियंकी छत

tower
mīnār
मीनार

cornice
cornice
कॉर्निस

pillar
khambhā
खंभा

cathedral
baṛā girjāghar | बड़ा गिरजाघर

styles • śailī • शैली

gothic
gothic | गॉथिक

architrave
prastarpād
प्रस्तरपाद

renaissance
renesāns | रेनेसान्स

baroque
bārok | बारोक

arch
mehrāb
मेहराब

frieze
chitr vallarī
चित्र वल्लरी

choir
gāyan sthal
गायन स्थल

rococo
rokoko | रोकोको

pediment
trikonikā
त्रिकोनिका

neoclassical
navśāstrīya | नवशास्त्रीय

buttress
puśtā
पुश्ता

art nouveau
ārṭ nūvo | आर्ट नूवो

art deco
ārṭ ḍeko | आर्ट डेको

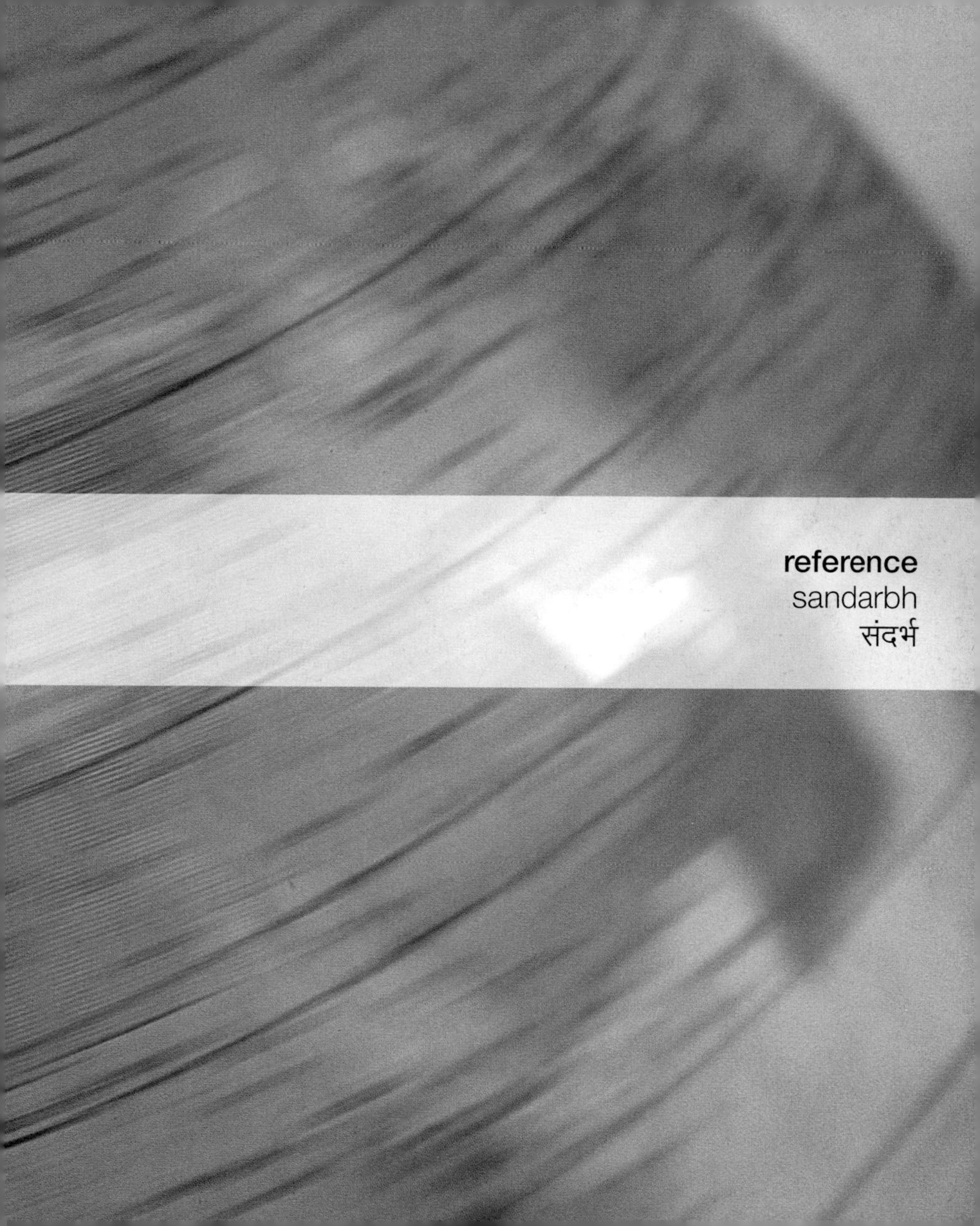

reference
sandarbh
संदर्भ

time • samaya • समय

minute hand
minaṭ kī sūī
मिनट की सूई

hour hand
ghanṭe kī sūī
घंटे की सूई

clock | ghaṛī | घड़ी

vocabulary • śabdāvalī • शब्दावली

second
saikanḍ
सैकंड

now
abhī
अभी

a quarter of an hour
pandrah minaṭ
पंद्रह मिनट

minute
minaṭ
मिनट

later
bād meṃ
बाद में

twenty minutes
bīs minaṭ
बीस मिनट

hour
ghanṭā
घंटा

half an hour
ādhā ghanṭā
आधा घंटा

forty minutes
chālīs minaṭ
चालीस मिनट

What time is it?
kyā samaya huā hai ?
क्या समय हुआ है?

It's three o'clock.
tīn baj gae haiṃ
तीन बज गए हैं।

five past one
ek baj kar pāṃch minaṭ
एक बज कर पांच मिनट

ten past one
ek baj kar das minaṭ
एक बज कर दस मिनट

quarter past one
savā ek
सवा एक

twenty past one
ek baj kar bīs minaṭ
एक बज कर बीस मिनट

second hand
saikanḍ kī sūī
सैकंड की सूई

twenty five past one
ek baj kar pacchīs minaṭ
एक बज कर पच्चीस मिनट

one thirty
ḍeṛh
डेढ़

twenty five to two
do bajne meṃ pacchīs minaṭ
दो बजने में पच्चीस मिनट

twenty to two
do bajne meṃ bīs minaṭ
दो बजने में बीस मिनट

quarter to two
paune do
पौने दो

ten to two
do bajne meṃ das minaṭ
दो बजने में दस मिनट

five to two
do bajne meṃ pāṃch minaṭ
दो बजने में पांच मिनट

two o'clock
do baje
दो बजे

night and day • rāt aur din • रात और दिन

midnight
ardhrātri | अर्धरात्रि

sunrise
sūryodaya | सूर्योदय

dawn
bhor | भोर

morning
subah | सुबह

sunset
sūryāst | सूर्यास्त

midday
madhyāhn | मध्याह्न

dusk
sāyaṃkāl | सायंकाल

evening
sandhyā | संध्या

afternoon
dopahar | दोपहर

vocabulary • śabdāvalī • शब्दावली

early
jaldī
जल्दी

on time
samaya par
समय पर

late
der
देर

You're early.
āp jaldī ā gae haiṃ
आप जल्दी आ गए हैं।

You're late.
āp der se āe haiṃ
आप देर से आए हैं।

I'll be there soon.
maiṃ jaldī hī pahuṃch jāūṃgā
मैं जल्दी ही पहुंच जाऊंगा।

Please be on time.
kṛpyā samaya par pahuṃcheṃ
कृपया समय पर पहुंचें।

What time does it start?
yah kis samaya śurū hogā?
यह किस समय शुरू होगा?

I'll see you later.
maiṃ āpse bād meṃ milūṅgā
मैं आपसे बाद में मिलूंगा।

It's getting late.
der ho rahī hai
देर हो रही है।

How long will it last?
yah kab tak chalegā?
यह कब तक चलेगा?

What time does it finish?
yah kab samāpt hogā?
यह कब समाप्त होगा?

calendar • kaileṇḍar • कैलेंडर

month
mās
मास

year
varṣ
वर्ष

January
janvarī
जनवरी

2010

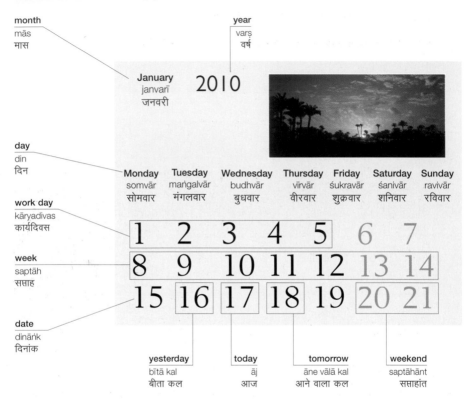

day
din
दिन

Monday	Tuesday	Wednesday	Thursday	Friday	Saturday	Sunday
somvār	maṅgalvār	budhvār	vīrvār	śukravār	śanivār	ravivār
सोमवार	मंगलवार	बुधवार	वीरवार	शुक्रवार	शनिवार	रविवार
1	2	3	4	5	6	7
8	9	10	11	12	13	14
15	16	17	18	19	20	21

work day
kāryadivas
कार्यदिवस

week
saptāh
सप्ताह

date
dināṅk
दिनांक

yesterday
bītā kal
बीता कल

today
āj
आज

tomorrow
āne vālā kal
आने वाला कल

weekend
saptāhānt
सप्ताहांत

vocabulary • śabdāvalī • शब्दावली

January janvarī जनवरी	**March** mārch मार्च	**May** maī मई	**July** julāī जुलाई	**September** sitambar सितंबर	**November** navambar नवंबर
February farvarī फ़रवरी	**April** aprail अप्रैल	**June** jūn जून	**August** agast अगस्त	**October** akṭūbar अक्टूबर	**December** disambar दिसंबर

years • varṣ • वर्ष

1900 **nineteen hundred** • unnīs sau • उन्नीस सौ

1901 **nineteen hundred and one** • unnīs sau ek • उन्नीस सौ एक

1910 **nineteen ten** • unnīs sau das • उन्नीस सौ दस

2000 **two thousand** • do hazār • दो हज़ार

2001 **two thousand and one** • do hazār ek • दो हज़ार एक

seasons • ṛtueṃ • ऋतुएं

spring
basant
बसंत

summer
grīṣm
ग्रीष्म

autumn
patjhaṛ
पतझड़

winter
śarad
शरद

vocabulary • śabdāvalī • शब्दावली

century
śatābdī
शताब्दी

decade
daśak
दशक

fortnight
pakhvāṛā
पखवाड़ा

this week
is hafte
इस हफ़्ते

last week
pichhle hafte
पिछले हफ़्ते

the day before yesterday
bītā parsoṃ
बीता परसों

weekly
sāptāhik
साप्ताहिक

monthly
māsik
मासिक

annual
vārṣik
वार्षिक

millennium
sahsrābdī
सहस्त्राब्दी

next week
agle hafte
अगले हफ़्ते

the day after tomorrow
parsoṃ
परसों

What's the date today?
āj kyā tārīḳh hai?
आज क्या तारीख़ है?

It's February seventh, two thousand and two.
āj 7 farvarī 2002 hai
आज 7 फ़रवरी, 2002 है।

numbers • aṃk • अंक

0 zero • śūnya • शून्य

1 one • ek • एक

2 two • do • दो

3 three • tīn • तीन

4 four • chār • चार

5 five • pāṃch • पांच

6 six • chhah • छह

7 seven• sāt • सात

8 eight • āṭh • आठ

9 nine • nau • नौ

10 ten • das • दस

11 eleven• gyārah • ग्यारह

12 twelve • bārah • बारह

13 thirteen • terah • तेरह

14 fourteen • chaudah • चौदह

15 fifteen • pandrah • पंद्रह

16 sixteen • solah • सोलह

17 seventeen • satrah • सत्रह

18 eighteen • aṭhārah • अठारह

19 nineteen • unnīs • उन्नीस

20 twenty • bīs • बीस

21 twenty-one• ikkīs • इक्कीस

22 twenty-two • bāīs • बाईस

30 thirty • tīs • तीस

40 forty • chālīs • चालीस

50 fifty• pachās • पचास

60 sixty • sāṭh • साठ

70 seventy• sattar • सत्तर

80 eighty • assī • अस्सी

90 ninety • nabbe • नब्बे

100 one hundred • sau • सौ

110 one hundred and ten • ek sau das • एक सौ दस

200 two hundred • do sau • दो सौ

300 three hundred • tīn sau • तीन सौ

400 four hundred • chār sau • चार सौ

500 five hundred• pāṃch sau • पांच सौ

600 six hundred • chhah sau • छह सौ

700 seven hundred • sāt sau • सात सौ

800 eight hundred • āṭh sau • आठ सौ

900 nine hundred • nau sau • नौ सौ

1000	**one thousand** • ek hazār • एक हज़ार
10,000	**ten thousand** • das hazār • दस हज़ार
20,000	**twenty thousand** • bīs hazār • बीस हज़ार
50,000	**fifty thousand** • pachās hazār • पचास हज़ार
55,500	**fifty-five thousand five hundred** • pachpan hazār pāṃch sau • पचपन हज़ार पांच सौ
100,000	**one hundred thousand** • ek lākh • एक लाख
1,000,000	**one million** • das lākh • दस लाख
1,000,000,000	**one billion** • ek arab • एक अरब

first pahlā पहला

second dūsrā दूसरा

third tīsrā तीसरा

fourth • chauthā • चौथा

fifth • pāṃchvāṃ • पांचवां

sixth • chhaṭhā • छठा

seventh • sātvāṃ • सातवां

eighth • āṭhvāṃ • आठवां

ninth • nauvāṃ • नौवां

tenth • dasvāṃ • दसवां

eleventh • gyārahavāṃ • ग्यारहवां

twelfth • bārhavāṃ • बारहवां

thirteenth • terhavāṃ • तेरहवां

fourteenth • chaudhavāṃ • चौदहवां

fifteenth • pandrahavāṃ • पंद्रहवां

sixteenth • solahavāṃ • सोलहवां

seventeenth • satrahavāṃ • सत्रहवां

eighteenth• aṭhārahavāṃ • अठारहवां

nineteenth • unnīsvāṃ • उन्नीसवां

twentieth • bīsvāṃ • बीसवां

twenty-first • ikkīsvāṃ • इक्कीसवां

twenty-second • bāisvāṃ • बाइसवां

twenty-third • teisvāṃ • तेइसवां

thirtieth • tīsvāṃ • तीसवां

fortieth • chālīsvāṃ • चालीसवां

fiftieth • pachāsvāṃ • पचासवां

sixtieth • sāṭhvāṃ • साठवां

seventieth • sattarvāṃ • सत्तरवां

eightieth • assīvāṃ • अस्सीवां

ninetieth • nabbevāṃ • नब्बेवां

one hundredth• sauvāṃ • सौवां

weights and measures • bhār aur māpak • भार और मापक

area • kṣetr • क्षेत्र

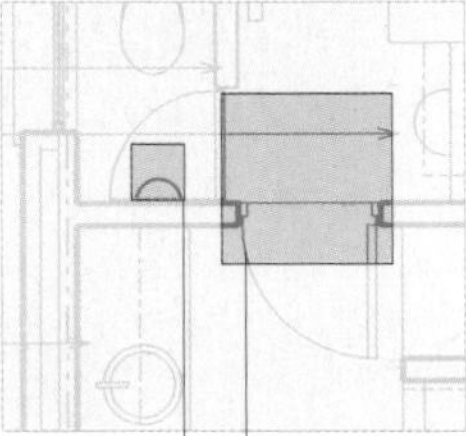

square foot
varg fuṭ
वर्ग फुट

square metre
vargmīṭar
वर्गमीटर

distance • dūrī • दूरी

kilometre
kilomīṭar
किलोमीटर

mile
mīl
मील

pan
pain
पैन

pound
pāuṃḍ
पाउंड

kilogram
kilogrām
किलोग्राम

ounce
auṃs
औंस

gram
grām
ग्राम

KRUPS

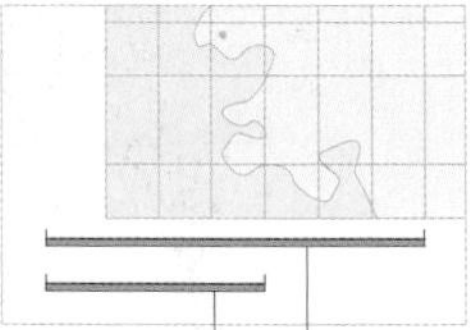

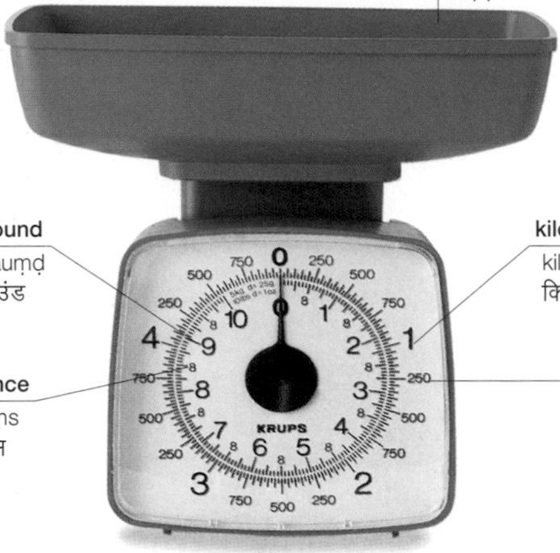

scales | tarāzū | तराजू

---

vocabulary • śabdāvalī • शब्दावली

yard	**tonne**	**measure (v)**
gaz	ṭan	māpnā
गज़	टन	मापना
metre	**milligram**	**weigh (v)**
mīṭar	milīgrām	tolnā
मीटर	मिलीग्राम	तोलना

---

length • lambāī • लंबाई

foot
fuṭ
फुट

HELIX

millimetre
milīmīṭar
मिलीमीटर

centimetre
senṭīmīṭar
सेंटीमीटर

inch
īnch
इंच

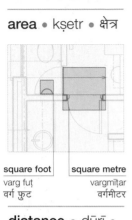

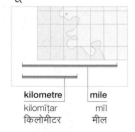

capacity • kṣamtā • क्षमता

half-litre
ādhā līṭar
आधा लीटर

pint
pāinṭ | पाइंट

millilitre
milīlīṭar
मिलीलीटर

measuring jug
māpak jag | मापक जग

volume
āyatan
आयतन

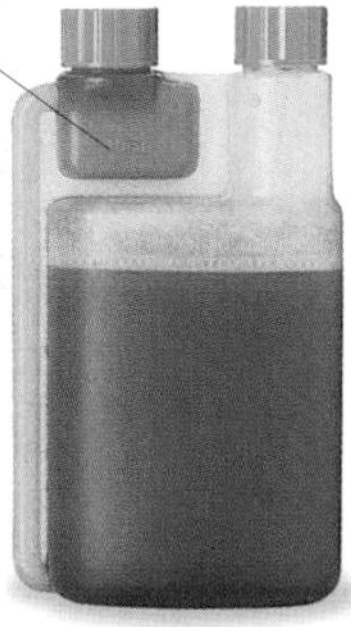

measure
māp | माप

vocabulary • śabdāvalī • शब्दावली

gallon
gailan
गैलन

quart
kvārṭ
क्वार्ट

litre
līṭar
लीटर

container • kanṭenar • कंटेनर

carton
kārṭan | कार्टन

packet
paikeṭ | पैकेट

bottle
botal | बोतल

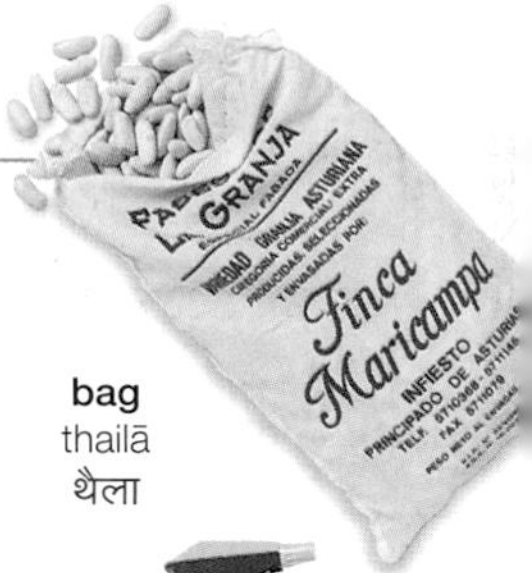

bag
thailā
थैला

tub | ṭab | टब

jar | jār | जार

can
kain
कैन

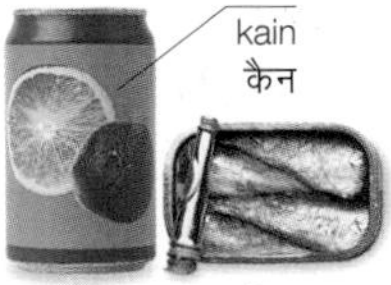

tin | ṭin | टिन

dispenser
ḍispensar | डिस्पेंसर

bar
ṭikiyā
टिकिया

tube | ṭyūb | ट्यूब

roll | rol | रोल

pack | paik | पैक

spray can
spre kain | स्प्रे कैन

world map • viśv mānchitr • विश्व मानचित्र

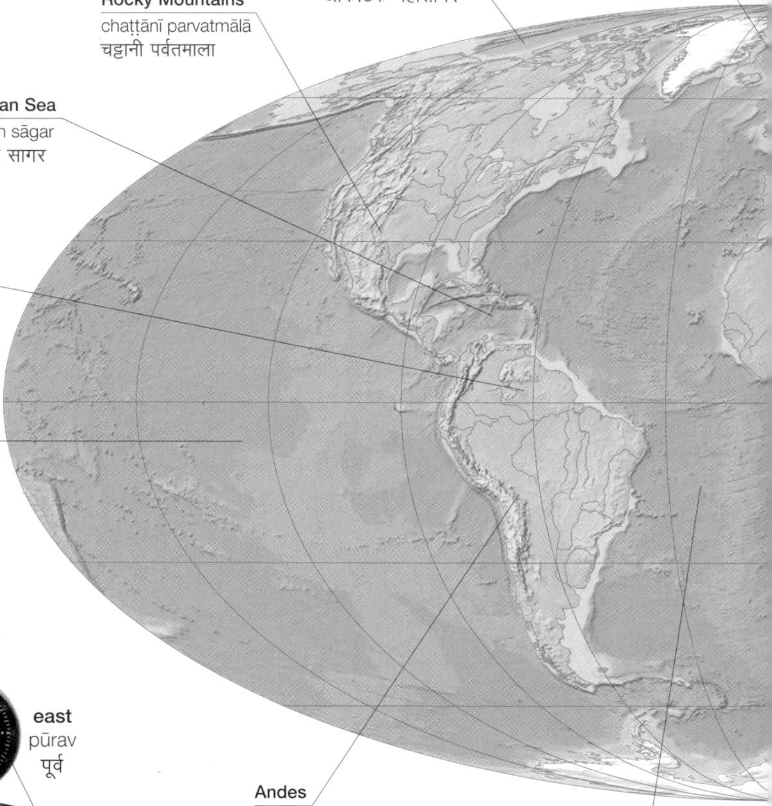

North Sea
uttarī sāgar
उत्तरी सागर

Arctic Ocean
ārkṭik mahāsāgar
आर्कटिक महासागर

Rocky Mountains
chaṭṭānī parvatmālā
चट्टानी पर्वतमाला

Caribbean Sea
kairībiyan sāgar
कैरीबियन सागर

Amazonia
amāzoniyā
अमाज़ोनिया

Pacific Ocean
praśānt mahāsāgar
प्रशांत महासागर

Andes
aiṅḍīz
ऐंडीज़

Atlantic Ocean
atlāntik mahāsāgar
अतलांतिक महासागर

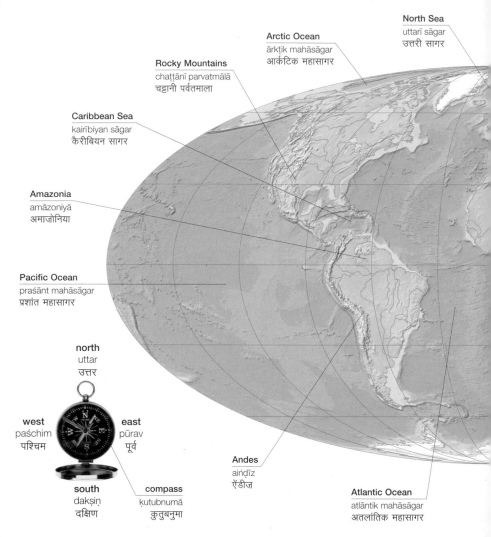

north
uttar
उत्तर

west
paśchim
पश्चिम

east
pūrav
पूर्व

south
dakṣiṇ
दक्षिण

compass
ḳutubnumā
कुतुबनुमा

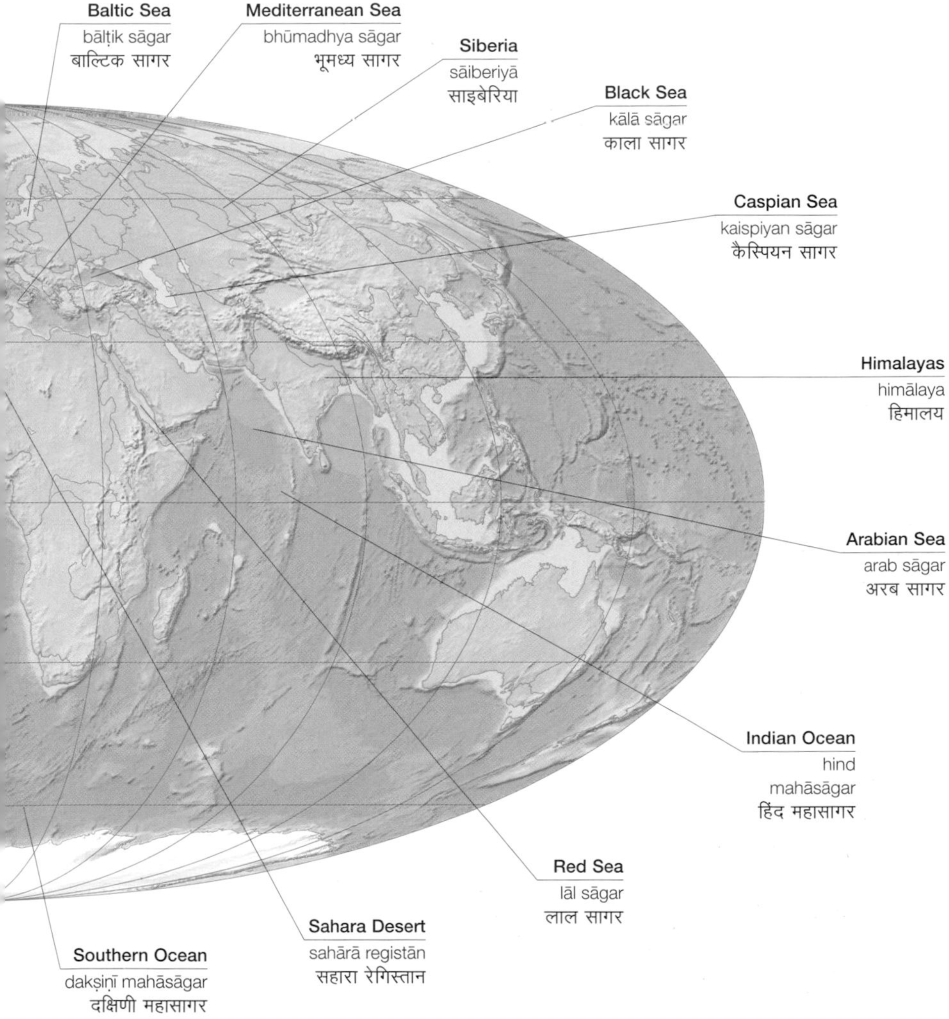
Baltic Sea
bālṭik sāgar
बाल्टिक सागर
Mediterranean Sea
bhūmadhya sāgar
भूमध्य सागर
Siberia
sāiberiyā
साइबेरिया
Black Sea
kālā sāgar
काला सागर
Caspian Sea
kaispiyan sāgar
कैस्पियन सागर
Himalayas
himālaya
हिमालय
Arabian Sea
arab sāgar
अरब सागर
Indian Ocean
hind
mahāsāgar
हिंद महासागर
Red Sea
lāl sāgar
लाल सागर
Sahara Desert
sahārā registān
सहारा रेगिस्तान
Southern Ocean
dakṣiṇī mahāsāgar
दक्षिणी महासागर

North and Central America • uttarī aur madhya amerikā • उत्तरी और मध्य अमेरिका

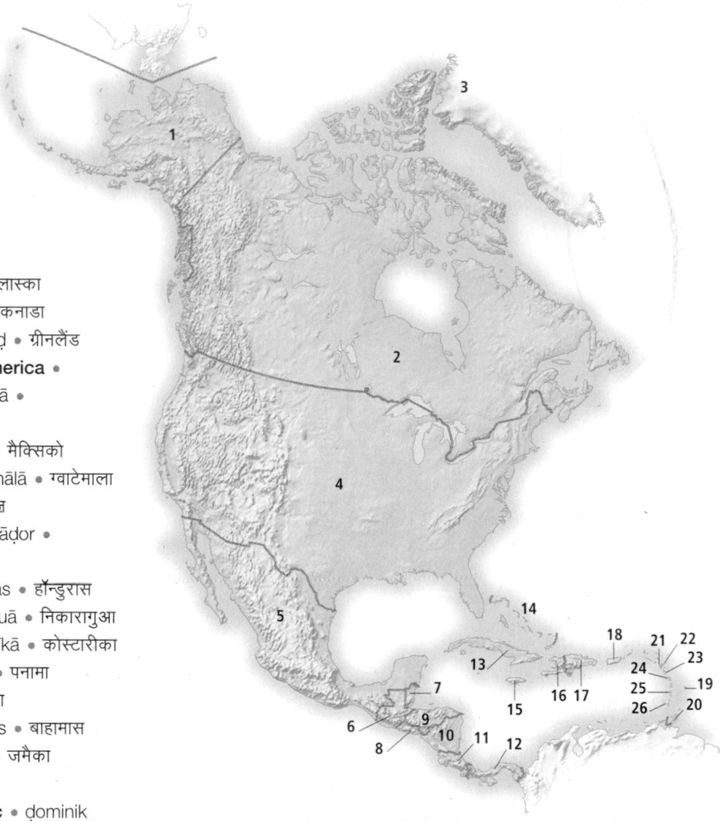

1 **Alaska** • alāskā • अलास्का
2 **Canada** • kanāḍā • कनाडा
3 **Greenland** • grīnlaiṇḍ • ग्रीनलैंड
4 **United States of America** • saṃyūkt rājya amerikā • सयुंक्त राज्य अमेरिका
5 **Mexico** • maiksiko • मैक्सिको
6 **Guatemala** • gvāṭemālā • ग्वाटेमाला
7 **Belize** • belīz • बेलीज़
8 **El Salvador** • el selvāḍor • एल सेल्वाडोर
9 **Honduras** • honduras • हॉन्डुरास
10 **Nicaragua** • nikārāguā • निकारागुआ
11 **Costa Rica** • kosṭārīkā • कोस्टारीका
12 **Panama** • panāmā • पनामा
13 **Cuba** • kyūbā • क्यूबा
14 **Bahamas** • bāhāmās • बाहामास
15 **Jamaica** • jamaikā • जमैका
16 **Haiti** • haiṭī • हैटी
17 **Dominican Republic** • ḍominik ganṛājya • डोमिनिक गणराज्य
18 **Puerto Rico** • puerto rīko • पुएरतो रीको
19 **Barbados** • barbados • बारबेडॉस
20 **Trinidad and Tobago** • trinidād evam ṭābāgo • त्रिनिदाद एवं टाबागो
21 **St. Kitts and Nevis** • senṭ kiṭs eṇḍ nevis • सेंट किट्स एंड़ नेविस
22 **Antigua and Barbuda** • enṭīguā aur bārbuḍā • एंटीगुआ और बारबुडा
23 **Dominica** • ḍominikā • डोमिनिका
24 **St Lucia** • senṭ luchiā • सेंट लुचिया
25 **St Vincent and The Grenadines** • senṭ vinsenṭ eṇḍ da grenāḍins • सेंट विन्सेंट एंड द ग्रेनाडिन्स
26 **Grenada** • grenāḍā • ग्रेनाडा

South America • dakṣiṇī amerikā • दक्षिणी अमेरिका

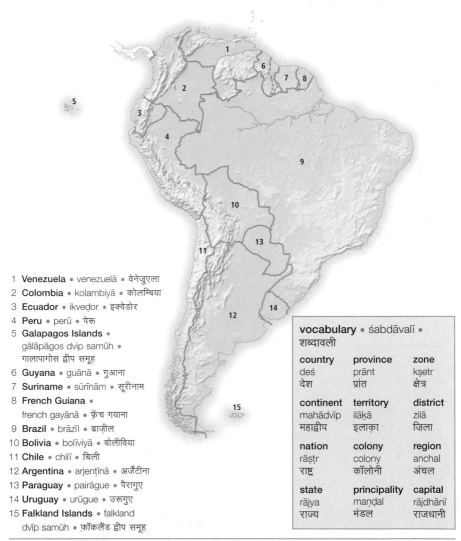

1 **Venezuela** • venezuelā • वेनेज़ुएला
2 **Colombia** • kolambiyā • कोलम्बिया
3 **Ecuador** • ikveḍor • इक्वेडोर
4 **Peru** • perū • पेरू
5 **Galapagos Islands** • gālāpāgos dvip samūh • गालापागोस द्वीप समूह
6 **Guyana** • guānā • गुआना
7 **Suriname** • sūrīnām • सूरीनाम
8 **French Guiana** • french gayānā • फ़्रेंच गयाना
9 **Brazil** • brāzīl • ब्राज़ील
10 **Bolivia** • bolīviyā • बोलीविया
11 **Chile** • chilī • चिली
12 **Argentina** • arjenṭīnā • अर्जेंटीना
13 **Paraguay** • pairāgue • पैरागुए
14 **Uruguay** • urūgue • उरूगुए
15 **Falkland Islands** • falkland dvīp samūh • फ़ॉकलैंड द्वीप समूह

vocabulary • śabdāvalī • शब्दावली

country deś देश	**province** prānt प्रांत	**zone** kṣetr क्षेत्र
continent mahādvīp महाद्वीप	**territory** ilāḳā इलाक़ा	**district** zilā ज़िला
nation rāṣṭr राष्ट्र	**colony** colony कॉलोनी	**region** anchal अंचल
state rājya राज्य	**principality** maṇḍal मंडल	**capital** rājdhānī राजधानी

Europe • yūrop • यूरोप

1 **Ireland** • āyarlaiṇḍ • आयरलैंड
2 **United Kingdom** • yūnāiṭeḍ kiṅgḍam • यूनाइटेड किंग्डम
3 **Portugal** • purtgāl • पुर्तगाल
4 **Spain** • spen • स्पेन
5 **Balearic Islands** • bailirik dvīp samūh • बैलिरिक द्वीप समूह
6 **Andorra** • anḍorā • अन्डोरा
7 **France** • frāṃs • फ़्रांस
8 **Belgium** • beljiyam • बेल्जियम
9 **Netherlands** • nīdarlaiṇḍ • नीदरलैंड
10 **Luxembourg** • lakzambarg • लक्ज़मबर्ग
11 **Germany** • jarmanī • जर्मनी
12 **Denmark** • ḍenmārk • डेनमार्क
13 **Norway** • nārve • नार्वे
14 **Sweden** • svīḍan • स्वीडन
15 **Finland** • finlaiṇḍ • फ़िनलैंड
16 **Estonia** • esṭoniyā • एस्टोनिया
17 **Latvia** • lāṭviyā • लाटविया
18 **Lithuania** • lithuāniyā • लिथुआनिया
19 **Kaliningrad** • kailinin grāḍ • कैलिनिनग्राड
20 **Poland** • polaiṇḍ • पोलैंड
21 **Czech Republic** • chek gaṇrājya • चेक गणराज्य
22 **Austria** • austria • ऑस्ट्रिया
23 **Liechtenstein** • liśtenastin • लिशतेनस्तिन
24 **Switzerland** • sviṭzarlaiṇḍ • स्विटज़रलैंड
25 **Italy** • iṭlī • इटली
26 **Monaco** • monāko • मोनाको
27 **Corsica** • corsica • कॉरसिका
28 **Sardinia** • sārḍīniyā • सार्डीनिया
29 **San Marino** • sān mārino • सान मारिनो
30 **Vatican City** • veṭikan siṭī • वेटिकन सिटी
31 **Sicily** • sislī • सिसली
32 **Malta** • mālṭā • माल्टा
33 **Slovenia** • sloveniyā • स्लोवेनिया
34 **Croatia** • kroeśiyā • क्रोएशिया
35 **Hungary** • haṅgarī • हंगरी
36 **Slovakia** • slovākiyā • स्लोवाकिया
37 **Ukraine** • yūkren • यूक्रेन
38 **Belarus** • belārūs • बेलारूस
39 **Moldova** • moldova • मॉल्डोवा
40 **Romania** • romāniyā • रोमानिया
41 **Serbia** • sarbiyā • सर्बिया
42 **Bosnia and Herzogovina** • bosniyā eṇḍ harzogovinā • बोस्निया एंड हर्ज़ोगोविना
43 **Albania** • albāniyā • अल्बानिया
44 **Macedonia** • meseḍoniyā • मेसेडोनिया
45 **Bulgaria** • bulgāriyā • बुल्गारिया
46 **Greece** • grīs • ग्रीस
47 **Kosovo (disputed)** • kōsōvō • कोसोवो
48 **Montenegro** • mōntenegrō • मोंटेनेग्रो

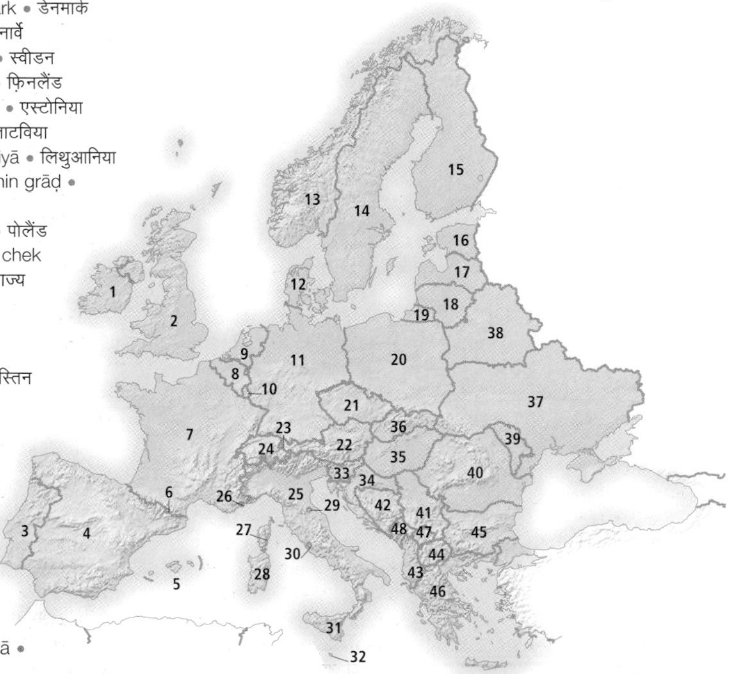

Africa • afrīkā • अफ़्रीका

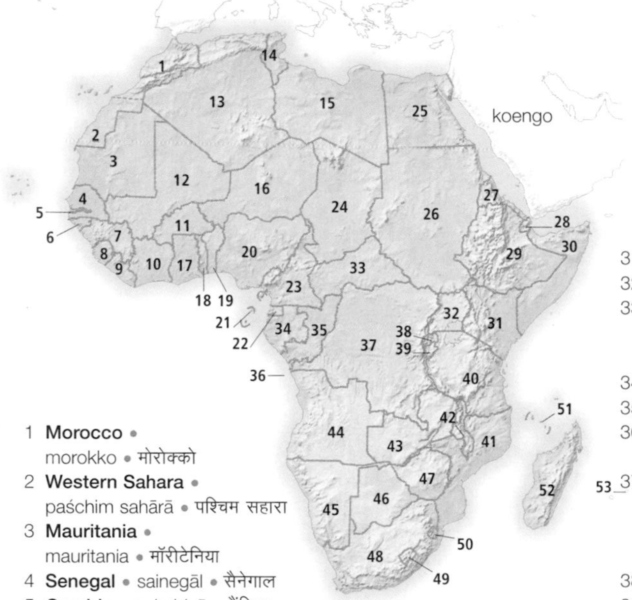

1 **Morocco** • morokko • मोरोक्को
2 **Western Sahara** • paśchim sahārā • पश्चिम सहारा
3 **Mauritania** • mauritania • मॉरीटेनिया
4 **Senegal** • sainegāl • सैनेगाल
5 **Gambia** • gaimbiyā • गैंबिया
6 **Guinea-Bissau** • ginībissāū • गिनीबिस्साऊ
7 **Guinea** • gini • गिनि
8 **Sierra Leone** • sierā lione • सिएरा लिओने
9 **Liberia** • lāiberiyā • लाइबेरिया
10 **Ivory Coast** • āivarī koṣṭ • आइवरी कोस्ट
11 **Burkina Faso** • burkinā fāso • बुर्किना फ़ासो
12 **Mali** • mālī • माली
13 **Algeria** • aljīriyā • अल्जीरिया
14 **Tunisia** • ṭyūnīśiyā • ट्यूनीशिया
15 **Libya** • lībiyā • लीबिया
16 **Niger** • nāijar • नाइजर
17 **Ghana** • ghānā • घाना
18 **Togo** • ṭogo • टोगो
19 **Benin** • benin • बेनिन
20 **Nigeria** • nāijīriyā • नाइजीरिया
21 **São Tomé and Principe** • sāo ṭom eṇḍ princhip • साओ टोम एंड प्रिंचिप
22 **Equatorial Guinea** • ikveṭoriyal gini • इक्वेटोरियल गिनि
23 **Cameroon** • kaimrūn • कैमरून
24 **Chad** • chād • चाद
25 **Egypt** • misr • मिस्र
26 **Sudan** • sūḍān • सूडान
27 **Eritrea** • eriṭriyā • एरिट्रिया
28 **Djibouti** • jibūtī • जिबूती
29 **Ethiopia** • ithopiyā • इथोपिया
30 **Somalia** • somāliyā • सोमालिया
31 **Kenya** • kīniyā • कीनिया
32 **Uganda** • yugāṇḍā • युगांडा
33 **Central African Republic** • madhya afrīkī gaṇrajya • मध्य अफ़्रीकी गणराज्य
34 **Gabon** • gaibon • गैबोन
35 **Congo** • congo • कॉन्गो
36 **Cabinda (Angola)** • kebindā (aṅgolā) • केबिंदा (अंगोला)
37 **Democratic Republic of the Congo** • congo loktāntrik gaṇrājya • कॉन्गो लोकतांत्रिक गणराज्य
38 **Rwanda** • ruāṇḍā • रुआंडा
39 **Burundi** • burūṇḍī • बुरूंडी
40 **Tanzania** • tanzāniyā • तंज़ानिया
41 **Mozambique** • mozāmbīḳ • मोज़ाम्बीक़
42 **Malawi** • malāvī • मलावी
43 **Zambia** • zāmbiyā • ज़ाम्बिया
44 **Angola** • aṅgolā • अंगोला
45 **Namibia** • nāmībiyā • नामीबिया
46 **Botswana** • botsvānā • बोत्सवाना
47 **Zimbabwe** • zimbābve • ज़िम्बाब्वे
48 **South Africa** • dakṣiṇ afrīkā • दक्षिण अफ़्रीका
49 **Lesotho** • lisotho • लिसोथो
50 **Swaziland** • svāzīlaiṇḍ • स्वाज़ीलैंड
51 **Comoros** • komoro • कोमोरो
52 **Madagascar** • maiḍāgāskar • मैडागास्कर
53 **Mauritius** • mauritius • मॉरीशस

Asia • eśiyā • एशिया

1 **Turkey** • turkī • तुर्की
2 **Cyprus** • sāipras • साइप्रस
3 **Russian Federation** • rūs • रूस
4 **Georgia** • georgia • जॉर्जिया
5 **Armenia** • ārmeniyā • आर्मेनिया
6 **Azerbaijan** • azarbejān • अज़रबेजान
7 **Iran** • īrān • ईरान
8 **Iraq** • irāķ • इराक़
9 **Syria** • sīriyā • सीरिया
10 **Lebanon** • lebnān • लेबनान
11 **Israel** • izrāyal • इज़रायल
12 **Jordan** • jordan • जॉर्डन
13 **Saudi Arabia** • saūdī arab • सऊदी अरब
14 **Kuwait** • ķuvait • क़ुवैत
15 **Bahrain** • baharīna • बहरीन
16 **Qatar** • ķatar • क़तर
17 **United Arab Emirates** • sanyukt arab amīrāt • संयुक्त अरब अमीरात
18 **Oman** • omān • ओमान
19 **Yemen** • yaman • यमन
20 **Kazakhstan** • kazākistān • कज़ाकिस्तान
21 **Uzbekistan** • uzbekistān • उज़्बेकिस्तान
22 **Turkmenistan** • turkmenistān • तुर्कमेनिस्तान
23 **Afghanistan** • afgānistān • अफ़ग़ानिस्तान
24 **Tajikistan** • tajākistān • तजाकिस्तान
25 **Kyrgyzstan** • kirgīstān • किर्गीस्तान
26 **Pakistan** • pākistān • पाकिस्तान
27 **India** • bhārat • भारत
28 **Maldives** • māldīv • मालदीव
29 **Sri Lanka** • śrīlaṅkā • श्रीलंका
30 **China** • chīn • चीन
31 **Mongolia** • maṅgoliyā • मंगोलिया
32 **North Korea** • uttarī koriyā • उत्तरी कोरिया
33 **South Korea** • dakṣiṇ koriyā • दक्षिण कोरिया
34 **Japan** • jāpān • जापान
35 **Nepal** • nepāl • नेपाल

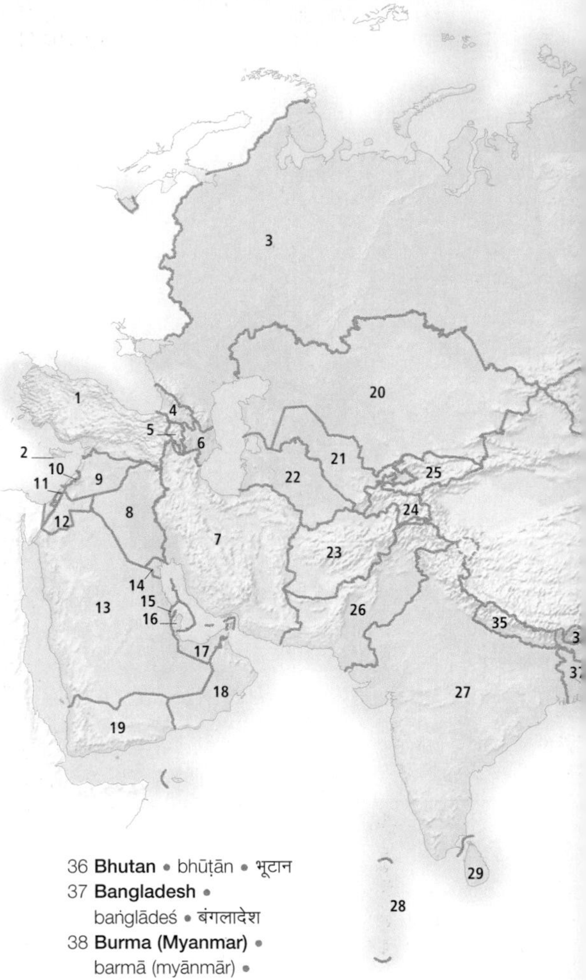

36 **Bhutan** • bhūṭān • भूटान
37 **Bangladesh** • baṅglādeś • बंगलादेश
38 **Burma (Myanmar)** • barmā (myānmār) • बर्मा (म्यांमार)
39 **Thailand** • thāīlaiṇḍ • थाईलैंड
40 **Laos** • lāos • लाओस
41 **VietNam** • viyatnām • वियतनाम

Australasia • australasia • ऑस्ट्रेलेशिया

1 **Australia** • australia • ऑस्ट्रेलिया
2 **Tasmania** • tasmāniyā • तस्मानिया
3 **New Zealand** • nyūzīlaiṇḍ • न्यूज़ीलैंड

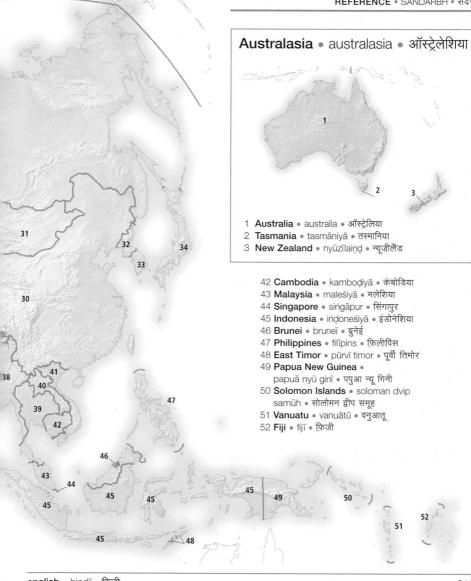

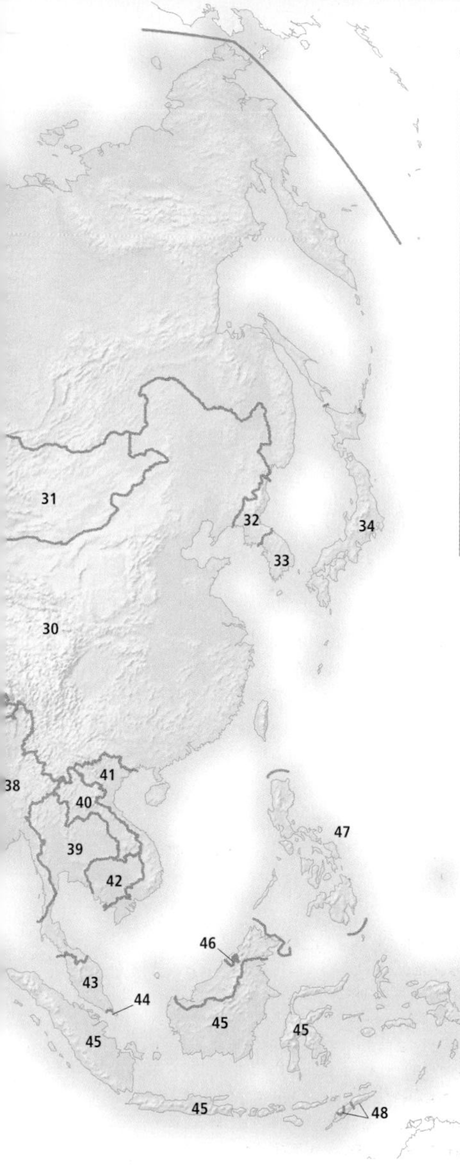

42 **Cambodia** • kamboḍiyā • कंबोडिया
43 **Malaysia** • maleśiyā • मलेशिया
44 **Singapore** • siṅgāpur • सिंगापुर
45 **Indonesia** • iṅḍoneśiyā • इंडोनेशिया
46 **Brunei** • bruneī • ब्रुनेई
47 **Philippines** • filīpins • फ़िलीपिंस
48 **East Timor** • pūrvī timor • पूर्वी तिमोर
49 **Papua New Guinea** • papuā nyū ginī • पपुआ न्यू गिनी
50 **Solomon Islands** • soloman dvip samūh • सोलोमन द्वीप समूह
51 **Vanuatu** • vanuātū • वनुआतू
52 **Fiji** • fijī • फ़िजी

particles and antonyms • upsarg, pratyaya aur vilom śabd • उपसर्ग, प्रत्यय और विलोम शब्द

to
ko • को

from
se • से

over
ūpar • ऊपर

under
nīche • नीचे

in front of
sāmne • के सामने

behind
pīchhe • पीछे

onto
ke ūpar • के ऊपर

into
ke andar • के अंदर

in
andar • अंदर

out
bāhar • बाहर

above
ūpar • ऊपर

below
nīche • नीचे

inside
andar • अंदर

outside
bāhar • बाहर

up
ūpar • ऊपर

down
nīche • नीचे

at
par • पर

beyond
pare • परे

on top of
ke ūpar • के ऊपर

beside
ke pās • के पास

between
ke bīch • के बीच

opposite
viprīt • विपरीत

near
nikaṭ • निकट

far
dūr • दूर

here
yahāṃ • यहां

there
vahāṃ • वहां

through
ārampār • आरम्पार

around
ghūm kar • घूम कर

for
ke lie • के लिए

towards
kī taraf • की तरफ़

with
sāth • साथ

without
bagair • बग़ैर

before
pahle • पहले

after
bād meṃ • बाद में

by
tab tak • तब तक

until
jab tak • जब तक

early
jaldī • जल्दी

late
der • देर

now
abhī • अभी

later
bād meṃ • बाद में

always
hameśā • हमेशा

never
kabhī nahīṃ • कभी नहीं

often
aksar • अक्सर

rarely
kabhī-kabhī • कभी–कभी

yesterday
bītā kal • बीता कल

tomorrow
āgāmī kal • आगामी कल

first
pahlā • पहला

last
āḳhrī • आख़री

every
harek • हरेक

some
kuchh • कुछ

about
lagbhag • लगभग

exactly
saṭīk • सटीक

a little
thoṛā sā • थोड़ा सा

a lot
bahut sā • बहुत सा

along
sāth-sāth • साथ–साथ

across
ke pār • के पार

large
baṛā • बड़ा

small
chhoṭā • छोटा

wide
chauṛā • चौड़ा

narrow
saṅkrā • संकरा

tall
lambā • लंबा

short
chhoṭā • छोटा

high
ūṃchā • ऊंचा

low
nīchā • नीचा

thick
moṭā • मोटा

thin
patlā • पतला

light
halkā • हल्का

heavy
bhārī • भारी

hard
kaṭhor • कठोर

soft
mulāyam • मुलायम

wet
gīlā • गीला

dry
sūkhā • सूखा

good
acchhā • अच्छा

bad
burā • बुरा

fast
tez • तेज़

slow
dhīre • धीरे

correct
sahī • सही

wrong
g̣alat • ग़लत

clean
sāf • साफ़

dirty
gandā • गंदा

beautiful
ḳhūbsūrat • ख़ूबसूरत

ugly
badsūrat • बदसूरत

expensive
mahaṅgā • महंगा

cheap
sastā • सस्ता

quiet
śānt • शांत

noisy • śor karne vālā
शोर करने वाला

hot
garm • गर्म

cold
ṭhaṇḍā • ठंडा

open
khulā • खुला

closed
band • बंद

full
bharā • भरा

empty
ḳhālī • ख़ाली

new
nayā • नया

old
purānā • पुराना

light
halkā • हल्का

dark
gahrā • गहरा

easy
āsān • आसान

difficult
kaṭhin • कठिन

free
ḳhālī • ख़ाली

occupied
vyast • व्यस्त

fat
moṭā • मोटा

thin
patlā • पतला

young
javān • जवान

old
būṛhā • बूढ़ा

better
behtar • बेहतर

worse
badtar • बदतर

black
kālā • काला

white
safed • सफ़ेद

interesting
rochak • रोचक

boring
ubāū • उबाऊ

sick
bīmār • बीमार

well
svasth • स्वस्थ

beginning
ārambh • आरंभ

end
ant • अंत

strong
mazbūt • मज़बूत

weak
kamzor • कमज़ोर

useful phrases • upyogī vākyāṅś • उपयोगी वाक्यांश

essential phrases
āvaśyak vākyāṅś
आवश्यक वाक्यांश

Yes • hāṃ • हां

No • nahīṃ • नहीं

Maybe • ho saktā hai
हो सकता है।

Please • kṛpyā • कृपया

Thank you
dhanyavād • धन्यवाद

You're welcome
āpkā svāgat hai
आपका स्वागत है।

Excuse me • māf kījiegā
माफ़ कीजिएगा

I'm sorry
maiṃ māfī chāhtā hūṃ
मैं माफ़ी चाहता हूं।

Don't
mat karo • मत करो।

OK • acchhā • अच्छा

That's fine
yah ṭhīk hai • यह ठीक है।

That's correct
yah sahī hai • यह सही है।

That's wrong
yah galat hai • यह ग़लत है।

greetings
abhivādan
अभिवादन

Hello
namaskār • नमस्कार

Goodbye
namaskār • नमस्कार

Good morning
suprabhāt • सुप्रभात

Good afternoon
namaskār • नमस्कार

Good evening
namaskār • नमस्कार

Good night
śubh rātri • शुभ रात्रि

How are you?
āp kaise haiṃ?
आप कैसे हैं?

My name is...
merā nām … hai
मेरा नाम ... है।

What is your name?
āpkā kyā nām hai?
आपका क्या नाम है?

What is his/her name?
unkā kyā nām hai?
उनका क्या नाम है?

May I introduce...
maiṃ āpko … se
milvānā chāhtā hūṃ
मैं आपको ... से मिलवाना
चाहता हूं।

This is...
ye … haiṃ • ये ... हैं।

Pleased to meet you
āpse milkar ḳhuśī huī
आपसे मिलकर ख़ुशी हुई।

See you later
bād meṃ milte haiṃ
बाद में मिलते हैं।

signs • chihn • चिह्न

Tourist information
paryaṭak jānkārī
पर्यटक जानकारी

Entrance
praveś • प्रवेश

Exit • nikās • निकास

Emergency exit
saṅkaṭ dvār
संकट द्वार

Push • dhakeleṃ • धकेलें

Danger • ḳhatrā • ख़तरा

No smoking • dhūmrpān
varjit • धूम्रपान वर्जित

Out of order
ḳharāb • ख़राब

Opening times
khulne kā samaya
खुलने का समय

Free admission
muft praveś • मुफ़्त प्रवेश

Open all day • pūre
din khulā • पूरे दिन खुला

Reduced price • kam
mūlya par • कम मूल्य पर

Sale • sel • सेल

Knock before entering
praveś karne se pahle
dastak deṃ • प्रवेश करने
से पहले दस्तक दें

Keep off the grass
kṛpyā ghās par na chaleṃ
कृपया घास पर न चलें

help • sahāyatā
सहायता

Can you help me?
kyā āp merī madad kar
sakte haiṃ?
क्या आप मेरी मदद कर
सकते हैं?

I don't understand
maiṃ samjhā nahīṃ
मैं समझा नहीं।

I don't know
mujhe patā nahīṃ hai
मुझे पता नहीं है।

Do you speak English, French...?
kyā āp aṅgrezī, french
… bolte haiṃ?
क्या आप अंग्रेज़ी, फ़्रेंच ...
बोलते हैं?

I speak English, Spanish...
maiṃ aṅgrezī, speniś …
boltā hūṃ
मैं अंग्रेज़ी, स्पेनिश ...
बोलता हूं।

Please speak more slowly
kṛpyā aur dhīre boleṃ
कृपया और धीरे बोलें।

Please write it down for me • kṛpyā ye mere
lie likh deṃ
कृपया ये मेरे लिए लिख दें।

I have lost...
merā … kho gayā hai
मेरा ... खो गया है।

directions
nirdeś • निर्देश

I am lost
maiṃ bhaṭak gayā hūṃ.
मैं भटक गया हूं।

Where is the...?
... kahāṃ haiṃ?
... कहां हैं?

Where is the nearest...?
nazdīkī ... kahāṃ hai?
नज़दीकी ... कहां है?

Where are the toilets?
śauchālaya kahāṃ hai?
शौचालय कहां है?

How do I get to...?
maiṃ ... kaise pahuṃch saktā hūṃ?
मैं ... कैसे पहुंच सकता हूं?

To the right
dāīṃ taraf • दाईं तरफ़

To the left
bāīṃ taraf • बाईं तरफ़

Straight ahead
āge jākar sīdhā
आगे जाकर सीधा

How far is...?
... kitnī dūr hai?
... कितनी दूर है?

road signs • mārg chihn • मार्ग चिह्न

All directions • sabhī diśāeṃ • सभी दिशाएं

Caution
sāvdhānī • सावधानी

No entry
praveś varjit • प्रवेश वर्जित

Slow down
raftār dhīmī kareṃ
रफ़्तार धीमी करें

Diversion • parivartit mārg • परिवर्तित मार्ग

Keep to the right
dāīṃ taraf raheṃ
दाईं तरफ़ रहें

No parking
pārkiṅg niṣedh hai
पार्किंग निषेध है

No through road
ām rāstā nahīṃ hai
आम रास्ता नहीं है

One-way street
iktarfā rāstā
इकतरफ़ा रास्ता

Other directions
anya nirdeś • अन्य निर्देश

Residents only
keval nivāsiyoṃ ke lie
केवल निवासियों के लिए

Dangerous bend
khatarnāk moṛ
ख़तरनाक मोड़

accommodation
āvās • आवास

I have a reservation
mere pās ārakṣaṇ hai
मेरे पास आरक्षण है।

My room number is...
merā kamrā nambar ... hai. • मेरा कमरा नंबर ... है।

What time is breakfast?
nāśte kā kyā samaya hai?
नाश्ते का क्या समय है?

I'll be back at... o'clock • maiṃ ... baje lauṭūṅgā • मैं ... बजे लौटूंगा

I'm leaving tomorrow
maiṃ kal jā rahā hūṃ
मैं कल जा रहा हूं।

eating and drinking
khānā-pīnā
खाना–पीना

It's delicious • yah svādiṣṭ hai • यह स्वादिष्ट है।

I don't drink/smoke
maiṃ śarāb/sigreṭ nahīṃ pītā
मैं शराब/सिगरेट नहीं पीता।

I don't eat meat
maiṃ māṃs nahīṃ khātā
मैं मांस नहीं खाता।

No more for me, thank you • mujhe aur nahīṃ chāhie, dhanyavād
मुझे और नहीं चाहिए, धन्यवाद।

May I have some more? • kyā mujhe thoṛā aur mil saktā hai?
क्या मुझे थोड़ा और मिल सकता है?

May we have the bill?
kyā hameṃ bil mil saktā hai? • क्या हमें बिल मिल सकता है?

Can I have a receipt?
kyā mujhe rasīd mil saktī hai? • क्या मुझे रसीद मिल सकती है?

No-smoking area
dhūmrpān varjit kṣetr
धूम्रपान वर्जित क्षेत्र

health • svāsthya
स्वास्थ्य

I don't feel well • merī tabīyat ṭhīk nahīṃ hai
मेरी तबीयत ठीक नहीं है।

I feel sick
maiṃ bīmār mahsūs kar rahā hūṃ
मैं बीमार महसूस कर रहा हूं।

What is the telephone number of the nearest doctor?
sabse nazdīkī doctor kā fon nambar kyā hai?
सबसे नज़दीकी डॉक्टर का फ़ोन नंबर क्या है?

It hurts here
yahāṃ dukhtā hai
यहां दुखता है।

I have a temperature
mujhe bukhār hai
मुझे बुख़ार है।

I'm ... months pregnant
mujhe ... mahīne kā garbh hai
मुझे ... महीने का गर्भ है।

I need a prescription for ... • mujhe ... ke lie docterī nuskhā chāhie
मुझे ... के लिए डॉक्टरी नुस्ख़ा चाहिए।

I normally take...
sāmānyataḥ maiṃ ... letā hūṃ
सामान्यतः मैं ... लेता हूं।

I'm allergic to...
mujhe ... se elarjī hai
मुझे ... से एलर्जी है।

hindi pronunciation

the hindi alphabet

The Hindi script, which is called Devnagari, is made up of 12 vowels and 36 consonants. In this book we have adapted the usual romanization of Hindi by dropping the "a" normally used to represent the Hindi vowel "अ" that is attached to all Hindi consonants. Roman consonants, such as "w", only have a sound of their own once they are joined to vowels such as "a" or "e", as in "water" or "wet". In Hindi, however, every consonant incorporates the vowel "अ", so is a complete sound in itself. The sound of the consonant changes when another vowel is added to it. For example, the Hindi consonant "क" is romanized as "ka". When more vowels are added it becomes "की" (kee) or "के" (ke).

In this book we have used Roman consonants to represent each Devnagari consonant, and its accompanying vowel. For example, traditionally "लोग" ("people") would be transcribed as "loga", but we have used "log" to help you pronounce it more accurately. The exception to this is the Hindi consonant "य", represented by the Roman "ya", where we have retained the "a" to keep the pronunciation accurate.

We have kept the Roman spellings for words such as ball, monitor, coffee, and sauce, which are commonly used in everyday Hindi.

hindi vowels

vowel	english equivalent	phonetic symbol	guide to pronunciation
अ	a	a	as "u" in cut
आ	aa	ā	as "a" in class
इ	i	i	as "i" in bit
ई	ee	ī	as "ea" in beat
उ	u	u	as "u" in put
ऊ	oo	ū	as "oo" in hoot
ए	e	e	as "a" in late
ऐ	ai	ai	as "a" in rack
ओ	o	o	as "oa" in goat
औ	au	au	as "o" in floppy
अं	un	ṃ	as "un" in clung
अ:	ah	ḥ	as "ah" in blah

hindi consonants

Instances marked with a bullet (•) have no equivalent in English pronunciation.

consonant	english equivalent	phonetic symbol	guide to pronunciation
क	ka	k	as "cu" in cut
ख	kh	kh	as "kh" in Khaki
ग	ga	g	as "g" in girl
घ	gha	gh	as "gh" in Ghana
ङ	angah	ṅ	as "ung" in clung
च	cha	ch	as "chu" in church
छ	chha	chh	•
ज	ja	j	as "ju" in jug
झ	jha	jh	•
ञ	yan	ñ	•
ट	ta	ṭ	as "tu" in turtle
ठ	tha	ṭh	as "th" in lothar
ड	da	ḍ	as "du" in dump
ड़	ra	ṛ	•
ढ	dha	ḍh	as "dh" in Dhaka
ढ़	rha	ṛh	•
ण	na	ṇ	•
त	ta	t	as "t" in Tashkent
थ	tha	th	as "th" in Pythagoras
द	da	d	as "the" in the (pronounced softly)
ध	dha	dh	•
न	na	n	as "nu" in nursing
प	pa	p	as "pu" in puckered
फ	pha	ph	as "fu" in fur
ब	ba	b	as "bu" in bubble
भ	bha	bh	as "bha" in bharat
म	ma	m	as "mu" in mutter
य	ya	ya	as "yu" in yuppie
र	ra	r	as "ru" in rub

... continued on next page

continued from previous page

consonant	english equivalent	phonetic symbol	guide to pronunciation
ल	la	l	as "lo" in love
व	wa	v	as "wo" in word
श	sha	ś	as "shu" in shut
ष	sa	ṣ	•
स	sa	s	as "si" in sin
ह	ha	h	as "hu" in hurt
क्ष	ksha	kṣ	as "ksha" in rickshaw
त्र	tra	tr	as "tr" in trinidad
ज्ञ	jna	jñ	•

combining consonants and vowels

To show how vowel sounds change, we have taken the consonant "क" (ka) and shown how the vowel sound changes when each of the 12 vowels is joined with it.

k क	+	**a** अ	=	**ka** क	**ka** as "cu" in cut
k क	+	**ā** आ	=	**kā** का	**kā** as "ka" in kamikaze
k क	+	**i** इ	=	**ki** कि	**ki** as "ki" in kiss
k क	+	**ī** ई	=	**kī** की	**kī** as "kee" in keen
k क	+	**u** उ	=	**ku** कु	**ku** as "cu" in cushion
k क	+	**ū** ऊ	=	**kū** कू	**kū** as "coo" in cool
k क	+	**e** ए	=	**ke** के	**ke** as "ka" in kate
k क	+	**ai** ऐ	=	**kai** कै	**kai** as "ca" in California
k क	+	**o** ओ	=	**ko** को	**ko** as "coa" in coarse
k क	+	**au** औ	=	**kau** कौ	**kau** as "co" in copy
k क	+	**ṃ** अं	=	**kang** कं	**kang** as "kan" in kangaroo
n न	+	**ḥ** अ:	=	**nah** न:	•

You can repeat this exercise with other consonants as the vowel sounds will change in the same way.

key to romanization

अ	आ	इ	ई	उ	ऊ	ऋ	
a	ā	i	ī	u	ū	ṛ	
			ए	ऐ	ओ	औ	
			e	ai	o	au	
क	क़	ख	ख़	ग	ग़	घ	ङ
k	ḳ	kh	ḳh	g	ģ	gh	ṅ
च	छ	ज	ज़	झ	ञ		
ch	chh	j	z	jh	ñ		
ट	ठ	ड	ड़	ढ	ढ़	ण	
ṭ	ṭh	ḍ	ṛ	ḍh	ṛh	ṇ	
त	थ	द	ध	न			
t	th	d	dh	n			
प	फ	फ़	ब	भ	म		
p	ph	f	b	bh	m		
य	र	ल	व	श			
ya	r	l	v	ś			
ष	स	ह	:				
ṣ	s	h	ḥ				
क्ष	त्र	ज्ञ					
kṣ	tr	jña					

A "~" over a vowel shows it is pronounced nasally.

A consonant with a dot below it, for example "ṃ", is an anuswar, or a half consonant, which means it is a consonant without an accompanying vowel sound.

Certain letters in Hindi, though pronounced differently, have been romanized with the same consonants, as there aren't enough characters in the Roman alphabet to represent similar sounds. For example:

hindi consonant	**roman transliteration**
द	d
ढ	ḍh
ढ़	ṛh
ध	dh
ड़ & ऋ	ṛ
ड	ḍ

We have used the *nukta* (a dot) below certain consonants to denote Urdu pronunciation. Consonants with *nuktas*, for example, have been romanized as follows:

क़	ख़	ग़	ज़	फ़
ḳ	ḳh	ģ	z	f

Some of these consonants without a *nukta* have been romanized as follows:

क	ख	ग	ज	फ
k	kh	g	j	ph

index • tālikā • तालिका

C

E

G

I

N

Q

R

U

V

acknowledgments • ābhār • आभार

DORLING KINDERSLEY would like to thank Tracey Miles and Christine Lacey for design assistance, Georgina Garner for editorial and administrative help, Sonia Gavira, Polly Boyd, and Cathy Meeus for editorial help, and Claire Bowers for compiling the DK picture credits.

The publisher would like to thank the following for their kind permission to reproduce their photographs:
Abbreviations key:
t=top, b=bottom, r=right, l=left, c=centre

Abode: 62; **Action Plus:** 224bc; **alamy.com:** 154t; A.T. Willett 287bcl; Michael Foyle 184bl; Stock Connection 287bcr; **Allsport/Getty Images:** 238cl; **Alvey and Towers:** 209 acr, 215bcl, 215bcr, 241cr; **Peter Anderson:** 188cbr, 271br. **Anthony Blake Photo Library:** Charlie Stebbings 114cl; John Sims 114tcl; **Andyalte:** 98tl; **apple mac computers:** 268tcr; **Arcaid:** John Edward Linden 301bl; Martine Hamilton Knight, Architects: Chapman Taylor Partners, 213cl; Richard Bryant 301br; **Argos:** 41tcl, 66cbl, 66cl, 66br, 66bcl, 69cl, 70bcl, 71t, 77tl, 269tc, 270tl; **Axiom:** Eitan Simanor 105bcr; Ian Cumming 104; Vicki Couchman 148cr; **Beken Of Cowes Ltd:** 215cbc; **Bosch:** 76tcr, 76tc, 76tcl; **Camera Press:** 27c, 38tr, 256t, 257cr; Barry J. Holmes 148tr; Jane Hanger 159cr; Mary Germanou 259bc; **Corbis:** 78b; Anna Clopet 247tr; Bettmann 181tl, 181tr; Bo Zauders 156t; Bob Rowan 152bl; Bob Winsett 247cbl; Brian Bailey 247br; Carl and Ann Purcell 162l; Chris Rainer 247ctl; ChromoSohm Inc. 179tr; Craig Aurness 215bl; David H.Wells 249cbr; Dennis Marsico 274bl; Dimitri Lundt 236bc; Duomo 211tl; Gail Mooney 277ctcr; George Lepp 248c; Gunter Marx 248cr; Jack Fields 210b; Jack Hollingsworth 231bl; Jacqui Hurst 277cbr; James L. Amos 247bl, 191ctr, 220bcr; Jan Butchofsky 277cbc; Johnathan Blair 243cr; Jon Feingersh 153tr; Jose F. Poblete 191br; Jose Luis Pelaez.Inc 153tc, 175tl; Karl Weatherly 220bl, 247tcr; Kelly Mooney Photography 259tl; Kevin Fleming 249bc; Kevin R. Morris 105tr, 243tl, 243tc; Kim Sayer 249tcr; Lynn Goldsmith 258t; Macduff Everton 231bcl; Mark Gibson 249bl; Mark L. Stephenson 249tcl; Michael Pole 115tr; Michael S. Yamashita 247ctcl; Mike King 247cbl; Neil Rabinowitz 214br; Owen Franken 112t; Pablo Corral 115bc; Paul A. Sounders 169br, 249ctcl; Paul J. Sutton 224c, 224br; Peter Turnley 105tcr; Phil Schermeister 227b, 248tr; R. W Jones 309; R.W. Jones 175tr; Richard Hutchings 168b; Rick Doyle 241ctr; Robert Holmes 97br, 277ctc; Roger Ressmeyer 169tr; Russ Schleipman 229; Steve Raymer 168cr; The Purcell Team 211ctr; Tim Wright 178; Vince Streano 194t; Wally McNamee 220br, 220bcl, 224bl; Yann Arhus-Bertrand 249tl; **Demetrio Carrasco / Dorling Kindersley (c) Herge / Les Editions Casterman:** 112ccl; **Dixons:** 270cl, 270cr, 270bl, 270bcl, 270bcr, 270ccr; **Education Photos:** John Walmsley 26tl; **Empics Ltd:** Adam Day 236br; Andy Heading 243c; Steve White 249cbc; **Getty Images:** 48bcl, 100t, 114bcr, 154bl, 287tr; 94tr; **Dennis Gilbert:** 106tc; **Hulsta:** 70t; **Ideal Standard Ltd:** 72r; **The Image Bank/Getty Images:** 58; **Impact Photos:** Eliza Armstrong 115cr; John Arthur 190tl; Philip Achache 246t; **The Interior Archive:** Henry Wilson, Alfie's Market 114bl; Luke White, Architect: David Mikhail, 59tl; Simon Upton, Architect: Phillippe Starck, St Martins Lane Hotel 100bcr, 100br; **Jason Hawkes Aerial Photography:** 216t; **Dan Johnson:** 26cbl, 35r; **Kos Pictures Source:** 215cbl, 240tc, 240tr; David Williams 216b; **Lebrecht Collection:** Kate Mount 169bc; **MP Visual.com:** Mark Swallow 202t; **NASA:** 280cr, 280ccl, 281tl; **P&O Princess Cruises:** 214bl; **P A Photos:** 181br; **The Photographers' Library:** 186bl, 186bc, 186t; **Plain and Simple Kitchens:** 66t; **Powerstock Photolibrary:** 169tl, 256t, 287tc; **Rail Images:** 208c, 208 cbl, 209br; **Red Consultancy:** Odeon cinemas 257br; **Redferns:** 259br; Nigel Crane 259c; **Rex Features:** 106br, 259tc, 259tr, 259bl, 280b; Charles Ommaney 114tcr; J.F.F Whitehead 243cl; Patrick Barth 101tl; Patrick Frilet 189cbl; Scott Wiseman 287bl; **Royalty Free Images:** Getty Images/Eyewire 154bl; **Science & Society Picture Library:** Science Museum 202b; **Skyscan:** 168t, 182c, 298; Quick UK Ltd 212; **Sony:** 268bc; **Robert Streeter:** 154br; **Neil Sutherland:** 82tr, 83tl, 90t, 118, 188ctr, 196tl, 196tr, 299cl, 299bl; **The Travel Library:** Stuart Black 264t; **Travelex:** 97cl; **Vauxhall:** Technik 198t, 199tl, 199tr, 199cl, 199cr, 199ctcl, 199ctcr, 199tcl, 199tcr, 200; **View Pictures:** Dennis Gilbert, Architects: ACDP Consulting, 106t; Dennis Gilbert, Chris Wilkinson Architects, 209tr; Peter Cook, Architects: Nicholas Crimshaw and partners, 208t; **Betty Walton:** 185br; **Colin Walton:** 2, 4, 7, 9, 10, 28, 42, 56, 92, 95c, 99tl, 99tcl, 102, 116, 120t, 138t, 146, 150t, 160, 170, 191ctcl, 192, 218, 252, 260br, 260l, 261tr, 261c, 261cr, 271cbl, 271cbr, 271ctl, 278, 287br, 302, 401.

DK PICTURE LIBRARY:
Akhil Bahkshi; Patrick Baldwin; Geoff Brightling; British Museum; John Bulmer; Andrew Butler; Joe Cornish; Brian Cosgrove; Andy Crawford and Kit Hougton; Philip Dowell; Alistair Duncan; Gables; Bob Gathany; Norman Hollands; Kew Gardens; Peter James Kindersley; Vladimir Kozlik; Sam Lloyd; London Northern Bus Company Ltd; Tracy Morgan; David Murray and Jules Selmes; Musée Vivant du Cheval, France; Museum of Broadcast Communications; Museum of Natural History; NASA; National History Museum; Norfolk Rural Life Museum; Stephen Oliver; RNLI; Royal Ballet School; Guy Ryecart; Science Museum; Neil Setchfield; Ross Simms and the Winchcombe Folk Police Museum; Singapore Symphony Orchestra; Smart Museum of Art; Tony Souter; Erik Svensson and Jeppe Wikstrom; Sam Tree of Keygrove Marketing Ltd; Barrie Watts; Alan Williams; Jerry Young.

Additional Photography by Colin Walton.

Colin Walton would like to thank:
A&A News, Uckfield; Abbey Music, Tunbridge Wells; Arena Mens Clothing, Tunbridge Wells; Burrells of Tunbridge Wells; Gary at Di Marco's; Jeremy's Home Store, Tunbridge Wells; Noakes of Tunbridge Wells; Ottakar's, Tunbridge Wells; Selby's of Uckfield; Sevenoaks Sound and Vision; Westfield, Royal Victoria Place, Tunbridge Wells.